AMERICAN

BEACH

Abraham Lincoln Lewis

AMERICAN BEACH

How 'Progress'
Robbed a Black Town—
and Nation—of History,
Wealth, and Power

Russ Rymer

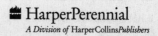

HarperPerennial
A Division of HarperCollinsPublishers

Parts of this book appeared in different form in *Harper's* magazine, *Vogue*, and the *Fernandina Beach News-Leader*.

PHOTO CREDITS:
Frontispiece: Courtesy of Johnetta Cole.
Cover: Vacation home of A. L. Lewis, American Beach, 1940s.
(Home next door belonged to his son, James H., and later to MaVynee Betsch.)
Courtesy of collection of Ernestine Latson Smith.
Back cover inset: Lewis Street, American Beach, 1940s. Courtesy of collection of Ernestine Latson Smith.

HarperCollins books may be purchased for educational, business, or sales promotional use. For information please write: Special Markets Department, HarperCollins Publishers Inc., 10 East 53rd Street, New York, NY 10022.

First HarperPerennial edition published 2000.

Designed by Liane F. Fuji

The Library of Congress has catalogued the hardcover edition as follows:

Rymer, Russ.
    American beach : how "progress" robbed a black town—and nation—of history, wealth, and power. / Russ Rymer.
    p. ill. cm.
    ISBN 0-06-017483-8
    1. American Beach (Fla.)—Race relations. 2. Afro-Americans—Florida—American Beach—History. 3. American Beach (Fla.)—History. I. Title.
F319.A45R96 1998
305.896'073075911—dc21   98-230257

ISBN 0-06-093089-6 (pbk.)

00 01 02 03 04 ❖/RRD 10 9 8 7 6 5 4 3 2 1

This book is for my parents,
Richard and Elizabeth Rymer,
who made me to know early on that
justice is also a matter of heart

Contents

Acknowledgments

This book was supported by a 1995 Whiting Writer's Award from the Mrs. Giles Whiting Foundation.

I'd like to express my gratitude to several who helped *American Beach* along: my assiduous editor, Sara Lippincott; my agent, Melanie Jackson; and my acquiring editor at HarperCollins, Lawrence Ashmead, who, acting on some irrational confidence, encouraged me on this story for longer than a decade before it even became a book idea, and before I'd even become an author of books. My thanks also to Jane Palecek, for her day-saving design work and editorial encouragement; to Bill and Gloria Broder for their wise counsel; and to Ben Ehrenreich for his research. And to Susan Faludi for excelling at the impossible task of living with the author even as he lived with the story, and for shepherding the course and shape of this book through a thousand conversations.

My thanks go especially to the residents of American Beach and Fernandina Beach, Florida, for receiving me so warmly as a neighbor while at the same time putting up with me as a journalistic infidel. Many among them who contributed lavishly to this tale make an appearance in the text, but some who do not appear (or who do not appear sufficiently) should be acknowledged. In particular, Gogo Ferguson and David Sayre, who, along with Louise Millette, offered a Cumberland Island refuge that was essential (more than they knew) to the project's sane progress. Retta McDowell's timely offer of her Fernandina house—"the little house of great transitions"—was a godsend almost equal to her warmth and youthful spirit. Donna Ballard, who has a better eye for intrigue (not to mention a truer heart) than most reporters, was always ready with a wild story and a helping hand. Pamela Selton and Carol Alexander, long-time companions of MaVynee Betsch, have been especially kind in keeping me abreast of events in Florida since my departure, just as they were in explaining them while I was there.

For their perspectives on Fernandina and Jacksonville, I am indebted to Ernestine Smith, Camilla Thompson, Charlotte Stewart, Hortense Gray, and Willie Mae Ashley, to Miriam Burney, Ben Durham, Frank and Emma Morgan, Harriett Graham, Arnolta Williams, and Florida Supreme Court Justice Leander Shaw, to Michael Stewart, Rudolph Williams, Jan Davis, William Watson, Leroy Tyler, Jeffrey Wilson, and Janice Ancrum, to Bill and Celeste Kavanaugh, Helen Litrico, Connie Hufstetler, Kathy Donaghy, *Florida Times Union* reporters Derek Kinner and Tonyaa Weathersbee, and to Mary Hurst, Sarah Bottoms, and Steve Hopper, formerly with the *Fernandina Beach News-Leader*. Bob and Karen Warner, proprietors of the Florida House Inn, were always liberal with their hospitality, as were Shirley and Butch Williams, and Joan Altman and her gracious daughter Julie.

My thanks also to Richard Long, Sibille Pritchard, M. J. Hewett, Ava Doppelt, Louise Wright, Fran Pignone, Lucy Ann Hurston, Stetson Kennedy, Laura Stewart, Lorelei Anderson Francis, and Tom Lewis for their insights into Eatonville, Orlando, and Celebration.

Because this book contains no source list, I have tried to express my reliance on other authors and books within the text. Several, how-ever, warrant special mention: *Black Business in the New South*, by Walter B. Weare (Duke University Press, 1993), *Mickey Mouse History and Other Essays on American History*, by Mike Wallace (Temple University Press, 1996), the works of Nathan Irving Huggins and of Lerone Bennett, Jr., and the anthology *Lure and Loathing*, edited by Gerald Early (Allen Lane, The Penguin Press, 1993).

Among a journalist's subjects there is always someone for whom he feels he is writing, and whose verdict on his labors he anticipates. To my sorrow, two such people who were generous friends to me and who experienced these stories are no longer alive to read what I have made of them: Ruth Smith and Annie Fout. They lived, I suppose, at oppo-site corners of a small southern town, but at the intersection of Hard Luck, Courage, and Grace they were close neighbors. May this book reflect the world they knew, and their very great goodness of heart.

My thanks go finally, and most importantly, to Johnnetta Cole, and to the person at this book's center, MaVynee Betsch, for their openness in inviting me into their lives, and into the story of their family.

The Road at My Door

The crabber on the courthouse steps, July 8, 1991.

Tuesdays during the years I lived on Amelia Island, I would drive down to American Beach and carry MaVynee Betsch back to Fernandina to go shopping. She could hardly have driven herself. MaVynee, who had grown up accustomed to Packards and Cadillacs, had sold her last car, a Pinto, long ago. She had no license and could probably not get a new one, considering the official confusion over her name—she'd amended "Marvyne" to remove the "R" when Ronald Reagan was elected—and the length of her hair and fingernails, either of which measurements would have qualified in the eyes of the Florida Department of Motor Vehicles as an impediment to the proper operation of an automobile. At any rate, she couldn't afford the gas.

In her current penury, her life was organized the way a millionaire's is, around foreseeable fluctuations in the markets, which meant, in MaVynee's case, that Tuesday was double discount day at the Nassau County Health Food store. The more holes they punched in her bonus card, the sooner she would earn a bumper crop of tofu and organic carrots when the card got full. So Tuesdays it was, and I would generally arrive in early afternoon and gather MaVynee into town. While she got her groceries, I would head around the corner to the Winn-Dixie for a bottle of her vintage of choice, a gallon of cranberry juice.

If her purpose was to stock up on provisions, mine (and I like to think part of hers, also) was to catch up on conversation. My anticipation of our talks was always freighted lightly with dread, for the least encounter with MaVynee could be an intense experience. To the island on which I was but a novice and a newcomer she had a long allegiance and a deep emotional attachment. Touring Amelia Island with MaVynee was like touring Troy with Schliemann. The least step on our journey could kick over some shard that, though dross in my eyes, shone in hers with moral significance and would instantly become an exhibit in her ongoing narrative. Her narrative had many ornate branches, hung heavy with folly and heroism, but they all sprang from a massive trunk: the betrayal of nature and humankind by the forces of progress and wealth. The island, it turns out, made an excellent case in point.

"Baby, let's go!" she would say when I picked her up. "We have so much to do!"

By that time, I would already have met the challenge of finding her, which was not always easy at the Beach, where she could be lost in the crowd or lost in solitude. American Beach has a permanent population of only 150, but it bursts with visitors on summer weekends. On Sunday evenings, when it is a popular party retreat for black teenagers from Jacksonville, the kids park their cars in yards and along the main street all the way back to the highway, and sheriff's deputies set up roadblocks and stand by in force, tensed for trouble. At other times, American Beach seems almost a ghost town, a cluster of aging, sun-struck, clapboard homes cupped in the palm of an enormous sand dune, its quiet narrow streets, under sheltering oaks, haunted (it often seemed) only by MaVynee. "I can go an entire week and not see a two-legged fool," she exulted to me. Usually I would find her at her mailbox, a bright orange tin contraption the size of an osprey's nest, set on an unsteady post by the beach and referred to by MaVynee as Revolutionary Headquarters, owing to the nature of the correspondence that flowed through it.

As we drove the sandy side streets back to the highway, the narrative would begin. She would point out for my enjoyment the phlox blooming on the huge dune's flank and the dense windswept tangle of live oaks at the edge of town. ("They're enchanted! An Enchanted Forest!") Or she would show me such monuments to municipal history as the house that sheriff's deputies had laid siege to one summer evening, blasting away until it was destroyed and its resident, whom they had come to question about a misdemeanor, dead. On the highway, she would identify the convenience store owned by a white man whose father had been especially generous to blacks in the bad years of the thirties, or the rundown roadside bar where, on the previous weekend, a black gentleman dressed in a suit had pulled up in a car with out-of-state plates, opened the trunk, retrieved a briefcase, walked inside, opened the briefcase, pulled out a shotgun and, turning to a customer at the bar, said, "You're the one," before killing him and neatly packing up the gun and returning the briefcase to the trunk and disappearing down the road. MaVynee's histories did not lack for drama.

Her critical eye was more commonly snagged by the ordinary run of things—how life was changing in this little world, how awful and absurd the changes were. "Tell me" she asked, as we passed one of the new luxury resort developments encroaching on American Beach, wherein palatial homes elbowed each other like factory shanties, "would you pay half a million dollars to listen to your neighbor's toilet flush?" The towers of the newly built Ritz-Carlton resembled those of a prison to her. Golf was a perplexity. One day, she could not forgo the opportunity the sport presented to compare one of her most admired species with the one that most disappointed her. "Look at the sea turtle," she instructed. "She comes here from afar to drop a little white sphere in a little hole, and she disturbs nothing and bestows life and ensures the abundance of nature. Now notice your white man; he comes from afar to drop a little white sphere in a little hole and destroys everything in his path."

And so we would pass through the middle reaches of Amelia Island—where the links had claimed vast acres of forest and had spread across the land like the scars of some emerald cataclysm; where one posh housing development was hardly up before the next was begun beside it; where the manicured lawns of resort "Plantations," in at least one instance, hid the buried corpses of antebellum plantation slaves— and eventually we would come to the busy outskirts of Fernandina, the island's principal metropolis and the Nassau County seat.

In town, the reaction to MaVynee was sharply divided: tourists and newcomers, on catching first sight of her, showed a marked tendency to gather up their children and run; the old-timers barely blinked. Fernandina is a small Southern rural county seat, accommodating of eccentricity within the family. A six-foot-tall, sixtyish black woman dressed in flip-flops and layers of felt, with eighteen-inch fingernails and a five-foot-long fall of hair festooned with political buttons, trained down her back, carried in a ball at her waist, and coifed into a foot-high cock's comb atop her head, drew hardly a double take from them. Crackers lounging in front of the ammunition store and rednecks passing in pickup trucks would give her a nod or a wave or stop to tell her that they did or didn't agree with her most recent letter to the editor. They called her MaVynee (her name, despite its altered spelling, is still pronounced to rhyme with "ravine") or Miss Betsch or Beach Lady. She would yell back, "Hey! Hey!" and give them a wave or a thumbs-up, and a score of bracelets would ripple and chime on her forearm. In addition to being a born-again pagan (as she describes herself) and a radical black feminist ecologist activist, MaVynee is a remarkably capable good ol' boy. I've known conservative Republican politicians to huddle with her over strategy and a Southern Baptist deacon and family man to confess on her shoulder his affair with a woman in the choir. Fernandina was MaVynee's town as surely as American Beach, as surely as Amelia was her island.

To the passing eye, Fernandina Beach (as the town is properly known to those not yet on a first-name basis) is an idyllic place, a picture postcard of small-town life, a sugar cone of confirming American pieties. With a skyline comprising white church steeples, the clock tower of its brick Victorian courthouse, and the masts of the shrimping fleet moored at its docks, with its brick sidewalks and quiet streets framed in Spanish moss that droops from stately overarching trees, Fernandina gives an impression of unsullied Arcadian innocence.

To the more experienced—or more jaundiced—inspection, Fernandina reveals something darker. Occasionally, as I drove or walked along its streets, I was seized by a momentary fear, as though a quick cold current from an unexpected depth had washed through my warm latitude. In the strange torpor of a downtown so clearly built for burlier commerce, in the blind eye turned to the secrets of fugitives and refugees and reigning town fathers in a town whose every father seemed a fugitive from something or somewhere, I sensed a gentle menace, a peril as impossible to locate within all that Arcadian innocence as the slave's corpse under the condo lawn. One day I mentioned these feelings to MaVynee as we drove through town. She was waving out the window to a passing friend as I spoke, giving her a boisterous "Hey, baby!" It was a beautiful Tuesday afternoon in the midst of a beautiful season, and whatever in the world was dark or troubling was hidden deep in glory. But when she turned to me her face was uncharacteristically earnest. "You know what the black folks say," she told me, neither particularly surprised by my notion nor in need of any elaboration. "'Fernandina is an evil place.'"

MaVynee Betsch was hardly the first of Amelia Island's residents, nor I the first newcomer, to mistake it for a separate world. I had originally stumbled on the island in the late 1970s, on a day when I was both hell-bent and distracted, which is to say I was lost. I reached the eastern end of a long straight low-country highway and found myself vaulting off the continent on the parabola of a steeply arched bridge. The bridge looped high at its center to clear the masts of pleasure yachts and the wheelhouses of grunting pushboats plying the Intercoastal Waterway, and cresting it permitted me a momentary glimpse of the land where I was about to arrive: a thirteen-mile-long spit of forested sand battered on one flank by the Atlantic and lulled on the other by tidal marsh—a barrier island connected to mainland Florida only by the single loose staple of the span over which I rode.

From that vantage, and at that instant, Amelia Island struck me as a self-contained kingdom, a shipwrecked Gondwanaland washed up against the coast of the New World by the force of some natural perversity: ancient hurricane, continental drift. It seemed, as I explored it, to have little in common with the vast inland low country through which I had just passed. Amelia had identity and presence, it had importance of place; the rural expanse I'd left behind on the other side of the bridge was the essence of endless nowhere. The island was a border province, and Fernandina a gateway port, between deep water and backwater, antithetical realms.

The island seemed steeped in roguish alienation. At the end of Fernandina's main street, in front of a tepee-shaped visitor's center, was a carved wooden peg-legged pirate, obviously the municipal mascot, inhospitably brandishing a cutlass. A brass plaque on a side street commemorated the Cuban revolutionary José Martí, who had holed up in a local boardinghouse while plotting a return to his homeland. The house itself, Martí's improbable Elba, lay that day in near collapse, though it was hardly more humble than much of commercial Centre Street, a collection of dusty dry-goods shops with sheet-metal façades. Fernandina seemed lost not only in space but in time. The cacti in the window box of one local restaurant, a waitress there informed me, had been planted by Al Capone.

The outlaw aura of Fernandina Beach was not just fanciful. In its heart, Fernandina is an Istanbul or an Andorra, a sentinel city on a contested and shifting border, full of strange piracies and villainous subtexts; even in the vitae of its historic first families, deed and misdeed are cheerfully confounded. In recent years, prominent residents have been investigated for contract fraud and political graft and arrested for drug trafficking; local shrimpers speak of hauls of "square lobster," meaning bales of marijuana. The island was a depot for gun-running during the Spanish-American War and again, it is rumored, during the Reagan administration's war against the Sandinistas. The CIA, it is also rumored, maintains a presence on the island in the form of a hangar in a field near the two-strip airport, and will occasionally send in an "engineer" or "designer" fresh from Tibet or Afghanistan, who spends his mysterious days alone in the hangar and pays his monthly lodging from a Haliburton case full of cash.

From its earliest days as a Spanish outpost on the English frontier, Amelia Island has lain just over the border from the law. For a while, in 1817, it was actually a renegade nation, ruled by Jared Irwin as defense minister and Ruggles Hubbard as civil governor, men who had been respectively a congressman from Pennsylvania and the high sheriff of New York. It was wrested from them by a career pirate, Luis Aury, who held the island for most of a year before American troops ran him out and restored the island to the Spanish crown. Four years after that, it became part of the United States, when Florida was admitted to the Union. When Florida left the Union during the War Between the States, Amelia Island left Florida; it was held by federal troops for the duration of the unpleasantness. An old island woman once described to me her earliest memory, extending back more than a century—of the V of gold buttons down the chest of the blue jacket of the officer leading a column of Union cavalry, who leaned from his saddle one summer morning to ask her the way to Fort Clinch.

The crenellated batteries of Fort Clinch still guard the island's north end, though the soldiers bivouacked there today are state park guides, as bellicose as bureaucrats. (I once saw them assembled sullenly in a downtown office in full Civil War regalia, head wounds bandaged, muskets stacked against a water cooler, attending a government-mandated lecture about sexual harassment in the workplace.) The narrow sound the fort overlooks is no longer a boundary between hostile nations but putative allies: Florida and Georgia. Shrimp boats and container ships leave through the sound from the Fernandina docks, and submarines glide through it headed for the sub base in nearby Saint Marys, Georgia. It is emblematic of Amelia's prickliness that the slim, peaceful channel to its north is the only state border in the nation defended by Civil War cannon and patrolled by a nuclear force.

Though I was at first entranced with Amelia's otherness, it was its commonness, its universality, that drew me back to live there some fifteen years later. I had visited many times over those years. By 1992, when I became a resident, the view east from the bridge was the same in my eyes as the view over my shoulder, only clearer, more distinct. I sought that clarity. Amelia was America distilled into something strong and clear. The heart of things is often revealed in their extremity. Why shouldn't the soul of a nation be discovered on an island off its coast? "Everything happens here, baby," MaVynee liked to tell me. "Why go anywhere else?"

In the large western city from which I'd come, "everything" was generally invisible; processes were hidden, institutions were dispersed. The industrial district lay as far from the government and retail districts as poor neighborhoods from rich; a citizen might exist in one realm and never know the other. Such would be inconceivable in Fernandina, where poor and well-off live cheek by jowl and the fishing fleet and the container port and the smokestacks of the pulp mills are for all intents and purposes right downtown. The modern American shrimping industry was invented in Fernandina by marooned Portuguese fishermen, and it dominated the local economy until Rayonier and the Container Corporation of America arrived in the 1930s to provide the local paycheck. Their two mills still supply the atmosphere with stench and noise, in the same abundance with which the Atlantic supplies the beach with brine and rote. There is no place in Fernandina's lovely historic district that is not perfumed on overcast days with sulfurous smoke and serenaded on spring nights with a graveyard-shift cacophony of murderous clangings and the hissing of pressure-tank release valves. To inhale that wafting halitosis on a beautiful subtropical morning while saying hello to the mayor or the newspaper editor or the harbor pilot or the high school principal on the sidewalk that extends from the docks to the beach past courthouse and post office and church was, in a funny and convincing way, to experience the world entire. In Fernandina, from the right perspective, the range of civic existence could be taken in at one glance, like the village you see through the window in an Easter egg.

Albeit a cracked egg. In nothing did Fernandina so resemble the greater world as in the strength of its internal divisions. Beneath the mantle and crust of surface civilities ran contests between countryside and township, between newcomers and natives, Northerners and Southerners, between resort developers and mill workers, between the wealthy and the poor. If it was discord you were after, MaVynee might say, why go anywhere else? Of course the deepest division and greatest discord was that between the races. About a fifth of Fernandina's 10,000 residents are black.

*   *   *

There are some to whom all black histories look alike, and the stories that make a place like Amelia Island what it is are drowned out in a chorus of slave chant and poor man's blues. Amelia's songs were brighter. I had come there to hear one of them—the history of a Jacksonville patriarch who founded Florida's first life insurance company, became one of Florida's first black millionaires, and built a town by the ocean where blacks could enjoy, in the phrase in use in its advertisements at the time, "recreation and relaxation without humiliation." The town was American Beach; the patriarch was A. L. Lewis—Abraham Lincoln Lewis. He was MaVynee Betsch's great-grandfather. I found it hard to separate his history and hers from those that surrounded and predated them.

Like the rest of the Sea Islands stretching from Charleston, South Carolina, down to Jacksonville—and making up, along with the littoral extending inland thirty miles, the region known to the Creek Indians as Gualé—Amelia was heavily invested in slavery. The island was blanketed with mammoth farms, like the Egan and Egmont plantations on the north end and the Harrison plantation girdling the island from sea to marsh below its equator, producing the mainstays of the Colonial low-country export economy: long-staple cotton, indigo, and rice.

Perched on the border with the English colonies and then the American states, Fernandina played a notorious role in that economy. When Thomas Jefferson outlawed the importation of slaves, in 1807, New England slaving families reregistered their ships under the Spanish flag and brought their cargoes to Fernandina to be smuggled across the border into Georgia by gangs of desperadoes known as "moccasin boys." Fernandina's traffic in "new" Africans became intense—its harbor sometimes hosted three hundred square-riggers at a time—and particularly horrifying. When British or U.S. men-o'-war attempted to interdict smuggling, smugglers would dump their incriminating cargoes overboard. When the cargo was human, black bodies washed up in the Amelia surf. The "evil" that haunts the island in the minds of modern-day black residents is, more than anything, the ghost of those drowned Africans.

Coincidentally, the island's border status also made it, for blacks, a sanctuary. Slavery was a different creature under the Spanish than it was under the English, and marginally more humane. Florida's Spanish colonists encouraged manumission and accepted and legally sanctioned interracial marriage. There were numbers of freed blacks in the area, and some of them owned plantations and slaves and found acceptance and status in white society. Mischievously, the Spanish encouraged slaves from Deep Southern states to rebel against their masters and flee across the Florida line. Even while it was a way station for U.S.-bound chattel, Fernandina was a terminus of an early, south-bound underground railroad.

The free black community thus established was shaped by Amelia's piratical proclivities. Pirate societies were egalitarian relative to the respectable societies they preyed upon. When they preyed upon slave ships, they might enlist the liberated cargo in their adventures. Luis Aury took and ruled Amelia with a crew of Negroes known as Aury's Blacks (just as Jim Floyd, a prominent blockade runner in the Spanish-American War and a black man, would smuggle guns to Cuba with an all-white crew). Even there the record is paradoxical, for Aury's pirates trafficked profitably in slaves. The blacks of Amelia Island early learned that liberation and subjugation might wear the identical face.

Amelia's free black population exploded during the Civil War. The island's whites briefly resisted Union encroachment, supplied with cases of ammunition from Confederate sympathizers in New York City (New York's mayor, Fernando Wood, reportedly foremost among them). But in March of 1862 they capitulated, and after the local whites fled west, slaves by the thousands came east out of the hinter-lands and crossed the sound to freedom. Many of the "contraband" enlisted in the Glory Brigades, black regiments that held Amelia Island and Hilton Head Island to the north, the only two pieces of the

Confederate coast to stay in Union hands for the duration of the war. In raids on their old plantation lands, the contraband troops fiercely contested the Confederate hold on north Florida. The old woman who described for me her memory of gold buttons on a Union soldier's uniform was black. So were the soldiers she remembered from her Reconstruction-era childhood.

Reconstruction was the prelude to Fernandina's golden age, and it was an age when the city and the region were led by blacks—black judges, mayors, representatives, and city and county officials. Fernandina had the first universal male suffrage in a black-majority voting district in the nation's history, and its elected officials were pioneers. Their legacy did not survive Jim Crow, however; nor has it been revived in the age of integration, affirmative action, and remedial racial gerrymandering. In recent years, there have been a few black officials in Fernandina and Nassau County, including a superior court judge and a mayor, but as of this writing there are none: no black city commissioners, no black county commissioners, no black judges, no black mayor, no black state or federal representatives, and no blacks on the county school board, though the student body in the county's public schools is even more heavily black than the general population. When Janice Ancrum, a black professional woman who worked for the Private Industry Council, a state-sponsored job-training and placement bureau, came within seven votes of winning the Democratic primary for the school board in 1994, the county commission reacted within days by passing a regulation forbidding any PIC employees not on leave from running for any county office. (Not that Ancrum would have made it; the Democratic candidate was defeated, in a race in which the largest forum was sponsored by the Christian Coalition, whose members alleged that the yoga classes recently introduced in the Fernandina Beach High School were exercises in communist mind control.) After one recent election reaffirmed Fernandina's conservative *revanche*, MaVynee put the news together with a coincidental newspaper account of a dog whom someone had decapitated, leaving the head impaled on a stick. "It's a mean season," she told me. "Just pure, indecent mean. It's happened before. It runs in cycles. It's something in the human psyche that will scare you most to death."

*   *   *

There was plenty to scare you in Fernandina's public commerce. The newspaper office was firebombed in 1993, the only newspaper in the nation so honored that year. A few years before that, county commission hearings on whether to ban automobile traffic on the beach became so rancorous that they had to be conducted under the protection of armed police. The violence manifested passions at loose on the island which were deeper than mere politics.

On a midsummer morning in 1991, Ronnie West, a fifty-year-old white man who lived on the marsh north of town and made his living fishing for crabs, pulled his pickup truck onto the sidewalk in front of the Nassau County courthouse, climbed onto the roof of the truck's cab, which he had draped with an American flag, and sat down. To protect himself from the summer sun, West wore a bill cap and dark glasses. Under his left ear, aimed at his head, he placed the barrel of a twelve-gauge shotgun. His finger was on the trigger. In the bed of the truck, he had mounted a sign, painted in rough red letters on a sheet of whitewashed plywood. It read: "WhERE IS JusTICE IN AMERICA."

As much as anyone, Ronnie West could be called the salt of Amelia Island, where his father had been a crabber before he was. West lived in the house his father had bought in 1960, which West bought from his stepmother ten years later, after his father's death. The property included a yard, and beyond the yard a bit of tidal marsh, and a catwalk winding through the marsh to a dock on Egan's Creek, where West kept his boat. For thirty years, the Wests had paid taxes on their plot of land, which, they understood, was listed in the courthouse as it had been laid out by the Spanish—in a square. But in the mid-1980s a group of powerful residents wanted part of the property for a commercial project they envisioned. They already owned the land across Egan's Creek to the north, land that had once belonged to an oil company. Using a 1901 map that divided West's lot into two triangles, they maintained that the oil company's old deed gave them rights to the northern part of West's land, also. They filed a quitclaim on the property. West took the matter to court and lost, and after thinking a while about the prospect of losing his land and his livelihood, painted his sign and loaded his shotgun and drove downtown to the courthouse.

The ensuing drama did not last long. The city police evacuated the

courthouse and closed off three blocks of Centre Street. Patrolmen surrounded West, aiming pistols, rifles, and shotguns at him. Snipers took
up position on nearby rooftops, and a negotiator was called in to talk to
him. After two hours, West lowered his gun and was led away sobbing.
The project, which turned out to be a sailboat and pleasure-craft
marina, went forward. The judge assessed the Wests liable for the legal
fees of their opponents—$91,000. "It doesn't matter," West's wife, Vera,
said to a friend on the sidewalk after the hearing. "It's impossible.
Ninety-one thousand is ninety-one million to me."

The incident galvanized Fernandina, and Ronnie and Vera West
became folk heroes. Residents held rallies and fish-fry fund-raisers for
them, and sold T-shirts with "WhERE IS JusTICE IN AMERICA"
dripping across the front. That the Wests' predicament was taken personally by so many indicated that it wasn't personal at all but universal:
Amelia Island was, behind all its civility, in the throes of a civil war
sparked by its rapid evolution from a working place into a tourist destination where visiting yachtsmen reigned and fishermen were a color-
ful anachronism. What happened to the Wests was notable for its bla-
tancy, but their fate was being replayed all over, and you didn't have to
know the individuals to see what was going on. On our drives,
MaVynee liked to count the FOR SALE signs on the beach road, where
longtime residents were being forced out of their homes by the higher
taxes of a newly affluent island.

Up until the late 1980s, the islanders had evaded that destiny. The
stench from the pulp mills had for a while inoculated Fernandina against
the rampant tourist development devouring Florida's Atlantic coast. The
town remained miraculously overlooked, an intact Victorian village and
an authentic working Southern county seat. But inevitably Fernandina's
very authenticity began attracting retirees and developers immune even
to the prophylaxis of pollution. The pollution has decreased in recent
years thanks to environmental regulation, and Fernandina is growing
and booming. Its downtown has been beautified. José Martí's crumbling
hideaway has been snugly refitted as the Florida House Inn, which touts
itself as Florida's oldest operating hotel. (Accurately so. Fernandina also
boasts the oldest working weekly newspaper in Florida and the oldest
working saloon.) The ludicrous tepee has been replaced with Brett's
Waterway Café, a chic glass-sheathed restaurant, and the pirate has been

relegated to a less conspicuous spot on the sidewalk; he is a spectator now to the parade of his town's improvement. The sheet-metal façades on Centre Street have been ripped off to reveal Victorian brick ornament and ironwork; inside are a welter of knickknack and sweatshirt shops, which have run off the last of the office-supply, auto-parts, general-merchandise, and grocery stores. Local residents trying to shop downtown for anything other than souvenirs can no longer even hear their town's distinctive noises: the high chiding of chimney swifts in summer twilight and the clanking of rigging from boats in the marina have been replaced by canned music oozing from speakers set in brick pedestals all along Centre Street, courtesy of town planners who have apparently concluded that being followed down the street by cheerful mall melodies will preclude, in the tourist mind, the fear of being followed by anything or anyone else. The beach area and downtown have succumbed to a blitzkrieg of country inns and bed-and-breakfasts: in 1991 there were three; today there are at least five times that many. According to the latest census count, the average rent for a house in Fernandina is $275 a month, rivaling the spring-season rate for a Saturday night in the cheapest room at the Ritz-Carlton, where the Presidential Suites go for $1,500. Somewhere in that differential is the equation of fortunes of Amelia's newcomers and old-timers, and the inevitability of tourism in the island's economy.

Fernandina is not the only American municipality in the 1990s to have surrendered its identity to an incursion of Lexi and lattes. Like other relatively modest cities that face an influx of sudden money, it finds that commercially and socially it is increasingly ruled by those who know it least. The fracture line does not neatly divide the races; in fact, the changes have forged an alliance between Fernandina's older blacks and whites, both of whom perceive that they are being run under by a yuppie juggernaut. Nevertheless, the progress has a color, and exclusion from it has a color, too. Fernandina's newcomers are almost exclusively white. Blacks aren't drawn there by opportunity, and indigenous blacks who are ambitious usually leave. Fernandina is a place with an immigrant class of entrepreneurial whites invested in its surface amenities of fairways and beaches and a black population cut off from its advancement and invested in its past. Of all the divisions on the island and in the town, this runs the deepest; it is an unbridgeable gap of perception between those who have the money and those who hold the memory. Perhaps because they lack the money, memory has become the special province of Fernandina's blacks.

At some point early in my residence, I arranged an introduction to Janice Ancrum, the woman who would almost crack the color barrier on the Nassau County school board. She met me courteously, but interrupted my greeting with a question: "Why are you so interested in black folks?" Aimed with the steady, level eye of suspicion, the question was so fundamental that it stumped me. Surely, I thought, the exceptional character of Amelia Island's black history was an obvious enough attraction for a nosy white journalist. But it wasn't really all that obvious; besides, I realized later, it wasn't the real answer. The truthful answer to her question about why I was so interested in black folks was: I wasn't. Not per se. An interest in black folks, however interesting they might be, was not what prompted me to write about race on Amelia Island. Granted, before I arrived I had known little of black insurance magnates and Southern black coastal resorts, much less of black pirates and black planters. But if I had at first been attracted by the uniqueness of local black history, it was the universality of that history that drew me back to write about it.

Black American history and black American experience are generally perceived as islands off the continent of mainstream American life. Important islands, perhaps—lovely and interesting, if you find them so—but ancillary. Many historians, usually white ones, find it possible to tell the American saga without mention of a significant black role. Other historians, often black ones, tout black relevance, but rarely to greater effect. The relevance is usually construed in one of two ways: The first holds that black subjugation gives the lie to the vaunted American ideals of freedom and equality. The second champions black participation in America's advance, noting that black slaves built much of the country's infrastructure; that a black entrepreneur opened the first hotel in San Francisco; that black leaders helped found several large American cities, homesteaded Chicago, and dominated the incorporation of Los Angeles; that blacks invented the carbon filament lightbulb and the traffic light, to say nothing of jazz, the pre-eminent form of American musical expression.

And so they were subjugated, and so they did contribute. And Amelia Island provides ample evidence of both, if that is what you are looking for. The escaped slaves that fled there during the Civil War were skilled craftsmen, many of them, and some of the antebellum freedmen were trained engineers; their handiwork is evident in the storefront brickwork, the ornate mantels of Victorian homes, the hulls of the shrimp boats, the chiseled marble headstones in Fernandina's Bosque Bello Cemetery. American Beach is itself an emblem of black innovation. The modern lily-white "plantations" that MaVynee Betsch so detests have their historical provenance in her great-grandfather's invention of a corporate-sponsored vacation enclave shut off from a hostile exterior world. That may have been some of what I wanted to show when I decided to tell A. L. Lewis's story: here was a man whose contribution had been neglected; here were histories missing from the books.

What I found was something else and something more. To champion A. L. Lewis as a black man of unsung success was to sell him short, to become enmeshed in the same web that trapped those historians touting Garrett Morgan's traffic light. In a strange and pernicious way, citing black contribution to majority culture concedes the majority's hegemony over the culture and marginalizes the cited contribution as well as the contributor. Annals of black American achievement are in this way self-defeating, for they involve only the most exceptional black people and enlist them in a supporting role. It is a demeaning equation. In the long run, the black person who contributed, and who must petition for recognition, is left as far offshore from America—as islandized—as the black man who stood apart as a reproach to America's hypocrisies. For even if racial experience is not an island, the issue of race is, and nothing that blacks achieve is perceived independent of it. If a black man walked on the moon, he would be "the first black man to walk on the moon" (in case you were wondering what the majority culture already is up there). No wonder there is a trend toward Afrocentrism and an imperative to record black achievement in the historical context of a majority black culture. Only in such a context, it would seem, can black endeavor shake off the onus of race and be celebrated for itself. Afrocentrism springs, to that degree, from a desire to be recognized as truly and fully American.

The fortress of American identity is all but impregnable because the foundations of American culture are so solid. Solid, anyway, in the popular imagination, which envisions the country as built on bedrock principles: the principles of equality and freedom expressed in our founding documents and the principle of Yankee ingenuity—a spirit of cultural dynamism, technological progress, and economic entrepreneurship. Black protest concurs in the centrality of these values, whether it honors them in the breach by throwing racism in their face or buttresses them with stories of black achievement. Ingenuity and equality and freedom are all indisputably part of the American character. But the country's foundation is laid in a deeper stratum than the bedrock of values—in the region of a molten, fluid question. The question preceded the founding fathers by two centuries; two centuries later, it is with us still, unanswered.

Homebrew American conservatives like to link the Constitution up with free enterprise and God, though the Constitution recommends no particular economic system and its framers were deeply and openly ambivalent on the nature of a deity. Nevertheless, the conservatives are right, in a way: the question of America was economic and religious, long before the Constitution was drafted. The New World was colonized during the Reformation and the European wars of religion, a protracted and bitter dustup between the domain of religious virtue and the secular domains of business and law. Commerce, for so many centuries constrained by the dictates of the church, wanted to break free, and its restiveness provoked the question: What *was* the moral obligation of business? Where did mankind's economic existence and moral existence coincide, and where collide, and where was the boundary between them? Can one truly render unto Caesar without also rendering to God? America, with its endless untapped resources and its capitalism unfettered by medieval tradition, became the great field for the resolution of that battle.

We are still confused about the nature of the fight: witness the fundamentalists who rage against secular humanism but favor free enterprise, that innately secular-humanist activity. While Americans enjoy arguing about rights and liberties as lofty abstract principles, the battle is really on the ground. The contest over our essential, founding American idea is the ongoing trench war between morality and money.

Should pornography be allowed to abide by the law of supply and demand so dear to libertarians? How about prostitution and gambling? Is society responsible for those who cannot make a living? Should television shows be predicated on marketability or on social responsibility? If you own your property, can you use it in whatever way you wish, even if that disrupts the common good? Can you cut down the last old redwoods and float them to Japan because you need the sudden profits to pay off a leveraged buyout? Does a company have a responsibility to retain those it hires, or to stay in a community that fostered it? When you have the quarter, can you pass the beggar by? If your economic advancement leaves out an entire category of citizen, is it acting impartially? If it *is* acting impartially, should it? Can the marina builders build whatever they want, if by doing so they destroy the life and livelihood of Ronnie and Vera West? Tellingly, the sign in the back of West's pickup truck read not "Where is justice in Fernandina?" or "Where is justice in Nassau County, Florida?" but "Where is justice in America?"

A hundred and forty years ago, the question that infused America's earliest glimmering brought it to the brink of dissolution. The hand of God might be seen in that, for those who see such things: He Who provided the grand stage for playing out the dilemma of morality and business placed on the stage the dilemma's most extreme expression, the issue of chattel slavery. The Southern planters contended that slavery was business; the Abolitionists called it iniquity. If the conflict was in fact a divine test, America passed, though barely. Its virtue as a society would be clearer of blemish if it had never chained a single slave, but because it did and because it fought to free that slave, its place in the long history of nations is unique. It is the only country that has gone to war with itself over the morality of holding slaves and risked its own destruction to confront its mortal sin.

Amelia Island was engrossed in that great test, with the special distinction that its black sons fought on the battlefield of their own emancipation. The least black male citizen of Amelia Island was enlisted in the very center of the nation's fate. He and his sisters still are. The battleground has moved, from feudal slavery to industrialization and now to a new service, entertainment, and information economy dominated by corporations and retail chains, which has come into

Amelia Island in the guise of tourism but is transforming every town in America. In significant regards, though, the battle remains the same. Our subjugation and our liberation still often wear the same face. We contest the old undiminished question, the line between money and what money cannot buy. No longer can it buy human beings, but it will buy culture and justice and history, if it may, just as it buys land and labor and goods. And people's souls are as caught in the transaction today as they were in the old slave South—as caught in Fernandina as in New York, on an island off the coast as in an Iowa field or Michigan factory, caught as surely if they are black as if their skin is white.

Precisely because they live so close to the fringe—ethnically, economically, geographically—the black residents of Amelia Island find themselves thrust to the center of the American experiment. This book is about their struggle, and so to some degree this book is about race: three stories of conflict in three black Florida communities. Being personal stories, personally observed, they do not suffice as allegory; experience on the ground is never as pure as the view from the bridge would imply. But they are more than just accounts of muddy experiences of race conflict. These are stories about progress and wealth and heritage—about the vital importance of memory, the personal nature of justice, the burden put on history and culture to be honest and true. They are stories about the importance of emancipating those things—culture, memory, history, heritage, and personal integrity—from the chains that modern commerce imposes on them. And they are stories about the importance of black experience to issues in American life that have nothing to do with race—issues that would be American predicaments even if race were not.

On our weekly rides into Fernandina Beach to go shopping, my conversations with MaVynee Betsch were journeys of their own, far outpacing the odometer. They launched me on my own more solitary wanderings through the public records and personal recollections of that corner of the Deep South. In my investigations I learned of a troubled man and the troubled policemen who shot him, of people trying to save a town's future by using its history, and of a patriarch who was important not because he was one of the earliest black millionaires or the founder of a black company and a black resort but because, as a businessman weighing his obligations to his race in the generation after slavery, he was made to grapple as no one else with the meaning of the American dream, the American dilemma. My journey would take me into an isolated and time-locked island and would eventually lead me back to the mainland—to an epicenter of average American experience and the new American world. But it would begin at my door, with a neighbor's scream at midnight, in a town that was evil, surely—just as evil as anyplace else.

2

Whom Shall I Fear?

© 1990 Bob Self

A storm hits American Beach.

For the last eight years, ever since their first big altercation with the police, Whilamena Wilson had hated to see her husband, Dennis, go out at night alone, and was reluctant to go out with him. This night was no exception. The next day—February 22, 1994—would be Dennis's birthday, his thirty-third, and he had wanted to celebrate its arrival. Perhaps his sister could take the kids, he told Whilamena, and the two of them could escape for the evening. He placed a call to the Elizabeth Pointe Lodge, the new bed-and-breakfast out on the beach road, to ask about reserving a room. His boss had given him tomorrow off, so they were free to lounge around in the morning and stay out on the beach until checkout time. But Whilamena nixed the idea. She had driven a long way that day to see her infirm mother—all the way into Georgia and back—and she was tired. And, anyway, it was foggy out. And, anyway, there was the problem with the police.

So Dennis Wilson worked until late evening in the side yard, filling in gopher holes with a shovel so that the lawn mower wouldn't tip into them the next time he cut the grass. Then he came indoors and headed into the bedroom to change out of his work clothes. Whilamena could hear the coins and keys from his pants pocket dropping into the china dish on the bedside table, and she hurried off into the kitchen to warm up his dinner in the microwave. But when he emerged, he said he didn't want to eat right then; he thought he might step out for a short while after all. He called into the bedroom to Demetrius, his twelve-year-old son, but the boy didn't hear him, or at least didn't respond. Then Dennis Wilson left the house and hopped in his car and drove off.

It was dark, and the fog was becoming dense. The Wilson home is on Florida State Road A1A, a four-lane highway that runs from Amelia Island and the island city of Fernandina Beach on the Atlantic coast, west through O'Neil and Yulee and Callahan, to form the spine of Nassau County. Wilson turned right out of his drive onto A1A in a direction that, had he continued, would have taken him out into the country, out past the Nassau County Sheriff's Office and the Florida Highway Patrol headquarters and the county jail, through the long, empty stretches of slash pines and saw grass and the stretches emptier yet where the pines had been harvested to feed the Fernandina pulp mills, out past the souvenir and orange stands and floodlit filling stations at the intersection of I-95. But at the first break in the median, he made a U-turn and aimed his Ford Probe back east, toward Amelia Island and the coast. In half a mile, he passed under the traffic light at O'Neil, glowing dimly overhead in the mist, and in another mile he was on the bridge. It was twenty minutes to eleven.

Later, Whilamena would remember exactly the time of her husband's departure. As soon as he had gone, she realized that it was past bedtime for their daughter, Dominique, and her glance traveled automatically to the clock on the wall over the television set. She was sitting on the living room couch, braiding Dominique's hair as the child sat before her on a hassock; when it was finished they went into Dominique's bedroom, and Whilamena knelt with her daughter for prayers. It was something Dennis would usually have done, had he been at home. With both children in bed, Whilamena washed the hair oil from her hands and put on a nightgown, but after a while, unable to sleep and compelled by a sudden worry, she made two personal appeals for her husband's safety. For the first, she would recall, "I got back down on my knees," but the second was more direct: she picked up the telephone and dialed the number of Dennis's car phone, which he had recently removed from their pickup truck and installed in the little Ford. "I wanted to tell him to come on back now," she told me. But mysteriously, the call wouldn't go through, and it was then, as she sat on the couch by the living room window with the phone in her hand, that Whilamena saw the lights, saturating the fog with blue emergency, a stuttering cold neon through the Venetian blinds: out on the highway, sheriff's deputies were racing for Fernandina. "They were going so fast," Whilamena said, and the way she said "fast" was a long, slow exhalation of awe and fear. "And I said to myself, 'Oh, please, don't let anything have happened to my Dennis.'"

At quarter to eleven, when Dennis Wilson was driving across the Amelia Island bridge, Paul Alberta was sitting in the living room of his mother's house on Vernon Street in Fernandina, watching a movie on television with his mother and his twelve-year-old daughter, Tunisia. His mind was on his daughter, who lived with her mother and stepfather and had been having troubles at home. Those troubles had been escalating, and Alberta was disturbed. A few hours earlier, he had phoned his friend Dennis to talk about it. Whilamena answered. Dennis was in the yard working, she told him, and promised to say that he'd called. Just checking up, Alberta told her, but Whilamena knew better. To the day and hour, she had known Paul Alberta as long as she'd known her husband, ever since the two men showed up in her hometown to watch a softball game and she'd encountered them in the bleachers. Whilamena had known Paul Alberta for more than a decade, and she knew when there was something on his mind.

Alberta had only recently returned to live in the town of his birth. After fifteen prodigal years, a dozen of them in the military, he'd been given an honorable discharge and a no-contest divorce, and had come home to help his mother, who was in Nassau General Hospital with what the doctors feared was terminal cancer. For the last two months, he had been living in her house; it was a house he hadn't lived in since he was a teenager at Fernandina Beach High School, back when his best friend, Dennis Wilson, had lived around the corner and a few blocks away. It was strange being back, a curious sort of dissonance, living in the camphored familiarity of his childhood home in a town he hardly recognized. Fernandina had changed from the close-knit village of his youth, becoming more divided and angry even as it had become more prosperous.

The people who welcomed Paul Alberta back to Fernandina Beach listed Dennis Wilson prominently among the things in town that had changed: he was angrier, they said, though more prosperous. Alberta's mother told him about his friend's legal troubles, and an aunt announced that Wilson was on the verge of violence and that if Alberta continued hanging around with him it would surely lead to trouble. Alberta had always known Dennis to be a confrontational guy, head-strong, hair-triggered, unapologetic: that's just the way he was. The two had had their fights back in their high school days, and had always smoothed them over. But his aunt's suggestion made Alberta mad. "Can't nobody make me get in trouble," he told her. "As long as I maintain my level, I can socialize with anybody."

He continued to rely on his friend. When he got a job as a diesel mechanic in Jacksonville, it was Wilson who drove with him to Sears a couple of days before Christmas to pick out twenty-three hundred dollars' worth of tools. And it was Wilson he called when he had a worry, like the worry he had tonight. "Dennis is a type of person I felt I could talk to," he would later tell me. "You know, a lot of people I went to school with are laying 'round here on drugs, all strung out. You know, you can't talk to them. So every time I came home on leave, me and him sit around and talk about this, talk about that. What happened was, me and Dennis had the type of relationship that if he had a problem he could talk to me, and if I had a problem I could talk to him."

Strangely, Wilson never talked much about his problems with the police. From Alberta's point of view, whatever had transpired seemed to have settled him down. When Wilson partied now, Alberta noticed, he preferred to party at home. He, at least, seemed to be maintaining his level, in a town that was in other ways slipping. And knowing Wilson as he did, Alberta was sure that tonight Wilson might or might not call him back but, considering his recent terror of driving after dark, would definitely not come by.

Nevertheless, just before eleven o'clock there was a crunch of tires on the wet dirt of the driveway, and Wilson was standing in the door. Dennis Wilson was six feet tall and weighed two hundred and fifty pounds. And he was strong. He had grown up helping his father on shrimp boats, wrestling the heavy nets to release their living cargo onto the swaying deck. Little wonder that as a grown man, Wilson had a tendency to fill whatever doorway he stood in. He stepped inside, but only long enough to ask after Alberta's mother's health and say hello to Tunisia. He didn't sit down; he wanted to go for a drive. He seemed animated, eager. "Do you know my birthday's at twelve o'clock?" he asked. Alberta invited Tunisia to come along with them, but she didn't want to miss the movie's ending. "Back in a while," he said to his mother and grabbed his red flannel shirt off a chair and walked out to the car with Wilson.

It was mild outside; an early draft of spring had slipped into town through the still air. Wilson was shirtless. He wore a black leatherlike jacket, unzipped, jeans, and a white baseball cap. As they got in the car, he told Alberta that he wanted to take him back out to the house to show him his latest project: a red flashing light he had just wired up in the yard to draw customers off the highway for a business he was starting selling seafood.

That was just like him, Alberta thought. Wilson was always engaged in something, and when he was done he had to show it off. He worked hard—always had. He inherited that exceptional drive from his mother, Miss Albertina. Miss Albertina was legend. "Big ol' crab-shuckin' woman," some people called her. As soon as any of her kids could walk and tote, she had them out picking up cans by the roadside and doing other odd jobs, and the lesson stuck. The house on A1A was early evidence of Wilson's domestic ambition; he had bought it when he was only eighteen, when no one else his age thought far past cars and partying. Recently, he'd been enlarging it and fixing it up, and he'd bought the two-acre lot next door and put in three mobile homes to rent out. Aside from his day job with a contractor, he was freelancing as a tree surgeon and selling firewood from the trees he cut. Now he was planning to sell shrimp and fish from his front door to customers drawn there by the blinking light. "Sure," Alberta said, "let's go see it." But they decided that first they'd get a beer.

Wilson backed out of the drive and headed the Probe into the fog as though navigating submerged channels—left onto Fir Street, right onto Twelfth. He glanced at Alberta, sensing his seriousness, just as Whilamena had sensed it earlier. "What's wrong with you?" he asked, and Alberta began telling him about Tunisia and her troubles. The subject occupied them as the Probe climbed north, up the ladder of cross streets that some Fernandina pioneer, in a contradictory passion for both nature and order, had named alphabetically after trees: Elm, Date, Cedar, Beech, Ash. They passed the town's athletic field and the Elm Street Recreation Center, the barber shop where Wilson's older brother Maxcell cut hair, and the white frame house where Wilson had grown up, but which had not been in the family since Miss Albertina died. No one at all was out.

Houses swam by, their dilapidation salved by mist. This was not the Fernandina of gingerbread and widow's walks and picket fences, which lay across Eighth Street to the west, in the city's historic district. Buildings were being restored over there; over here they got rehabbed. East of Eighth and south of Beech was the neighborhood commonly thought of as the black part of town. Most of its houses were ranch-style, of brick veneer or painted concrete block, modest in size, meager of ornament. Some had fenced yards, and among the fences those that were chain-link outnumbered those that were picket. There was little in the way of sod lawns or boxwood hedges, but a great number of dahlias, hydrangeas, begonias, and potted caladiums were set out front along swept walks, an observance that implied not ostentation but defense: in the same way that blue paint on a porch roof warns away evil spirits, the flowers guarded the border between dignity and decline. The houses east of Eighth Street straddled that border. Many were handsome, others less so: small wood-framed cottages set on red-brick pilings, shotgun shacks leaning over hard dirt yards. The neighborhood seemed to Alberta to have changed for the worse in his absence. Violent crime was making an appearance, and on Ninth and Tenth Streets crack cocaine was being sold heavily.

On Atlantic Avenue, Wilson pulled over in front of the Li'l Champ convenience store. It was past eleven now, but the store was still open, its light flooding white across the avenue through the fog. Wilson had promised Whilamena he would stop drinking, but she had given him a dispensation for his birthday and he was inclined to take it early. "I haven't had a beer all week," he said to Alberta, and it was unclear whether it was a boast or a complaint. They bought a four-pack of Schlitz Malt Liquor, and as Wilson began the drive back down Ninth Street they each popped open a can. To go out to Wilson's house dictated a right turn at Jasmine, so that they could continue south on Eighth Street to the bridge. But Alberta suddenly recalled that today was his Aunt Paulette's birthday, and they decided to drive out to Paulette's place to see what was going on. Paulette lived on South Fletcher, the beach road. So Wilson turned left and headed down Jasmine toward the coast.

For a city street, Jasmine is a long, dark stretch of lonely. Along much of its length it has no neighbor except marsh and scrub forest, with an occasional new-style subdivision of the sort that separates itself from the road and the world with a high blank length of fence. The result is that Jasmine is overlooked by almost no windows at all for the mile between Fourteenth Street and South Fletcher. Paul Alberta had been cheered by unshouldering his problems. The Staple Singers were playing on the tape deck, and the discussion had turned to happier things. They reached Fourteenth Street, and Wilson stopped at the red light before continuing ahead on Jasmine. Soon after that,

Alberta noticed the headlights close behind them. Wilson was driving slow. "Let 'em around," Alberta said, and just past the derelict Fourteenth Street Shopping Center, Wilson pulled the Probe over into the wet grass, and the lights passed.

It was a police car.

Reflexively, Alberta took the open Schlitz Malt Liquor cans and put them back in the paper bag and put the bag beneath his seat. Wilson seemed unconcerned. He brought the Probe back onto the pavement and followed the cruiser's taillights. After a while, the lights brightened and slowed and bumped off onto the shoulder. Wilson pulled around and Alberta glanced in the passenger-side mirror to see what was up, hoping the cruiser would turn and head back into town. Instead it fell in behind them, and the two cars traveled that way in a slow, short procession until they reached the end of the road.

After its long flat unremarkable straightness, Jasmine meets South Fletcher with a bit of a topographical fillip, cresting the coast dune and dropping down into the intersection off a slight rise. From the top of that rise, on a clearer night, one can look out over the road to the beach and over the beach to the Atlantic. The shoulder of the sea on those nights is beaded with the running lights of coastal freighters, and the rising moon casts a wide white path that, coming at you out of the east, can seem like Jasmine's continuation by other means into another realm. Tonight, the only impression Alberta had was one of thick fog thickening. Overhead, two red blinking lights issued a monotonous warning. Jasmine widens in its last twenty yards from two lanes to three, and the middle lane is marked with a left-turn arrow, faded to near invisibility by sun and traffic. Wilson stopped at the light and then pulled left onto South Fletcher. He was still accelerating when the cruiser's blue lights came on behind him. There was no siren. Wilson pulled over onto the shoulder and cut his headlights, but left the parking lights on and the engine running, and rolled down his window.

There were footsteps, and the face of James Norman appeared. It was not a face Wilson knew. Norman was a patrolman with the Fernandina Beach Police Department. He asked for Wilson's license and registration, and asked Wilson whether he knew why he was being stopped. "No, I don't," Wilson said. Norman told Wilson that he had not been fully in the proper middle lane before turning left onto South Fletcher. Alberta leaned over Wilson to protest that it was mighty foggy out and the street markers were hard to see, but he heard no response. Wilson handed his license through the window and Norman disappeared to sit in his own car under the blinking blue lights.

In a while he returned and asked Wilson to get out. The two men walked around to stand in the hard beach sand behind and to the right of the Probe. Alberta sat alone in the car, listening to the Staple Singers. They were singing, "I'll Take You There." He strained toward the passenger mirror and could see Wilson in the cruiser's headlights, touching his nose with his finger and doing the other minute calisthenics of a field sobriety test; a flashlight shone in Wilson's face. Finally he returned, and closed his door and sat in the driver's seat waiting. "What's going on?" Alberta asked him. "Did you get your license back?"

"No," Wilson said. Alberta did not think his friend seemed upset or angry.

"Why not?" he asked.

"I don't know," said Wilson. "He's trippin' with me. That's all—he just trippin' with me."

"Mercy," the Staple Singers sang, "I'll take you there!"

"I've dealt with these people before," Wilson said.

Across Fernandina, at Beech Street and Fourteenth, Police Sergeant Denny Bell sat in his cruiser, watching for speeders and listening to the radio with an alert idleness born of endless habit. The radio scratched out a staccato account of what was going on in town. There was nothing going on. Bell was shift supervisor, and so he paid more than casual attention to the location of each of his officers. In addition to the dispatcher downtown at the station house, there were four of them out patrolling: himself, Gregory Rozier, Alfred Smith, and Jim Norman. Following the other three cars by their radio dispatches was like tracking the gyrations of storm birds in occasional flashes of lightning.

The radio crackled and Bell heard Norman's voice, calling in from car nineteen. "HQ," he said. "Nineteen. Ten-twenty-eight, Florida." A 28 was a request for information on a license-plate number, and as soon as dispatch responded, Norman read it out: "Florida, Kilo, Mike,

Zulu, five, six, Zulu." Norman was on Jasmine, apparently following a car; nothing to worry about. On a typical midweek night shift, a patrolman might run 28s on several cars, checking for stolen vehicles and leaving a record of the identification of those cars he intended to stop. Just for safety's sake. In a moment, the radio crackled again. Dispatch was responding. "Two-door '90 Ford," the dispatcher said, and then relayed information that alarmed Denny Bell. "Registered to Dennis Wilson . . . Dennis Wilson." Bell headed his cruiser out rapidly in the direction of Jasmine Street.

Some minutes would pass before Norman's request for a 35, the code for backup, but Bell didn't need to wait. Norman was Fernandina's youngest patrolman—twenty-four years old, newly graduated from the police academy, second year on the force. There were things he did not fully appreciate about Fernandina, and Wilson might be one of them, even though Bell included a rundown on Wilson in his initiation of every new cop on the beat. At forty-seven, Bell was Fernandina's oldest and most experienced cop, and he knew Wilson well, knew his long arrest record and knew he could be provocational with no cause and belligerent when confronted. Bell had encountered him plenty of times in the station house when Wilson came in to complain of police harassment. Officer Alfred Smith, too, when he heard Wilson's name over the radio, was hit with a surge of adrenaline, left his beat, and headed for the beach.

Bell was halfway across town before Norman's voice came back on the air to ask if there were any outstanding warrants on Wilson. Again, the pause before the response. In the same way that Bell could envision his shiftmate walking alone through the fog to check on a car beside the highway, he could picture the scene in the yellow warmth of headquarters: the dispatcher in the narrow paneled room, facing two computer monitors and the tape machine that recorded the incoming calls. To check on the warrants, the dispatcher would dial the county sheriff's office on the telephone to ask if Wilson was wanted. The sheriff's dispatcher would look the information up on her computer and relay it back. With all the million-dollar technology at headquarters, warrant retrieval through dispatch still worked with the logistical efficiency of a bucket brigade.

Finally, a voice, confirming that Wilson was indeed fugitive. "Ten-four. Resisting arrest," dispatch said to Norman, and Bell listened intently for the crucial phrase, which came. "With violence." Resisting arrest with violence was a felony. Bell reached to the dash switch and turned on the blue lights.

"Ten-four," he heard Norman saying to dispatch, "I'm gonna need a thirty-five."

In Bell's imagination, he was already too late. If Wilson had heard the warrant announced over Norman's radio, what then? An incident could already be in the works. But when Bell reached South Fletcher and pulled his cruiser in behind Norman's, everything seemed under control. Norman was standing behind his car, the safe position for an officer waiting for backup—these young academy grads knew procedure—writing out a citation for the improper left turn. He walked over to Bell to tell him the situation. He was writing Wilson up for the traffic infraction and for violating a home-to-work provision on his license, Norman said. He had smelled beer in the car and on Wilson's breath, and had attempted a field sobriety test, but Wilson had been uncooperative, turning his head constantly so that Norman could not inspect his eyes with a flashlight. Nevertheless, Wilson did not stumble or weave or in any way appear to be drunk, so Norman was overlooking this. Bell warned him about Wilson's disposition and sent him out to serve the warrant.

Norman approached the Probe and knocked on the driver-side door. The window rolled down, and he told Wilson to get back out of the car. Bell and Norman would remember what ensued this way: The door opened and Wilson stepped out, asking how come, but as soon as he saw an additional policeman, he knew the answer was serious. "What's he doing here?" he asked, and fell back into the crux of the open door. The opening of the door had sent Norman toward the front of the car; he was now standing by the corner of the fender, and Bell was within the doorframe, facing Wilson. "There's a warrant for your arrest," Norman informed him. "Step out of the car and put your hands up." Wilson stayed jammed behind the half-open door. He seemed to Bell irrational and agitated. He denied that there could be a warrant out for him and refused to be arrested. He said that he wasn't going to jail. And then he got back into the car.

At that point, Bell and Norman both drew weapons. Patrolmen in Fernandina Beach are issued 9-millimeter Glock 17s as regulation sidearms. The Glock is a semiautomatic, and requires a pull of the trigger to fire each shot. It normally holds eighteen bullets, but by injecting a round into the chamber and then overcoming a stiff clip spring to top off the clip with an extra round, the gun can be made to hold a total of twenty bullets. Department regulations require that a patrolman empty his pistol at the end of each four-day work cycle and load it at the beginning of the next, and that's what Norman had done. He believed in the margin of advantage of a fully loaded weapon; his Glock held twenty rounds.

Repeatedly, the policemen ordered Wilson out of the vehicle, in language they would later recall as cordial, though insistent: "Please get out of the car. Please get out of the car. Get out of the car *now!*"— more and more loudly as Wilson refused to respond. From within the car, Alberta insists, the language he heard was more threatening: "*Try anything, nigger, and we'll blow your fuckin' head off!*" Alberta was getting scared. "Dennis, what's going on?" he asked, and told his friend to do what the policemen wanted, that he would drive the car home and tell Whilamena what had happened. But Wilson told him he wasn't getting out, that he had had too much trouble with Fernandina cops.

The door was still ajar, and Bell reached through and grabbed Wilson's jacket at the elbow and tried to drag him out. From his position by the front left wheel well, Norman watched Wilson through the windshield but couldn't see his hands. Wilson pulled against Bell's grasp; one hand fell to the stick shift and he put the car in gear and as he started driving forward Norman felt the fender hit his leg. He twisted back, and the car accelerated, and the fender hit him again. Norman's arm was outstretched, the Glock aimed into the windshield from no more than a couple of feet away. He yelled at Wilson to stop, but the car kept moving. He squeezed. The pistol jumped loudly in his hand. He squeezed again.

The first four shots entered the windshield, leaving a neat, close trail of holes just above the corner of the glass. The car passed Norman, and he swung around and continued shooting, firing four more rounds through the open driver-side window and several at the rear of the car. Bell had been holstering his Glock, with the idea of freeing both hands to grab Wilson, but as the car took off and his partner began shooting, he drew again and fired until Norman's back obscured the fleeing taillights. The Probe continued down South Fletcher, seemingly unfazed, and disappeared into the fog. Both policemen ran for their vehicles.

Inside the besieged car, Paul Alberta was yelling at his friend. He could feel a burning pain in his left leg, like a bee sting that wouldn't subside. "Slow down, Dennis!" he yelled. "I've been shot." He opened the passenger door and dragged his foot in the sand, wanting to hop out, but the car was gaining on a telephone pole or a roadsign, and he pulled himself back in as it swept by. He cowered against the glove compartment and looked up sidelong, terrified. Wilson was silent; he slumped toward Alberta but then he righted himself and with a visible effort pulled the wheel hard to the left.

A quarter of a mile to the north, Sarah McCarthy was driving down South Fletcher in her parents' Jeep Cherokee, with her friend Lisa Young. Both women were in their early twenties. They had spent the evening in the Palace Saloon downtown, and now they were groping their way home through the fog. Lisa saw the car first, approaching them in their lane with only its parking lights on. *My God, a drunk*, she thought, and called to McCarthy to watch out. Before McCarthy could switch lanes to avoid a collision, the oncoming car left the road altogether and jumped a ditch, mowed down a mailbox and a Century 21 sign, and bumped across a driveway. The two women watched, transfixed. As the car crossed the drive, the passenger door opened and a man fell out onto the ground. The car continued through a hedge and across another driveway, hit the corner of a house, and stopped. There was a moment's eerie silence—just the two of them and the still car and the man writhing on the ground. Then, as Lisa Young would recount, there was a roar of engines. "Police cars came out of the fog like out of nowhere," she said.

Policemen leapt out with drawn weapons, and McCarthy wheeled the Jeep around and fled north. Within five minutes, she had turned and come back, drawn by the fear that they had done something wrong by leaving the scene of an accident. There were three police cars now—Patrolman Smith had arrived. The man who had fallen out the door of the car lay facedown on the driveway; his hands were cuffed behind him. Another man, wearing a white baseball cap, was slumped behind the wheel of the crashed car and was being checked by police. Young and McCarthy were, apparently, the only witnesses to the crash. They got out of the Jeep and a policeman approached them. They remember him saying, "You saw him try to run me over, didn't you?" Young replied that they hadn't seen anything except the crash, but the patrolman came back a moment later and repeated the question, the women recall: "You saw him try to run me over, didn't you?" His insistence and the sight of the crash disturbed the two women. At home later, Young was distraught.

Midnight had arrived by then, and with it the advent of Dennis Wilson's birthday. By the time he turned thirty-three years old, he was nearly as cold as the mist.

There is hardly a modern social problem that does not end up in the vicinity of Amelia Island, requiring the attention of the Fernandina police. In the summer season of 1994 alone, a raft that had apparently carried Cuban refugees washed up on the beach, a serial killer who had left a trail of murdered homosexuals up and down the East Coast began picking his prey in local bars, and the grieving family of John Bayard Britton, a local physician murdered by an antiabortionist in Pensacola, required an armed escort at his funeral service, where "pro-life" protesters from out of county yelled racial taunts at local black police and offered marksmanship trophies to future successful assassins. In a public-safety debacle that made the networks, five people drowned in the ocean within minutes of each other along fifty yards of beach. But what put Fernandina that summer directly at the center of America's social turmoil was the killing of Dennis Wilson. Race tensions were the engine driving that turmoil, and the kind of event that most frequently and reliably inflamed them anywhere in the country was the killing of an unarmed black man by white policemen. In that sense, Fernandina's distress had the effect of making it a very ordinary American place.

Some might say that the unremitting outrage over police brutality was absurdly exaggerated. In no minority community in the country is police brutality a leading or even a significant cause of wrongful death, compared with deaths inflicted by criminals. In recent decades, police brutality and excessive use of force have declined, even as black-on-black predation has increased. Nor are they as pervasive as those other insults to purse or culture or health that define the black dilemma in

America. Nevertheless, a bullet fired from a police gun at a black subject is invariably a political as well as a physical missile—it traverses, at 1,500 feet per second, the great untraversable schism in American society. And when it does, the schism broadens. Not only because of the policeman's role as antagonist but also because of his more ordinary role as emissary. If the races are better neighbors in America today than they were in the past, it is the sort of neighborliness that necessitates strong fences; our peace is preserved by the maintenance of a no-man's-land. Our lives are less intermingled. Our business is conducted by messenger. More than ever before, we have appointed the police the messengers; our diplomats are armed. That is why a bullet fired from a police gun rends a community on its way to finding its mark, why police shootings are more than just a blemish in our broad and varied relations: our relations are not broad, not varied. Between adversaries whose only remaining contact is diplomatic, a diplomatic breakdown is catastrophic.

Often, when the catastrophe hits big cities, as it did Miami in 1980 and 1989, and Los Angeles in 1965 and 1992, and Washington in 1991, the passions are played out in the media and in the pronouncements of practiced spokesmen, with predictable results. Subtleties are overrun. The arguments become abstract and politically symbolic. The more the symbols compel the nation's attention, the more the personal, internal complexities of the original incident are forgotten. In a more remote, less noticed America, things remain closer to the bone. Instead of spiraling outward, becoming more and more public, the issues burrow deep into a community's private heart. In a place like Fernandina, whose families tend to know each other, relations between a cop with a gun and the person who takes a bullet, even in this age of tense division, are more than likely familiar. The civic agony is worse for being in all ways personal.

The weeks following the night of Dennis Wilson's killing would strain Fernandina Beach almost to rupture and bring it to the edge of riot and legal siege. Rumors of retribution circulated; whites downtown and on the beach road warned each other to draw the blinds at night and stay indoors even in the day. Children were kept out of school and some white families left town. Law enforcement agencies from surrounding counties were pulled in to augment the local police or were placed on alert. Police rode two or four to a car and responded to even minor calls with a swarm of cruisers. Fueled by the preaching of an implacable minister, a march for justice would take place through downtown and a militant redress committee would be formed by Fernandina's angrier black residents. An official inquest would be held in the courthouse, but despite its findings black and white would find themselves pushed farther apart than ever, in a little city that was becoming big but was not yet big enough to accommodate the distance.

There are two phone lines into Bernard and Patricia Thompson's home on Beech Street, and the first call came in on their personal line. It was twenty-five minutes to midnight. "Did you hear?" a voice asked, and the news it delivered hit Patricia Thompson from all sides. Thompson is Paul Alberta's aunt, and since the day two years earlier when her father married Dennis Wilson's older sister, Geneva, she was also—at least, officially—Dennis's niece. Patsy, as everyone knew her, was a good friend of both men. Bernard had helped Dennis renovate his house, and she had employed Whilamena in her day-care business. Oh, Thompson thought: Whilamena! She hung up and dialed the Wilson house.

"Is Dennis home?" Thompson asked, knowing the question was odd at that hour, but not knowing how else to finesse things.

"He went to pick Paul up," Whilamena said.

"I heard Paul's sick and at the hospital," Thompson said lamely, and as she spoke her other phone rang, the one that would ring almost incessantly over the next days. It was the business line of the Nassau County branch of the NAACP. Patsy Thompson was president of the branch, and her husband was head of the organization's legal redress committee. "You better come to the hospital," she told Whilamena.

A click announced a call coming in through Whilamena's call-waiting service, and she put Thompson on hold. "Hey, Whilamena," someone said, and all Patsy Thompson's diplomacy fell in shards. "I heard Dennis was dead."

For the rest of the night the lights coming on in houses traced the phone lines around Fernandina like an impulse down a broadening pattern of nerves. Thompson went to Nassau General Hospital, where she paced the bright linoleum and gleaned bits of news from nurses and nervous cops. Just before one o'clock, Whilamena arrived with her children and Wilson's sister Jeanette Baker. A policeman took Whilamena into a back room to confirm the bad news. Then the relatives, near and distant, headed for South Fletcher. A crowd had gathered there, blocking the road, pressed against the police tape in the gray fog—a surreal congregation, parting to let the widow through. A hundred feet away, Whilamena could just make out her own family car, surrounded with the ghostly figures of policemen.

Urgent calls also went out along that other, more restricted nerve, to those who needed to know within Fernandina's law enforcement and government. Fernandina's police chief, Walter Sturges, was away at the state capital for a conference, and it fell to his assistant, Captain Hoyt Johns, to get dressed, drive down, and size up the scene. He was met by Nassau County Sheriff Ray Geiger and Geiger's deputy, Major Tommy Reeves. Reeves was head of the investigation unit in the sheriff's office, and since it wouldn't do for the Fernandina police to investigate an incident involving their own department, that duty would fall to him. When Reeves arrived at Jasmine and South Fletcher, the place was nearly deserted. The road was closed with yellow tape. An evidence technician was stooped over, spray-painting orange circles on the macadam as though preparing it for some child's innovation on hopscotch. Each circle held a spent shell casing.

The north end of the crime scene was not so lonely. Thirty or forty people were gathered in the road—all of them black, Reeves noticed, in a neighborhood that was largely white. The car was resting against the house, with its parking lights still on and the tape deck blaring, because the patrolmen had not wanted to tamper with the evidence. Of the limp figure in the driver seat Reeves recalls, "He was unquestionably dead." He counted the bullet holes in the windshield glass and seat cushions. He inventoried the little Probe, noting the smell of spilled malt liquor, and also Norman's cruiser, where a citation lay half-completed on the front seat with a license clipped to it. The face on the license belonged to the man now slumped over the wheel of the wrecked Ford, being serenaded by the Staple Singers. In the photo, the face was smiling broadly.

Evaluating the scene took hours, much longer than usual. "The humidity was a hundred percent," Reeves recalled to me later. "My hair was dripping, my clothes were sopped. I couldn't keep my paper dry, and my pens wouldn't write." But the main trouble was the assembly behind the police tape, which Reeves could not see clearly from a hundred feet away but could certainly hear. "These people were not a friendly crowd," he said. "They were hostile. They were yelling. Their general mood was anger and wanting retribution against those officers involved. They were demanding to go up to the car where the body was. I told them we just could not allow that. I needed that crime scene to be undisturbed. We fought this battle the whole time, to keep them behind the police tape. We had to call out extra officers to keep them from overrunning the crime scene."

The Florida Department of Law Enforcement brought up generators and floodlights from Jacksonville for site inspection and photography, but they were afraid to turn the lights on, lest the illumination of the car and the body inside it further incite the crowd. "It would have tripped the trigger," Reeves said. At three A.M. they could wait no longer, and the yard around the car leapt into brilliance. No riot ensued. That left Reeves with one remaining problem: removing the body. In Jacksonville, where he used to work, that would have been simple—an ambulance would have whisked it to the medical examiner's office. But from Fernandina, the ride to the Jacksonville morgue was an hour each way, and only the funeral homes would do it. Therein lay a problem. "I don't know what the deal is," Reeves said to me, a bit reluctantly. "I'll tell you and you can make what you want of it. The white funeral home up there will not pick up black people." I knew the mortuary he meant, and that it only handled a black funeral once in a blue moon. "We called for Huff and Battise, the black funeral home, and my God, we waited! It must have been two hours. It was a long time before they came."

A call to Huff & Battise meant a call to C. T. Smith. Smith, in his seventies, was a quiet-spoken son of one of Fernandina's old black families. You can measure black mortality in Fernandina by the ringing of the red phone on the sideboard in his parlor. When it rang that night, the caller told him nothing of the circumstances, just a place. So it looked like business as usual to Smith when he got there: car off the road and a mailbox down, your standard late-night mismatch between a driver's desire to go home and his incapacity to get there. Two things seemed out of the ordinary—the size of the crowd and the reticence of the police, who usually told him what was up, but tonight did not. The man he had been called to handle was no stranger to Smith—he had known Dennis Wilson from the day he had been born.

Smith loaded Wilson's body into the hearse, and just before daylight, as the fog began to tatter, he sent it down the long road into Jacksonville. The crowd had kept its vigil. It seemed as though every member of local law enforcement, uniformed and plainclothes, was at the scene, and every black person in town. With the exception, that is, of the two police officers and the two black men who had been there at the start.

By dawn that morning, opinion on the street had already divided into opposing sides. One side's story was that Dennis Wilson was a dangerous man with a criminal record who had confronted the police one too many times and gotten what he asked for. The other was that Wilson was someone the police had long targeted and finally found their chance to eliminate. The former was of course the official choice, as Sheriff Ray Geiger made clear in an afternoon press conference. He announced that an investigation by his office was already underway headed by Major Reeves, and in a preemptive move of support for the policemen's decision to shoot he displayed Wilson's record of twenty-three arrests since the start of 1982 and relayed the medical examiner's finding of Wilson's blood alcohol level—.13, sufficient to make Wilson legally drunk. "This was not your go-to-Sunday-school type of man," Geiger said.

"Are you glad he's dead?" a television reporter asked.

"What kind of question is that?" snapped Geiger.

At the inquest, seven weeks later, Whilamena Wilson would take the stand at her own request, and would go through her husband's arrest record, noting that in one after another of the most serious charges Wilson had been found not guilty by judge or jury. He was, in fact, not much of a criminal in the usual sense. Wilson had never raped anyone or shot or stabbed anyone, nor had he committed any crime he might be seen to profit from—never burgled a house or robbed a convenience store or sold or bought drugs or torched his neighbor's barn or forged someone's name on a check or traded stocks on an inside tip.

He was certainly rough. He had been violent to Whilamena and had accosted other women. Any number of Fernandinans had run afoul of his temper. When he'd been drinking, he was a handful. Not everyone who thought Dennis Wilson was overdue a comeuppance and that the world would be better off without him was white. His first arrest was for buying a stolen bicycle, when he was ten. He gave it back and the charges were dropped. In 1980, he paid a fine for driving with a suspended license, and that began an epic litany of serious and minor traffic infractions; the first seven arrests on Wilson's record since 1981 involved driving without a license. His last repetition of that particular offense came in January, the month before his death. Increasingly, over the past dozen years, he had also been charged with angrier crimes: disorderly conduct, breach of the peace, and firearms violations.

His tendency to violence did not surprise some of his relatives. "It's a Wilson trait," one his nephews told me. "When I get mad, I'll say anything to anybody. It's like an uncontrollable rage that comes over you, and if you can't control it, you'll hurt somebody. It's Wilson, man." Yet this nephew, like other Wilsons I knew who were closely related to Dennis, was among the most steady and pacific people I've ever met. If some black Fernandinans diagnosed Dennis Wilson's famous temper as inherited, just like his work ethic, others described it in sociological terms: perhaps an inherited work ethic had brought Wilson inexorably up against the barrier past which no amount of ambition would carry him in Fernandina—the barrier that one friend familiar with Wilson's struggles called the "blank white wall."

There was a time in Dennis Wilson's life, before the trouble with the police, before the arrests and arguments and harassment complaints and lawsuits, when he seemed to have given Fernandina the slip. He joined the army. The military draws many of Fernandina's sons—Denny Bell served in the army in Vietnam—and for many of its black sons, it is a popular avenue of escape from the stultifying sureties of a hometown future. Paul Alberta chose the same escape, though he chose it circuitously, through an accidental encounter that showed something of Fernandina's inescapability. Alberta's mother had sent him out to Seaside, California, after graduation, to stay with her sister, away from the aimlessness of his Fernandina peers. A few days after he arrived, he was walking down the street to the store when, to his amazement, he ran into his favorite peer, his schoolyard buddy, Dennis Wilson. Wilson was stationed at nearby Fort Ord. "We had a nice talk," Alberta told me, and after Wilson flashed his steady paycheck and signed Alberta onto the base for dances, Alberta was persuaded to enlist. He would go on to serve in Panama and Kuwait. A year after Alberta's enlistment, Wilson was discharged, honorably, but under a cloud. In a preview of his resentment of uniformed authority, he had refused to obey a lieutenant's orders.

What Wilson did next surprised Alberta. "The last thing I ever expected Dennis to do," he told me, "was go home." When, later, Alberta also returned to Fernandina, just in time to attend at close range the killing of his friend, the town itself seemed almost animate in their fate.

Defenders of Dennis Wilson would note that he had his first violent altercation with the local police after he went to the aid of some white civilians. He didn't have to go far; that particular piece of trouble came straight to him.

Dennis and Whilamena had spent the evening of August 22, 1986, dancing at Mr. P's, a nightclub in Jacksonville. About one-thirty or so, they headed home, and as they pulled into their drive and got out of the car, all hell broke loose. All hell had started in Fernandina, when the driver of a white 1979 TransAm committed a traffic infraction and then tried to outrun Fernandina police. The infraction was ordinary; the pursuit was spectacular. By the time the chase made it over the bridge and into the county, sheriff's cars were waiting. They had formed a moving wall blocking the oncoming lanes with their lights flashing and sirens blaring. The TransAm ran through the cordon with its headlights dark at more than 100 miles an hour, tipping one sheriff's car into a ditch, where it rolled twice and landed on its roof. Then the fugitives' luck exploded, literally. The TransAm blew its engine and coasted to a steaming stop on the shoulder by the Wilsons' mailbox.

Two men were in the car—Rudolph Reeves Yeagle and his friend Jon Hatfield. Yeagle was driving. They were on an extended visit from Kentucky, and they had brought with them a felicity of country expression that made their later depositions marvels of ironic understatement. "You knew you were running away from the police?" an attorney asked Hatfield. "Well," Hatfield allowed, "they were chasin' us."

"When we stopped," Hatfield testified, "I jumped out and immediately went face-first down on the ground, spread eagle."

"Why?" the attorney asked.

"Because I seen it on TV," Hatfield told him. "That's what you're supposed to do."

What happened next wasn't supposed to, at least in Hatfield's opinion. He and Yeagle were kicked by the Fernandina police and the sheriff's deputies and hit with clubs and zapped with stun guns.

"What happened? They just beat you up?" the attorney asked Hatfield.

"Yes," Hatfield said.

"For no reason? They just walked up and hit you?"

"As far as I know," Hatfield said.

"For no reason?" the attorney pressed.

"The reason was, I was on the ground," Hatfield explained, "and they come up and hit me on the back of the head."

Watching the melee from their front doorstep were Whilamena and Dennis Wilson. They berated the police in terms the police described as obscene, telling them to get off their property and turn off the lights and halt the beating. Whilamena told me that she and Dennis intervened only to save the white boys' lives. When the white boys were handcuffed and thrown in the back of a police car, official attention turned to Dennis and Whilamena. Sergeant Lee of the sheriff's office placed both Wilsons under arrest. Then, as Lee testified later, Dennis put his hand on Lee's chest and pushed him backward. Lee and another officer thereupon threw Wilson to the ground. From the back of the cruiser, the Kentucky boys watched the action.

"How well were you able to see the officers and Dennis Wilson?" a lawyer asked Yeagle in a deposition.

"Like a motherfucker," Yeagle said.

"Like a motherfucker?" the lawyer asked.

"'Excellent,'" Yeagle interpreted.

Hatfield described the activity: "I saw what looked like eight or ten people in a circle beating something."

"What were they doing?" an attorney asked. Hatfield's response was described by the court reporter as "a clubbing motion."

"They was stingin' him with the sting gun," Whilamena said in her deposition, of the treatment given her husband by the officers.

"Stun gun, you mean?"

"Yeah, whatever you call it. . . . They was just stingin' him all over."

"How many times did they hit [Dennis]?" an attorney asked.

Whilamena replied, "Oh, they beat him. Ain't no doubt about it."

Whilamena Wilson spent the night in jail, and Dennis Wilson did, too, after his head had been sewn up at the hospital. Yeagle and Hatfield were found innocent on charges of battery on an officer, aggravated assault, and disorderly conduct, and so were the Wilsons. Afterwards the Fernandina Beach Police Department and the Nassau County Sheriff's Office settled a brutality suit brought against them by the Wilsons. The amount of the settlement was not disclosed, but it was rumored to be $35,000. It was enough money, anyway, to give Wilson a new way to taunt the police. "See what y'all bought me?" he would yell at them in town. What they had bought him was a brand-new 1990 red Ford Probe.

The years following that incident were years of some trouble for Dennis and Whilamena Wilson. Miss Albertina died, and in memoriam Dennis named his property on A1A after her: Tina's Point. Out on a corner of the lot, on an embankment by the highway where everyone passing could see, he spelled her name with white-painted bricks. The greater tragedy happened on what was meant to be a holiday. Whilamena and Dennis and their two sons had gone to spend the day swimming at American Beach. The boys ran ahead while Wilson unloaded the beach chairs from his car; by the time he caught up, the oldest, his stepson, had been trapped in a fast outbound current and disappeared. The ocean off American Beach is known for malicious currents, just as the beach is known as the best on the island; sometimes in a heavy surf a massive runout appears right in the center of the beach, and people can drown in it, as five people did on Memorial Day, 1994. The current that caught Wilson's stepson wasn't quite natural, though: it was a by-product of Amelia Island's resort economy. A big dredge was working offshore, pumping sand and water into tunnel-size pipes. The beach end of the pipes spewed water that washed back out to sea, leaving its freight of sand behind to rebuild and replenish the beach. That was the runout that had swept the boy away. His body washed up a day later and a mile up the beach. He was eight years old. Encouraged and guided by American Beach resident MaVynee Betsch, Wilson filed a wrongful death suit against the county, which was settled out of court, just like his suit against the police.

Wilson's success in his brutality suit did not assuage his anger. Increasingly, after 1986, Wilson's arrests were for resisting arrest, with or without violence, and battery on a law enforcement officer. The law certainly reciprocated his antagonism. Sheriff's Deputy Fuller Crews was on duty at the county jail one night when Wilson was brought in on a charge. The arresting officer had not handcuffed him, and Wilson bolted from the car into the woods. Crews and another jailer tracked him down through the dark and rain, and when they found him, Crews recalled, "We tightened him up a little."

Wilson's antipathy for anyone in uniform was so ecumenical that Paul Alberta once presented it to me as evidence of Wilson's lack of racial animus. "Dennis would help anybody, whether you were black, white, whatever. He would help anybody, if he liked you," Alberta said. "But if he ain't liked you, he didn't care nothing about you. That's the way he was. He wasn't no prejudiced person, and he didn't like no law enforcement, white or black."

On November 14, 1989, Jerry Cameron, who was then the police chief in Fernandina, addressed a letter to Rodney Gregory, Wilson's lawyer. The letter read, in part:

> The reason I am writing you is that Mr. Wilson's confrontations and threats against police officers are becoming more frequent and more serious. He, at one point, went into a gun shop and requested to see a gun that would make a lot of blood, that the police were not going to "____" with him anymore. On another occasion, he remarked to an officer and a civilian that he was going to take out one of my officers, and could do it very easily while the officer was working at his off-duty job. He most recently threatened Sgt. Johns, commenting to another police officer, "I've got the guns, I can do it." He then came to the Police Station, became involved in a confrontation with Sgt. Johns, and was arrested for having a con-

cealed firearm. Of much more concern is that he, on this past Saturday, went to one of my officer's home; had a shotgun laying in the back seat of the car; told the Officer he wasn't going to take it anymore, that he was not afraid to die. He had obviously been drinking on this occasion.

To continue to threaten the lives of police officers, and to show up in various places with firearms, is creating a situation that is likely to result in serious harm to Mr. Wilson or to a police officer. All officers of this Department are justifiably concerned that Mr. Wilson has taken certain steps to carry out his threats and that they can no longer be considered idle threats. Consequently, when Mr. Wilson is in their presence, they are in extremely defensive posture.

We have now reached the point that I am genuinely concerned that additional confrontations could be disastrous. It appears, from my perspective, that Mr. Wilson may actually want a confrontation where he is exposed to great bodily harm, or possibly death.

Cameron closed, "In the hope of defusing a very dangerous situation, I remain, Very truly yours."

Soon after Dennis Wilson's death, I met with Jerry Cameron in the courtyard of a Fernandina café. Cameron was no longer either a Fernandina resident or a city employee. He had resigned as police chief in 1992 and moved to a Caribbean island to teach scuba diving at some place called Pink Gin Beach. He had had enough of law enforcement. On the wall of the police station, in a row of other chiefs, is his photograph, in which he is short-haired and pale. The man who met me in the café was as dark as an old oak desk, wearing shorts and sandals, with a long blond ponytail and two turquoise bracelets, one of which he wore around an ankle. His memories of Dennis Wilson were fresh and unleavened, though, and when I asked him about Wilson's penchant for annoying the police, he shook his head. "He would tell my men that he was teaching his little girl to shoot, and was using pictures of policemen as targets," Cameron recalled. "I had Dennis in my office every two months. I said, 'Dennis, you cannot do this! You're making my men so nervous, you're going to get hurt.'"

Still, the provocations increased. "He would go out of his way to find blue lights and get in a fight," Cameron told me. "If he hadn't been shot on the night he was, it would have been somewhere else, some other time. He wanted to commit suicide by cop."

*   *   *

In times of conflict and crisis, Fernandina's different factions—black and white, newcomer and old-timer—search for explanation in different realms, using different rules of evidence. For many, the history relevant to Dennis Wilson's death extended no deeper than his rap sheet, his penchant for bad behavior, and his clear insubordination in the minutes preceding his shooting. He had provoked and had been punished. He had certainly disobeyed and probably even assaulted an officer of the law, and the consequence, however lamentable, was foreseeable. That's as far as it went: case closed. Few middle-class whites could imagine any circumstance wherein they would flout a policeman's orders, much less expect to get away with it. For other residents, including most blacks, the issue had little to do with Dennis Wilson's personality or his official sins. For them, the roots of the tragedy ran to the far corners of Fernandina society and deep into its past, and the obvious facts of the matter were only a place to start.

The split reflected a more general division in Fernandina's mindset, a gap in perception that had been widening as the town lost its old industrial and fishing economy and became the fiefdom of a new class of tourist entrepreneurs and retail merchandisers. The newcomers, unrooted in history, perceived the place geographically, and their analysis of any event proceeded from the point of its occurrence, like a ripple on a pond, as shallow as a spreadsheet. Was the violence near their neighborhood? Would it inconvenience their customers?

To the old-timer in Fernandina, the present hour and surface geography are of secondary import. The old-timer didn't come to his position over land but over time, through his experience in one single place, down through the generations. His assessment of any occurrence goes perpendicular to the assessment of the businessman, to the bottom of his personal, and then his ancestral, memory.

The historical viewpoint is even stronger in Fernandina than it might be in other old, small Southern towns, because Fernandina is a fishing town, an old pirate port on a treacherous, hurricane coast. The fisherman's fortunes are always obscured beneath waves or over the horizon; his wealth is hauled from unseen depths and his disasters lost to them. For the old Fernandinan, what is visible on the surface is not to be taken at face value but read for sign and portent: the fins that follow the fisherman are either friend or predator, but never both. Sometimes they belong to the dolphins, who are said to save drowning men, sometimes to the sharks. The truth of things barely breaks the surface, and the meaning that accrues to an event accumulates through dark channels. How you read the news of Dennis Wilson's death, if you were a Fernandina citizen, depended on who you were and which model of perception you decided to trust—on whether you saw in the surface of life its face, or saw the veil.

In his hospital bed the morning after the shooting, Paul Alberta related something to Patricia and Bernard Thompson which made them think that maybe the incident on South Fletcher had been something more than an unplanned encounter between a motorist and two cops. In the last moments before the bullets began flying all around him, Alberta had witnessed a distinct apparition through the passenger-side window: a man who was not Denny Bell and not James Norman, standing in the beach sand beside the road. Alberta later told the official inquest what he had seen. "I looked around, and I saw another man with a gun standing five feet to the right," Alberta testified, and described the man as short. "He didn't have on a uniform, to the best of my recollection. . . . I don't know if he was a police officer, but he had his gun pointed."

Alberta thought that this mysterious gunman was the source of the bullet that had pierced his left leg. But at the inquest Alberta's third man was derided as a phantom. There were no footprints in the sand, no shell casings on that side of the car, no holes from an inbound bullet in the Probe's passenger door. Alberta, it was suggested, must have seen a reflection in the glass.

For black listeners at the inquest, however, the third gunman remained a tangible presence. If he wasn't concrete, he was nevertheless convincing—an embodiment of all the unseen forces attending the confrontation between black civilians and white power. If anyone wondered why Dennis Wilson (or any black man) might not jump to obey a policeman's orders, the phantom offered an historical explanation.

On the morning of February 23, Patsy Thompson's living room, its lace curtains pulled over lowered miniblinds, was full of people—two relatives of Dennis Wilson and rotating teams of area newspaper and television reporters who had come to interview them. Wilson's family was extensive; he had close to twenty siblings (including a sister who lived across the street from me, and whose screams when she heard the news had awakened the neighborhood). Representing them all were Maxcell Wilson, Dennis's older brother, who sat mostly quiet in an easy chair in the corner, and Jeanette Baker, who was as animated as her brother was impassive. Baker is a military nurse but was dressed this day in mufti: blue jeans and a San Francisco sweatshirt. "This was not just a murder," she said to Sarah Bottoms, a reporter from the weekly *Fernandina Beach News-Leader*, "and not just a killing. It was a lynching. They said, 'We planned to get this guy, and we bided our time.' Everybody knew that the police were after him. Everybody knew that the police had even told him that they were going to get him. And now that they have him on a dark street in a white area, it looks like mud, and it's beginning to smell even worse."

The phone rang, and Thompson answered it as she always answered her second line, "Hello, NAACP." As she talked, Sarah Bottoms and the Wilsons continued their conversation in lowered tones. "Aren't you angry?" Bottoms asked Maxcell Wilson. He deliberated for what seemed a long time before answering. "It was uncalled for," he said.

With her ear still pressed to the phone, Thompson jotted out a note and passed it to me. It read, "4 black young men have been killed by police in a short period of time."

This, then, was the first submarine layer of relevant history. While defenders of the white policemen focused on Dennis Wilson's violent tendencies, black Fernandinans were examining the tendencies of the police. The gist of the issue, the history that circled ominously beneath the official explanation, was the point of Patsy Thompson's note: Dennis Wilson was not just a black man shot and killed by local law enforcement. He was the fourth such in the last five years.

The first was Andeaz Clark, a nineteen-year-old graduate of Fernandina Beach High School, whose only crime on the night of February 12, 1989, was having the extreme bad fortune to be in the back seat of his friend Michael Dennison's car. Clark and Dennison and a third local boy had just been to a ball game and were looking for some trouble or a fight to round the evening out. Dennison was amusing himself by spinning his Buick Century in donuts around a dirt parking lot when the Fernandina police spotted him. He was younger than Clark by three years but already had a record to show for his troubled adolescence. He had returned to Fernandina from the juvenile detention center in Daytona Beach only two days earlier. As he told his passengers when the police tried to stop him, he had no intention of going back. So he ran. And the police pursued.

The Buick sped down Eighth Street and over the bridge into the county. Dennison plowed across the median to avoid a roadblock and continued in the oncoming lanes of A1A at 85 miles an hour. When he reached the intersection of Highway 17, at Yulee, his path was blocked by a patrol car. He rammed it out of his way. Both of his passengers were pleading with him to stop and let them out. At the intersection with I-95, Dennison climbed an exit ramp and roared south on the northbound side of the interstate. By the time he reached Jacksonville, twenty miles later, he had at least switched to the correct side of the road. His tail was as bright as a comet's: cars from the state patrol, the sheriff's offices of two counties, and the Jacksonville and Fernandina police. They fired some twenty shots at the Buick—Nassau County Sheriff's Deputy Stanley Hurst was shooting from the driver's side of his speeding patrol car while his friend and seatmate Rickey Pope leveled a shotgun through the passenger window. Pope was a civilian, along that night just for fun; he had brought his own shotgun, a 12-gauge, pump-action, 20-inch-barrel Remington. He emptied four shells at the Buick as they careened down Jacksonville streets, blowing out its left rear tire. On Florida Avenue, Dennison collided with another cruiser and turned into a cul-de-sac, throwing sparks from rubberless rims, and finally went off the road. Three of his tires were flat, and he was trapped by so many police vehicles that they filled the street and the last of them had to go elsewhere in search of a place to park. The first officer to approach the car later said that everything was under control at this point. The second officer, Deputy Stanley Hurst, opened fire anyway. Hurst said later that he was under the impression that Dennison was still trying to flee, and that he was shooting at the last remaining tire. If so, he missed badly: he put a 9-millimeter copper-jacketed hardball slug through the back of Andeaz Clark's head.

Police response to the killing differed in town and county. The Fernandina police shift supervisor that night was Denny Bell. He had called off most of the city police cars, allowing only the first to continue the pursuit, and had phoned Chief Cameron at home to tell him that there was a disaster in the making. Bell and Cameron had then driven to Jacksonville to view the scene. "The car looked like it had been in Vietnam," Cameron told me. "Bullet holes everywhere. A front fender was missing. I sat and analyzed this, and I said, 'There's no way to make anything good out of this.'" By the time he and Bell got back to Fernandina, Cameron had decided what to do. "I got on the phone and I called all the black leadership, and I called my captain, and I said, 'There's going to be a very important meeting tomorrow at two o'clock.' And we had a meeting, and I brought the goriest pictures I could get and showed them up there—I was determined to upstage the media on this—and I said, 'This is a tragedy, and there's no way I can justify it.'"

Days later, Chief Cameron attended Andeaz Clark's funeral, and brought some other white officers with him. At the funeral, Clark's father shook his hand. "I was treated courteously," Cameron told me. His forthrightness surprised and pleased the black ministers and other black leaders, but it opened a breach between him and Nassau County Sheriff Laurie Ellis that never healed. Cameron recalled for me his attempt to enlist Ellis in his community meeting: "Laurie said, 'Tell them to piss off'—that if they caused any trouble, he'd arrest them."

Hurst and Pope were accused of perjury and tampering with evidence during the investigation of the case and eventually pleaded guilty to obstruction of justice. That seemed to settle things: moral turpitude (as the prosecutor referred to the perjury and evidence tampering) was sufficient reason to keep Hurst out of the sheriff's office for good. Instead, immediately after the sentencing hearing, at which Hurst received probation, Sheriff Ellis told reporters that Hurst still had his job, "and we're glad to have him." Clark's seventy-five-year-old grandfather, Lewis Faison, called the rehiring of Hurst "a slap in the face."

Law enforcement in Nassau County had always had its shadow of racism. One Depression-era police chief of Fernandina was an avowed member of the Ku Klux Klan, and Klan parades down Centre Street were escorted by the town's one police vehicle, with the chief waving from behind the wheel. But the Fernandina police were always seen as benign compared to the county sheriff's office. The character of the law in Nassau County, Florida, was established by the head of that office, a former road contractor and chain-gang foreman named H. J. "Cap" Youngblood, who ruled Nassau County from 1940 to 1968 and is still storied, three sheriffs and thirty years later. "Cap was a *man*," one ex-deputy told me, as though the inference in that would be evident, to which another added, with portent, "He ran a tight county." Translated, that meant Youngblood got brutal when he needed to, and was not often brutal arbitrarily. "I don't care if you were black or white," Ben Sessions, another ex-deputy, told me. "If you made him mad, he'd put a foot through you."

A certain degree of brutality was considered a recommended survival tactic by lawmen in that time and place, whether they were white or (like Ben Sessions) black. Northeast Florida was, and often still is, a Wild West sort of place. With three deputies patrolling hundreds of square miles of tough small town and lonely backwoods, meaningful backup was an absurdity and any lapse of authority could get you killed. Youngblood had authority. To arrest a man, he generally called him on the telephone and told him to report to jail. One story of Youngblood's talent for suasive apprehension concerns the night Ben Sessions had trouble breaking up a bar brawl in Hilliard, a small outpost in the extremity of the county. Youngblood drove over, marched into the bar, and made an offer to the hostile crowd. "If y'all can whip me," he said, "y'all can all go home." Upon consideration, everybody sat down. Youngblood said, "Fine. Be at my office at nine A.M. tomorrow."

Under successive sheriffs, and especially under Laurie Ellis, the brutality had continued while Youngblood's finesse in administering it did not. The office developed a reputation for excessive force. Fuller Crews, the deputy who ran the county jail for a while in the 1980s, recalls turning away prisoners brought in for incarceration and sending them to the hospital instead because they had been beaten too savagely. A three-part TV-news exposé of the sheriff's office by reporter

Winston Dean of Jacksonville station WTLV alleged the faking of jail-breaks, the tipping off of drug dealers, and a history of excessive force. The series was titled "Fist of Justice," and it struck a raw nerve in Nassau. Even in their own defense, sheriff's deputies suggested their brutal natures: Ellis's second in command, Rocky Mistler, said of a man who had been beaten when he was apprehended, "I should have killed him then." Another deputy, refuting the drug dealers who had implicated him in illicit activity, described them as "just dogs, that's all—they're dogs, and they'll fight each other." These attitudes doubtless underlay the outbreak of suspicious shootings in Nassau County in the late 1980s and early 1990s.

The second of those shootings occurred a year and a half after Andeaz Clark was killed, when Sheriff's Deputy Larry McDonald responded to an attempted break-in at the Pepper Tree Village apartments on Lime Street. It was late at night when McDonald reached the scene; he saw a man behind the Fourteenth Street Shopping Center whom he took to be the burglar. He called for him to stop, and when the man turned around, McDonald thought he saw a weapon. McDonald fired and hit Alvin James Oliver in the head. Oliver was a career burglar who had been released earlier that year after serving eight months of a four-and-a-half-year sentence. He was carrying a flashlight, some socks, and a pair of pliers, but no weapon. Within a day, the sheriff's office announced its conclusions in the matter. "A preliminary investigation indicates it was a justifiable shooting," Colonel Rocky Mistler said. In the course of the following month, the state's attorney's office and a judge both concurred. McDonald was a respected officer. Fellow deputy Chuck Moser said of him, "He was a straight-up deputy. Oh, he could be a little rough. But in a hands-down situation, if I had to choose someone to back me up, it would be McDonald. He'd pop a cap on somebody if he had to. But he wouldn't do it unnecessarily."

In fact, McDonald had earned a reputation as the man the sheriff's office called in when "popping a cap" was called for. Only three months earlier, he had killed another suspect, a white man who raised a rifle toward him. He was cleared in that shooting as well.

Despite the official exonerations, a public dissatisfaction was brewing. It found its champion in Andrew McRae. McRae is a Baptist preacher—burly and short, with a stance that displays the low pugnacity of a street fighter, all explosive reach, no strike zone. His real reach is verbal. His voice approximates the throttled power of a subway under a restaurant; he knows how to make the Wedgwood tremble. His vowels loiter, and he has a knack for driving home a rhetorical blitzkrieg with a shy and calculated stutter, which he does without fail whenever he takes the pulpit. On the night Andeaz Clark was killed, McRae was packing boxes in Saint Augustine, the home of his previous ministry, and getting ready to move his family to smaller and more peaceful Fernandina, where he would preside over First Missionary Baptist Church, on Ninth Street. More than a hundred and thirty years old, First Missionary was one of the deepest wells of black tradition and sentiment in Fernandina. Like most black churches on the island, it is a shouting and clapping church, whose parishioners show up with a Bible in one hand and a tambourine in the other, and know the hymnal by heart. Its gospel choir is considered the best around, and its congregation is not one to just sit back and listen. In the midst of a minister's perorations, spontaneously but seemingly on cue, the congregants at First Missionary will begin to hum, and then to sing low, and then louder, hymns that become the counterpoint to the sermon, accompanying and directing the preacher's progress.

The active role of First Missionary's worshippers in their Sunday service reflected the active role that Fernandina's churches, black and white, have long played in their town's racial, political, and commercial conflicts. When black longshoremen went on strike in 1888, the bell pealing from the steeple of the First Presbyterian Church on Fifth Street was the designated call to arms for white vigilantes, who called themselves the Minute Men. Likewise, when the enormous Egmont Hotel was built in 1877 to service Fernandina's first tourist boom, it dedicated itself to finding a way to drive off its nearest neighbor, the Northern Colored Methodist Church. A *WPA Guide to Fernandina* published in 1940 describes the results: "The Negroes refused to sell because they profited from the generosity of the hotel guests. Church services resembled those of the Holy Rollers, where singing and shouting continued far into the night. The hotel managers solved the problem by erecting a bowling alley adjacent to the church, and for weeks there was a battle royal between the crashing pins and the exhorting of the pastors. Finally the bowlers won out and the church was moved."

White and black churches are often institutional kin—their congregants worshipped together before the Civil War, and their affiliation is still acknowledged in many parish programs. Nevertheless, Sunday morning, as the saying goes, is the most segregated time of the week, and the churches attended by black Fernandinans have an altogether different role than those attended by whites. The mainstream white churches beatify the status quo that the black churches, to some degree, wish to subvert or challenge. For white parishioners, the church is but one institution of a generally orderly existence that includes such sister institutions as government, finance, and insurance against disaster. The black church is omnibus. The days are past when it had to provide the insurance and the finance, but it is still a court of grievance and a political boiler room, offering blacks the prospect of refuge and recompense that whites seek in the courthouse. Punishment, reward, and justice in general are handled a bit differently in the two venues. But then the system of narrow argument and quantifiable observation that prevails in the courthouse has never been entirely satisfying to blacks (or to any disfranchised people); it too often overlooks the emotional and empirical depths of their experience. If they are churchgoers, they may win their case on appeal, to God, on Sunday.

The dichotomy between secular law and spiritual law, between rational law and emotional law, was understood by some of Fernandina's leaders. "You just don't tell a community that's bleeding from a dozen different wounds that this wound was justified, and that's it, and that's the end of it," was how Jerry Cameron put it. Ilona Preliou understands this, too, professionally as well as personally. She was the personnel coordinator for the City of Fernandina—her office sat directly across Second Street from the police department—and her husband, Johnell Preliou, was the head of the NAACP at the time of the Andeaz Clark and Alvin James Oliver shootings. "Johnell said something once that really made me love him," Ilona Preliou told me. "They were talking about the Andeaz Clark shooting, and there was a quote in the paper where he said, 'People know that it's wrong. And if you don't know in your head, you know in your heart.' And that's true. You can't deny a wrong. It will nag at you somehow."

From the pulpit of First Missionary, Reverend McRae did more than nag. As soon as he arrived in town, he became the most vocal of Andeaz Clark's posthumous advocates and Sheriff Laurie Ellis's committed critic. "His philosophy is racist," he said. "Every sermon I preach, I'm going to mention what Ellis does. And during election time, if anybody is running against him and it's a close race, he's going to be in trouble."

To such criticism, Ellis responded in the newspapers, "No matter what I do, there's a small group of people I can't please."

McRae's conviction on the matter was sealed by his own experience. He was sometimes enlisted in presenting complaints to the Fernandina police on behalf of a parishioner who felt mistreated. But he quickly had incidents of his own to report, including one that happened after a revival, when he was pulled over while driving a visiting evangelist back to his hotel. When the patrolman acted rudely, McRae squared off: "I said, 'Officer, I respect you as an officer of the law, but you better call for some backup. Because I'm a preacher, and you're not going to talk to me like that. I'm a man. And I demand you treat me that way.'" When another patrolman arrived and suggested that a trip to jail might do the preacher good, McRae said, "No problem."

"I said, 'I'm ready to go to jail or, better than that, I'm ready to go to the cemetery. But wherever I go, I'm going as a man. And I'm not going as a child, and I'm not going as a thing.' I said, 'You do what you gotta do.'"

Eventually, they wrote him a ticket for having one of his two license-plate lights out. But the episode took most of a half hour and nearly escalated into an incident worthy of mention in the *News-Leader*. McRae was left with the feeling that he had been caught in the dragnet like a porpoise in a haul of shrimp—taken up with no regard for his real identity. It's a feeling he shares with many black Fernandinans who have been stopped by the police. To be black, and especially black and male, is to be regularly mistaken for a perpetrator, in Fernandina as in so many other places, and the solidarity that that creates is not between the police and the law-abiding citizen. It is one piece of the agony of the black middle class, and for some among them it approaches the level of chronic rage or pain. No people need police protection more in defense of their persons and culture, for the simple reason that their neighborhoods are poorer and more of their sons are criminals. But precisely because more of the criminals are their sons, they also have more to fear from the police.

It was hard to get protection without drawing affront. It seemed to the law-abiding black populace of Fernandina, who so badly needed the help of the police, that "To Protect and Serve" sometimes meant only to Protect the World from Blacks and Serve Them Warrants. It was as though the police and the thugs had conspired to corner the law abiders, and when the law abiders looked around them, they were unsure to whom they should appeal. The inclination was toward the police more often than outsiders supposed, even when the policeman was a sheriff like Laurie Ellis with a departmental history of brutality.

The tendency frustrated Andrew McRae. "Black people said, 'Naw, that's Mr. Ellis. We're going to vote for him,'" McRae told me. Even as he berated Ellis from the pulpit, the parishioners in black churches all over town were fanning themselves with paper fans that bore a photograph of a reverential-looking black family on one side and on the other the motto "Compliments of Laurie Ellis, Sheriff, Nassau County."

Within a couple of years, Laurie Ellis would fall from grace of his own weight. It was discovered that he and Rocky Mistler had been running a major drug concession from their evidence room. The citizens of Nassau County voted him out of office. The May following his ouster, Ellis was up on charges, and was sentenced to sixteen years in prison. For black Fernandinans, the episode confirmed their feeling of being squeezed between the lawless and the law: it turned out that the two forces had been engaged in the same line of work. Adding to their disgust was an incident two months before Ellis's ouster: the third killing of a black man by sheriff's deputies. The black man, this time, was the son of Fernandina undertaker C. T. Smith, of Huff & Battise.

"When the sheriff's office did what they did to the Smiths, it forced black people to start thinking," McRae told me. "Because of who C. T. is, they struck at the power source. C. T.'s son was killed. This was not just a black that has a record. It's a man who has a standing in our community, and you can't do that. And that's what turned the tables on Laurie Ellis. Not because of the fact that he killed another black man, but what black man he killed."

*   *   *

July 21, 1992, was a perfect Saturday at American Beach until early afternoon. The call that brought sheriff's deputies to the small black township was something more than a nuisance call and something less than an emergency. A neighbor of C. T. and Ruth Smith's beach house claimed that Chuck Smith, their thirty-eight-year-old son, had threatened her with a knife. No one had been hurt, and there was no crisis in progress. When a car with two officers reached American Beach, they saw Chuck Smith walking up the road toward his house and stopped to question him. C. T. Smith joined them, and his account of the initial conversation differs from that of the deputies in one regard: the deputies remember Chuck Smith drawing a knife while arguing with them; C. T. remembers his son jabbing an aggressive finger at the deputies but is sure that the knife he carried remained in its sheath. Whatever the case, both deputies drew guns. C. T. pleaded for calm. The guns went back in their holsters and Chuck turned and walked across Leonard Street and into the Smith house.

The deputies called for backup. Eventually every available deputy in the county would be on Leonard Street, a short, unpaved dead end with half a dozen infrequently used vacation homes on it. The deputies barricaded the street's entrance and surrounded the Smith house. They asked C. T. if there were guns inside. He said there were. They were going to get Chuck out, the officers said, and everyone else in the house needed to leave, in case things got rough. C. T. went in to get his wife, who was wheelchair-bound and suffered from advanced Lou Gehrig's disease. Chuck held the front door open for his mother and stepped outside to help guide her chair down the ramp. C. T. wheeled her around the corner onto Julia Street, where she wouldn't see what might be about to happen. Chuck went back inside the house, and a siege began that lasted into the night.

Several years earlier, when Chuck Smith had come home to Amelia Island, Ruth Smith felt that things were bound to go well for her son. He was educated and disciplined: he had a degree in sociology from the University of California at Berkeley and had been a Navy Seal. He was equal parts generosity and belligerence, but it was generosity that brought him home—his help was needed in caring for his invalid mother. And he needed her, too, because he suffered from paranoid schizophrenia that was generally invisible but occasionally crippling. Smith's calm could be disrupted by a word—suddenly he would be threatening and seemingly dangerous. In particular, Smith was easily provoked by the police, who stopped him for minor things. Denny Bell once stopped him for riding his bicycle through a stop sign, and Smith struck a ninja stance and ended up in jail. The police seemed afraid of Smith's strength and military training. They saw only his belligerent side. "Chuck was as helpless and benign a guy as you'd ever want to meet," Jerry Cameron told me. "But if you didn't know him and you got into an altercation with him, you'd want to call for a helicopter. His eyes spit fire."

Through a public address system, the deputies surrounding the Smith beach house called for Chuck to surrender. They also called him on the phone, sixty-nine times in the course of three hours. Nine times Smith answered, and his voice seemed to officers incoherent and irrational. It would be noted on a subsequent grand jury report that "Mr. Smith's mental condition was apparently well known to the Nassau County Sheriff's Office." In fact, the report noted, each of four hospitalizations Smith had undergone for paranoid schizophrenia "were preceded by encounters with police authorities." At five-fifteen, ignoring C. T. Smith's pleas that they call off the confrontation that was already in its fourth hour, deputies began firing crowd-control tear gas canisters through the windows on three sides of the house. They lobbed twenty-five canisters in all, followed by a series of "flash bangs," which the lawmen hoped would disable Smith. Flash bangs are small exploding missiles. They are designed not as a disabling tool but as a diversionary weapon whose noise and flame impersonate larger munitions. Nevertheless, they are capable of killing someone. "A predominant theme of Mr. Smith's paranoia appears to have involved police authorities," the grand jury report continued, "and his belief that the police meant to harm him."

An hour passed while the tear gas settled, but no one came out of the house. A SWAT team tried to enter through a kitchen door. They were repulsed with a single shot from Smith. They fired back. In the retreat, one officer stumbled to the ground. The others turned to help him, and Smith fired again. Officers spent the next several hours shooting sporadically into the house through windows and even

through walls with rifles and shotguns. Large rocks and cinder blocks
were thrown through every window, to knock out whatever remnant of
glass the canisters and bullets and flash bangs had missed, and
Venetian blinds and curtains were torn away to improve the view of
the interior. Rocky Mistler tried to pull debris from an obstructed
window just as night was falling. Smith fired, and again drew a barrage
in response. Electricity was cut to the house, and spotlights were
shone into it by the Fire Department.

In their glare, it was determined that Smith was holed up in the
bathroom; it was the only place not exposed by torn-out windows.
Mistler and Lieutenant Mike Hurst (who is not related to Deputy
Stanley Hurst) went to the rear of the house. They could see through a
bedroom to a bathroom wall. A ramrod was fashioned to reach
through the bedroom, and a hole was poked through the wall. First,
though, Hurst fired into the wall with a shotgun, to soften it up.
Through the hole, they glimpsed a swatch of Smith's clothing. They
yelled at him to surrender, but got no response, and shot him through
the hole with a shotgun. The blast hit him in the groin, and he fell to
the bathroom floor. A team of deputies tried to enter the house to
reach him. The tear gas, which Smith had endured for seven hours,
repulsed them almost instantly. They made another, smaller hole high
in another bathroom wall, from a closet on the porch. Deputy Larry
McDonald and Lieutenant Hurst poked a flashlight through the hole,
and the barrel of a shotgun. Smith was lying on the floor. He tried to
raise his torso. Two shotgun blasts from McDonald and Hurst, one to
the head and one to the chest, knocked him back down. Beside him on
the floor lay a cocked revolver.

His body was loaded onto an ambulance stretcher and brought out
past the crowd of American Beach residents pressing against the barri-
cade, past his parents. The ambulance took him to a Medivac helicopter that whisked him to a hospital in Jacksonville—which refused
him. "Why are you bringing me this?" the receiving doctor asked the
police in evident outrage, and sent the body straight to the coroner.
Before he died in his bathroom, Chuck Smith had hemorrhaged mas-
sively, internally and externally. He took multiple bullets to his torso,
head, and limbs during the twelve-hour siege—eighteen penetration
wounds in all, and two through the brain.

Three months after Chuck Smith's death, I walked through what remained of the house at American Beach. It was being rebuilt at county expense. "You fire one round into a house, it's yours," one of the workman explained to me. The workman was white and of a redneck mien, overalled and beer-bellied. He showed me the bathtub they had just loaded onto the debris truck. Its enameled steel had been perforated with more than a dozen high-powered rifle rounds. So much firepower had been poured into the house that its exterior walls were aerated and interior wallboard was frayed and feathered like carpet shag. Now the workers were tearing out the wallboard and loading it onto the truck. Inside, the sting of tear gas was still sharp. Every wall and ceiling had to be replaced. The damage hit every room—the refrigerator had eight rounds through the freezer door alone, cereal was shot off the shelves, and the kitchen doorsill was blasted inward as though by an explosion— but the damage increased in proximity to the bathroom. There the fusillade had been so withering that, as you could see with the wallboard torn away, the structural studs had been shattered.

"This was overkill," the workman said. He rubbed at a smudge of blood on the bathroom floor with the edge of his boot. When the workmen had opened up the house that morning, a wide swath of blood still led from the bathroom to the kitchen. "They dragged him out," the workman told me, and then, lest I think he meant it only as factual representation and not as a statement of disgust, he repeated himself with emphatic slowness. "They . . . *dragged* . . . him." Shards of flesh still clung to the bathroom ceiling. "You know how it is when you're shot," the worker said. "It tears you apart."

As with Oliver and Clark, no official punishment was meted. "The Grand Jury is outraged by the incompetence exhibited by the Nassau County Sheriff's Office during this crisis and feels that excessive force was used. We believe that different courses of action could have saved Mr. Smith's life," the grand jury report concluded, but went on to say, "Despite these findings, we do not conclude that the death of Charles T. Smith, III, was the result of a criminal act."

In the wake of Dennis Wilson's death, Reverend McRae again became the standard-bearer for black anger. Tensions were high and rising on all sides. A letter postmarked Gainesville, Florida, arrived at the

Fernandina Beach Police Department, announcing a planned protest rally on the courthouse steps at one P.M. on March 12 by robed members of the Bedford Forrest Brigade of the Ku Klux Klan.

It was signed, "Respectfully." Saturday came and went, and the klansmen failed to materialize. Outside offers were coming in on the other side, as well. In a sermon, McRae made his response plain. "I told them, 'Naw, stay home. This is a Nassau County affair, and we'll settle it among ourselves.'" His stand drew applause from the assembled. Rumors of protests and possible riots caused white residents to lock up their houses and keep their windows dark at night, so as not to become the target of a drive-by shooting. Some left the island altogether. One Friday, the courthouse and all government offices were closed early so that employees could get home safely before the beginning of a rally that promised to be angry. The rally never materialized, either. McRae found white concern over violence insulting. "One thing I resent," he told me, months later, "was the continued insinuation that we were going to use violence. You know, at no time did we ever advocate using violence, and everybody came on television talking about 'Calm, calm, calm,' you know. We're *not* calm. But we're not violent. If we were violent people, after the mess we've been through we'd be standing knee-deep in blood."

A protest march was held; it began in front of the Huff & Battise Funeral Home and wound past City Hall and the police station and down Centre Street to the courthouse, stopping at each place for prayers and speeches. Paul Alberta led the procession in his wheelchair, his braced right leg held straight before him like a prow—not the leg that had been shot but the one whose knee had been crushed in the fall out of Wilson's car. Store owners watched the march from behind cash registers, and tourists clutching packages and ice-cream cones gawked from across the street: the specter of racial discord against the backdrop of Saturday retail fervor was as astonishing to visitors as the appearance of so many of Fernandina's black citizens on Fernandina's main street was to residents. The line of protesters snaked for three blocks, a rendition of "We Shall Overcome" sagging like taffy along its length. McRae did most of the speaking.

By the day of the march, McRae's long crusade against police brutality in his adopted home had already passed its apogee, at Dennis Wilson's funeral. The Saturday of the funeral dawned with a brilliance.

An early spring had come to Fernandina. The redbuds were blooming in front of First Missionary Baptist Church in an unruly profusion of purple. A crowd stood around on the sidewalk and on the church steps, scuffing heels and saying little. When Whilamena arrived, they pushed outward against the stair railings so that she could enter. She collapsed on the steps, her knees knocked out by what appeared an impossible weariness, but was caught at each elbow by relatives. As they supported her down the packed center aisle, she began wailing, and her cries from the front pew and the sound of the organ floated out the front door from the sanctuary onto the sidewalk under the redbuds, under the perfect spring sky. Wilson's coffin lay just below the pulpit. There were more people than could fit into the church, even with the aisles bursting full and the balcony groaning. Reporters unable to shove their way through the front door walked around back and slipped into the loft with the choir.

Friends and clergy gave eulogies. An usher fanned Whilamena's face with a funeral parlor fan. The American Legion Jacksonville Post 197 presented Wilson with the initiation certificate of membership that he had been slated to receive the next Friday. The coffin was opened, and the congregation filed by, with the deacons and the choir going first and the family last, to lay a hand on his lapel, kiss his cheek, sob on his chest, or, in the case of one of his elders, to shake an admonishing finger in his face and give him a last angry lecture on his comportment.

The messages from the pulpit were aimed in great part at the comportment of the larger community, and much of the language was angry. "I stand here today, I try to make sense of all this. What's been happening in this community?" demanded Pastor Charles Wilson, one of Dennis's brothers, who was visiting from Palatka, Florida. "Last year, a brother died. Year before, a brother died. As the pastor of this church has already said: Black men, I call your attention. We're in serious trouble. We come in, we grieve, we mourn, and we bury. We get ready for the next one. That's gotta stop."

"We need to come together," Andrew McRae stammered softly when it was his turn to sermonize, before bellowing, "*And we need to come together at some point other than a funeral!*"

Rodney Gregory, who had been Wilson's lawyer and would later represent Paul Alberta and Whilamena in civil suits against the Fernandina Beach Police Department, took the pulpit to admonish, "Folks, don't get confused. We all know how Dennis's life has gone. It's gone by a bullet. But that bullet did not discriminate. It could have been fired by a black man or a Filipino. Just because that bullet happened to come from the gun of a white man doesn't mean you start a race war. You don't take your problems, you don't take your concerns, you don't take your tears out on white folks, or black folks, or any folks."

His conciliatory rhetoric reached few white ears. Except for the reporters in the choir loft, the only white faces anywhere in the vicinity were to be seen when the funeral let out: police watching through the windshields of cruisers from the Fernandina Police Department and the Florida Highway Patrol. They were on hand not to clear traffic for the funeral cortege but in case the mourning developed into a protest rally that would require armed containment.

Even as McRae saw his church fill with a thousand people adamantly concurring with his admonitions about the dangers of police brutality, he was aware that he was presiding over quite another sort of funeral, that of his ministry. His long advocacy had brought a backlash among the very group of citizens he meant to help: black Fernandinans. McRae heard some black people saying that he hated whites, heard black people calling *him* a racist.

"It's something you even have to be careful how you talk about," McRae explained to me. "The problem, I guess, is that a lot of blacks don't want to accept the fact that racism exists—that there *is* a problem. Then others who enjoy certain luxuries feel threatened—feel that their relationship is threatened with our white brothers and sisters if they get involved in talking about the relationship between the races. This kind of attitude is very prominent around oppressed people. They feel that if they're not attached to certain people—say, white people, people of privilege—then they feel they're not anyone, you know. So they're not going to say anything to jeopardize, and anytime you say something they feel is going to threaten that, they tend to retaliate. But that's the way it is."

The deeper problem was that McRae, like many of the Fernandina whites he railed against, was a newcomer to town. Whatever his intentions, his understanding of local history was imperfect. Beneath the first level of that history—the history of police brutality and institutionalized racial conflict—was a more bedrock level that had to be considered, a history of racial cooperation and affection. While it was true that a former Fernandina police chief used to escort Ku Klux Klan parades down Centre Street, it was also true that the same police chief would go home and sit down to table for a family dinner with black friends—his family, his table, his friends, at his invitation. On the level of personal relations, things became complex.

In Patricia Thompson's living room two days after the killing, when the Wilson family was being interviewed by the press, it was clear that only part of the outrage they felt was over the persistent evil expressed in Thompson's note, *4 black young men have been killed by police in a short period of time*. The deeper outrage was not about confrontation but betrayal—about something that had been lost, abandoned. "We played together with white boys and girls," Thompson told one reporter over the phone. "We didn't know nothin' about racism. We didn't know no color in Fernandina. We had a very good relationship, the blacks and the whites. We didn't have no killings."

Jeanette Baker, who had just called her brother's death a "lynching," also described it as a part of a general loss of innocence. "If racism is allowed in any part of the community, it's going to bore through all of it," she said pleadingly to Sarah Bottoms of the *News-Leader*. "See, somebody's doing this to us. Somebody is manipulating me and you. It's like we're pawns. We're on this chessboard, and we're being manipulated to hate each other. I don't think this is a normal thing. Somebody's planting manipulative seeds, and those seeds have been planted over here and over here and over here. And they're using us. They're using us. And we're being destroyed by it. And the country itself is going to be destroyed."

The history of what had been betrayed was explained to me by Ilona Preliou, herself a relative newcomer. She had grown up outside Birmingham, Alabama, the daughter of a black landowner who had white sharecroppers. Her race experience defied stereotype, but even she found Fernandina mystifying. "I get the feeling this was a special place," she said. "There are rumors that most of Fernandina was owned and operated by black people years ago. It was like a little paradise, a little escape for black people. I know that the Catholic school here used to produce some very, very talented people. People who played the violin and all. There was just a very strong black middle class, indicating that these were people who believed in good, middle-class values. They're still here. I mean, their values are still here. That's probably why we don't have riots in Fernandina—because they have the middle-class consciousness. I think that consciousness keeps the lid on things."

Even during Jim Crow and disfranchisement, Fernandina enjoyed an unusual closeness between the races. Housing was mixed and much of social life, and black businesses thrived on Centre Street west of Third. Two well-known black sisters who paid childhood visits to their relatives in Fernandina, Sarah and Elizabeth Delany, authors of the best-selling memoir, *Having Our Say*, remembered Fernandina as a place where their obliviousness to Jim Crow could be maintained—strong testament to the gentleness of Fernandina's society in a cruel era. There were black doctors and pharmacists, saloon and hotel keepers, grocers and butchers and hairdressers and barbers, florists and launderers, and black-owned and black-operated seafood processors and fishing boats. The idea that, even in a segregated society, whites and blacks were made for different jobs had to be imported; it came in during the early 1930s with the establishment of the pulp mills. There the jobs were designated black or white, with different hiring offices, pay schedules, and unions, and contracts stating how much less a black person would be compensated for doing the same work as a white, if perchance he happened through inadvertence or necessity to be put into that role. The mills also imported a lot of new white talent from the hinterlands of north Florida and south Georgia. Even as black businesses were falling on hard times, the local culture changed and a cracker sensibility took up residence next to Fernandina's traditional tolerance, and neighbors became uneasy. Black Fernandinans refer to those days as "The Separation."

"I don't think they want to be together," Ilona Preliou told me, of her black and white townspeople today. "And there was a time when they *were* together. And I think what changed it was probably when the power changed—when black people lost property and all the other things they had."

C. T. Smith and his wife Ruth represented, as much as anyone, the traditional black establishment; undertakers are a part of that limited firmament of black professionals who were allowed to prosper anywhere in the South even in Jim Crow times. They both grew up in Fernandina, and they remember the era of closeness and the coming of The Separation. The Smiths were married at the beginning of the mill era—C. T. worked at Rayonier before becoming an undertaker— and they remember the town's peculiarities, good and bad. "White people were livin' side by side with black people," Ruth recalled. "And we all—if anything happened in a black neighborhood, the whites were there, and if anything happened in a white neighborhood, the blacks were there, to come see what they could do for them. It was just like it was one big family."

Ruth Smith had spent some years in New Jersey, where she lived with an aunt while going to school, and she knew how novel such closeness was. "There's a lot of white people in the North who are very prejudiced," she told me a month before Wilson's death. "Because I've lived North, too. I've been exposed to white people who are not particular about you bein' around. The old saying is: Northern white man don't care how high you get, as long as you don't get too close. A Southern white man don't care how close you get, as long as you don't get too high."

For decades, Fernandina had allowed exceptions to its "don't get too high" rule. But as the mill era lengthened, the penalty tightened. "Long years ago," Ruth Smith told me, "there was a Dr. Freeman, and they ran him out of town. He was black, and they didn't want him in town: he was too high for them. He was getting too rich for them. So they ran him out. It got so bad, until he had to leave and go to Jacksonville. We had a black pharmacy—they just closed it up. Whatever any ol' redneck felt like doin', he'd just go ahead and do it, and the law would back him up." After the black drugstore closed, blacks could get their prescriptions filled only by waiting outside the back window of the white pharmacy.

The beaches were similarly segregated: at the end of Atlantic Avenue (Centre Street's extension to the ocean) there were two pavilions, one to the north for white residents, and one for blacks to the south. Mysteriously, the black pavilion burned. Afterward, local blacks went south to American Beach. Ruth and C. T. Smith took their children to American Beach to learn to swim, a skill that would propel their son Chuck into the Navy Seals, and eventually they bought a lot and built a house there, in which their son would die.

The resurgence of tourism promised the decline of the hegemony of the mills, and a close to that post-Depression era that had seen Fernandina so arbitrarily divided. But it didn't work as it was supposed to. Ruth Smith saw how Fernandina was changing, and it seemed to be for the meaner. The influx of Northerners, the cosmetic improvements demanded by the tourist trade, the town's burgeoning prosperity and politeness and progressiveness, served perversely to further the isolation and exclusion of blacks. The newcomers were appalled at the old Southern regime of Jim Crow, because they found injustice unsightly—a blemish on their image of themselves and a tarnish on the respectability of their business. But businesswise, the newcomers found blacks, especially poor ones, as unsightly as racial oppression, and so the confluence of Southern and Northern mores turned a difficult equation into a nearly impossible one for blacks on the island: Don't get too high, the word seemed to be, and don't get too close, either.

Sitting in their living room in November 1993, a year and four months after their son's death, Ruth and C. T. Smith considered that phenomenon. "Really, it was like this," C. T. said of the old days. "There was a line, and you didn't go over it. But really, things were friendly. There were black stores. All of Second Street was black, and all of Third. Fourth Street was white."

Ruth seemed to want to nod, but couldn't. She was seated in her wheelchair behind a card table on which her immobile arms were propped. Her paralysis from Lou Gehrig's disease had progressed steadily, climbing from her lower limbs as a tree is climbed by a choking vine. She could still speak, and move a finger to press the button on a speakerphone, and she could turn her eyes to look out into the yard, but nothing more. Her voice, though, was a nimbus of joy and cultured civility, even when she was discussing devastating subjects. "And now what do you see?" Ruth asked C. T.

"Well, you can sit downtown two hours and never see a black person, unless they're going to the post office or the courthouse or the bank. That's all."

Ruth said, "We're more separated than we've ever been. It used to be we played together when we were kids. And we would work together. And if you wanted a cup of sugar, you went and asked for one, black and white, it didn't matter. And some of the black stores were bigger than some of the white."

One day in 1992, Ruth Smith had confronted one of her white friends in the Episcopal church they both attended. "Did you ever stop to look at Centre Street?" she asked her. "It's lily white."

"What do you mean?" the friend asked.

"When you get a chance, go down there, store to store. Tell me, when you get back, any black people you see working in any store. Then you tell me how many black people are shopping down there."

The woman came back and said, "Ruth, you're absolutely right. What's the problem?"

Ruth said. "They won't hire us, and we won't support them. They haven't said anything to us, and we haven't said anything to them. But we discuss it among ourselves."

The friend said, "Ruth, I never thought about it."

And Ruth said, "Think about it."

If the Depression and the mill era had brought an end to Fernandina's era of racial cooperation, the onslaught of tourism brought the death of something almost greater: the memory of that closeness, and the memory of black eminence in Fernandina's birth and growth. The history survived in the minds of a few old-timers, like Ruth and C. T. Smith. When Ruth Smith talked about those times, the paralysis that had claimed her movement and would eventually claim her voice and breath seemed almost a partner to the general oblivion that would eventually smother the memory of all she described.

The tourism touted history, of course; that was the irony. Fernandina's attractiveness to visitors was based largely on its illustrious past. But it was safe history, which is to say not threateningly relevant. Tourists and developers ask little enough of history, after all: only that it stay demurely apart from the present, in the realm of the completed and the certain. History of that more decorous sort has become such a hot commodity locally as to take on extravagant forms: one Fernandina B&B touts itself as "A Historic Bed and Breakfast with a Heritage of Elegance"; its owner assured me that it originally belonged to a man who returned from the Civil War to run the house as an underground railroad. "A haven for slaves after slavery?" I asked the owner, a recent immigrant from New Jersey. "We can't be sure of the exact dates," he said. I asked, "What kind of man would that have been, to run an underground railroad in postwar Fernandina?" The innkeeper leaned toward me and gave a half whisper, half hiss of reverential vehemence. "A . . . perfect . . . Southern . . . gentleman," he said.

Such fungible fantasy is typical. "Prepare for passage through a past more fanciful than fiction in armchair comfort as a docent sets the focus of the action using three remarkable maps," read an ad for the Amelia Island Museum of History in the local telephone directory, and so on one day in 1993 I did, accompanied by MaVynee Betsch, who is known islandwide as the unofficial mayor of American Beach. The museum has a worthy side, a research library that has published a series of useful booklets on local history. But even that serious effort was scarred by a near-total omission of black involvement (an omission the library has begun to try in the last few year to rectify). In the museum, African descendants made cameo appearances as plantation slaves but contributed nothing voluntary to the island's progress. Betsch became more and more aggravated with each successive diorama. Her aggravation crested as the docent pointed out a model of the archaeological digs of the Indian burial grounds, complete with stratifications of different colored soils. "Did you know there are twenty-eight shades of brown on this island?" the docent said, her awareness of soil subtleties far outpacing that of the subtleties of race. Betsch stormed out. But others have flooded in. That year the museum had 14,500 visitors. Those visiting Fernandina history far outnumbered those who were living it.

There is a danger in such glossy recollection. The eradication of black history has done more than weaken the bond between Fernandina's black generations, though it has done that. It has also eradicated all evidence of the old collaboration between black and white on the island and in doing so has obliterated a bridge between the races. It was a bridge all the more needed as modern commerce forced the races apart. More and more, the only bridge left seemed to be the police.

*   *   *

Amelia Island's tourist boom rides atop a new apartheid. Oddly, it is not as though black Fernandina and white Fernandina were traveling different roads: they are both in flight from a former innocence toward a new sophistication. The identical road just leads them to different destinations. The charter cynicisms of commerce being different from the cynicisms derived from poverty, sophistication is bringing different gifts to black and white in Fernandina, symbolized in their extremity by bric-a-brac on Centre Street and crack cocaine on Tenth. One Fernandina minister I met marveled at the correlation between the escalating price for a bottle of fine wine from the cellar of one upscale restauraunt and the escalation of drug sales in the restaurant's parking lot. In 1994 the island still retained a few black enterprises—Benjamin Cab Company and Maxcell Wilson's Barbershop and several small juke joints like the 501 Club, where a group called the Hurt Me Hurt Me Girls performed on summer Saturday nights. But by and large, the new divisions have meant that commerce is the property of whites, who imagine that disrupting it is largely an activity of blacks. In this climate, law enforcement is no longer able to maintain the image of protecting each citizen individually, and instead seems to be defending the business of one race from the predations of the other.

When the business being protected is tourism, it must be defended from more than crime. Even the appearance of anything unpleasant or complicated can be the equivalent of a looting. And so the police, in containing crack and crime, are protecting more than property; they are sworn to defend the insouciance and blithe oblivion of a society at play from the unsettling desperation of a society out of work, right next door. Those societies have seemed to be at actual war, on occasion—as when a group of black teenagers in 1992 pulled a car full of white Ritz-Carlton employees over for what was meant to be a robbery, until one among the robbers saw the two women in the backseat writing down a license number and shot them both to death. The teens were promptly turned in by their mothers. They were sentenced to multiple life terms.

The Fernandina Beach Police Department's unsought role as the bridge between the races is emphasized by its internal integration. Chief Sturges liked to point out that his department has a better representation of blacks and women than almost any in Florida. Law enforcement in Nassau County was integrated by Sheriff Cap Youngblood after an occurrence at American Beach. In Youngblood's time, American Beach drew its clientele from all over the South, and many arrivals recounted being harassed by deputies as they made their way through the county along the route they called, unaffectionately, the "Youngblood Trail." One July day in 1950, at the Beach, there occurred what Ben Sessions (who was at that time an agent for the Afro-American Life Insurance Company, which had founded the town) describes as "a cutting." A white deputy was dragged from his car by two men and virtually vivisected; he was saved by the intercession of a black doctor who was a Beach resident. Instead of clamping down, Youngblood approached black civic and business organizations with a proposal so innovative that it had as yet been tried in only one or two other venues in the state: why not, Youngblood asked, hire a black deputy?

The first black deputy, Jerry Maddox, was not provided with a car or a uniform and he could arrest only black folks. Even with that, Youngblood's farsightedness was too far-fetched for some. "Youngblood had some white men tell him at a commission meeting that if he didn't get rid of that so-and-so they weren't gonna vote and put him in office no more," Sessions told me. "He told them if they didn't never vote for him again, he was keeping his black deputy as long as he wanted to, nobody was going to tell him how to run his office. So he kept him."

Deputy Maddox got flak, too. "The biggest people, really, to be against Jerry was his own people," Sessions said. One Saturday morning, Maddox was called to a house on Eighth Street and Gum to intervene in a domestic dispute, "and it wasn't two minutes until he was dead," Sessions remembered. "He got out of the car, and started around the front. Fellow was standin' at the corner of the house with a carbine, blew him down." Sessions was in the vicinity and arrived just barely in time to catch his friend alive. "I said, 'Jerry, please don't die on me.' Breath passed. So I was right there when the last breath left him. And it was another black man killed him."

Sessions had helped talk Maddox into taking the deputy's job. After the shooting, he took the job himself, and along with another black deputy, Curtis Telfair Sr., confronted Youngblood over the limitations of their role. "We said if we were going to be deputies, we were going to arrest white as well as anybody else. And he accepted it."

Even with those full powers, integration did not alleviate the distrust between blacks and the county sheriff's office: the new black deputies were liked in some ways even less than the white ones, and suspected of being overseers for white interests. Curtis Telfair Sr. went on to become one of the first black policemen in Fernandina Beach. His grandson, Curtis Telfair III, still works for the department. When Denny Bell first joined the force, in 1969, it was Curtis Telfair Sr. who taught him the ropes. When Bell went off patrolling on his own, he borrowed Telfair's pistol.

Integration, though, was only the beginning of reform challenges for local law enforcers. Nassau County's new sheriff, Ray Geiger, worked hard to dispel the unprofessionalism of the Ellis era through better pay and training and stricter procedures, just as the Fernandina police worked to replace the outdated model of enforcement that the layman might describe as repressive or brutal but that in the parlance of Fernandina police officers is called Neanderthal. Captain Hoyt Johns calls it that, and Johns is a confessed reformed Neanderthal, as his "enforcer" bears ample witness. That's how he refers to his right hand, on which his middle knuckle has been driven so far back toward his wrist that his "social finger" (as he refers to his middle finger) is shorter than those to either side. Residents of the black neighborhoods of Jacksonville, where he used to work narcotics and street crime, called him Cracker John. Now, in Fernandina, he is in charge of patrolling. For the officers cruising the streets of Fernandina, Chief Sturges was the war secretary, but Johns was their general in the field. The chief taught a class called "Verbal Judo"; Johns applied it to the street. "You know, you can always get tough if you have to, hopefully," he told me. "You can always escalate. But it's hard to downsize a situation. I tell the guys, 'If you get out with a gun in your hand on a traffic stop, where do you go from there? Do you shoot? Or do you stick it in your ear and go home?'" Johns preaches the new, more diplomatic alternative, where handcuffing a suspect and getting him into the car is called "escort technique" and convincing an antagonist he doesn't really want to resist is known as "redirecting."

"When I was first in law enforcement, there wasn't no redirect-ing," Johns told me. "Redirecting was a stick. This was back in the late sixties, early seventies. There was just a different mentality of police work then. A lot of the officers initiated violence. It didn't matter what color you were. There were a lot of stitches passed out years ago that didn't need to be passed out."

Evolving from the Neanderthal is a confusing process for any police force. By common perception, brutality and corruption were handmaidens of the good-ol'-boy system of hiring and policing, where the enforcement was personal and the justice often partial. But cold professionalism can, in itself, seem heartless and repressive, as citizens of Los Angeles know: since the 1950s, the premier reform "profes-sional" big-city force in the country, as well as the best integrated, has been the same LAPD so infamously scarred by incidents of brutality. Fernandina is catching up. Its police department is being transformed as the town is being transformed, by an influx of young professionals—men like James Norman, the patrolman who pulled Dennis Wilson over and fired the first shots into his car. The new recruits are hired from the academy, where they are taught "community policing" as a professional ideal. Johns sees an irony in that. "On the one hand they're saying you need personalized law enforcement, and on the other hand they're saying take personality out of it," he complained. "What do you do, have two officers? One who lives here and one who doesn't, so they can play good guy, bad guy? I don't know. It's a hard thing to balance."

The personification of personal policing, locally, was Sheriff Youngblood. But Youngblood's approach—dropping by the house or telephoning to tell a suspect he had to report to jail—has burdened Youngblood's heirs. "When a deputy goes to arrest someone who in the past has been told they could 'come in,' what happens?" Johns asked me. "You have an incident like on South Fletcher."

Academy training offers little insurance against that situation. "The police academy does not teach discretion," Chief Sturges told me. "You learn discretion on the street." The average age of Sturges's officers had dropped during the previous decade from thirty-seven to the mid-twenties. "We're a young department," Sturges said, "and a young department goes by the book. An old one is more in tune with the community."

Denny Bell, like Sturges a local boy, agreed with his chief. "When you get on the street," he told me, "you don't deal with the situation by the book. You can't. Situations don't go by the book. It takes an instant for a situation to go the opposite way from the way the book says it's going to go. Only thing I know you can do in the street by the book is write a traffic ticket in six minutes flat. But nothing else applies. Nothing applies." In Bell's estimation, there was one thing in particular that didn't come in books: compassion. "It's not learned," he said. "It's something you find in yourself." And finding it takes time, with the result that as police departments reform themselves by recruiting young and better-trained professionals, it's often the older Neanderthals who are the easiest going on the street.

On the street, the old-time cop could find himself strung perilously between extremes: not only between "professional" and "personal" policing within his department, but between the emergent professional class in a town like Fernandina, and such a town's black citizenry. It was a dangerous place to be. The barrier that Dennis Wilson found so maddeningly impassable, and that a friend of his likened to a "blank white wall," was a barrier the street cop experienced more as a void or vacuum or gap, a moat over which he had to stretch each time he walked or drove his beat. Daily the moat grew wider. And if you slipped, it could swallow you up.

On the evening of February 21, 1994, as Dennis Wilson made his visit to his friend Paul Alberta, Sarah Bell sat at home alone, listening to her husband's voice crackling simultaneously from two police scanners. One was in the kitchen; the other, in the bedroom, was a Christmas gift from Denny. When the scanners erupted, she thought there must have been an accident. Then she heard her husband's voice telling dispatch to call his wife with a 77. A 77 meant that he was unhurt. She thought, "What is going on?"

Sarah and Denny Bell were, even in their late forties, a picture-book couple, she persimmon-lipped pretty, he with shoulders as implausibly straight as those of a Corn Belt scarecrow. They had been married for almost twenty-five years, and that's how long it had been since Denny had joined the police force. He took the job because he couldn't afford to marry her on his salary at the mills. In order to make ends meet, he had already had to sell his orange 1969 Camaro, which had cost $3,000 new, the car they had courted in. When he started on the force, all he knew of police work was the salary: $3,600 a year.

After six months, Bell had been in a number of situations where he had helped someone or confronted someone, always for the best. He liked the job and people liked him. Of all officers in the Fernandina Beach Police Department, Denny Bell had perhaps the best reputation in the black community, where he was generally received informally rather than officially, as family instead of enforcer.

"We've known Denny since before he was a police," Ruth Smith told me. "He spent half his life with us."

"He's been very good to blacks," Patsy Thompson said. She remembers Sarah and Denny both being part of an older, closer, albeit segregated Fernandina. Bell had coached Thompson's all-black, all-girl softball team back in 1969; Sarah, then his fiancée, played on a rival team. Among Bell's black acquaintanceships was a long-standing one with Dennis Wilson's mother. He used to stop by to see her on his way to work, back in his bachelor days. When she saw him coming, she set an extra place for breakfast. "Miss Albertina, she's dead, but she was a fine lady," Bell recalled. "She always put a hug on my neck when I came by, and I would give her a hug. I don't know if that's professional, but that's how we did."

At times over the years Bell had had occasion to draw his gun in the course of his duties, when he was threatened or someone else was. He had never had to fire it. Things had always worked out. He had two years left till retirement, and if you had asked him before February 21 if he had the least idea that he might shoot someone before finishing his career, he would have told you no.

Sarah Bell searched for her husband at Nassau General Hospital and caught up with him at headquarters, where Hoyt Johns had driven him and James Norman to placate the angry crowd on South Fletcher. The patrolmen were standing out back in the parking lot. Norman was nervously kneading his hands, and Bell was pacing in circles. He was as upset as Sarah had ever seen him. He told her, "I see it all being wasted."

His lot was already worse than he could know. On the highway to Jacksonville at that hour, Major Tommy Reeves was following Dennis

Wilson's body on its trip to the Jacksonville morgue. Reeves was a part of the post-Ellis regime at the Nassau County Sheriff's Office, and had suggested one element of its reform—that detectives be required to attend the autopsies of people whose deaths they were investigating. In the early morning hours of February 22, 1994, he abided by it. That's what had him tailing a hearse in the fog. The duty was made immensely unhappier by something that happened as soon as Reeves reached the morgue. Mary Bomgardner, the supervisor of the sheriff's communications staff, paged him, and what she had to tell him was not going to advance the reformist image of the sheriff's office. "It was terrible news," Reeves told me. "You can't believe how bad it was."

Bomgardner had gone through the records relating to the night's events, and had discovered that the information the sheriff's dispatcher had given the Fernandina police dispatcher was simply not true. There was no outstanding warrant for Wilson's arrest. There had been, a week earlier. Wilson had come in and satisfied it, and a clerk at the sheriff's office had entered the event in the computer, but in the wrong column. Just one of those little things—a discrepancy whose irregularity an experienced dispatcher would probably have noticed and corrected when relaying information to the town. The dispatcher on the night shift on February 21 did not. She had been on the job a week. She passed on what she saw on the screen. When Dennis Wilson told Bell and Norman that he was under no warrant, he was correct. No wonder he felt paranoid about the policemen's intentions. For several minutes between the dispatch and his death, he had been both an innocent man and a declared fugitive.

Ray Geiger announced the miscommunication during his press conference on the 22nd; the revelation brought tinder to flash in Fernandina. At about the same time, Bell learned of the dispatcher's error at the state's attorney's office, where he went to give a sworn statement to the attorney and Major Reeves. The sergeant was feeling a bit hung out to dry. Little was reaching him officially; the department was not telling him or Jim Norman much of what was going on. As he sat waiting for his turn to be deposed, Bell overheard two people talking about Wilson's arrest warrant—the warrant that had convinced Bell that he was dealing with a violent felon at large and had thus led to the shooting. They were saying that the supposed warrant had been a mistake. Seven weeks later, at the inquest, Bell would learn the full horror of the mistake: after the sheriff's office erred in telling the Fernandina police dispatcher that there was a warrant out for Wilson for resisting arrest without violence, the Fernandina headquarters—"my own dispatcher," in Bell's words—relayed the information inaccurately over the radio, upping the charge to resisting with violence, thus making it a felony requiring action.

Even learning only half the chain of fatal miscommunications, Bell came home crying. The emotional freight was accumulating. Bell wouldn't tell Sarah what had happened. She thought it was because he wanted to be tough, but he professed another reason. He wanted his account to stay accurate, he said. If he rehearsed his account over and over informally, then by the time he related it to a judge it would have taken on a life of its own, and would have grown and changed almost willfully from the truth. All his experience with witness accounts told him that at such a sensitive time he was endlessly self-suggestible.

He was soon to find out just how suggestible. Bell had told Reeves that he shot only at the tire of the fleeing vehicle: that's what he had convinced himself was true. But Reeves was suspicious. There was a bullet in the tire, sure enough, but only one, and there were too many bullet holes in the back of the Probe to have come from Norman's gun alone. After the shooting, the police department sent Bell down to a psychiatrist in Jacksonville to be counseled through any trauma he might feel. It was a routine thing. Jim Norman went, too, and it helped. Norman, the product of Fernandina's constabulary improvements, had been inconsolable for several days after the shooting, but he was soon back on his feet and back on the force. Bell fared differently. During the counseling session on March 2, the counselor explained to Bell how traumatic events create mental blocks, and in the course of the discussion a horrifying realization surfaced, an opening of memory almost unbearably painful.

The following afternoon, Major Reeves got a call from Bell, who wanted to come in and discuss the case. Immediately. Reeves told Bell that he should probably have the attorney from the Policemen's Benevolent Association there to represent him, and that anyway the interview would have to be cleared with the state's attorney. Five minutes later, Sarah called. Denny was on his way, she said. She seemed worried, and told Reeves that Bell was having trouble handling the aftermath of the shooting, and that his therapy had brought up something he needed to talk about. When Bell arrived, Reeves received him but wouldn't ask him any questions without a lawyer present. So Bell gave him a soliloquy, going over the details of the shooting from the moment he arrived at the scene all the way through to the moment the car began to move. "As the tires gripped the pavement," Reeves reports of what Bell told him, "the car shot forward. At the same time, Norman started shooting into the windshield and was struck two times by the car. Bell lost his grip on Wilson's jacket sleeve, and as the car moved away he brought his pistol up and shot four times within a distance of eight to ten feet. He shot the four rounds in a period of approximately two seconds. The first shot possibly hit the left tire and the others could have been higher in the back of the car. He emphasized that the pistol was rising as he came up with it, and the shot in the rear car window could possibly be his."

That was the revelation that all the rehashing led up to: Bell hadn't just shot at the tire. He remembered now. He had shot at the car. He had shot at Dennis Wilson, and one of the shots may have been the one that entered Wilson's back between the shoulder blades and just to the left of the spine and that the medical examiner had retrieved from behind Wilson's sternum—one of the three shots, of the seven that had wounded Wilson, that the medical examiner said was sufficient to cause Wilson's death.

On a gentle evening the following May, I talked with Sarah and Denny Bell over fried fish and hush puppies at the Marina Restaurant on Centre Street. Sarah was staunch in her husband's defense, with a fervor that betrayed how terrible she felt his burden was. The first thing she said to me, with an emphasis that brought her forward over the restaurant table, was, "This is not your average cop."

"The way I look at it," she said, discussing the number of times Wilson had been freed on charges she felt he should have answered for, "Dennis Wilson was a man who had been spared time and again by slipups in the system, and eventually a slipup in the system is what killed him." That inexperienced dispatchers were responsible for the "slipup" seemed of little consolation to her husband. He felt ostracized within the department, and was enraged by his perception that even while the department was holding him at arm's length it was eagerly using his own hard-won reputation with Fernandina's blacks to excuse its problems and contain a bad situation. People in town had been coming up to Bell and saying, "Well, if you shot Wilson, I know it must have been justified." Of all the things that were said to him, that was the hardest, Sarah told me, as we stood on the sidewalk after the meal. "They tell Denny, 'Wilson was trouble for so long that sooner or later someone was going to have to get rid of him. We're glad if it had to be someone, it was you.'" At this, her husband, usually so controlled in his bearing, paced away from us into the street and circled back, kicking at the curb. "They mean this as supportive," he explained. "But they don't know how it sounds." His voice was full of distress, and when he caught sight of his wife's face he stopped short. Her lips were pursed and she was staring hard at nothing down the street and her eyes were glazed with tears. Bell stepped back off the curb and looked up for a moment at the spring sky, while his chest heaved. Then he stepped back again, and the question he asked did not seem addressed to either of us, because he knew we did not have an answer. Still, it was too insistent to be rhetorical. "What am I supposed to say to that?" he asked, and then concluded, "I don't know what to say."

The inquest on the death of Dennis Wilson opened on April 14. The courthouse was secured as though it were the target of a heist, cordoned off with barricades and police tape and garrisoned with sheriff's deputies and policemen. Fifth Street, which runs beside it, was closed. But the crowds envisioned weeks earlier did not show. Inside the hundred-year-old-courtroom, the pews were not empty, but they weren't packed either, and the only people left standing in the halls were police on sentry and witnesses in the breach. Within the courtroom well, Sheriff Geiger and Chief Sturges took up positions in straight-back chairs under the tall windows, the long morning light slanting warmly over their shoulders, and waited vigilant and poker-faced for things to explode or resolve. Geiger could watch the chief's discomfort with a particular if slim satisfaction. This time, unlike the last three times, it was not the Nassau County Sheriff's Office on the hot seat.

At a preliminary conference, the presiding judge, Richard R. Townsend, who had been brought in from Green Cove Springs to fend off any appearance of local favoritism, explained how he would conduct his hearing: by strict rules of evidence. Only he and the state's attorney would be empowered to ask questions, and only the propriety of police actions on the night of February 21 would be considered. The hearing would be devoted to "nothing but the truth." Evidently the "whole truth," with all its history, context, implication of racism, and examples of police brutality, would be beyond the hearing's scope.

This intention was imperiled by the very first witness. Paul Alberta limped through the gallery gate on a bamboo cane and led the court through the last evening of his friend's life. He recalled the policemen's request for Wilson to get out of the car: "*Try anything, nigger, and we'll blow your fuckin' head off!*" and described the apparition he saw through the passenger window. Alberta also recalled that after the shooting, as he lay bleeding on the driveway, a fireman had come up to him and delivered a fighting challenge: "Look at this face! Remember this face!"

The invoking of ghosts and conspiracies out of the mist around Wilson's car threw the case of Wilson's partisans into disrepute. An emergency medical technician, who had been at the scene in his fireman's boots, testified that he had repeatedly told Alberta to look into his face so that he could check Alberta's pupils for signs of incipient shock. What Alberta took as fighting words, it seemed, had been attempts to help.

Still, Alberta's allegations struck a chord of recognition in the gallery, feeding black suspicions that there was something pernicious at work beneath the surface. By their very vagueness, the allegations were made real, made to resemble the locus of misfortune and miscellaneous hazard that could never be pinpointed but which blacks in the gallery knew in their hearts existed. As the inquest turned to rebutting Alberta, it became a referendum on two systems of belief, on the surface versus the depths, the dry, constrained facts versus the underlying conviction that things in the world weren't right.

The court worked hard to return the river to its banks. At the beginning of the second day, the questions directly addressed the propriety of the policemen's actions. The state's attorney called Jim

Norman as a witness, and with an icy determination the young patrolman described all over again his drive down Jasmine to the beach road and the turn his life had taken there, how he had approached the Probe and tapped on the window and stepped toward the front when the door opened, and how the guns came out when Wilson got back in. "I was focusing on Dennis Wilson's hands," he said. "I could see him putting it in gear. I wasn't sure if he was reaching for a weapon." The vehicle accelerated once, he recalled, and "nudged" his leg. Then, within seconds, it accelerated again, and hit Norman's leg again, hard enough to back him up, and he started shooting as soon as he recovered his footing. As the vehicle went by him, he testified, he was worried that it was going to hit him. "I was on automatic," he said. "I wasn't really thinking." And he kept shooting, even after Bell had stopped, aiming at the taillights from forty or fifty feet away. "He had committed a violent felony," Norman said of Wilson, "and I was trying to keep him from escaping."

The next morning he awoke with a back pain, he said, from the battering he took from the automobile, and went to Nassau General's emergency room to seek attention. His leg was neither scratched nor bruised.

With that, the state's attorney was finished, and the judge turned toward the witness to ask a few questions of his own. Norman assured him that he had never used the "F" word or "N" word and had never threatened Wilson with his weapon or with violence if he did not cooperate.

The room became almost electrically still, a held-breath suspension so quiet that it seemed somnolent, the lazy turnings of the ceiling fan a windlass drawing the tension tighter. Words fell individually, like coins into counting hands, measured for size and heft. The judge asked a question and, in a slip, referred to Wilson as "the defendant" and had to correct himself. "I say 'the defendant'—I mean the suspect at this time." A slight scuffling broke out in the visitors' seats, and a thin agitated keening grew as the questioning continued. The judge suggested, "You used deadly force to keep him from escaping from a felony."

"No sir," Norman replied. "I used deadly force to protect myself from bodily injury."

Neither the judge nor the state's attorney pressed the questions that had buzzed through Fernandina for weeks and through the gallery during recesses. If Norman had been too close to the car to step away, how did he have time to fire four shots through the windshield? If, as he stated, he was shooting to save his life, was it shooting that saved it? Or stepping out of the way? And if it was stepping out of the way, why did he shoot? To protect his pride? His authority as a police officer? If he was protecting himself and others from a fleeing felon, were he and they really safer from a car being driven by a dead or wounded man than by an unhurt Dennis Wilson? And what of the safety of the innocent bystander, Paul Alberta?

The judge did ask Norman, "On reflection, would you do anything differently?"

"No, sir," Norman replied.

In the visitors' section, one of Wilson's sisters fainted, and in a commotion of banging wooden pews and urgent whispers, was half hauled and half led from the room. She returned fifteen minutes later, to sit crying quietly as testimony continued. By then, Norman had stepped down, as defiant and jut-jawed impassive as when he walked in, and another policeman had taken the stand—one who seemed as haunted and worn as his predecessor had seemed fresh and hard. "Theo Denny Bell," he said when asked to state his name. His testimony was a wound probing, more agonized as it drew closer to the moment when the wheels began to turn and the bullets began to fly.

"The driver of that vehicle was going to hurt Jim Norman," Bell said. "It appeared for a time that he was absolutely going to run over him."

The judge asked him if he viewed the car as a weapon or as a vehicle of escape. "A weapon," Bell said.

Couldn't they have let Wilson go, the judge asked, and gone to arrest him later at his house? The question was poised precisely on the border between new and old, professional and personal policing, and Bell thought a long time before responding—long enough that it seemed the question held some philosophical ramification, long enough for Bell to reflect on the era when he would have done just that, would have gone to the house, and Miss Albertina, Dennis Wilson's mother, would have greeted him at the door with a hug. But that was an era that was past. "I can't answer that," Bell told the judge, "because I don't know for a fact that I could."

As Denny Bell left the stand and walked the gauntlet of the Wilson family on his way back out of the courtroom, a voice whispered at him as he passed, "How could you? You sat at our table!"

In the inquest's last hour, after all the subpoenaed witnesses had come and gone, the state's attorney ushered another person through the court rail and advised the judge that she was there of her own volition and had not been called or commanded to come, but had asked to. Whilamena had been all but incapable of speech at the funeral and the protest rallies; now she let her voice be heard.

"Mrs. Wilson," the judge asked her when it came his turn to question, "is there anything else you feel that I need to know?"

"Well, I feel like, from my personal feelings, I think they should get reprimanded," Whilamena said. "For me, the only thing—I don't want nothin' bad to happen, I just want justice."

The state's attorney pressed her, "Is there anything else you think that you want the judge to hear?"

"Well," she said. "I would like to say like this: If you aren't in this shoe, you don't know, and it's like I don't care what nobody say, it's murder to me. You know. And it's like they took a lot from me and my household, from my kids. Their wives have their husbands; I don't have my husband. My kids' father is taken away from them.

"Understand," Whilamena told the judge, "my husband was not a bad type of person."

Four days later, Judge Townsend presented his recommendations to the state's attorney's office. Dennis Wilson's death had become Case No. 94-1-IQ, and was summed up in seven and a half pages, comprising twenty-one findings of fact and two conclusions:

1. There is no probable cause to believe that the death of Dennis Bernard Wilson was a result of a criminal act, criminal negligence, or foul play.

2. The evidence clearly establishes that Patrolman James Norman and Sergeant Theo Denny Bell were justified in the use of deadly force. . . .

On a burning summer afternoon several months later, I climbed the rambling wooden steps to the upper story of the rectory of the First Missionary Baptist Church to talk to Reverend Andrew McRae. McRae was leaving Fernandina. His critics had won. Two days after the

Wilson inquest, the church elders had presented him with a list of complaints about his pastoring; behind the details, he sensed the same old grudge—that his rhetoric had offended the decorum of a congregation that still cherished the belief that they and the local whites were partners in the destiny of their town. On the evening of his final Sabbath, the church that had last been packed for Wilson's funeral was packed for another send-off, and McRae took the pulpit for a last rolling sermon. "I preached it the way I received it," he told his tormentors, "but because I say it's wrong to kill four people, I've been called a racist, and called a troublemaker."

In the rectory, he summed up for me the episode that presaged his eviction. "We didn't do anything to get justice for Dennis Wilson," he said, but he did think the protests put the government and the police on notice. "This one was tougher for them, because it bordered on the brink of that explosion I've been talking about," McRae said. "They were right at the wire, and they realized it, and that made a difference. And more black people spoke out against this than ever before. We didn't get justice out of it. But I think they know now: when they kill a black person, they're gonna have to present more than his record. If we didn't get anything more out of this, we got that."

Some in Fernandina read McRae's departure as a hopeful sign of returning civic equipoise, others as an indication that the town would never learn. For the rest of that year, events would be weighed on that same scale, as Fernandina recovered from its wounds.

Repairs on Ruth and C. T. Smith's house at American Beach were completed in the summer of 1994, and Ruth and C. T. held an oyster roast for friends. In the mail, bills still occasionally arrived from the county for the Medivac helicopter that had flown Chuck Smith's body to Jacksonville; C. T. refused to pay. On a December day, right after she awoke, Ruth asked C. T. not to put her in her wheelchair, as usual, but in her old easy chair in the living room. There, in midmorning, as C. T. worked in the kitchen, she died.

In May, almost four months after the shooting, Denny Bell finally resumed active duty on the street, watching with an alertness born of endless habit for the troubles petty and otherwise that can plague a little town. He also watched warily over his shoulder for the experience he couldn't quite shake. Captain Hoyt Johns observed Bell's reentry into his profession carefully. "I'll tell you something," Johns said to me of both Bell and James Norman. "If they're policemen for fifty more years, it will haunt them. It's always there. That's one of the bad things about it."

It apparently haunted them in different ways. Within a year and a half, Jim Norman would land in more trouble for wrecking a new patrol car and for again shooting at a fleeing vehicle, and Chief Sturges would recommend that the city fire him. Norman would contest the firing, and the city would file suit to prevent his reinstatement, but ultimately he retained his job. Bell, meanwhile, served quietly and bided his time until retirement, fantasizing about embarking on the political career he had often considered, some office grander than his longtime position on the Mosquito Control Board. It was a dream made almost whimsical by the event that had forever attached his name to an image of violence and hate. On July 5, 1996, on the night before the last day of his four-day shift, Denny Bell suffered a heart attack and died in his sleep. He was 49 years old, and his wife had no doubt about what had contributed to his early death: his horror at the incident on South Fletcher, his guilt over his own dispatcher's error, his anger at the harsh treatment he felt he had received afterwards at the hands of his own department. Sarah Bell declined an official police funeral, and buried her husband in his business suit in Bosque Bello Cemetery, not far from Dennis Wilson. James Norman was a pall-bearer. A number of black mourners attended. Patricia Thompson, who was out of town, sent condolences on behalf of the NAACP.

Paul Alberta still bears the scars of his foggy night's encounter with mayhem. The mayhem seemed to surprise him less than the emotion it generated in him; he could describe with equanimity being shot at during the American invasion of Panama or pinned with another soldier under a truck during the Persian Gulf War (the other soldier died), but when he talked of his grief a tiny note of wonderment crept into his voice. "You know, every now and then, it bothers me," he told me. "It bothers me a lot. Especially when I'm alone, you know." A psychiatrist Alberta went to see in Jacksonville told him there was nothing really wrong with him. "It's because I been knowing Dennis for so long," Alberta told me. "And not like in the Persian Gulf you might know somebody for a year and see them get killed—something like that you get over. But this, it bother with me. It eat at me."

His leg also bothers him. He has had several operations and a lot of therapy to repair the shattered knee, but has not been able to resume his career as a diesel mechanic; he is afraid he might never be able to. He gets around, even gimp-legged. "I'm in the Elks," he told me. "Every Sunday we give a little dance, down on American Beach."

One summer Sunday at the Elks' dance, a tune came on the jukebox which Alberta reacted to before he even recognized; it was the lyric invitation to a secret place where no one weeps, and no one worries, where there "ain't no smiling faces, lying to the races."

"Mercy," the Staple Singers shouted, and then they sang the refrain, "I'll take you there!"

"I can remember hearing that song," Alberta said, "and I just started crying."

Out on Highway A1A, the Wilson property has undergone a minor alteration. Not to the house, where a year after the shooting a wind chime hung silent in the eaves, its clapper missing, and Christmas lights Dennis never took down were faded to white by the Florida sun—but out on the corner of the lot, where he had spelled TINA in painted bricks in memoriam to his mother. Whilamena arranged some new bricks there. They spell DENNIS. Whatever else his death wrought on his community, these were its tangible monuments: a name in bricks beside the highway and carved in granite at Bosque Bello Cemetery, and the circles of orange spray paint that still marked the macadam on the beach road just north of Jasmine. The circles there were like the graffiti of surveyors or utility crews, undecipherable to the visitor—a telltale code to some arcane piece of submerged city infrastructure, necessary, permanent, and hidden.

3

Ancestral Houses

A. L. Lewis and Mama Zone on vacation in Africa, 1937.

Courtesy Johnnetta Cole

For most of the years I've known her, MaVynee Betsch has lived on a chaise longue on the beach in front of the house her great-grandfather built. The house is not one he would recognize. After his death, of old age and a tired heart in 1947, it fell out of the family, and has lost to successive renovations the formal white clapboard and latticework gingerbread and the dark, top-hung shutters over heavy sash windows that give it such an air of staid nobility in old photographs. The building has been streamlined: clad in plywood, stuccoed, and painted beige, with the sliding glass doors and weathered wooden deck that typify the standard-model modern vacation bungalow. The people who own it live in a distant corner of Georgia and come to relax on occasional summer days. When they're not around, MaVynee sets up her chaise on the wide porch and writes her letters and reads her books and presides over the panoramic oceanfront of American Beach just as her great-grandfather, Abraham Lincoln Lewis, once presided.

She calls him Fafa, the man whom no adult not in the family would have thought of calling anything but "Mr. Lewis" when he was alive, the dark-skinned man with the peanut-shaped head and the soft, otherworldly voice and calm demeanor, whose unfathomable ocean of anger was never tossed by surface storms of temper, who came out of the turpentine farms and lumber mills and cigar factories of Reconstruction Florida to become the preeminent figure in the black economic life of that entire corner of the South.

MaVynee recalls him from her early years, his last. "Oh, that man," she told me one day. "There's no way to describe the effect he had on people just by walking into a room." She remembers him arriving at the beach house he had built with his fortune in the town built by his company, remembers how he wouldn't spend any time looking back up the hill at the results of all his labors but would stand on his porch in his suspenders and tie—while Mama Zone, his second wife, aired the house and his valet drew the bath and his chauffeur, Ollie, garaged the car—staring wordlessly out across the Atlantic as though by patience and penetrating gaze he could perceive something known to all, but hidden even from him.

"And what was he looking at?" MaVynee asked me one day, waving a braceleted arm out over the white sand and constant surf and the vast blue emptiness to the east. "Africa, baby! That's Africa out there. He was looking at where he was from!"

On her chaise longue on the beach, in front of the house that Fafa built but would no longer recognize, in the town he founded, which has now, in its central precincts, nearly fallen down, MaVynee lives in an edifice of memory, in the ruins of a history, with her gaze trained on a past she knows lies just beyond the horizon, invisible to common sight.

Occasionally she will be asked to lead a tour. A bus will pull into American Beach packed with students from a black college or a public high school, and MaVynee will narrate a ride through town, standing in the aisle with her back to the windshield as the diesel grumbles idly through tight streets. Sometimes, as once when the bus bore students from Bethune-Cookman College in Daytona Beach, I'd take a seat. The Bethune-Cookman students were less impressed with their destination than with their guide, at least at first. MaVynee Betsch is nothing if not scenic. For tours, she wears her formal gown—a bright, crisp kente cloth wrapped into a skirt, under a draped felt serape. She ties a scarf of black lace tightly across her forehead, with a turquoise cloisonné butterfly perched in its meshes just between her eyebrows. Her great topiary circle of gray hair rises so high above her crown that on this day it bent against the ceiling of the bus; the mass of her hair disappears down the neck of her blouse and emerges at her waist to fill a hair net the size of a beach ball, which she cradles in the crook of her left arm. The hair is studded with buttons advertising liberal political causes.

On a visit to American Beach some years ago, when I had only heard of MaVynee's existence and doubted it, frankly, I interrupted a group of men working on a car in a driveway and asked them if they knew where the Beach Lady lived. (That was the name I'd been given.) "No," they answered; then I told them that she had big hair. "Oh, yeah," one of them said. "The lady with the fingernails." And sure enough, when I found her, on the porch of A. L. Lewis's house on Gregg Street, her fingers were amply endowed. The nails of her right hand were relatively short (for utility, I presumed). But those on her left hand extended almost to her ankles, spiraling around each other like the roots of some ambulatory mangrove. To protect them, she carries them in a plastic bag she grasps with her thumb. She lacquers them with Revlon. She was, on our first meeting, as exotic as she had been described, but no one had warned me of her most extraordinary feature, a voice of such vaulting, lilting clarity and speech of such evident culture that soon after she began to talk I had forgotten the strangeness of her appearance altogether. As I would find out, MaVynee, in her youth, had been an opera singer.

Now her voice began its work on the students. "When I was young," she began, enunciating into a microphone and steadying herself with a hip against the bus driver's shoulder, "were black people allowed to visit most Southern beaches?" She made a comic, exasperated face. "Unh-unh!" she cautioned, and let out with her favorite exclamation of extreme repudiation: "*No . . . way, . . . Jo . . . sé!* So what did we do? Well, my great-grandfather, A. L. Lewis, was president of the Afro-American Life Insurance Company in Jacksonville, which was the first—wait a minute, that's right—the *first* insurance company in the state of Florida. That's first, *period*, baby—black or white. And in the early 1930s, the company decided to build a resort where blacks could come, and this is it: American Beach."

The result of the Afro-American Life Insurance Company's initiative was once described to me by a service station owner in Fernandina, a white man named Topsy. He viewed it with an outsider's dispassionate objectivity. "It used to be on weekends we could only go so far down the beach," he said, "and then you'd look down there and as far as you could see were t-h-o-o-u-u-s-s-a-a-a-n-d-s of blacks. And if you got closer, you saw the buses, big Greyhounds all lined up side by side.

"They had the best beach," Topsy told me. "There was more going on."

It's the consensus locally that "they" had the best beach in general, cupped in the curve of the island, where the strand was widest, under the brow of the island's largest sand dune—a beach sequestered from the rest of the world by square mile upon square mile of undeveloped live oak and palmetto forest that stretched in all directions. And indeed, as MaVynee told the students, the buses came. They came for four decades, from the late 1930s into the 1970s, from Atlanta and Chicago and Birmingham and Charleston, arriving by caravan halfway through the summer nights, and the pocket hotels had bellhops to unload the luggage, and big-name bands and burlesque troupes played the clubs, and the restaurants were mobbed, and the motel was booked up years in advance, and the summer houses were inhabited by eminent people in the forefront of their generation in Jacksonville and the South—pioneering black dentists, doctors, lawyers, preachers, educators, undertakers, and, as you might expect, insurance company executives.

MaVynee can list the Beach's illustrious visitors—Cab Calloway, Ray Charles, Ossie Davis, Zora Neale Hurston, Joe Louis, Hank Aaron, Paul Robeson, and Billy Eckstine among them—and she can call each house by its owner's name. Some of the names are contemporary—the actress Barbara Montgomery, of *Amen!* fame, Emory University psychology professor Eugene Emory, jazz drummer Billy Moore, Cleveland dramaturge Alexander Hickson, Jacksonville educator Emma Morgan, former Howard University dean Edna Calhoun, Florida State Senator Arnett Girardeau, Federal Judge Henry Adams, Florida Supreme Court Justice Leander Shaw, Jacksonville historians Camilla Thompson, Charlotte Stewart, and Hortense Gray, and television journalist Lydia Stewart. But the houses MaVynee holds in highest reverence are those whose names are old: the house built by Dr. Harry Richardson, Tuskegee educator and the first black graduate of Harvard Divinity School (whose wife, Selma, a former Tuskegee professor now nearing a hundred, still comes down from Atlanta); the house of Ida Guzman, also of Tuskegee, who was a friend of George Washington Carver; the house of Dr. I. E. Williams, medical director of the Afro-American Life Insurance Company, and his wife Arnolta, friend of W. E. B. Du Bois and honored by presidents as recent as Ronald Reagan; the house of I. H. Burney, a president of the Afro-American, and Miriam Burney, the first black woman to graduate from Mount Holyoke College; and the house of Gwen Sawyer-Cherry, the first black woman legislator in Florida.

That generation has largely died off, and the names were strange to the Bethune-Cookman students, staring from the windows of the only bus to come through in a very long time. As the bus crawled along the main street—Lewis Street—from its juncture with highway A1A, I thought how little had changed since my own first trip down Lewis Street fifteen years earlier, on a day when I was kiting down A1A headed for Jacksonville and stopped and doubled back because the name I had passed on the road sign—"American Beach"—was nowhere on my map. The acres of oak and palmetto jungle that once insulated the Beach are diminished now. Housing developments, like Summer Beach to the north, and golf resorts, like Amelia Island Plantation to the south, crowd it on all sides. But now, as before, American Beach's long straight narrow main street is a hallway to a hidden realm. It loiters past a small white wooden church and a score of modest brick or frame homes set on a wooded plateau, before reaching the flank of the great sand dune, which rises to its south. There the world ahead opens up and falls away to expose an enormous sand caldera, a nearly treeless, terraced amphitheater open to the sea.

The students seemed stunned by the view. Homes lined the terraced streets; the house closest to them, across Lewis Street from the dune, had dropped its balcony into the yard and was tumbling onto its face. In the bottom of the bowl of sand were a cluster of square buildings, a central grassy square, and a string of sentinel houses along the beach. The houses were kempt, generally. A couple were even new. But the largest, a concrete fantasy known as the Blue Palace, through the very center of which a driveway extended all the way onto the beach, was an empty cinder, filling with drifted sand. The commercial buildings, except for a low brick beachside bar called the Rendezvous, looked derelict, their windows missing and their doors boarded, the gay palm trees and inviting flowers painted on their walls fading from the punishment of too many summers. The effect from the crest of Lewis Street was of stumbling out of the forest onto a lost civilization and wondering at its apocalypse. It was that beautiful, that compellingly mysterious, and one had the impression that the sand walls of American Beach were like the murderous funnel of the doodle bug— that once having fallen into the vortex of the town's history, you might never again scramble back out.

One day on the beach, MaVynee was approached by a white woman out on her jaunty constitutional from a neighboring resort, who said to her, in an apparent effort to be helpful, "Why don't you people clean this place up?"

"Lady," MaVynee shot back, "I've been to Athens and I've been to Rome. You have your ruins. These are ours."

American Beach, for MaVynee, is in its entirety a shrine—its landscape no less than its buildings. Her walks around its streets are a solitary Panathenaic Procession. She calls the sand dune NaNa, the African name of affection for a female ancestor, and as it shadows with cloud or blossoms with springtime she observes its face with an intensity of concentration she might otherwise expend on a lover's face. "I have a spiritual connection with this beach," she told the students. "Maybe it's because my parents honeymooned here." Her soprano dropped into a suggestive throatiness worthy of Lauren Bacall. "I think I may have been conceived here!" she deadpanned and then grinned large, delighted to be both at home in her town and at home on a stage, albeit in the front of a bus. "I'm serious!" she shrieked as the students laughed. "I'm sure of it!"

Whether or not she was conceived there, American Beach would not be a good place for MaVynee Betsch to elude her identity. Its road signs read like a *dramatis personae* of her life and lineage. Of the eleven streets that cross or parallel Lewis Street, several—Waldron Street, Price Street, Lee Street, and Gregg Street—bear the surnames of men who huddled with A. L. Lewis in a church study in Jacksonville in 1901 to plan the formation of the burial society that became the Afro (as the company is known to its familiars). Several more, such as Ervin Street (after the Afro's first sales agent) and Burney Road (after one of its last presidents), are named for those who labored under Lewis to keep the enterprise going.

The other streets are kin. Julia Street is named after A. L. Lewis's mother, about whom MaVynee knows little except that she was born a slave and lived in the Florida Panhandle. James Street is named after James H. Lewis, A. L. Lewis's son, whose beach house still stands next to that of the patriarch and who succeeded him as president of the Afro and held that office into his senescence, retiring in 1967 to be nursed toward death by his daughter, Mary, and her daughter, MaVynee—only to outlive the one and be reviled by the other, who calls him the Riverboat Gambler. "Whooo, God!" MaVynee burst out when I asked her if James H. Lewis the son was anything like A. L. Lewis the father. "*No . . . way, . . . Jo . . . sé!* I used to tease my grandfather that Fafa had a cold the day he was conceived! I damn sure did!

Those two were as different physically as they were mentally, sexually, and spiritually."

Three blocks after James Street comes Leonard Street, honoring J. Leonard Lewis, who was James H. Lewis's son and became the Afro's legal counsel after graduation from New York University Law School; who competed with his brother-in-law John Betsch, MaVynee's father, to become the Riverboat Gambler's heir apparent; and who won the rivalry but never gained the Afro's presidency, dying shockingly young not long after his rival's own untimely death.

And then, up in the forest, shrouded in trees, comes Mary Avenue. MaVynee tells people that the name honors Mary McLeod Bethune, founder of Bethune-Cookman College, friend of her great-grandfather, and sales agent and later board member of the Afro-American Life Insurance Company. She tells them the street is also named for A. L. Lewis's first wife, and also for his granddaughter, Mary Lewis Betsch, who was the daughter of James H. Lewis, sister of J. Leonard, wife of John Betsch, and mother of three children: Johnny, Johnnetta, and the oldest, MaVynee. Mary Betsch was a graduate of Wilberforce University, in Ohio; after the death of her husband and brother, she left her college registrar's job to work as a bookkeeper at the Afro and rose to become its first female top administrator; she was the force behind the building of its new Jacksonville headquarters in the 1950s, and might have taken the company's helm herself—for she was decidedly tough enough—had she not had the tougher job of succoring her father, the aging ex-president, the Riverboat Gambler, in his ornery last days and administering to the broken health of her eldest daughter, who would never outlast her influence.

As MaVynee reads out the street names to students on her tours, Mary Avenue is the one she invokes most quietly or lingers over longest. She may pass it by without mentioning it at all, or she may tell them how Mary Betsch directed the church choir and infused her children with a love of music, how she brought the retail life of Jacksonville nearly to a halt over the matter of a broken watch, when a white jewelry store clerk had the temerity to summon her by her first name. And once in a while MaVynee tells the story of her mother on her deathbed, in 1975. MaVynee sat with her through that time, in the antiseptic, air-conditioned hospital room in Jacksonville that would contain their last concentrated intimacies before containing those of strangers, in an acute-care ward sealed away from anything to do with their lives. And then one day the air conditioner broke and the nurses threw open the windows. It was the last day of Mary's life. The breeze bore in the noise and heat of the city, and something else, too—the faint scent, from fifteen miles away, of salty ocean air. Mary Betsch turned her head on the pillow to face the breeze and for the first time in a long time her pain faded and her voice had a young wonder in it, as though she had glimpsed the shape of sanctuary in some sustaining memory. "The beach, MaVynee. The beach!" she whispered, and they were the last words she spoke to her daughter.

In the perverse geography of human affairs, one can often see farther from the valley than from the heights. For blacks in Jacksonville, 1975 should have marked one of the heights. The long struggle for integration had been won—Florida schools were integrated in 1970—and black fortune, so long constrained by economic apartheid, could now proceed unfettered. Surely those institutions that had toughed out the bad times would prosper in the good. The keystone of black fortune in Jacksonville, the Afro-American Life Insurance Company, was preparing to celebrate its diamond anniversary, in its modern granite-and-glass headquarters on Union Street, whence it had moved almost twenty years earlier, among the most prestigious commercial buildings in Jacksonville. James L. Lewis (MaVynee's cousin, and like her a grandchild of James H. and a great-grandchild of A. L. Lewis) became in 1975 the third man in the family to assume the company's helm. "The barriers to equal business throughout all communities are decreasing," he wrote in announcing his accession. "The mood of this new beginning is excitement."

Looking back now from her chaise longue in the bottom of the Beach, MaVynee remembers 1975 as the year when the shadow crossed the lawn and a canker was in the rose, when every lush thing was dying or beginning to die. The casualties went beyond her mother and her grandfather to include much of what they loved. Her cousin James L. Lewis, the heralded heir to the Afro succession, would soon fall into debt and disrepute. He was arrested for running drugs in a shrimp boat that bore his name; the patronymic that had served as a beacon of respectability for generations of Jacksonville blacks now graced the police blotter of the DEA. He would die in 1992, of a heart attack. During his presidency, the Afro-American Life Insurance Company began a precipitous slide toward bankruptcy, dissolution, and (in 1987) receivership by the state. American Beach also began its final slide into neglect. MaVynee herself was ill, battling what she feared might be a fatal cancer, and though she recovered, she was changed and began her own transition, into a flamboyant but reclusive pauper. All around, the brightest of prospects dimmed. For MaVynee, the vista of American Beach presents not only the landscape of achievement against great odds but the landscape of defeat at the hour of triumph. One day, after one of her tours, she stood where the bus had dropped her off, surveying the land she had just described to students in grandiloquent terms. There was nothing grand in her voice. "Russ," she addressed me, though from her tone of aching lament I knew she was speaking to herself. "What went wrong?"

The decline she mourned was as global as it was particular. The evil that killed the Afro and afflicted the Beach also decimated the city of Jacksonville, whose wealthy black neighborhood and black business district have been razed and whose old black middle-class neighborhoods have been savaged by poverty and neglect and crime. The conditions that spawned that evil—underlying corruptions of environment and society—still plague the nation and the larger world, despite all the talk about progress and advancement. "It's the fourth-act syndrome," MaVynee told me one day. "That's what I call it. The opera's ending and the lady's dying and she's singing and dying and singing and dying and finally you say, 'At last!' We're in the fourth act. We're making lots of noise and dying, slowly."

In the late 1970s, MaVynee set out to thwart that death. She would have saved the world, but the money ran out. She spent her inheritance (a considerable one, since she was an heir to the fortune of one of Florida's first black millionaires and Florida's largest black landowner) funding butterfly studies and rain forest reclamation efforts and anti-whaling protests. She became, she says, the first black woman environmentalist. "I'm a terra-ist," she told me. As a result, a textbook on butterflies has been dedicated to her, and a right whale has been named after her by the scientists from the New England Aquarium, whose cetologists migrate to Amelia Island each winter to observe the whales swimming southward from their Nova Scotia breeding grounds. Every three years, MaVynee, Right Whale No. 1151, comes past Amelia on her way to calve, and the scientists give her namesake a full accounting. "It's so romantic," MaVynee says. "She's my Flying Dutchman."

She worked to stop the construction of a coal-fired power plant in Jacksonville, and lost. She worked to stop the development of Fort George Island, a coastal atoll just south of Amelia, and won. The ride down A1A from American Beach into Jacksonville is now a victory lap for her. The stretch of highway that would have been bordered by manicured gardens and golf courses is bordered instead with a rampant riot of pines and palms.

Lately, MaVynee's efforts have become even more local, focused by constraint of poverty. She lobbies by letter and worries about affording the postage. She relies on the kindness of intimates. Her sister, Johnnetta, who lives in Atlanta, sends her $150 a month for living expenses; MaVynee gives $25 to good causes and lives off the remainder. She is effective within her reach. She has convinced some American Beach residents not to mow down the indigenous plants in favor of water-thirsty lawns and to shield their streetlights and porch lights during the sea turtle nesting season lest the hatchlings march inland to their death, mistaking Edison's invention for the shimmer of moonlight on the ocean. Partly at MaVynee's urging, the island hosts a volunteer turtle patrol, mounted on dune buggies, which scours the thirteen-mile length of beach for incoming mothers, marks their buried nests, and attends the hatching of their eggs on the night when the strand erupts with thousands of shiny green coins scurrying for surf.

As a conservation watchdog, but also as a glutton for spectacle, MaVynee haunts the meetings of the Fernandina City Commission and the Port Commission and the Nassau County Commission. At the latter venue, her high-coiffed, flip-flop-shod, kente-wrapped figure is as common a fixture as the flag. I once heard a commissioner drawl, "I guess we can begin now. MaVynee's here." She sits in the back of the room. "I kid people it's because of segregation," she told me. "But really it's because all the deals are made in back. They pretend they're getting a Coke and come back and talk, and I listen." She makes it a point to miss the Pledge of Allegiance, which affronts both her pagan and her anarchic sensibilities, but when she is caught with no escape she recites the ending: "One nation, indivisible, with liberty and justice for all white folks got money." ("It's how we used to say it," she whispered to me, with a giggle.)

The commissioners are country to the core; their chivalry is long-suffering. "Thank you, MaVynee," they say. She presents her case with the polish of a practiced advocate, and makes the commissioners feel that she is on their side despite her gadfly agenda. "I grew up in a very public house," she told me. "We practiced the political graces over the dinner table every night."

She repeatedly petitions the county's Mosquito Control Board to use natural predators instead of poison spray to combat pests, and rallies moratoriums on the massive dredging operations that replenish Amelia's eroding beaches with coarse, shell-sharded, clay-clogged, bottom sand dug up offshore and blown onto the coast through four-foot-diameter iron tubes—operations that conservationists call counterproductive, because they disrupt the natural cycle of beach creation. In recent years, the dredging efforts have not blown sand on American Beach, thanks to MaVynee's lobbying, but the pipes—spray-painted DANGER/STAY OFF—still run along the beach to connect the dredges to neighboring resorts, and MaVynee lies awake at night listening to the eighteen-wheelers passing on the sand and the incessant back-and-forth of earthmovers. When the cranes drop off the heavy new sections of iron pipe, the thudding shakes every house in town.

"If I don't have a heart attack by the time I'm sixty, I guess it's a miracle," MaVynee said when she was fifty-eight, in 1993. (The miracle has since occurred.) That was the year of the most recent beach dredging, and MaVynee let off steam by threatening to move to Belize to live with a friend who farms butterflies, and channeled her frustration into music. She has been writing an opera for as long as I've known her, but all she will reveal about it is that the female lead dies in the first act but is later revived by mosquitoes; that it will be sung on NaNa, the sand dune; and that it will be composed of nature's sounds, though not exclusively. "I'm using the bulldozers in my opera, you know," she told me one particularly cacophonous beach-reclamation day. "*Beep . . . beep . . . beep*—that noise they make when they back up? I'm using it as a leitmotif."

In the county meetings, MaVynee bird-dogs every new housing development that borders beach or marsh, asking for wider buffer zones and setbacks, for restrictions on water use and sewage output, and (usually in vain) for the saving of as many trees as possible. Developers know the ropes; they consent to what's asked and then do what they want, to the degree they can get away with it. "Nothing seems to ever stick in their brain," MaVynee says. Doing what they want often means mowing down nearly every vertical living thing before laying the first foundation. In 1995, a company from Texas bought a prime piece of real estate on the north end of Amelia Island for a new housing development. The acres of rolling sand lay cool under a canopy of twisted maritime oaks, of the sort that Hollywood might seek out for a Faulknerian or at least Gumpian epic of the mythopoetic South. The company called in the earthmovers and converted the property to a vast sand parking lot, pocked for a season with smoldering pyres of stumps, and plunked down mammoth square homes on the hot expanse, like hotels on a Monopoly board. Then in front of each house they planted one or two nursery saplings, staked as though readied for public execution.

"People have got to *do* something to nature," MaVynee explained to me on one of our trips. "They've got to *impose*. They don't think nature is beautiful until they destroy it and replace it with a version of their own. They don't enjoy the subtlety of the beach shapes and the wild plants, they don't understand that *that's the beauty, dummy! That's what we came here for!* It's like someone who needs Wagner, with all the hoopla and costumes and garbage, going to see Debussy and missing the whole subtlety of the opera. You're not going to get the big opera, you're not going to get the big screaming, you're not going to get the big orchestra, the big dramatic scene. But if you're listening for Debussy, it's beautiful. I guess that's why I never got married. I could never find a man who understood that."

The town shared MaVynee's horror over the fate of the maritime forest, which had been taken for granted as one of the island's distinctive amenities for so long that no one had thought to protect it. In the uproar over its desecration, the city zoning inspector was fired and the county zoning inspector let go in a "restructuring." He was given a new job by Amelia Island Plantation, the resort adjacent to American Beach founded by Charles Fraser, developer of the father of all such Sea Island utopias, Sea Pines Plantation on Hilton Head in South Carolina.

The greater outrage in the affair of the maritime oaks was that people bought the houses. This was MaVynee's deepest fear made manifest—not just the fall of unbridled nature but its replacement by a regime of willful conformity. It defied her comprehension—a culture so rapacious to such insipid ends, in which money and sweat were expended in pursuit of an infantilized maturity. The privilege of living in "Plantations," playing on "links," and shopping in "chains" sounds suspiciously like slavery to her. As someone whose own history is a commitment to idiosyncrasy, she reads in the lust of the rich for petty regimentation her personal extinction and her culture's disaster.

"So, here comes Mrs. von Snooty Snooty with all her money, and where does she want to live?" MaVynee asked me one day. "In a place named 'Summer' or 'Palms' or 'Ocean,' in a house that looks just like the one next door and the one next door to that, sitting all in a lit-tul row on a street that could be anywhere, to look at it. It's so *boring!* You'd think they'd want to keep some trees for privacy, or novelty, or at least for some shade. But no, they cut 'em down and hole up in the heat with the air conditioner on and play golf on the weekends, and plant their lilies all in a lit-tul row. Yuck! Why does everything always have to be the same?"

"Look at that!" she commanded on another occasion, pointing to a row of high-priced and starkly conventional beachside condominiums. "What does that remind you of? The *projects,* baby. We call those projects, where I come from." Of the mammoth Ritz-Carlton, which poked out of the forest as obtrusively as a ziggurat out of a Yucatán jungle, she said, "I could design that on my drunk night, and I don't drink."

One day in the early spring of 1994, as MaVynee and I headed into Fernandina to do some grocery shopping, we took the back route and stopped at a new development just getting under way. She had been paying particular attention to it, because it bordered American Beach directly to the north, and whatever it turned out to be, American

Beach would have to live with or at the very least next to. The development would be set in a mature live-oak forest that had served as a buffer between American Beach and the Ritz-Carlton and Summer Beach. It was to be named, with the creative abandon so characteristic of developers, Ocean Village.

"At least it won't be another Plantation," MaVynee said as we got out of the car and began walking down a rutted path into the property. The overhanging oaks shielded our steps in a tracery of shadow, but all was not peaceful: soon we could hear the leitmotif. A machine was loose in the forest. "Okay, the walkover should be right up here," MaVynee said as we proceeded, referring to a slatted wooden walkway that was to stretch over the dunes to the beach. "There it is. We bitched and bitched to get a public beach access and a buffer zone. Now . . . Oh, my God! Look where they've got the fence. Baby, they're right up there to it, look!" And in fact the buffer at Ocean Village's border seemed to dwindle to nothingness in places. MaVynee's voice rose to rival the roar of the equipment. I had seen her outraged before, and it had never concerned me. Outrage was a form of composure for her—she was girded with high dudgeon. But now as she looked at the sidewalk-wide strip empty of significant vegetation that the machine operator was leaving between the project and its neighbors, the wind seemed to go out of her and a quavering hysteria crept into her voice. "Oh, damn it! This is supposed to be a park in here. I *told* the inspector he should have come on down here! It's too late once they've torn everything down. Damn it! They'll be right on top of us." Struggling to recover herself, she rehearsed a bureaucratic remedy. "We can find out from—um, go by—um, yeah, the zoning office. I think this is supposed to be fifty feet. You think that's fifty feet? It looks more like twenty to me. Oh, me!" The machine's noise was getting louder, and suddenly it broke into view, a juggernaut of belching yellow, a house-size backhoe on caterpillar treads. Its forelimb was raised roof-high as it approached, battering through the crown of a century-old live oak, and with a hydraulic flex the bucket came down, splintering the tree through the middle with a prolonged crack, followed by a hiss of raining foliage. The backhoe grunted backward for leverage and reached up for the rest. "Let's go!" MaVynee yelled at me, and ran stumbling back along the path. She was sobbing, whom I'd never once seen cry, even in the grip of her highest histrionics. "Oh, you bastards!" she yelled back over her shoulder. "I can't *believe* it!" But her voice was drowned out by another rending crack.

Even before Ocean Village brought the suburban desert to the north border of American Beach, MaVynee had been fighting an ongoing battle on American Beach's southern flank. She was seeking to save a pocket rain forest known as the Harrison Tract. The Harrison Tract was a remnant of the seven-hundred-acre Harrison plantation, which had been ceded by the Spanish king to a South Carolinian named Samuel Harrison in the late eighteenth century. In the mid-1930s, when the Afro-American Life Insurance Company was assembling property to form American Beach, it bought a hundred-acre corner of that old grant, lying south of Lewis Street and east of the highway, which was then just a rutted dirt road paved with oyster shells. A. L. Lewis never developed the parcel, and James L. Lewis, during his luckless Afro presidency, sold it off to speculators. A broad thicket of palmetto and magnolia and fern and twisted live oak, bisected by a sullen tannin creek and draped at its edges in Spanish moss, the Harrison Tract was a reminder of what the island used to be. Since 1984 the property had been in real estate limbo. A FOR SALE sign beckoned forlornly beside the highway, fading to pastel in the Florida sun, attracting infrequent nibbles. A trucking company considered buying the land for a storage depot, and a kennel wanted to put a dog run there, but they both backed out. The sign stayed, a goad in MaVynee's side. The prospect of losing her beloved ancestral land to grunting tractor trailers or the yelping of imprisoned animals was more than she could countenance, the more so because the parcel included, on its eastern edge, NaNa—the great sand dune itself, the defining natural monument of American Beach. NaNa was for sale, and getting her back was more than territorial imperative and more than conservation. It was a matter of family and racial pride: it would represent an answer to all that had gone wrong, a symbolic reversal of historic betrayals, extending back past the betrayal of A. L. Lewis's legacy by James L. Lewis's improvidence to the ancient and greater betrayal that marked the family's first exposure to Western commerce, when A. L. Lewis's ancestor was sold by another African into the white man's chains.

The asking price was not that high for so significant a salvation:

$3 million. It was more than MaVynee had on hand. So, over the years, she spent her postage and worked the pay phone up by the highway, and on occasion pressed me into service to drive her into Fernandina to meet with lawyers or into Jacksonville to meet with state regulators, to try to arrange some way that the land could be returned to the Beach or set aside by the state so that it would not fall into the Philistine hands of developers.

Our rides into Jacksonville also achieved some of my own aims, when we visited with those people who knew the city's black history and were old enough to remember MaVynee's parents and grandparents and the heritage they represented. Occasionally, when MaVynee's attention was diverted or she had left the room, the old people would turn to me with a query of their own. Just the sight of MaVynee provoked them to anger or to sorrow, and it became apparent to me that, in their minds, the twin mysteries of "Whatever happened to black Jacksonville?" and "Whatever happened to the Afro?" could be distilled into another more personal mystery: "Whatever happened to MaVynee Betsch?"

"MaVynee went abroad one time and stayed for some time, you know. It was years ago," Maude Aveilhe, a former employee of the Afro, told me. "Looks like when she came back she was a very different personality or something, but she's quite a person. She's nice."

Leota Davis, another Afro veteran, expressed it with more bitterness. MaVynee and I had spent a couple of hours in Davis's living room, talking of past times, the glory of the Afro in its heyday, the promise it had once held out, the heartbreak of its collapse. Afterward the three of us walked outside into another, more general collapse— the remains of a once proudly middle-class west Jacksonville neighborhood. Davis's eyes scanned the wreckage that surrounded her lovely home, the teenagers lounging menacingly on a car hood (mine, as it happens), and the boarded-up houses and buckled pavement along her street, and they lit at last on MaVynee, who had wandered on ahead of us. "Her mother would die if she could see what has happened to her," Davis said. "She would just die."

"They think she's crazy," Carol Alexander, a friend of MaVynee's, told me. "Most of the black people in Jacksonville do. You know—with her hair and her nails and living on the beach." Alexander, who lives in one of the posh subdivisions in southeast Jacksonville, had enjoyed something like the opposite of MaVynee's evolution: she grew up on the modest side of Philadelphia, the daughter of a hair shampooer and a handyman, and ascended into hard-won wealth. Still, and despite her prominence in civic causes, she was not (and could never be) a member of Jacksonville's old black bourgeoisie, and for that reason she had made something of a study of it. "What compels people?" she asked me one night after a dinner at the Ritz-Carlton. We were sitting in the lobby bar drinking margaritas, and a jazz quartet was playing, but her concentration was firmly on her subject: children of wealth and privilege, and what happens to them when they are black and grow up in a Southern city like Jacksonville.

Soon after Carol Alexander had moved to Jacksonville, she told me, she encountered one of those children, a prosperous tradesman's daughter who had built an international career as a stage performer, had come back home to take care of her dying mother, and then had decided to stay on, in the house where she grew up—"a real mansion, with chandeliers and wooden mantels with lions so finely carved their eyes follow you around the room." Alexander made a slit with her fingers in front of her face and peered through it, moving her eyes ominously back and forth, to demonstrate. The great house, she said, was moldering away, the ceiling falling in so that you could see the lathes, and cobwebs hanging in the corners, and the woman living alone there, alone in the glorious ruins.

So much of old black Jacksonville seemed enshrouded in that same dust. "Look at MaVynee," Alexander said. "When she was young, she and her sister were the most eligible girls in the city. They were aristocracy. They came out as *debutantes*. They were supremely educated. MaVynee goes to Oberlin. She graduates in some high position in her class."

"Thirteenth," I offered. I had heard the stories, too.

"Thirteenth," Alexander said. "She sings opera in the Oberlin Conservatory. She goes to live in Paris and becomes a diva in Germany. And then comes back. Her mother dies, and her grandfather, and she gives away her fortune to charity so she can live on the beach with as near to nothing as possible. Why?"

It was getting late in the Ritz. The musicians had packed up and the waitress had served the last drinks and gone home. The lights had risen, the cleaning crew arrived, and still Alexander sat. She loved MaVynee, she said, but the mystery of her collapse was a wall between them. She had heard the explanations—that MaVynee had suffered a mental breakdown as a result of racism she encountered in Germany, or gotten sick from the smog in London. Neither of those explanations sufficed, she said, in the face of what she knew about MaVynee's strong constitution and stronger personality. She suspected something closer to home, something right there in Jacksonville. "In town, they say it was a love affair," Alexander said. "But MaVynee's never mentioned anything about it, and I still don't understand. Why does someone give up a profession and status and fortune? What makes a person lay it all down?"

A few days later, I pursued the question with MaVynee—gingerly, as ever. As ever, she eluded me, with an elliptical defiance. "Baby," she growled. "I've been free so long it's frightening."

Shortly after the encounter with Ocean Village's backhoe, I heard the first rumblings that MaVynee's refuge was about to come under serious assault. It was May, the thick of sea turtle nesting season, and friends of mine—a poet and professor who was active in the turtle patrol and her husband, a real estate broker and developer who worked for Amelia Island Plantation—called to say that they had heard that a large adult turtle had washed ashore in mid-island, hurt. They were going out to see if they could find her. We met at a public beach access between the Ritz-Carlton and American Beach and, carrying our shoes and some tools in one large pail and a picnic dinner in another, began walking south, scouting the surf line. It was evening and the last light was fading by the time we spotted her, tossing in the roil without resistance, already dead. She was enormous—her shell the size of a coffee table, her flippers like palm fronds, her noble, hawk-beaked head as smooth and large as a bowling ball—a *grande dame* of a loggerhead. How many years had she swum through how many oceans, and almost, almost made it back home to drop her eggs in the sand that had spawned her, only to meet with mishap? The developer waded into the breakers and grappled her onto the sand and turned her right-side-up. The story was written in her carapace, scored with deep, long, parallel gashes, the signature of a ship's propeller. We studied her by flashlight as the sky went black, and then, while the professor spread a picnic on the beach's high shoulder, the developer retrieved a pruning saw from his tool bucket and set to work, struggling against the surf until he had secured his souvenir. He walked a little way off to wash in unbloodied water, and then we sat in the dark and ate, watching the string of ships' lights move slowly along the horizon. Directly behind us was the live-oak forest that was falling to Ocean Village bulldozers, and I told the couple about MaVynee's distress. From his silence, I could tell that the developer was deliberating. Finally he said, "MaVynee's going to have a bad summer, I'm afraid."

The professional secret that prompted his forecast was one he had not divulged, at that point, even to his wife: Amelia Island Plantation was in the process of buying the Harrison Tract, and preparing to announce its plans to build a new golf course and a new neighborhood of homes, perched directly on the edge of American Beach and called Plantation Park. MaVynee, like the rest of us, would soon enough learn the details of Plantation Park, and the developer was right about their effect, for she would have a bad summer and a bad few years to follow, and the Beach would be split internally, even as its existence was pressured from without. When the three of us had finished our picnic, we walked back north towards the bright lights of the Ritz, the remnants of our dinner in one pail, and the turtle's head grinning up at us from the bottom of the other.

Amelia Island Plantation and American Beach have never coexisted comfortably. When Charles Fraser's Sea Pines Company, creator of Hilton Head, first set its sights on Amelia Island in the early 1970s, it saw the proximity of American Beach as a bemusing problem—the company had no doubt, one former Sea Pines executive told me, about how the white retirees who were their prospective buyers would view their new black neighbors: pretty much as they viewed the great white sharks in the water. The company tried to confront the issue diplomatically in its 1972 Property Buyers Guide, but it wasn't diplomatic enough. The text read:

American Beach borders the north end of Amelia Island Plantation and covers two thousand feet of beach frontage. It is the vestige of an era that is fortunately passing from the American scene—be it however slowly.

For years, American Beach has flourished as a segregated, all-black recreational area. Fifteen years ago, it was an extremely popular, thriving beach resort whose population swelled greatly in the summer months.

Such is no longer the case. The reason is clear; as integration becomes a way of life—as "separate but equal" becomes simply *equal*—the need for an acceptance of black beaches is rapidly disappearing.

This is not to say that American Beach has disappeared. There is no reason to assume it will soon. It still has a summer season, and attracts people from the nearby inland communities. There are stores and restaurants that open for the summer, and do an active business. But American Beach does not seem destined to keep its special identity much longer. Five years from now American Beach will be unrecognizable, as it changes from "black beach" to "beach" and blends into, and is absorbed by, the growing island around it.

And so it should be. It once served a need. The need is now gone.

The brochure—as Jack Healan, Amelia Island Plantation's current president, noted to me—had not been meant to telegraph a racist opinion. Nevertheless it did. Especially with the telltale phrase about the disappearing "need for an acceptance of black beaches," and especially with the photograph across from the text showing an idyllic couple on the beach—two people who were beautiful, young, and, like everyone else pictured in the brochure, white. In the era of the new equality, it seemed to American Beach residents, the Beach was to be absorbed into the island before anyone of their complexion could be absorbed into the Buyers Guide.

Amelia Island Plantation did not take a passive role in the "absorption" of American Beach. During the Plantation's early years, company representatives and their proxies visited American Beach property owners and purchased options on their homes, one by one. Some residents fought the incursion: Frank and Emma Morgan, who reside in one of the original oceanfront homes and also own the town's central grassy parking lot, canvassed their neighbors, urging people to stay put. The Plantation nevertheless ended up with rights to much of the property from ocean to highway. Then an ill wind blew American Beach some unexpected good. The Sea Pines Company, the Amelia Island Company's corporate parent, went through bankruptcy reorganization, and by the time they unloaded their Amelia Island property onto its current owners the options on American Beach homes had lapsed. The Plantation's new administrators—as Jack Healan points out—have never bothered to publish a similar brochure or mount a similar takeover effort. The effort could not in any case have been repeated: the first one had wised up the Beach, whose residents were ever after resistant to the Plantation's goodwill.

Notwithstanding that victory, the impression lingered that American Beach was a vestige, not long for the world. What had overtaken the Beach was more than just the passing of the era of segregation—it was the passing of a system of belief. But if the need for a segregated beach was gone, the need for the system of belief was all the greater. In all its shabbiness, American Beach was still the preserve of a conviction. In its shininess, Amelia Island Plantation could not aspire to be anything more than commodity. One state was passionate, the other actuarial. The contest between them would attest to the importance of American Beach, and offer an explanation for the mystery of MaVynee Betsch.

The past that MaVynee inhabits so tenaciously comprises continents and centuries. Africa before the Diaspora and slavery after it afflict her imagination, as does that more particular exodus that brought her great-grandfather A. L. Lewis out of poverty in rural Madison, Florida, at the age of thirteen in 1878 to help seek his family's fortune in Jacksonville. Really, MaVynee's past began with the birth of that fortune at the turn of the century, an event coinciding almost precisely with the birth of modern Jacksonville.

No one has ever accused Jacksonville, Florida, of putting on airs. It is, in the 1990s, one of the South's least graceful cities. Its sparse outcropping of corporate skyscrapers, surrounded by unrestrained

generic-American urban sprawl, gives the impression of salted earth, a
desiccated soil in which nothing sophisticated or genteel can thrive.
Even Jacksonvillians, or especially Jacksonvillians, consider their home
a backwater—or enough of one, at least, to require defending against
the charge. In 1993, the city lobbied for a National Football League
franchise, arguing that Jacksonville was not, as its competitors had
claimed, "a hick town." But a football team—or for that matter a franchise of any sort—seems ill suited to provide what Jacksonville lacks: a
notable individuality, founded on a notable past. A hundred and eighty
years after its first settling, Jacksonville still seems a rambling squatters' camp awaiting its charter, empty of mission, bereft of history.

It didn't have to turn out that way. The Saint Johns River, which
the downtown straddles near its confluence with the Atlantic, is as aus-
picious a site for a model metropolis as the Ashley and the Cooper, or
the Charles or the Willamette or the Savannah. In its great breadth
and stately pace, the river offers a natural beauty and commercial
advantage that Jacksonville's pioneers, including those who pioneered
in bondage, turned to early profit.

The city also, of course, has a history, a prominent one. The history stays invisible because the prominence resides almost exclusively
on the black side of town. James Weldon Johnson and J. Rosamond
Johnson were born in Jacksonville, A. Philip Randolph was raised
there, Mary McLeod Bethune and Zora Neale Hurston worked there,
Paul Laurence Dunbar was inducted into the Masons there and rose to
the third degree, and the pioneer aviatrix Bessie Coleman died there.
Every one of them has been commemorated by innumerable biogra-
phies or postage stamps, but meaningful local memorials would be
hard to find. As of the mid-1990s, there was hardly more than a plaque
to honor any of them.

Jacksonville wasn't just a town that contributed exceptional black
talent to the greater world; for a while in its daily commerce it offered
a prospect of street-level racial cooperation and high-level black participation. In the late nineteenth century, Jacksonville was poised as
few cities in the South to lead the benighted region, and thus the
nation, into a brighter day. James Weldon Johnson noted of
Jacksonville at that time that it was "known far and wide as a good
town for Negroes . . . long after the close of Reconstruction." Within a

quick couple of decades, though, it had transformed itself, becoming, as Johnson noted in his biography *Along This Way*, a "one hundred percent Cracker town." In 1919, after the latest of a long series of Jacksonville lynchings, Johnson wrote in the *New York Age* that "one is taken up entirely with the shame of this city."

Jacksonville's fall from grace was gradual and incremental. But just as an interrupted lifeline on a human palm reveals to the clairvoyant the trace of a near-death experience, the arc of Jacksonville's history is sundered by a moment of sharp catastrophe. The division between old and new Jacksonville occurred on the afternoon of May 3, 1901.

Until twelve-thirty on that day, the century had proceeded smoothly for the city. The *Florida Times-Union* had called 1900 a "banner year" for Jacksonville business, especially for the budding tourist industry, which had recast the town as "the Winter City in Summerland" and kept the big hotels open from November to March to accommodate the Yankee trade. Sixty-three trains full of Yankees had arrived in Jacksonville in January 1900 alone, and 15,000 tourists lived the entire winter in the city—not bad for a place with a permanent population of fewer than 30,000.

Blacks, who made up most of that populace and provided almost all of the semi- and unskilled labor in Jacksonville's lumber mills, cigar factories, and tourist hotels, also partook of the centennial optimism, albeit from a lower perspective. They had a growing middle class to celebrate. There were in town 49 black ministers, 69 teachers, 6 doctors, 3 lawyers, and a pharmacist. Blacks owned 131 businesses, and their place in Jacksonville society was championed by such leaders as Joseph Blodgett, a builder and the state's first black millionaire; Jerome Milton Waldron, who was minister of Bethel Baptist Church; and James Weldon Johnson, the second black man to pass the state's bar exam and the principal of its one black high school, Stanton. For the annual black celebration held on February 12, Abraham Lincoln's birthday, to commemorate Emancipation, Johnson unveiled one of his new poems, which had been set to music by his brother Rosamond and was sung for the assembled crowd by a choir of five hundred schoolchildren. It went, in part:

Stony the road we trod
Bitter the chastening rod,
Felt in the days when hope unborn had died.
Yet with a steady beat,
Have not our weary feet
Come to the place for which our fathers sighed?
We have come over a way that with tears has been watered.
We have come, treading our path through the blood of the
slaughtered.
Out of our gloomy past,
Till now we stand at last
Where the white gleam of our bright star is cast.
Shadowed beneath thy hand,
May we forever stand.
True to our God,
True to our native land

"Lift Every Voice and Sing" would later be adopted and enshrined by the NAACP. What is sung today as the "Negro National Anthem" was originally an ode to Jacksonville's black *début de siècle* prospects.

Then came that May afternoon in 1901, and the infernal frailty of progress floated skyward on a spark up the chimney of a pineboard shanty in Hansontown, a black and poor neighborhood west of the central business district, and wafted across a yard on the strength of a northwesterly breeze and settled on the outdoor docks of the Cleveland Fiber Factory, where mats of Spanish moss had been laid out in the sun to dry. The moss caught the sparks, and the wind caught the flames, which spread, according to a contemporary newspaper account, "with the rapidity with which a man could walk." By nightfall, 466 acres, comprising the entirety of downtown, 146 city blocks, and 2,368 buildings had succumbed to what another reporter called a "thundering, mighty, lurid, storm-wave of fire." Incited by the heat over the river, a waterspout stalked along the wharves, as though one of nature's elements had risen to pace ringside at the rampage of another. Photographs of the scene the morning after show an ashscape pre-monitory of Dresden or Hiroshima—a stumpy forest of unattached chimneys in a plain of smoldering snow, as far as the eye could see.

Like San Francisco or Chicago after their respective conflagrations, Jacksonville rebuilt quickly, and was spiritually invigorated by the rebuilding. The city that arose was a brasher, better, twentieth-century city, with an unapologetic entrepreneurial ethos exemplified in the thrust of its new skyscrapers, the tallest of which was eleven stories high. But its modernity was intimately coupled with another shift: the Jacksonville that burned had been, for all its simmering racial hatreds and significant social disparities, a somewhat integrated city. Not so the city that arose. As James Crook, professor of history at the University of North Florida and author of *Jacksonville after the Fire*, expressed it: "Jacksonville developed as two cities in the years after the fire, one white and one black." Legions of laborers and militiamen flooded into the city from south Georgia and rural Florida, none of them having much experience with or tolerance for the urbane ways of urban blacks. James Weldon Johnson, for one, found this out quickly. Several days after the fire, he was beaten and nearly killed by a posse of militiamen for walking and conversing with a light-skinned woman whom they mistook for white. Then he was arrested.

Fortunately, out of the fire as out of Pandora's box, hope escaped with the furies. Unmentioned in the newspaper accounts of the disaster, a young black woman named Eartha Mary Magdalene White scurried in and out of a burning building on Ocean Street, hoisting armloads of boxes onto a commandeered wagon and driving them to safety. They held records and receipts of the Afro-American Industrial & Benefit Association, a company that had opened only a month earlier to provide burial benefits for Florida's blacks. Eartha M. M. White was clerk of the company, which, surviving the fire with enough of its ledgers intact, would continue in business. She delivered the boxes to 621 Florida Street, which was one of the only houses in Jacksonville's downtown to survive the fire—that of the company's treasurer, Abraham Lincoln Lewis.

Insurance companies created and run by and administering to blacks were perennial in the postbellum South: they were the direct result of the remarkable eagerness of freed slaves to participate in the civic life of the nation, and of the nation's reluctance to let them. The eagerness was perhaps surprising; the nation's economic system had hardly shown blacks its friendliest face, nor had its system of law, yet blacks displayed an avidness for American business and government practice that evinced a hopeful patriotism.

Jacksonville blacks were better prepared than most to pursue this patriotism because of their adventures during the recent war, when hundreds had escaped from the plantations to serve the Union in the First, Second, and Third South Carolina Regiments, the black Glory Brigades. Dan Schafer, chairperson of the history department of the University of North Florida, inspected the records of those units. "The white officer of one all-Florida company wrote that they were the best-looking troops he ever had seen," he told me. "They'd drill in the morning, then they'd have rest time, then school. They'd drill and then they'd have meetings and they'd talk about the time ahead, and train for citizenship. They became an active force after the war. They mustered out and settled in the town, became tradesmen, worked for the lumberyards. They played, I think, a very important part in the kind of race relations that was established during Reconstruction. They wanted to be involved in politics, had been trained daily in literacy and citizenship."

Things started off well enough. In 1867, at the inception of Reconstruction, blacks met in Bethel Baptist Church, and under the guidance of their minister, J. Milton Waldron, they chose a ticket for city elections. Waldron was an ardent "race man," a disciple of Booker T. Washington who later adopted the more militant ideas of W. E. B. Du Bois and would end his career ministering in South Africa. He positioned his Jacksonville church as a fortress in the fight he saw coming, incorporating it so that it could better run relief programs. He professed the belief that "Bethel should stand as a refutation of racial inferiority and an object lesson of the better side of Negro culture and progress in the South." As they chose their first political ticket, his parishioners adopted a proclamation reading, "Resolved, That we have become bona-fide citizens of Florida and the United States: that there is no distinction between the white and black man in political matters."

Blacks held open-air rallies and fife-and-drum-corps parades and elected delegates to the Florida State Constitutional Convention and representatives to the Jacksonville City Council and the Duval County School Board. They became policemen, marshals, judges, and justices of the peace. One of black Jacksonville's own, Jonathan Gibbs, became the Florida secretary of state in 1868, and later Florida superintendent of public instruction, in which post he initiated the public education system still used in the state.

Their going was hardly easy, however. Even their liberators made unreliable champions. In February 1869, less than two months before the lifting of the federal occupation of Jacksonville, white federal troops marched into town and went on what Jacksonville historian T. Frederick Davis describes in his 1925 book *History of Jacksonville, Florida, and Vicinity* as a "race rampage," shooting at any blacks they encountered while yelling ostentatious commands of "Ready, aim, fire!" Blacks stayed off the city streets for days, and one black man was killed; the soldiers later protested that it was all meant in fun and they were only firing blanks. Other predations were less "playful." Jacksonville partook of the escalating violence that would eventually give Florida the highest lynching rate of any state in the South.

Jacksonville blacks fought back, striking to secure labor rights and taking up arms on repeated occasions to forestall injustice. The "riot" of 1892 illustrates. On July 4 of that year, Frank Burrows, "a young white man," in T. Frederick Davis's not unbiased description, was struck over the head and killed by Ben Reed, "a giant negro." Reed was arrested, and, as Davis reports, "when the news spread . . . feeling ran high and there was talk by indiscreet persons of lynching." To prevent that eventuality, blacks began congregating on Liberty Street, across from the jail. By ten o'clock that night the jail was surrounded by a throng of five hundred black people, many of them armed with pistols and Winchester rifles. "The city was entirely in their control," Davis writes. They posted sentinels on street corners, and any passing white person was interrogated, then escorted to his destination block by block by a prearranged series of coded whistles. The mob seemed intent on insuring justice, not obstructing it, and when twenty policemen arrived, the crowd quietly let them through into the jail. The next day, Governor Francis Fleming mustered the state militia, and black marksmen took up positions in trees and house windows, "apparently," in Davis's estimation, "waiting for a war to begin." After three tense days, the prisoner Ben Reed was delivered to court and eventually convicted and sentenced to four years in jail, having been spared the rope that likely awaited him without the intervention of what Davis calls "a dangerous demonstration." "The incendiary talk by crowds of negro women," he writes, "was one of the most disturbing elements through-out the trouble."

Partly as a result of their prickliness, local blacks maintained their political muscle even after the lifting of Radical Reconstruction. "Jacksonville was the one exception in Florida to the decline in Republican fortunes," the historian Peter Klingman notes. "Negroes and white Republicans managed to maintain a voice in Duval County politics to a degree unmatched elsewhere in the state or in the South." This alliance met its Donnybrook after the election of 1888. That year the city elected a Republican mayor, C. B. Smith, along with eighteen aldermen, five of whom were black. It also boasted a black municipal judge, a black chairman of its Board of Police Commission, fifteen black policemen (out of twenty-three) and two police sergeants. Davis primly remarks that "this administration was entirely distasteful to the majority of the white people of Jacksonville."

It was also unpopular in Tallahassee, the state capital, where the legislature decided to do something about the state's wayward largest city. It passed House Bill No. 4, nullifying Jacksonville's charter, dis-banding its popularly elected government, and replacing it with one appointed by the governor. The new, more tasteful appointees were hardly men of demonstrated probity: within a couple of years the new city marshal had tried to murder the new mayor and his replacement had absconded with $1,400 of city funds, not to be seen again. But House Bill No. 4 had the desired effect. The new government, includ-ing the police force in its entirety, was lily white. The resolution of Bethel Baptist parishioners that "there is no distinction between the white and black man in political matters" had been proven false by leg-islative fiat. When House Bill No. 4 took effect in 1889, it marked the beginning of a significant rollback of black rights. A poll tax and a five-minute time limit on voting were imposed, and Jacksonville's black sixth ward was gerrymandered away. Jim Crow arrived in 1905.

The repression had a hidden consolation: as blacks lost freedoms and political power, they began building, for the first time in the United States, a self-reliant economy. During the Afro's first decade, Jacksonville blacks enjoyed the nation's first black-run daily newspa-per, the short-lived *Daily American*, founded and edited by James Weldon Johnson, and were operating their own transit system, with four trolleys running on a fixed schedule. After the trolley company closed in 1905 and the municipal transit was segregated by state law the same year, Eartha M. M. White, the Afro's clerk, swore she would never ride Jacksonville transit again, and didn't: she walked.

On January 15, 1901, four months before the great Jacksonville fire—on a night described in a 1941 official commemorative history of the Afro-American Life Insurance Company as "bleak" and "wintry"—Pastor Waldron summoned six men to a meeting in Bethel Baptist Church. They were, in the words of the company history, "Negro men of sturdy, rustic character, racial pride, hopeful vision and indomitable will." Among that little peerage, A. L. Lewis was an anomaly. The group, a local elite, included two preachers, two merchants, a contractor, and a physician. Lewis, at thirty-six, was an uneducated laborer and machinist who had worked in Jacksonville sawmills for twenty-two years. He was a Methodist, and his thrift and gravity and his leadership in Mount Olive African Methodist Episcopal Church, along with the ambition he had displayed by investing in Jacksonville's first black-owned shoe repair business, had brought him to the attention of black leaders, including those convened with him on this night.

The group sat in the prayer room of Bethel's parsonage, "reviewing the unhealthy surroundings, the presence of poverty and the absence of adequate relief in times of dire distress," according to the history, "and discussed prayerfully among themselves ways and means of alleviating the suffering, giving care and treatment to the sick and providing for the respectable burial of the dead." After a long conversation the men agreed to contribute $100 apiece to capitalize an insurance association, "an institution that was destined to be the greatest Negro business concern of the state of Florida, one whose path of progress was to lead our people to the dizzy heights of national reputation, give preferable and profitable employment to thousands of our men and women and relieve the distress of millions of our people." A. L. Lewis was appointed company treasurer, and on April 1, 1901, Florida granted a charter to the Afro-American Industrial & Benefit Association, making it the first insurance company chartered in the state. The company had achieved the first of its dizzy heights. Five weeks later it burned to the ground.

And was reborn in the back room of Treasurer Lewis's house. The fire forged a new role for Lewis. The other men in the Afro's founding committee, being men of higher affairs, were called away to rebuild their respective institutions. It fell to the machinist to rebuild the company. J. Milton Waldron, preoccupied with construction of a new sanctuary for Bethel Baptist Church, pleaded with Lewis to quit his job at the sawmill, and Lewis did, adding to the duties of Afro treasurer those of secretary and general manager. The company history notes:

> Having accepted the position as General Manager, Abraham Lincoln Lewis demonstrated undeniably the wonderful forces that had been concealed and lay dormant in the breast, heart and soul of an humble laborer in the saw mill. The forces of magnetic leadership, commanding executive ability, instantaneous initiative, far-sighted vision, keen perspective, racial pride, patient endeavor and indomitable will power, are but a few of the characteristics of this matchless leader—Indeed, a Master Builder!

"They called him the black Lincoln," MaVynee once told me. "And it's true he was an economic liberator." Even in the light of a more sober retrospect, the Master Builder was suited to the role of majesty. "He was extremely formal," MaVynee's sister, Johnnetta Cole, told me one day in her office at Spelman College in Atlanta. "I can't ever in my childhood really recall Fafa just relaxed, laughing over something silly. I can't imagine my great-grandfather in some setting of men drinking beer and laughing, can't imagine it. I can't even recall him in clothes other than vested suits. If I force myself, I can remember him at American Beach, in which case he would take off the jacket and put on a sweater. I think I can even remember the tie staying on. He was very formal."

I said, "The image I get of him is that he presided over the Beach."

"The recollection I have is that A. L. Lewis was presiding over wherever he was," she answered. "I'm really pulling this stuff up from early childhood. But A. L. Lewis was not a man who would walk away and leave you without an impression. Don't forget, Fafa dies when I am twelve. But I don't think I've ever encountered anyone like him since."

The man described to me by both great-granddaughters was hard on himself and others, demanding of subordinates, intolerant of sloppiness, scrupulous with money, devoted to his church, with an implacable sense of justice that made him a fair executive and a firm race advocate. "There was always a streak of controlled emotion when my great-grandfather talked about the white folks," Cole went on. "He would be quite controlled, and yet his outrage at the injustice would be clear. This is not a man who could scream. This is not a man who would pound on the desk. He would never lash out and curse. I think that A. L. Lewis never cursed. I mean, the idea would be repulsive to him. Outraged, yes. Particularly if it had to do with black folks not being treated properly."

Lewis's low beginnings were not unique among the leaders of black financial empires (or of white ones, for that matter: their rags-to-riches roster includes the likes of Leland Stanford, John D. Rockefeller, Jay Gould, Collis P. Huntington, and Marshall Field, and also—famously— Andrew Carnegie, who wrote approvingly of the humble births and absent educations of the era's captains of industry and finance). The Afro's sister company, Atlanta Life Insurance, founded in 1905, was led by a former barber, and North Carolina Mutual was founded (in 1898) by another barber, John Merrick, who had been born a slave. I asked Cole how it was that such men prevailed. "I wish I knew the secret— why a man who had so little could dream in such big terms," she said. "If we could find the answer, we could figure out how to socially reproduce men like that. Where do these people come from? I heard the story of the founding of that insurance company a million times. And it's always the same story, because Fafa would downplay any individual's role, and he would over and over again tell the story, and this is what sticks in my mind—that something had to be done. Because every Sunday the deacon would come around with the plate, because Brother Jacob needed this or Sister Mary didn't have any food. And he'd tell the story over and over again: *We had to do something*."

The need to "do something" is evident to anyone reading the local turn-of-the-century census figures. Black wages were dismal and living conditions were worse. Black neighborhoods—the "unhealthy surroundings" discussed in the Bethel prayer room—had little paving or plumbing, and the many unscreened outhouses fostered the spread of typhus. The difficulty of black life was most vividly displayed in the local mortality rates: black mortality in 1900 was 50 percent higher than that of whites, and infant mortality was double. The historian James Crook notes that in the early years of the century, more blacks died in Jacksonville than were born there. The high rate of black disease and death was not peculiar to Jacksonville, of course—it was a scandal nationwide, and the statistics were not lost on the major life insurance companies. Unfortunately, as with other such misfortune, the scandal was itself turned against blacks, compounding the difficulty of their lot. Major insurers, notably the Prudential Insurance Company, began offering reduced benefits to blacks—a third less than those they offered for a similar price to whites.

The deep reasoning behind this formula was laid out in 1896 in a book called *Race Traits and Tendencies of the American Negro*. *Race Traits* was written by a Prudential statistician named Ludwig Hoffman, whose central contention—that "we find in race and heredity the determining factor in the upward or downward course of mankind"— could serve comfortably as the thesis of latter-day books of similar leaning, such as Arthur R. Jensen's *Genetics and Education* and Charles Murray and Richard J. Herrnstein's *The Bell Curve*. *Race Traits* was the *Bell Curve* of its day, a poisonous apple of racial determinism polished on the sleeve of science. The respectability of *Race Traits* was arguably greater: it was sponsored by the estimable American Economic Association. Like *The Bell Curve*, it was taken seriously at the time of its publication. Its author was accorded a sober legitimacy, especially by himself. "Being of foreign birth, a German, I was fortunately free from a personal bias which might have made an impartial treatment of the subject difficult," he wrote, and congratulated himself on "making exclusive use of the statistical method and giving in every instance a concise tabular statement of the facts." But behind his charts and graphs and harumphing objectivity lay a polemical venom.

Hoffman held that slavery had been salutary for the black man, who had been "healthy in body and cheerful in mind" while snug in its grip but had since been burdened by a "misdirected education and an extravagance of charity" so clearly corrupting as to form "a most severe condemnation of modern attempts of superior races to lift inferior races to their own elevated position." "Generally speaking, it detracts from a negro's efficiency to educate him," Hoffman wrote, and noted that the African's physical constitution, naturally frailer than that of the "Aryan," was weakened further by miscegenation (for "neither good white men nor good white women marry colored persons . . . and good colored men and women do not marry white persons") and by an inherent inability to abide by moral strictures. Hoffman's evidence for this last point took a novel tack: the black man's penchant for evil acts is quantifiable by the violence required to curb it. "The fact is fairly proven that lynchings in the South are not the result of race antipathy," he wrote. "The rate of increase in lynchings may be accepted as representing fairly the increasing tendency of colored men to commit" rape. Thus even lynching was enshrined as evidence of the white man's relative gentility and elevated humanity. Hoffman let loose another barrage of actuarial tables to buttress this "proven" point.

His larger conclusion, and the one to have the most direct effect on American society, was that black people, lacking both the physical vitality and the moral fiber to prosper, and with a "race tendency to premature death," were faltering in their effort to keep up with "higher races." "The most threatening danger, numerical supremacy [of blacks], may be considered as having passed away, if indeed it ever existed," Hoffman wrote with evident relief, and predicted that black people would eventually become extinct in the New World: "Their fate is not difficult to read." Following the publication of *Race Traits and Tendencies of the American Negro*, the Prudential and other companies stopped writing life insurance policies for blacks altogether. Shortly afterward, the Afro was established.

Other black businesses were starting up, too. The appetite of the emancipated slave for success, ironically, found nourishment in a climate of increasing discrimination. Although opportunity was predicated on adversity, the shape and the nature of black enterprise were founded on something deeper. "The existence today of a Negro economy is the result of a long process of evolution caused by . . . pressure from the outside, and . . . a nationalism within the Negro group," the sociologist James B. Browning wrote in 1937, "but perhaps farthest removed in point of time was the cultural heritage which was filled with the cooperative spirit, [and which] was not crushed in the days before the Civil War but emerged in the form of a Negro economy."

That African cultural heritage was especially strong for insurance companies, which had direct antecedents in the *gbe* and *so* mutual-aid societies of the West African Dahomeans and the *esusu* of the Yoruba. The Afro was, in effect, husbanding an African cultural survival. In leading a response to the privations of the American South, A. L. Lewis was (as MaVynee would have it) looking for guidance across the ocean, back to where he came from.

The Afro's provenance was evident in its initial purpose, to provide for proper burials. Ludwig Hoffman had pontificated on the subject of the Negro "indifference to a burial in the 'potter's field.'" "Whoever has witnessed the pauper funeral of a negro, the bare pine box and the common cart, the absence of all that makes less sorrowful the last rites over the dead," he wrote, "has seen a phase of negro life and manners more disheartening perhaps than anything else in the whole range of human misery." His assumption that the "common cart" was voluntary was not untypically wrongheaded, and over ensuing decades he would be contradicted by such eminent anthropologists as H. W. Odum, who noted in his 1910 book, *Social and Mental Traits of the Negro*, that "it is a consolation to the Negro to know that he will be buried with proper ceremonies and his grave properly marked," and Hortense Powdermaker, founder of Queens College's Department of Anthropology and Sociology, who observed during her residency in Depression-era Mississippi (in a county seat served by the Afro-American Life Insurance Company) that in black homes the insurance receipt book was often kept tacked prominently to the wall. "Burial insurance is usually the first to be taken out and the last to be relinquished when times grow hard," she wrote in *After Freedom*.

Such concern had little to do with the civilizing influence of European culture. "Whatever else has been lost of aboriginal custom," the anthropologist Melville Herskovits wrote, forty years after Hoffman, "the attitudes toward the dead as manifested in meticulous rituals cast in the mold of West African patterns have survived." He observed that "the funeral is the true climax of life" in Africa, where "the dead are honored with extended and costly rituals."

That connection electrified Johnnetta Cole. "I wish I could say that A. L. Lewis told me, 'You know, we brought this idea from Africa,'" she said to me. "It would make a wonderful story. But I don't remember any reference like that. But he was a race man, who really believed in the race. And anyone in 1901 that would name a benefit society 'Afro-American' clearly had some consciousness that was not ordinary for that period of time. When I was eight or ten years old, I'd never heard of anthropology, and I wasn't smart enough to ask him, 'Why did you name this thing Afro-American?' I never asked."

It wasn't too long, however, before anthropology heard from Johnnetta Cole. In the 1950s, after a stint at Fisk University, she followed her older sister to Oberlin, where MaVynee studied music and Johnnetta studied mankind. She pursued her master's degree and Ph.D. at Northwestern, where Melville Herskovits had founded the nation's first African Studies program. Herskovits became her faculty adviser, while A. L. Lewis still served as her unofficial mentor. "I can tell you right now that one of the most unbelievable moments in my life was when I was studying to be an anthropologist," Cole told me, "and I was reading Powdermaker's book *After Freedom*, and she talks about black insurance companies—and the Afro-American, especially—and there it was, an explanation of how this man in my family was the carrier of African culture."

In 1960, in pursuit of her Ph.D., Johnnetta went to Liberia to research a dissertation about the effects on African men and on the societies of African villages when those men left home to become wage-earners in the Western-style economies sweeping the continent. She returned to become a prominent academician and consummate professional, as comfortable in corporate boardrooms soliciting tens of millions of dollars for educational endeavors as she is on campus putting those funds to work. "When you talk with her," MaVynee had instructed me on the eve of my interview, "remember, she's going to be far more sophisticated, cool, and methodical, compared to me. And I'm the older. But she has a whole different personality. Johnnetta and I are in different worlds. She's into humans, and for me, humans are—" She gave a thumbs-down and mouthed a raspberry. "I'm with the animals. Our connection is feminism. It's just like in music—Miles Davis will take a theme and he won't play the same thing as Coltrane. You don't sing *La Bohème* the way you sing *Traviata*."

But in fact I'd already met Johnnetta Cole, by chance, when I overheard a conversation behind me in a crowded hotel lobby in mid-Manhattan, and recognized the unmistakable timbre, accent, and lilting rhythm of my Florida friend's speech. But the speaker wasn't MaVynee. "Excuse me," I said to the tall woman in conservative suit and pearls and the closely cropped graying curls and the eyes, at once lambent and piercing, that were as immediately familiar as her voice. "You must be Dr. Cole." And I was right.

Our first interview took place a year and a half later, in 1994, at Spelman, where she was then president. Cole's office and her on-campus residence, Reynolds Cottage, were adorned with artifacts from her African journeys. Tucked amid them were artifacts of an earlier fascination. The crystal chandelier in the dining room of Reynolds Cottage was from the dining room of A. L. Lewis's house in Jacksonville, a house he built and moved into after departing Florida Street. The house was on Eighth and Jefferson, in Sugar Hill, the city's wealthiest black district. The desk in Johnnetta Cole's foyer was from his study. Her Havilland china belonged to his second wife, Mama Zone, and sat in his first wife's china cabinet. In the mid-1940s, when A. L. Lewis moved with Mama Zone into another Sugar Hill residence, he gave the house at Eighth and Jefferson to his granddaughter Mary, and that is where the Betsch children finished their growing up.

The walls of Reynolds Cottage and of Cole's presidential office were lined with family portraits from those times: A. L. Lewis stepping out of the portico of a grand hotel in Zurich in 1937, carrying a cane and wearing a soft tweed cap; A. L. Lewis with Mama Zone in Egypt, each in a fez and riding a camel in front of the great pyramids at Giza; A. L. Lewis in the Afro offices in 1945, being feted by employees on the occasion of his penultimate birthday. There was also a photograph of a Craftsman-style mansion, three stories of brick and shingle, with verandas and porches and copious windows, surrounded by a wrought-iron fence and topiary trees. "This is A. L. Lewis's house," Cole said. "This is the house at Eighth and Jefferson in Jacksonville where MaVynee and I lived, that is now a damn piece of parking lot for some medical center. And believe me, that hurts."

The keepsakes in Cole's office and in Reynolds Cottage were relics of that grand home—tangible evidence of what had been, and what had been annihilated. Cole's collection made a curious whole—the fastidiously Victorian china cabinet and the carvings from Liberia—but an organic one. The culture Cole had visited in Africa, which decreed the importance of the funeral to American blacks and informed the creation of the Afro-American Life Insurance Company, was a culture of, more than anything, kinship and memory. The photos and keepsakes were Cole's observance in her own life of the custom she had observed in the land of her distant heritage. In that home country, at the pinnacle of that culture of memory, and explaining even the reverence for the grave, was the absolute importance of the ancestor, a fixation so strong that Herskovits referred to it as a cult. "The elaborateness of funeral rites [in West Africa] is cast in terms of the role of the ancestors in the lives of their descendants," he wrote. "The relationship between the ancestors and the gods is close. . . . The power of a man does not end with death."

"Look at this one," Johnnetta Cole urged me as she led me through the gallery on her office wall. The photograph she pointed to was a family portrait taken on the front steps of the Lewis house in the 1940s, a few years before the patriarch's death. It's Easter morning, and the portrait is formal: the men wear suits and ties and their jackets are buttoned. The cast of A. L. Lewis's descendants is all there: among them James H. Lewis, the son; Mary Lewis Betsch and J. Leonard Lewis, the grandchildren; and John T. Betsch, the grandson-in-law. Before them all, in high collar and vested pinstripe, one hand folded behind his back, is A. L. Lewis himself, dark-faced, bald-headed, wearing a short gray brush of mustache over the only smile I had ever seen him display to any camera. Though it is still a wry, straight line of a smile that hardly dimples his cheek, it telegraphs an unreserved contentment and delight. His great-grandchildren stand in a chaotic little medley at his knee: among them two little girls in satin dresses and white, puff-sleeved blouses, their hair pulled back in tight braids, one gazing at the photographer with chin-down suspicion, the other, smaller, not facing the camera at all. "That's MaVynee, looking out as straight as she can," Johnnetta Cole told me, pointing to the taller of the two girls. "And that one's me: the adoring one. I just cannot keep my eyes off of my big sister."

In the autumn of 1993, several months before this conversation took place, Johnnetta Cole, concerned about MaVynee's alfresco lifestyle, had bought her a home at American Beach. That is, she bought her a motor home. MaVynee's friend Carol Alexander picked it out, and I drove MaVynee into Jacksonville to pick it up. It was parked among a hundred other recreational vehicles in a vast ugly lot on one of Jacksonville's bleaker commercial boulevards. The sales office was lousy with bad toupees and double-knit suits and gaunt men glowing with subcutaneous nicotine and provisioned by vending machines displaying such a cornucopia of cheese snacks as to suggest a dietary cause and effect between the ingestion of artificial flavors and raiment in synthetic fibers. The intended motor home was a used one, its once-Simonized earth tones faded to grunge. It had been done up at the factory in American kitsch: Indian motifs were ubiquitous in the foam-cushioned interior, and a chromed eagle was mounted on the grille. The model was called the Titan, and I supposed that its decoration was meant to suggest to the more usual customer—say, a geriatric gypsy ready to make the rounds of national parks and battlefields—a sort of gather-no-moss, Chautauqua independence. But as I watched MaVynee stoop down the short center hallway between canyon walls of peeling woodgrain pressboard, beneath a sky upholstered in polyester shag, and plunk her kente-clad figure into the booth in the back of the rolling kitchenette, the enterprise seemed more End of the Road than On the Road. She looked suddenly tired and old and defeated and sad, cringing there in the gaudy geode of plastic and Formica, trapped at last by a middle-brow conformity that even the talisman of her eccentricity was not strong enough to ward off.

I needn't have worried. Occasionally, over the years, American Beach homeowners have let MaVynee house-sit their properties, and I had seen what transpired, for MaVynee Betsch and Martha Stewart are evenly matched across the decorating divide. Her inimitable touch would transform the Titan. I left town for a while after the motor home's delivery, and when I returned, I found it parked in a vacant lot across Gregg Street from A. L. Lewis's beach house. The grass was already growing around its tires. MaVynee had surrounded it with seashells and driftwood and dime-store pinwheels and Spelman College pennants. Inside, her flair for organization was apparent. For years, her belongings, such as they were, had been stored in the unlocked, dirt-floored basement of another house on Gregg Street, where she would also take refuge in inclement weather (though the weather could be worse inside than out, owing to the basement's proclivity to flood). Now the collection was on sunnier display. MaVynee had plastered her unrivaled selection of bumper stickers across every available surface. The fold-down bed over the driver's seat had been permanently lowered, the mattress discarded, and the resulting deep shelf filled with manila folders holding all the information MaVynee had ever been able to collect on the Afro, on ecology, on race relations, on feminism, and on Jacksonville history. She had engraved the subject categories into the bulkhead with a ballpoint pen. Other issues had their special archival crannies. Open the oven and you would be treated to an exposition on health foods: not the foods themselves, articles about them. The freezer was an airtight repository of sea turtle and marine mammal lore, and the shower stall was indexed from *Ashanti* to *Zulu*. Books were stacked everywhere: on counters, on racks. The dinette had become a study space as grave in its intent as any carrel in the back stacks of Widener Library. She called it the Seminole Room. "Isn't it wonderful, baby?" MaVynee whooped. "American Beach has *needed* a museum!" Her joie de vivre had returned in force. She left the door of the Titan unlocked, so that any visitors could avail themselves of study privileges, and departed for her chaise longue, still parked on A.L.'s porch.

"God, I tell you. I don't have any mementos from my great-grandfather," MaVynee said, still thinking archivally as she surveyed the vast empty view. Way off over the beach, a crew of white fishermen worked to free their car, which had gotten stuck in the sand. It was low tide, and their intricate labors in the midst of the great expanse were the picture of busy futility.

"That's why I'm so close to American Beach," she continued. "It's like he's still here. That's what protects me. I'm *serious!* You know I've never been robbed, even sleeping in the outdoors?"

I was sure she was also protected by novelty; there were some who were convinced that the Beach Lady was a witch, among them no doubt the would-be muggers who had approached her chaise longue one midnight on the beach. She let them get up close before she sprang to her feet and routed them with a few bars of Wagner, her mosquito netting drifting about her like the corrupted rags of Alberich. Her heritage, a ring of fire limned by a patriarch, has afforded her another sort of protection—even as a child, she could trespass without fear, because people knew who her family was—and occasional sustenance, too. One day in Jacksonville, an elderly woman walked up to her and pressed a $100 bill into her hand. "Aren't you the daughter of John Betsch?" she asked. "He helped me get a divorce." I'd seen the same gratitude expressed less extravagantly by others. "And I wouldn't know them from Adam's house cat," MaVynee said. "But that's why I don't ever worry about anything. Because my great-grandfather said, 'Look,' he said. 'It will come back to you.' And it's true! How many times did my daddy get up in the middle of the night to get someone out of jail?" MaVynee's daddy, John T. Betsch, was in comportment a much looser man than A. L. Lewis. "Looser" is Johnnetta Cole's description. "Let's just say A. L. Lewis would not have worn spectator shoes or a Panama hat," Cole explained. Or run a pool hall, which is one of the things John Betsch did on the side while he was an executive with the Afro. But Betsch shared with A. L. Lewis a proclivity for community service and the conviction that money was a secondary form of wealth.

"My great-grandfather always told us: money is like manure," MaVynee would say, in explaining her vow of poverty. "Too little, the plant won't grow. Too much, you kill it." Clearly she calibrated the demarcation between sufficiency and excess differently than would, say, almost anyone else. "My favorite black person to admire was George Washington Carver," she told me once. "The whole time at Tuskegee, he never made more than $1,200. He lived in a dorm. I think of Mozart, who died a pauper—of Schubert. Deep down in my soul, they were my role models. Then George Washington Carver set it all in concrete."

On another occasion she said, "The desert is my favorite ecosystem, because it's what I am. In the desert, nature takes the least—*the least*—and makes the most out of it. It's another thing I like about being a singer: it takes nothing except breath, and not much of that. Do you know you can produce as much power pianissimo as forte? I never shall forget it, when I saw Zinka Milanov sing Aïda in Cleveland. When she hit that ending with the high A, you could have heard a pin drop, and she held it for a minute and a half, pianissimo, and—oh, chile!—every hair on you stood up."

The lesson is reiterated everywhere. On the beach, the effort to get the car unstuck was failing. The more the men labored, the deeper it was mired. "You see," MaVynee observed, "sometimes you can be soft and powerful at the same time." She was rooting for the beach, and the odds were looking good; the turning tide was bringing up reinforcements. After a while she said, "The white man is going the way of Fat Sam."

On Sundays, the Betsch children would go to church. Mount Olive AME was (and remains) a religious and social pillar of eastside Jacksonville, and serving as its pastor during the Lewis era must have been a brilliant tribulation. "I do remember needing to figure out who was really in charge in the church," Johnnetta Cole told me. "Interesting memory. Because there was the minister, but there was also A. L. Lewis. And where A. L. Lewis sat was always important, and when he stood up to report as a deacon or as superintendent of the Sunday school—I mean, that was a high moment in the service!"

Mary Betsch was in no less a position of power. "Mama was organist," MaVynee recalled. "That's why I loved her. You know how people get long-winded? Well, the organ has this power knob on the left that you push with the foot, and I could see it, because we always sat on that side of the church. When the preacher would get rolling, she would lean into that organ and drown him out. Mother had gorgeous hips, boy—and she'd swing that hip over and hit that knob, and I'd say, 'Go, Mama! Get him!'"

Afterward, the children went with their great-grandfather to the cemetery, where A. L. Lewis would sit a while on a concrete bench in front of the marble mausoleum that held his first wife's remains, and then they would go on to the mansion at Eighth and Jefferson for dinner. The meals were sumptuous, in the Southern Sunday, collards-and-springpan-corn-bread style. A. L. Lewis—a particular eater who folded his napkin into his collar and went without drink of any sort at the table—insisted that all fried foods be prepared in expensive olive oil instead of common lard. The corn bread, too. "I remember that corn bread. Oh, God!" MaVynee exclaimed. "Mama Zone was some good cook!" But these occasions weren't the most fun a kid could think of having. "We weren't allowed to play things that were in any way in violation of the sacredness of the day, which meant we could play school or we could play Sunday school," Johnnetta Cole remembers. Nevertheless she calls the meals a "privilege," because they were a child's chance to absorb an old man's lessons.

"I have a memory—and I don't know what year it was, but I have a memory—of sitting with MaVynee when we were little and playing with pennies," Cole told me. "And I remember Fafa standing over us, and just going over and over again about denominations and the relationship between pennies and nickels and the importance of saving. He really believed that, and he had a life to prove it."

The Betsch girls absorbed another lesson from their Sunday visits: A. L. Lewis might be prosperous, but he wasn't free. Sugar Hill was separated from the white neighborhood of Springfield by the green expanse of whites-only Hogan Creek Park, and the Lewis home offered a privileged prospect of prejudice. Johnnetta Cole remembers standing on a balcony of the house and looking down into the white pool and tennis courts she was not allowed to visit. Despite their exclusion, the Lewises were not isolated in their prosperity. Blacks in Jacksonville, as unwelcomed by white business as the Betsch girls were in the local pool, had built a city within a city in the decades after the fire. By 1925, the number of black-run businesses had increased fivefold, to around six hundred. Even after the worst of the Depression, most of those survived. There were black drugstores, taxidermists, a hospital, a college (Edward Waters, among four private black colleges in the immediate area), nursing homes, three newspapers (in addition to the Negro supplement printed by the *Florida Times-Union*), three department stores, a taxicab company with a hundred cabs, and a country club. And of course, the Afro-American Life Insurance Company, which, being the largest black financial institution in town, lent the money that made many of the other businesses possible.

The central artery was Ashley Street. Because of its early status as the only paved thoroughfare in black Jacksonville, Ashley lent the name The Bricks to the surrounding commercial precinct. At its height, through the 1940s and 1950s, Ashley Street was a dense urban corridor, with its buildings sporting contiguous iron balconies over sidewalks alive with commerce in every conceivable commodity, from quick sin to high salvation. Along Ashley and its side streets were large theaters—the Strand, the Ritz, the New Frolic, and later the Roosevelt. There were ballrooms, like the Linape, the KP Room, Manuel's Tap Room (serving twenty-four hours a day), and the Tropicana, and the massive Masonic Hall, whose construction A. L. Lewis funded when he was the Masonic treasurer. "I mean, Ashley Street was *it!*" one longtime resident told me. "People used to dress up on Sunday and go strolling on Ashley, just like in New York you used to stroll on 125th Street."

Or on Auburn Avenue in Atlanta, or Central Avenue in Los Angeles, or any number of thriving black boulevards in cities around the nation. The economy of those streets was small compared with the surrounding white economy, but it was at least complete. "We didn't have to ask the white man for nothin'!" MaVynee remembers. "*Nothing!* Now you go to the hotel, but don't own it. You go to a restaurant; you don't own it. No. The white man owns it, and you're going to his place, and you give the white man your money. Back then, you could go from sunup to sundown and never bother with white people. That's how self-contained it was."

Being self-contained, this world was invisible to whites. Especially invisible was the "high society" world of black cotillions and supper clubs and literary societies and theater groups—of anything that smacked of black education and achievement. In James Weldon Johnson's novel, *Autobiography of an Ex-Coloured Man*, published anonymously in 1912 when Johnson was the United States consul in Corinto, Nicaragua, a post he'd assumed during Teddy Roosevelt's administration, the protagonist passes through Jacksonville, and his critique of the black social structure is anything but fictitious. "I shall give the observations I made in Jacksonville as seen through the light of after years; and they apply generally to every Southern community," Johnson wrote. He divided blacks into three classes, "not so much in respect to themselves as in respect to their relations with the whites." The lowest of the three was what he called "the desperate class" of criminals and ne'er-do-wells and sub-subsistence laborers, which class, while only a "small portion of the black people . . . often dominates public opinion concerning the whole race." The prominence of these impoverished was proportionate to the fear they engendered. Johnson wrote, "This class of blacks hated everything covered with a white skin, and in return they are loathed by the whites," who regarded them "as a man would a vicious mule, a thing to be worked, driven, and beaten, and killed for kicking."

The second class was the one most visible to whites—Johnson called it "the connecting link between whites and blacks"—the class of servants and domestics, whose natural goodness, however good that might be, was supplemented by the etiquette of contractual sub-servience. These were the "good Negroes," held up as examples of what the race was capable of and might be suffered to aspire to. (The example is an unthreatening one of dependent mediocrity, and there-fore debased as a model of aspiration; the white Southerner who eulo-gizes his "Mammy" or his kind housekeeper is transacting in that cur-rency.)

The third class, "as far removed from whites as the members of the first class," comprised the independent tradesmen and well-to-do and educated blacks. Here Johnson deserves to be quoted at length, because his description is as a shard of cuneiform, a rare glimpse of a lost civilization:

> These people live in a world of their own. I concluded that if a coloured man wanted to separate himself from his white neighbours, he had but to acquire some money, education, and culture, and to live in accordance.
>
> This latter class of coloured people are well-disposed towards the whites, and always willing to meet them more than half-way. They, however, feel keenly any injustice or gross discrimination, and generally show their resentment. . . .
>
> The[ir] position . . . is often very trying. They are the ones among the blacks who carry the entire weight of the race question; it worries the others very little, and I believe the only thing which at times sustains them is that they know that they are in the right.

Johnson considered the invisibility of these people a problem as important as the mistreatment of the "desperate class": "There is to my mind no more pathetic side of this many-sided [race] question than the isolated position into which are forced the very coloured people who most need and who could best appreciate sympathetic co-operation; and their condition grows tragic when the effort is made to couple them, whether or no, with the Negroes of the first class I mentioned."

The coupling, however arbitrary, had its great advantage: the black community, denied integration with the surrounding world, remained integrated within itself. Surely, there were resentments and distinctions between the poorer members and the wealthy blacks they derided as "sadiddy." But the very strength of those distinctions arose from the forced proximity of all black citizens. Sugar Hill bordered Blodgett Homes, a housing project, and Black Bottom, largely a slum, and Black Bottom bordered The Bricks, and the borders in every case were porous. MaVynee, who couldn't swim in Hogan Creek Park, took her piano lessons from a teacher in the projects and played her recitals there. The plight of the least was known to the highest, in concrete and personal terms.

This made for a further integration central to the role of the black businessman—an integration between the onus of success and the onus of serving a community. It was a personal integration and, insofar as it was also religious, it had a provenance: Melville Herskovits has noted that one characteristic distinguishing African from American society was the degree to which religion in Africa was "an intimate part of . . . life," indistinguishable from "the considerations of everyday living," and not a thing in itself with a designated day and place, separate from one's ordinary commerce. The separation of morality and commerce is not only ingrained in American life; it is celebrated. In the century between the Gilded Age and Reaganomics, the separation became something of a doctrine, like the separation of church and state: the only sacred and central duty of the businessman, the doctrine went, was to turn a profit and make money for his stockholders. In Johnnetta Cole's estimation, this perspective had historical roots in antebellum slavery. But even today, long severed from those roots, the perspective still bears its same strange flower.

"There's no question in my mind about the ability of early Americans of means to dichotomize their lives," Cole told me. "You own these slaves, but you're a Christian. So you go to church and give generously. That was the solution. Not to abolish slavery. Go to church, and give generously. That ability to dichotomize, I think, is very deep in that period of American history."

Virtue had made a few spectacular raids against Jacksonville capitalism over the years, but they were all of the most Pecksniffian sort. Carry Nation came through in 1907 to inveigh in white and black churches against the saloon and the whorehouse, and eventually won: Jacksonville opted for temperance even before national prohibition forced the issue. Later, the fight against iniquity was carried to the movie industry, which had set up shop in a network of Jacksonville studios. For a few short years, it seemed that Jacksonville might become an eastern Hollywood—many of the Buster Keaton and Laurel and Hardy films were made there—until the accompanying car chases through the Jacksonville streets, and the fast living among the film colony, and their habit of shooting location scenes on Sunday, when all good people were in church, incurred the good people's ire. The industry became the burning issue of the 1917 mayoral race, after which the industry was invited out of town. Both outbursts of commercial moralism, ironically, blew up in the face of blacks. Temperance (like women's suffrage in turn) was sold on the basis of its racist appeal: to wit, it would keep good white men from fraternizing with loose black women in the sections of town where saloons and brothels thrived. For their part, the movie studios in Jacksonville included a few run by blacks, producing such features as *The Green-Eyed Monster*, whose posters advertised "an all-colored cast." When the industry moved out west, the black studios closed down, and nothing significant grew up in Hollywood to replace their lost point of view.

The partition between business and its obligation to society—what Cole calls the "dichotomizing"—remained a perennial issue within the Jacksonville business community in the years after the great fire. The single-minded self-interest of the businessman was relieved by philanthropy. But white business philanthropy was crucially different from that practiced by blacks. For one thing, prominent white families divided their responsibilities by gender: the man handled the shop, mill, or bank, and the wife—whose servants did the housework, thus rendering her idle—handled the philanthropy, often with her husband's money and in his company's name. This division is implied in James Crook's description, in *Jacksonville After the Fire*, of the aim of Jacksonville's activist women to "awaken this New South city to concerns beyond economic growth and development." In the black community, things were different: nearly all the women worked, and those men and women who chose to engage in philanthropy did so as part of the job.

The paragon of the type was Eartha Mary Magdalene White. White had, it would seem, several careers before assuming her clerkship at the Afro-American, and would have several more afterward, but her name would be associated—even in White House ceremonies honoring her achievements—with charity. When she died in 1974, at ninety-seven, after breaking a hip at her workplace, she was known around Jacksonville as "the Angel of Mercy." White was raised in Jacksonville by her adopted mother, Clara, who had been a slave on Amelia Island until Emancipation, who had seen her own parents sold away on the auction block, who had seen nine of her natural children die and the remaining one disappear, and who brought her adopted daughter up into the obligation of service, with a parental exhortation to "do all the good you can in all the ways you can for all the people you can while you can." Eartha's own self-exhortations included one she scrawled with a pencil in her diary: Stanford White's definition of a skyscraper, which Eartha White applied to the stature of a person's character: "It must be tall, every inch of it tall."

She graduated from the National Conservatory of Music in New York, and remained there in her twenties as a professional singer before returning home to become a schoolteacher, Florida's first black registered real estate agent, a charter member and the official historian of Booker T. Washington's National Business League, organizer in her own right of the Jacksonville Business League, the only black member of Woodrow Wilson's Council on National Defense (which met at the White House), an enumerator for the Census Bureau, a county social worker with a desk in the county courthouse, and creator, owner, and proprietor of a department store, a taxicab company, an employment agency, a home-cleaning service, and a steam cleaner called the Service Laundry, whose slogan was "Put your duds in our suds; we wash everything but a dirty conscience."

Eventually, White was rumored to have become a millionaire, but she still dressed for the office in secondhand clothes and sneakers. Her business acumen was entirely at the service of her philanthropy. She used her civic influence, club associations, and profits to found and run the Old Folks Boarding Home for indigents, the Mercy charity hospital, an orphanage, a "boy's improvement" club, a treatment center for alcoholics, a home for unwed mothers, soup kitchens, relief programs, and a park for blacks (really for anyone, but mostly blacks came) staffed by a private recreation department whose salaries she paid from her own pocketbook. She also ran the Clara White Mission, a relief mission that had been founded by and named after her mother, which grew in size and status until eventually it moved into its own multi-story building on Ashley Street, where Eartha White ate with the transients. At the end of long days, when she was too tired to make it home on foot, she slept in her office on a cot. The mission abided by the slogan of the black Community Chest, which Eartha White chaired: "It's Everybody's Job."

It was certainly the job of every black businessman; there was no way, if you were black, to escape a particular sort of moral obligation. It was fine for the white businessman to make his money and go home happy; if he didn't make money or made it nefariously or spent it only on himself, his failure damaged no reputation but his own. It especially did not reflect on his race, to which he had no conspicuous obligation. The black businessman labored under a heavier burden, and enjoyed an enhanced opportunity. His every success or failure was a racial omen. He was judged by white and black observers alike as a race representative, and as his success increased, so did the moral stature he had to consider and maintain. He was a performer, watched with the same nervous tension with which James Weldon Johnson watched his brother Rosamond perform on a London stage in 1905, with a surfeit of "pain and pleasure . . . more keenly felt by Negroes than by any other people. For them the central persons are not individuals, they become protagonists of the whole racial cause."

The moral onus was inescapable. When the NAACP magazine *The Crisis*—in its January 1942 issue, devoted to a profile of Jacksonville—critiqued the city's black businesses, it highlighted the remarks of dentist William L. Redmond to the Negro Business League, warning of "the danger to Negroes when members of the race, for purely selfish purposes, entered into certain types of business which are designed to drain the Negroes' purses but are destined never to lift the race one iota, either economically or morally." The distinction he drew between the sporting and gambling enterprises and those of more sober and industrial concerns such as the Afro represented one of the clearest internal divisions in the community.

Moral imperatives not only constrained black business—they also elevated it, from the drab status of enterprise to the grander one of mission. "The Pride of a Race demands that it be willing to be self-sustaining," an early brochure for the Community Chest proclaimed. Every business effort that contributed to that self-sustenance was judged in community terms and was self-consciously a black business. The result was the second crucial difference between black and white philanthropy: among blacks, there was no such thing as philanthropy, really—no way to separate commerce from service and to call the service philanthropy. Work and race responsibility were organically connected. As Eartha White wrote to a friend, "Service is the price you pay for the space you occupy."

The higher the barriers between the surrounding white world and the black community, the greater the internal integration of the latter. Added to the geographic proximity of poor and wealthy, the commensurate roles of women and men in community service, and the intermixture of work and service was a unity within the individual personality. "When I think about my great-grandfather, probably one of the things that I would come to say is that this man seemed to have very few discontinuities," Johnnetta Cole told me. "His life really was fairly smooth. You didn't have the feeling that A. L. Lewis was now at the Afro and a businessman but he's not thinking about Mount Olive AME Church. Or that A. L. Lewis is now at Mount Olive but he really isn't thinking about the YMCA. His life, it seemed to me, was very, very integrated."

In 1919, A. L. Lewis assumed the presidency of the Afro-American Life Insurance Company. In short order, he instituted some progressive changes, organizing a Pension Bureau that would secure an employee's retirement for a small weekly contribution, and formalizing the weekly inspirational meetings, held in the auditorium every Saturday noon. The meetings were compulsory—the offices closed early to accommodate them—and A. L. Lewis attended and usually spoke, giving sermons on Christian responsibility. He adopted as the "President's Message" a verse from Micah. It would appear forthwith on Afro publications and employee guidebooks and be framed in calligraphy and hung on the wall over Lewis's desk. After his death, when his granddaughter Mary helped oversee the construction of the new Afro headquarters on Union Street, she had the message chiseled below the roster of company founders into a large slab of polished green granite and set into a wall of the lobby. Bible verses make easy advertising for companies in the Bible Belt; they reflect an exculpating piety and cast the aim of the business in terms consoling to the customer and flattering to the character of the concessionaire. Lewis's own friends, watching his statesmanlike demeanor on an overseas trip, decided that he exemplified the Proverb "Seeth thou a man diligent in business, he shall stand before kings." But A. L. Lewis chose a different creed for his message, one tangential to the purpose of promotion. It did not portray the organization but was directed at the individual, and lying between challenge and chastisement could not be made to comfort. It was a business slogan that ostentatiously excepted business from the essential concerns of the day. It read, "He hath shewed thee, O man, what is good; and what doth the Lord require of thee, but to do justly, and to love mercy, and to walk humbly with thy God?"

Even for a violent era, 1919, the year of Lewis's accession to the Afro presidency, was exceptional. The summer of that year would be known, whether in reference to the rage vented or the blood spilled, as Red Summer. White rampages erupted in twenty-five cities, including Knoxville, Omaha, Longview, Texas, and Chicago, where two blacks trespassing on a white beach sparked mob violence that killed twenty-three blacks and injured hundreds more. In Washington, D.C., blacks were chased on the street and pulled from streetcars and beaten, some of them to death, during a three-day spree that James Weldon Johnson, now living in Harlem and working with the nascent NAACP, called a "pogrom." In Jacksonville, two black men accused of killing a white insurance executive (employed, oddly, by a company that sold policies to blacks) were abducted from the jail and lynched north of the city. The body of one was tied to the bumper of a car and dragged back into town and dumped in the central square. Seventy-six other blacks were killed by lynch mobs nationwide; eleven were burned at the stake. In Phillips County, Arkansas, between two hundred and three hundred blacks, in Johnson's estimate, were hunted down and shot ("like animals," he said) in retaliation for a church meeting of black farmers to petition for higher cotton prices. Survivors were herded into a courtroom, where, after a forty-five-minute trial on charges of conspiring to seize white land and kill white landowners and five minutes of deliberation by a white jury, twelve black farmers were sentenced to death and sixty-seven others to life imprisonment. They were all later freed by the United States Supreme Court, where the NAACP defended them.

The Jamaican émigré Claude McKay wrote of the violence of Red Summer, "Like men we'll face the murderous, cowardly pack,/Pressed to the wall, dying, but fighting back." But fighting back was no simple thing for people indicted as murderous even while being murdered. Blacks were presented with the curious problem of defending themselves simultaneously against white barbarism and against the white assertion that blacks were inherently uncivilized. While no amount of violent reaction would suffice to protect blacks physically, the least amount disqualified them from white esteem. While no amount of refinement would suffice to make blacks socially or professionally acceptable, the least display of it could qualify them for violent sanction. In the years after the Great War, black veterans were singled out for terrorism and lynching by the Ku Klux Klan because, the Klan argued, they had already killed white men on the battlefield and consorted with white women in European cities and would have an appetite for killing and consorting again. Also, it was said, they had been shown respect and needed to be reminded of their place. Some were lynched in uniform.

The "invisible" class of well-to-do blacks was hardly invisible in this regard. A 1917 paper in the *Psychoanalytic Review* by a psychologist named J. E. Lind shows how A. L. Lewis may have been viewed by many of his white colleagues. "Because he wears a Palm Beach suit instead of a string of cowries, carries a gold-headed cane instead of a spear, uses the telephone instead of beating the drum from hill to hill and for the jungle path has substituted the pay-as-you-enter street car, his psychology is no less that of the African."

There were many such critiques of what Lind called the "savage heart beneath the civilized exterior," and they complicated horribly the lot of middle-class blacks. Once that denigration had been mouthed, it could not be escaped: their every aspiration could be mocked by whites and poorer blacks alike as emulation (of whites) or refutation (of white opprobrium). They were judged not by what they did, but by who they did it for—or, more precisely, whose world they did it in. In that context, acting in accordance with white mores amounted to nothing more than an aping of white manners: minstrelsy, a defensive sort of whiteface routine, robbed of integrity. Acting in conscious defiance of those mores was hardly more independent and amounted to much the same thing. This was the great Conundrum, the trap that tightened no matter which way you pulled. Even the black man who saw the bourgeois blacks as Uncle Toms was caught: he, too, was judging his brothers by how they were judged by whites.

The Conundrum left no way out but one: owning outright some corner of the culture. In cities large enough to have an independent black economy—where, in MaVynee's words, you "didn't have to ask the white man for nothin' "—middle-class blacks could pursue success and refinement in their own right, without the insinuation of subservience to someone else's standards. Pursued in their own right, and precisely because they were not meant as response, the Havilland china in A. L. Lewis's china cabinet and the mansion in which it resided—like any achievement, material or social or intellectual—represented an angry retort on the behalf of all his race to all the Linds of the world. It was the final ingredient in the internal integration of the community; the mixing of race responsibility with what could be called a Radical Respectability.

The formula was a touchy one: respectability, even slightly mishandled, presented a new set of limitations and restrictions instead of liberation. The Harlem Renaissance novelist Zora Neale Hurston, among others, diagnosed this problem. She had a brief but thorough introduction to Jacksonville's Sugar Hill society, when she married Albert Price III in Fernandina Beach in 1939. Price wasn't quite wealthy, but was well connected. His grandfather had been a co-founder of the Afro-American Life Insurance Company and A. L. Lewis's predecessor as Afro president; his grandmother still served on the company's board. When the marriage fell apart (after less than a year),

Price retained as his divorce lawyer J. Leonard Lewis, MaVynee's uncle. After that and other experiences with what she called a "fur-coat peerage," Hurston became convinced that wealthy blacks were bound no less than poor ones by the gossamer conventions of race. In her phrase, she "saw them pacing a cage that wasn't there."

Proving black sufficiency was a perilous task in the hothouse atmosphere of critical inspection. The dangers were on vivid display in late April 1930, when Bessie Coleman came to do an aerial show in Jacksonville. Aviation expositions had come to town before—in 1921 Lieutenant William DeVoe Cone set down in a Liberty-powered DeHavilland after flying from San Diego in 22 hours and 17 minutes, lopping three and a half hours off the transcontinental record. (He was feted in Jacksonville for a month, and was killed in a crash on the day he left, trying to best his own time East to West.) Still, the Coleman arrival was spectacular, for Bessie Coleman was black, the world's first black licensed pilot and the world's only black woman pilot, and her exhibition was touted as a victory for the race. She was sponsored by the Jacksonville Negro Welfare League, and her flight was preceded by days of celebrations, parades, athletic events (including a bicycle race by Western Union messengers), speeches, and church rallies in the black community. The morning before the event, she and another pilot, a white man from Texas named William D. Wills, went aloft in his plane to practice for one of her stunts, in which she would parachute from the plane's open cockpit. A loose wrench jammed in Wills's foot controls and the plane did a barrel roll at two thousand feet. Coleman, who was wearing neither a seat belt nor a parachute, fell from the cockpit and landed in a field. The plane straightened out, but not quickly enough to avoid a tree, which flipped it over, crushing Wills inside. On his body, rescuers found a telegram announcing the birth of a daughter he would never get to see and a book in whose flyleaf he had written, "Experience is what you get when you're looking for something else."

The *Florida Times-Union* of the next morning called the deaths of Coleman and Wills tragic, but was not too impressed to resist spending a half column on an accompanying article attesting to a silver lining: "Tragedy sometimes solves the commonplace worries of life. It so happened yesterday. . . ." Mrs. W. L. Meadows, arriving at the accident, which had occurred in her field, found her missing guinea hen's nest next to the offending tree, containing a dozen guinea eggs. They had not been broken in the crash. For the black community, packing Bethel Baptist Church for Coleman's memorial service, the disaster was unmitigated. Its lasting effects were apparent to me, more than sixty years later, when I mentioned Coleman's fateful flight to a black pilot and his wife, residents of American Beach, and received a stony silence of the sort that means one has trespassed in someone else's minefield.

Later I understood the reason, when I was looking through old articles in the Eartha White Collection of the University of North Florida. The articles about the accident had been clipped by White—that she had saved them until the end of her life was a testament to their significance—and they contained the unspoken part of the story. After the plane had crashed, as people were trying to pull Wills's body from the wreckage, a spectator, a member of the Negro Welfare League who had worked to bring Coleman to Jacksonville and had handled publicity for the event, nervously lit a cigarette, and his carelessness ignited gas fumes, causing the plane to burn and then explode with Wills still inside. The spectator was arrested and held several hours in the Jacksonville jail, crying inconsolably. His compounded humiliation and despair were chronicled by the newspapers, which identified him as "John T. Betsch, negro." He was MaVynee and Johnnetta Cole's father, and what must have been one of the worst days of his life—when his attempt to showcase for his city the achievement of a race pioneer had not only resulted in that pioneer's death but had made the papers as yet another demonstration of Negro mishap and shame—was a day of which they had never heard a word, from their parents or anyone else. "It was never talked about in my childhood," Johnnetta Cole told me, shortly after she learned the story. "And I wouldn't have any trouble imagining why. It must have been a frightening memory for him. It must have just done him in." She considered a while, then emerged from her thoughts optimistic. "But it's all so much my father. Who would bring a black woman pilot to Jax? John Betsch would do that. Great flash! Great style! He was a race man. Oh, was my father a race man!"

"He's another reason I can't get married," MaVynee once told me. "My daddy was *fun!* God, he made you laugh! After him, men are just so boring." Until my account of it, she hadn't heard of her father's misfortune either.

The foundation of black respectability wasn't air shows or other such carnivals but a commonplace conservatism. It pervaded the community. "The difference was that in that era the whole town read you," said Billy Moore, a son of Jacksonville and a current American Beach resident, a man of MaVynee's generation who remembers when The Bricks and his own youth were both dominated by Big Jim, the steam whistle on the waterworks that blew every afternoon at five, giving him exactly ten minutes to get home. ("I knew that when Big Jim blew I had to pedal that bicycle," he said.) "That was just the society at the time. You could go to any house and say you were hungry and be fed. I mean anywhere. And if you were acting up and somebody knew you, they would just call your name and discipline you on the spot and you would pray they didn't call your house and tell your father and mother. They could give you a whippin' and nothing said about it."

Moore's family was solidly of the invisible class—his father worked as a chemist formulating black hair-care products for Sophia Nickerson Stark's factory, salon, and beauty college on Fifth and Myrtle. He also worked in the post office. Billy's mother was Alpha Moore, who was one of the undeniable pillars of the community, being a music teacher at Stanton High School. The family had a house at American Beach. Sitting in that beach house one hot summer afternoon, Moore told me a story of a time when he offended his mother's standards. In the early 1950s, Moore attended Florida A&M University in Tallahassee, which had a prestigious music program. He was on a scholarship. He played drums, and when his virtuoso reputation spread he began staying out until two in the morning playing jazz in smoky juke joints around the Black Belt of Georgia and Alabama, making a lot of money but slighting his classes, and his grades fell and he was expelled. Soon after his parents got the expulsion letter, Alpha Moore showed up at the door of his dormitory room. She grabbed Billy and, in his still-astonished words, "She slapped me all the way down the hall. In the men's dorm!"

Along the way, she reminded him that she was the top black music

educator in the state of Florida, and that he had shamed her. Alpha
Moore was a classical pianist who had done her postgraduate work at
Columbia University. Early in Billy's life, she had taken him to
Carnegie Hall and told him about opera diva Marian Anderson and
how Anderson had done the impossible by getting to sing there when
no black singers could. It was a pointed lesson in racial promise and
personal perseverance. Shaming Alpha Moore's expectations was no
light thing.

His father was waiting outside the men's dorm in the car. It was
night. As they drove the many hours back across the state, they discussed the boy's fate. Then they reached a crossroads. Moore's father
stopped the car and said, "If I turn left, you're enrolling in Edward
Waters College in Jacksonville. If I turn right, you're going to Florida
Normal in St. Augustine. Which will it be?"

"Normal," Billy said. It was three A.M. when they reached the campus of Florida Normal College. Alpha Moore got the president of the
college out of bed—ringing the doorbell until the porch light went
on—and had Billy enrolled on the spot, and had him put immediately
on probation and confined to the dorm and library and class. And
then, before driving off and leaving him there in the dark, she told him
that if he didn't make the honors list she was digging a pit in the back-
yard and putting his drums in it and dousing them with kerosene and
burning them. Moore looked at me at this point in the story; we were
sitting at his dining table and he was in his swim trunks with his shirt
open, having just returned from the beach, and the sound of the surf
filled the high, bright room with a distant lulling roar. "She meant it,"
he said, and his face wore a forty-year-old expression of panicked
admiration.

Throughout the community of that day, in The Bricks, in Black
Bottom, in Sugar Hill, music reigned, whether it was from the corner
lamppost on Ashley Street across the intersection from the Clara
White Mission, where pickup blues musicians (among them a young
Ray Charles) loitered purposefully, waiting for a break, or from the
altar of Mount Olive AME Church, where Mary Betsch presided from
the organ bench. On their way to church, the Betsch children passed
the open doors of the evangelist churches, where the congregants
shouted and fell over in raptures and the music was loud and sancti-

fied. "Oh, the tambourines!" MaVynee says. "I loved it! *Yahoo!*" But that's not how it was in Mount Olive. "Mama played classical stuff—Haydn, Mozart." And hymns, including a rare spiritual. The regimen was identical at the other established denominations. At Bethel Baptist Church, J. Milton Waldron's old congregation, Handel was leavened with an occasional "Climbing Jacob's Ladder," sans clapping or tambourines. "I don't want to say we didn't have gospel," Ernestine Smith, an American Beach homeowner and Bethel congregant, told me. "But we didn't shout. If you shouted, you were escorted out or tapped on the shoulder. We didn't even say good loud Amens."

In the echelons of Radical Respectability, nothing ranked higher than a classical music education and classical music ability. The echoes of its importance reverberate throughout accounts of Jacksonville society. James Weldon Johnson's mother, like Billy Moore's, was a music teacher—his parents had met at one of her recitals. His brother Rosamond was an accomplished composer and a graduate of the New England Conservatory, and after James joined him in New York as a lyricist, the two brothers dominated the international light opera and vaudeville scene of their day, until George and Ira Gershwin assumed their mantle. Their example was allegorical—that through music you could buttress your community against the brutalities aimed at it, and also one day, if you were good and lucky, you could surpass those brutalities and break out of that community and succeed. It was the lesson Alpha Moore taught her son when she took him to Carnegie Hall, and the lesson stuck. Her son eventually provided his own surpassing example. He did make the honors list at Florida Normal, and his drum set wasn't burned, and he went back to Florida A&M, where he graduated with honors before proceeding to Columbia, where he got his master's.

Soon thereafter, Billy Moore invited his mother to join him in New York and told her to bring her best dress. A limousine picked her up at her hotel and brought her to Carnegie Hall, where a seat was waiting for her in the balcony, front row, center. He had told her that he would meet her at the hall, but the seats beside her were taken. After a while the announcer came out and said, "Zanuck presents the Ray Charles Orchestra," and the curtain went up, and the only performer onstage, the only one not waiting in the wings, was Billy

Moore behind his drum set. And Alpha Moore, music teacher at
Stanton High School, who had demanded that her son be home when
Big Jim blew on the waterworks and had slapped him all the way down
the hall of the men's dorm of Florida A&M, stood up in the balcony,
and threw her hands to the vaulted ceiling and yelled, "Thank you,
Jesus! Thank you, Jesus! Thank you, Jesus! Thank you, Jesus!"

Moore went on to play percussion with the likes of Lena Horne, The
Four Tops, Stevie Wonder, and Diana Ross (until 1996, he led Atlanta's
African-American Philharmonic Orchestra), after touring the country
with Ray Charles. For the duration of that tour, whenever Billy Moore
got back on the band bus everyone would yell, "Thank you, Jesus!"

There were two pianos in the house in Sugar Hill during the time that
the Betsches lived there—an upright in the upstairs den and a baby
grand in the glassed-in downstairs porch. Half a block down Eighth
Street, MaVynee's grandfather, James H. Lewis, had a concert grand in
his parlor. The children had started their music and dance lessons
before they started school—ballet for the girls and tap for brother
Johnny. Piano all around. The piano teacher started the sisters out on
Duke Ellington arrangements. When they played four-hand duets,
Johnnetta took the high end; MaVynee preferred to rumble around in
the bass. After a while, Johnnetta got bored and switched to violin.
Johnny, when he reached the age of discretion, took up drums. But
MaVynee stayed on the keyboard and the keyboard got her to college.
Her choice of college was itself the result of a musical intervention,
when operatic baritone Todd Duncan came through town and stayed
at the Betsches' house. "So I played my little piano for this famous
baritone. And he was the one who said, 'Why don't you go to
Oberlin?'" MaVynee said. "*Oberlin!* I had planned to go to Fisk. So I
made a tape of—I never shall forget it—Beethoven's *Pathétique. Dom*-
da-dee-da-deeee-dum. *Dom*-da-de-da-deeee-dum," she sang, and then,
thrilled with the memory, let out with a delighted "*Whooo!* And you
had to make a tape of a Romantic piece. I did a Beethoven sonata, and
then I did some sort of classical—I think I did a Haydn something. I
did it on Grandpa James's grand. And I sent it off."

And was accepted into the conservatory. And went to Oberlin to
major in piano. She had found her campus, but not yet her calling.

If music was the highest peak in the range of respected pursuits, opera was its pinnacle. This was as true in white society as in black. Jacksonville had initiated its first grand opera house in 1884 to great fanfare, a twelve-hundred-seat theater built of heart pine. It was dedicated with a nationally acclaimed performance of Gounod's *Faust* and soon thereafter it burned down. When it was rebuilt, three years later, the new house opened with a homegrown minstrel show. Such is the story of Jacksonville.

In the closed environment of pre-integration black America, opera had an especially pointed role, serving the aims not only of snobbery but of social protest as well. Sometimes that role was workaday; for years, the regular out-of-town venue for the home company of the Metropolitan Opera was Atlanta. While the Met was there, the black singers lent themselves to local causes. When the Wheat Street Baptist Church ran out of construction funds before it could put a roof on its new cathedral on Auburn Avenue, the job was completed with money raised by black Metropolitan Opera singers, who performed benefits in the starlit shell of the cathedral's sanctuary. At other times, the victory of music over prejudice could be spectacular, as it was in the most famous of such encounters, in 1939, when the Daughters of the American Revolution refused to let Marian Anderson sing in Constitution Hall in Washington, D.C., provoking Eleanor Roosevelt to resign from the DAR and inspiring an invitation to Anderson from the Secretary of the Interior to give her concert from the steps of the Lincoln Memorial. She accepted. Seventy-five thousand people attended. Thirteen years later, when Marian Anderson came to sing in a black auditorium in Jacksonville, whites were upset that they couldn't attend the concert: they were barred by laws against interracial theater seating. Anderson refused to do an extra, all-white show. So for the duration of her visit, Jim Crow was suspended. It was a delicious victory—one that blacks could gloat over graciously in black tie, offering an ironic hospitality to their overlords in a house mixed racially, seat by seat. Anderson stayed with J. Leonard Lewis's family, and reported to the black press that the Lewis home was a very fine home indeed.

The position of opera in black esteem was not accidental. It was launched by troupes of black singers such as the Colored Opera Company of 1873, the Oriental-American Opera Company of 1895, and the Theodore Drury Opera Company of 1900. The goal of such companies was, culturally speaking, defensive. In the age of blackface and minstrel show, the comic, light, Step-'n-Fetchit operetta farce, they aimed to prove to the world that black performers were capable of higher and harder things—of the real thing, grand opera. The Oriental-American, organized in New York City with funds provided by a Syracuse philanthropist, toured nationally and throughout Europe in its brief but successful existence. In its cast were some Jacksonvillians—J. Rosamond Johnson, who was its music director, and a young soprano recently graduated from the National Conservatory, the Afro-American's future first clerk, Eartha Mary Magdalene White. While announcing the advent of blacks to opera, their success also trumpeted the coronation of opera as part of the promise of the coming century to blacks.

In her second year at Oberlin, MaVynee Betsch went with her classmates to Cleveland to hear the great Yugoslavian soprano Zinka Milanov as Aïda, the role that was so much her signature that not only is she identified with it but the role is forever identified with her. Perhaps it was fate that MaVynee's first exposure as a student to the operatic stage should feature a European prima donna in the guise of an Ethiopian princess. By the time Milanov had hit the final pianissimo (and devilishly difficult) high A, MaVynee had switched ambitions. For her senior recital at Oberlin Conservatory, she sang Purcell and a set of German songs by Schubert and then a modern song cycle in French, composed by a fellow student.

With her graduation, MaVynee was poised to do more than begin a career. She was poised to make good on a societal aspiration over four generations in the building. In her, the threads of Radical Respectability would come together: the thread initiated by A. L. Lewis when he set out as an uneducated laborer to create a dynasty whose worldly success would be crowned by service and cultural refinement, and the thread initiated by Eartha Mary Magdalene White when she set sail from a Manhattan pier with the Oriental-American Opera Company to show the world that the American children of Africa were rightful heirs to the jealously guarded heart of European culture.

One Lewis protégé, writing shortly after his death, noted: "Even though Doctor Lewis [A. L. Lewis received an honorary doctorate from Wilberforce University in 1936] firmly believed in interracial cooperation and harmony, he believed that improved race relations could only come when the Negro attained industrial competence and economic sufficiency." Lewis's vision of self-sufficiency, then, was aimed at the prospect of eventual harmony. Beyond the task of creating an independent black economy was the promise of one day entering the larger world unburdened by the Conundrum, free to aspire and achieve without the stigma that the aspiration and achievement were somehow motivated by the need to emulate. MaVynee graduated from Oberlin in 1955, the year after *Brown v. Board of Education*. It was a time when that vision of self-sufficiency seemed on its way to being realized. She was the prominent heir to the family that ran the company that was the largest employer of black people in the state of Florida, a company that was the linchpin of the black economic infrastructure of Jacksonville and a major contributor to the economies of other cities and towns throughout the South. The foundation had been laid. A. L. Lewis, among others, had laid it. It fell to MaVynee's generation to reap the promised reward, to take that economy public, as it were, to secure their place as unapologetic partners in the greater culture and so prove that the struggle of almost a century had not been predicated on a delusion.

Some would see it as delusional. The year of MaVynee's graduation, the high stakes of her coming adventure were spelled out by the black sociologist E. Franklin Frazier of Howard University. Frazier derided the entire concept of Radical Respectability. In an influential work entitled *Black Bourgeoisie*, he held that the effort to adopt white culture and ideals served only to divorce middle-class blacks from their folk roots without gaining them entry into white society, thus leaving them a people "suffering from nothingness," and "in the process of becoming NOBODY." One of Frazier's clearest examples was musical. The truest expression of black culture, he felt, was the Negro spiritual, born in the old black church. The dilemma of the middle class was evident in its rejection by respectable black churches of the good loud Amens of "religious emotionalism." Churches, that is, like Jacksonville's Mount Olive AME, whose predilection for Handel and Haydn Frazier would certainly have characterized as a rejection of black roots.

Frazier's analysis may have fit some members of the black bourgeoisie, but it did no justice to the motives of black musicians. At A. L. Lewis's funeral at Mount Olive, in 1947, the mourners, whose number included all blacks and most whites of prominence in Jacksonville, viewed the body to the accompaniment of an organ arrangement of Dvořák's *New World* Symphony. It was only when MaVynee heard it again in Oberlin that she discovered what the *New World* was and perceived its amalgamation of Czechoslovakian folk song and Negro spiritual. Even before Antonín Dvořák was introduced to the latter form by the black classical composer (and James Weldon Johnson collaborator) Harry Burleigh, European song and Negro spiritual were linked in the minds of black performers. They were linked by the terms of the Conundrum. Though white Americans applauded spirituals as the first authentic American music, though they recognized that the songs of slaves could be as haunting in their expression as those of Mahler and Schubert, they nevertheless stigmatized blacks for their creation. The black spiritual singer was cast as a new variety of noble savage, a genetic minstrel possessed of a "natural" gift and thereby incapable of the discipline demanded by high European art. The pioneering black classical singers—Marian Anderson among them—were intent on dispelling this myth. Some of them listed that mission foremost among their motivations. They constructed their concerts not to distance themselves from spirituals but to champion them as worthy fare for academy musicians. Just as A. L. Lewis had wanted the platform of economic self-sufficiency from which to declare that his tastes and desires were truly his own and not the product of emulation, so black singers wanted the platform of classical achievement—a sort of industrial competence—from which to declare that their native music, like their other choices in life, was not something they did because they couldn't do anything else.

MaVynee didn't sing any spirituals at her senior recital, but as she mapped out her plans she summoned the example of the first black solo tenor to tour the European stage: Roland Hayes, a man who was a part of Lewis family lore because he was an acquaintance of J. Leonard Lewis, MaVynee's uncle. Hayes had compiled a book of spirituals, which MaVynee bought and studied. She took it with her to Chicago to visit Johnnetta, who introduced her to Melville Herskovits— "Johnnetta's *god*, you know, *the* anthropologist to end all anthropologists," MaVynee says—and Herskovits talked to her about music. "He said, 'For God's sake, MaVynee, when you do the spirituals, strip them down, don't do the arrangements. Make them simple and pure, as they were intended to be.'" When she got to West Germany, she followed his advice. She sang her spirituals a cappella. Entire European orchestras listened silently in the pit.

On an evening in mid-1993, I received a telephone call in my home in Fernandina. I had hardly said hello before a woman's voice, thick with the sort of leisurely but commanding drawl that bespeaks a sure sort of Southern aristocracy, said, "Mr. Rymer, we are strangers." There was a momentary pause, just long enough to permit me to accept her sentence as both cosmic verity and adequate introduction, and then the voice said, "But we share a common interest."

The voice, it developed, was that of Adele Fishler, a Fernandina resident and the widow of Herbert "Heimey" Fishler, attorney at law. Our mutual interest was A. L. Lewis. Mrs. Fishler had come into possession of a piece of correspondence written by Lewis to her husband more than fifty years earlier, and she offered to let me see it. The name Fishler was already familiar to me; only a few weeks earlier, it had been associated with deep disappointment.

Throughout the building of the Afro-American Life Insurance Company, A. L. Lewis had enjoyed the good offices of various powerful whites—notably attorney John C. L'Engle and William Barnett, the president of Barnett Bank, the state's largest. They were from Jacksonville's Brahmin families, of such brassbound genealogy and secure station that they could afford to ignore the cracker impulse to fortify their well-being with another man's misfortune, and so were friends to blacks, though generally behind the scenes. At crucial moments in the history of the fledgling Afro, they did for it what they also did for white companies of similar youth and promise—they threw their professional muscle and institutional worth into guaranteeing a loan or warning off a corporate bully. When A. L. Lewis decided to build a town on the coast of Amelia Island in neighboring Nassau County, he required the offices of someone local to handle transactions in land and cash, someone who knew the courthouse blindfolded and the registrar of deeds by nickname. He settled on Heimey Fishler, one of Fernandina's foremost attorneys.

Nassau County was certainly not a place to enter unprotected, as Lewis was to find out when the Ku Klux Klan demonstrated against his plans. Even at a much later date, when American Beach was an accepted reality, Lewis would contract with the state police to provide escort for his employees headed there for the annual company picnic, in order to protect them from the depredations of Nassau County law enforcement. MaVynee recalls her childhood fear on trips to the beach house, her prayer that no mechanical or pneumatic failure would strand them in Klan country. Every summer, the Lewis family would go to Washington D.C., or to visit John Betsch's parents in the North Carolina mountains, and the drives through the South were episodes in unease. A black man at the wheel of a fine car was such an invitation to retribution from any envious bigot that Dr. Richard Moore, friend of the family, president of Bethune-Cookman College, and member of the board of the Afro-American, kept a chauffeur's cap in his glove compartment to wear during his passage through white precincts, especially when he was traveling with white friends, who then had to sit in back. MaVynee and her sister both recall their panic the night their car had a flat tire beside a lonely north Florida highway, and sure enough a car pulled up behind them onto the shoulder and there was a glare of undimmed headlights and a slamming of car doors and they were confronted by four white men in galluses. Then, after a few quiet words with John Betsch, the men retired, wishing the family Godspeed on its way. When MaVynee begged an explanation for the miracle of their deliverance, her father pointed to the pin in the lapel of his jacket, the jacket he had been careful to slip back into as he stepped out of his car. The leader of the reception committee, he said, was a ranking Mason. So was Betsch, thirty-second degree.

I had heard about Heimey Fishler's role in the creation of American Beach early in my investigations, and I had been excited at the prospect of going through the wealth of correspondence that must have transpired between him and A. L. Lewis—a correspondence that would surely spell out for me step by step how that creation happened. It was a necessary record, because so much—so much—else was lost. I had intended to examine the rise and fall of the Afro-American Insurance Company in the archives of such newspapers as the *Florida Star*, an historic black weekly, but the newspaper's building, containing the only complete collection of its back issues, burned to the ground in 1993. I had searched for the records of the Afro-American itself—ledgers, letters, stock offers, and property liens from 1901 on—records that should all have gone to Tallahassee when the company was put into receivership in the late 1980s. The Florida Department of Insurance informed me that whatever they had received they had transferred to the Florida Black Archives on the campus of Florida A&M; its director told me that the Archives had gotten only a scrapbook and a few similar items. MaVynee told me of a black trucking executive in Jacksonville who had kidnapped the choicest of the documents at the time of the company's bankruptcy, perhaps in lieu of payment, and was holding them for ransom. The family hadn't agreed to his terms. These documents were languishing in an unknown location, or perhaps they had already been destroyed.

When I lamented the scarcity of Afro papers to one beach resident, a Jacksonville historian who had been connected with the Afro, she implied to me that their loss might not be accidental: there were individuals, she said, who feared what the records might reveal about the running of the Afro in its final years.

The Afro's missing documents were a symptom of a larger lost history: black Jacksonville's. Oral accounts of the town's progress should have abounded, but they were silenced by modesty, an amnesia for mundane detail among persons accustomed to considering their lives inconsequential as history. They were also guarded by suspicion. I grew used to hearing that any candid history of black society would be used only to embarrass blacks. Many held the opinion of the waitress in a Fernandina restaurant who interrupted my interview with one of the community's black leaders to warn the woman not to tell anything to a white man, or even recite any history in a form where whites might get to hear it. On another occasion, a street-fair vendor rushed from his booth to berate MaVynee for speaking to me and me for being white and taking notes. I was inclined toward sympathy with the position—if it was based on the ground that a people robbed of so much, including the right to be the arbiters of their own story, had little left except history to call their own and could expect to see that history mangled in strange hands. MaVynee had already raged to me about her encounter with a newspaper reporter, a well-meaning white woman who had come to the beach to do a sympathetic profile, but who still ran afoul of MaVynee's ire. "I resent people coming here assuming they can just interview black people and they don't know a damned thing about our culture—nothing," MaVynee said to me. "I told this woman, 'You insult black people coming in here with this.' She said, 'Well, MaVynee, I don't understand.' I said, 'I know you don't. You are an example of what I'm talking about. You come here just assuming you're going to come to American Beach and write a story. You are not *bringing* anything to it. This is a two-way street. *Two-way*. You *bring* something. You *understand*. And when you interview, there's an interplay. It's like music—you show up with your violin and you haven't even practiced the piano part.' *Oooh*, God, that woman got teed off!"

I could only guess how much of MaVynee's replay was meant as a caution to me, but I found it more eloquent than the vendor's argument, which consisted of referring to me as a canine and a probable pedophile, as were all white men, in his opinion. When MaVynee protested that I was writing a history of American Beach, he hooted, "Oh, so the Jew wants to get rich off our ancestors' experience?" He seemed to be doing pretty well on his forebears' bones himself; he was selling T-shirts that featured a black man over a cartoon caption reading, "It's Reparation Time!" The T-shirt cartoon and the T-shirt vendor both struck me as variations of the infamous trucker who held the Afro history for ransom: the vendor, too, regarded history as a commodity, profitable in caricature but in its true nature subject to theft, and better left to languish unseen than set out in the open where it might well be pilfered by white villains.

My experience wasn't unique. White and black historians alike related to me stories of the same resistance. Black researchers met it when they represented a large—that is, white-run—university; just that fact could be enough to get them barred from some privately held collections in Jacksonville and any number of privately held memories. When Eartha White died in 1974 many of her possessions were at the Clara White Mission, where they still reside, available to scholars, with many on display. Other belongings stayed in White's home, which was eventually abandoned and vandalized, and where squatters used her valuable collection of documents to fuel fires. She might have been gratified to know that her work was still providing comfort to the indigent, but others were horrified. Eartha Mary Magdalene White, who some seventy years earlier had risked her life to save the Afro's records from the great Jacksonville fire: Now her own personal estate was being torched. With the encouragement of Dan Schafer, White's heirs donated her remaining papers, some with singed edges, to the Carpenter Library at the University of North Florida, the only establishment in Jacksonville with the resources to catalogue and preserve so large a collection; for their efforts, Schafer and the university have been vilified as colonialists and race pirates.

Partly as a consequence of these attitudes, the society whose invisibility to whites James Weldon Johnson lamented had now become invisible to itself. Young blacks in Jacksonville, even those of race consciousness and Afrocentric ideals, had little comprehension of the long preeminence of black people in local and national affairs. There was in the area no publicly accessible, standing exhibit of black history better than MaVynee's homemade archive in the Seminole Room of the Titan. But even the Titan drew few visitors from among the young partyers at the Beach. They descended on the weekends with no notion of the Beach's significance, just as, back in town, they drove past the boarded-up Afro-American Life Insurance building on Union Street with no idea what it had once housed. Their ignorance went beyond the affairs of the Afro to include seemingly the entirety of their community's twentieth-century past. White disregard and black suspicion had conspired to erase black history altogether. The culture of memory had collapsed.

So when I learned of Heimey Fishler's involvement, it was with a great sense of relief. Fishler died in 1984, but his partner, a younger man named Arthur "Buddy" Jacobs, had inherited his files, and in early 1993, I visited Jacobs in his Fernandina office to ask permission to go through them. In his waiting room, when I explained my mission to his secretary, she said, "Oh, we burned Mr. Fishler's papers just last week." They had been held for a certain number of years, the decent interval required by law with old legal documents, Jacobs himself explained, and then incinerated, all.

"Our history!" MaVynee said when I told her. "That's unreal. Oh, I am sick! We're just like the Indian—not extinct, just treated that way."

And so on the appointed day, I went to see Adele Fishler. The letter she produced was not one that had been left to her by her husband. A friend had found it in a flea market and, recognizing the name of the addressee, had picked it up for a dollar. Fishler pulled it out of a scrapbook and laid it on a coffee table, a single sheet of stationery notable because the entire top third of the page was taken up with a logo of the Afro-American Pension Bureau and a panoramic halftone of American Beach. In the photo, several hundred people are clustered on the beach in long dresses and long-sleeved dress shirts; a queue of black sedans is parked along the high-tide line. It was apparently a day soon after American Beach's establishment, for the Lewis home, its skeleton of roof trusses visible over another building, is still under construction. A celebration is going on; could it have been the township's dedication? One of the Afro's annual company picnics? Front and center in the photo, an American flag snaps from its pole in an offshore breeze.

The letter's substance was a simple piece of business, dated July 29, 1941. "Honorable Sir:" it began,

If you remember, some time ago I informed you that Dr. F. D. Patterson, President of Tuskegee Institute, spent four or five days at American Beach. He told me that he would get busy and try to help us in the matter of the property on his return. I sent him some blue prints and other data and am enclosing to you a copy of his reply.

You will read the letter and see what he says in regard to the matter. I thought that I would give you this information and that if need be, you can get in touch with him and other parties.

I think, however, that by going direct to the President and Mrs. Roosevelt, we will get some quick action. I am very much interested in the temporal welfare of my people in the South.

I trust you received the other information in my other letter I sent you.

Yours very truly,
A. L. Lewis,
President

Ordinary enough, but the letter resonated with all I had been told of its author. "He would be quite controlled, and yet his outrage at the injustice would be clear," Johnnetta Cole had said to me. She had also said, "You didn't have the feeling that A. L. Lewis was now at the Afro and a businessman but he's not thinking about Mount Olive AME Church. Or that A. L. Lewis is now at Mount Olive but he really isn't thinking about the YMCA. His life, it seemed to me, was very, very integrated." And here, in the brevity of a page, business meshed so seamlessly with race responsibility that the transactional "I trust you received the other information" followed directly from the transformative, from a sentence so measured—so controlled—in its reprise of an ardent belief, a sentence so unbidden, so unnecessary to the secular business at hand between a client and a lawyer, that its inclusion seems purely catechetical: "I am very much interested in the temporal welfare of my people in the South." In the history of what A. L. Lewis was trying to do—build a resort—that sentence, by itself, would distinguish him.

By 1935, when the Afro began purchasing land on Amelia Island for American Beach, it had already declared itself in the business of creating recreational amenities for blacks. A. L. Lewis had built a golf course on Sentelle Road in Jacksonville, the Lincoln Golf and Country Club, where black celebrities from around the country— most notably Joe Louis—came to play or dine. His company had also expanded from providing mortgages for individual homes to funding the construction of entire housing developments. All of that was only a dry run. Lewis wanted to put the real estate, home building, and recreation together and make a town, a complete resort.

Lewis was not the first American millionaire to ride his fortune to the beach. The tendency is older than the Republic. Considering that the Pilgrims began journeying to Stafford Springs (in eventual Connecticut) on example of the local Nipmuck Indians, the desire for a private but communal oasis is older than Colonial occupation. In the late nineteenth and early twentieth centuries, a period roughly coinciding with the span of A. L. Lewis's life, it was required of the powerful and wealthy that they congregate at least annually—or, in more elevated cases, almost continuously—at a series of elite resorts. This was Radical Respectability for the robber-baron class; not to show up at Bar Harbor or Newport or Southampton or Palm Beach was to abdicate one's role in society and to some degree one's public duty. The grand resorts included inland spas like White Sulphur Springs and Saratoga, but the greatest were on the Atlantic, where the conditions were ideal for the desired mix of social and athletic intercourse. As J. P. Morgan phrased it, "You can do business with anyone, but you can only sail a boat with a gentleman."

Even better than a beach was a beach on an island. "Being on an island is everything," one woman resident of Fishers Island told Cleveland Amory in the 1940s. "It's that little jump over the water that makes all the difference."

As Amory reported in *Last Resorts*, his biting paean to the gilded age of conspicuous leisure, the "difference" was significant when it came to power and commercial influence. Resorts had been a part of the business cycle ever since antebellum days in Newport, Rhode Island. The season at what would become the grandest of grand resorts began in late spring when the Southern planters arrived on the packets picking up fertilizer for their cotton fields at the Fall River fertilizer mills, and ended in the autumn when the planters left on the packets that had just dropped off the cotton at the Fall River textile mills. A century later, the resort was hosting even more of an oligarchy: in 1930, a Newport denizen noted that of "the fifty-nine men who ran America," fifty were his fellow resorters.

Resort culture was at its most concentrated and occult in the Sea Islands extending north from Amelia through the Georgia and South Carolina coasts. These became millionaire fiefdoms—several of the most renowned Northern industrialists and bankers each bought an individual Georgia island and bought jointly the island in the middle, Jekyl, as a place where the Rockefellers, Carnegies, Fergusons, Macys, Sloans, Vanderbilts, Astors, McCormicks, Fishers, Goulds, Whitneys, Pulitzers, and Morgans could all congregate. The one hundred or so members of the Jekyl Island Club represented a shadow United States government and, by accepted local estimate, one-sixth of the world's wealth. Jekyl's importance was international, from 1886, when the Jekyl Island Club was opened, to World War II. The Federal Reserve System was invented there, by six men meeting secretly—which is to say, off season—and the building of Harvard Business School was funded there in its entirety in the course of one casual dinner conversation. The first public transcontinental telephone line connected San Francisco, the White House, and the Jekyl Island Club, where Theodore Vail, the president of AT&T and a man so avid for the innovative capacities of wealth that he had had a toilet installed in his motor car, took the first call. William Rockefeller and J. P. Morgan eavesdropped from nearby chairs, and Woodrow Wilson listened in from Washington. The phone call lasted most of an afternoon, during which the men took meals and naps. Before them on the club lawn was a memento of their country's economic foundations, the cook's kettle of the *Wanderer*, the last slave ship to bring its cargo to North America, which landed on Jekyl in 1858.

The largest of the millionaires' islands was larger than Manhattan: Cumberland Island, Amelia's twin and neighbor, lying a long stone's throw to the north just over the Georgia border. It belonged to the Carnegies, whose descendants live there on a compound (where they run one of the family's old mansions, Greyfield, as an inn), along with a smattering of Rockefellers. The rest of the island is now a national seashore, thanks in some small degree to the efforts of a local lobbyist, MaVynee Betsch. MaVynee, though, has never gone to Cumberland Island and won't, because she says it was the gathering spot among the islands where the cotton planters kept breeding huts for forced couplings of slaves, much the way horses or cattle were bred by the same owners for strength, size, and endurance. If that's true, she would doubtless see evidence of it if she went. She would also certainly see evidence of a saga that paralleled her own family's fate.

The layers of Cumberland's history, unobscured by development, lie close to the surface. At the bottom, there are Indian middens heaped with calcified oyster shells and chipped stone tools. Then the tabby walls of old plantations, the brick chimneys of the slave cabins set in orderly rows under the knowing oaks, the tidy graveyard where Light-Horse Harry Lee was once interred (until he was moved to Virginia in 1913 to rest near his son, Robert E.), and where still repose relatives of Revolutionary War General Nathanael Greene and friends of Eli Whitney, inventor of the infernal cotton gin. And there are newer, more prominent ruins of the most recent civilization to rise and decline there, that of the Carnegies themselves, whose several mansions dot the forest, moldering away where they haven't caved in outright, the marbled indoor swimming pools empty, the stables collapsed, the tennis courts buckled, the servants' bells silenced, the fountains that once rained dizzy, ambitious life all dry. And under the high, gloomy paneled ceilings behind padlocked doors, the Tiffany lamps that Louis Tiffany designed himself and autographed still hang over the vast parquet and the gold-rimmed china and monogrammed crystal are set at table for an ornate dinner delayed by generations, garnished with the carcasses of bats. Facing Amelia from the island's southern end is Dungeness, the largest of the mansions, a windstrewn castle through whose once-grand galleries the love vine climbs and armadillos amble. Dungeness burned in 1959, torched, it is said, by a poacher from Fernandina angry at his expulsion from the Carnegie preserve.

For a brief time, the Sea Islands seemed to have a different and more proletarian future in store, as part of an independent black nation. While marching through Georgia, William Tecumseh Sherman had mulled over the problem of what to do with the slaves he was liberating into the ashes of a decimated economy—a problem much on the official mind in Washington, where the emancipated were flooding across the Potomac. With Lincoln's blessing, Sherman issued Special Field Order 15, declaring the region known as Gualé—the Sea Islands and the Southern coast from Charleston to St. Augustine and inland to thirty miles—a black territory, where white civilians would no longer be allowed (except in St. Augustine, Fernandina, Jacksonville, Savannah, Beaufort, Brunswick, and Charleston), and where blacks would be repatriated onto abandoned Confederate land, attracted with a come-on so catchy it has become a stock phrase in the American lexicon: forty acres and a mule. Two years later, Congress rescinded both the land-and-livestock promise and the charter of the nascent territory, but the islands stayed overwhelmingly black. The land was good for subsistence farming and not much else, and the islands were so isolated that African folkways and the African-English patois known as Gullah continued there undisturbed. So did the Africans, until the very isolation made their islands attractive to Rockefellers and Carnegies and Morgans and Astors and anyone else with an oceangoing yacht and a pedigree.

The pedigree had to be pretty good, at any of the grand resorts. Exclusivity was the motivating ideal. Even the Nipmucks of Stafford Springs, Cleveland Amory writes, reserved the right to refuse service to the déclassé Podunks. When the Pilgrims took over management of the Springs, they likely excluded Nipmucks. At the grand resorts, exclusion was the central art form and having the ferocity and subtlety to divide "the right people" from "the wrong people" was an essential skill. Eleanor Roosevelt, admitted into Newport society at the age of eighteen, was made aware that not even her crisp lineage could elevate her to anything more than "country cousin." "I still get shivers when I think of it," she recalled decades later. Anti-Semitism was endemic and, at many resorts, constitutional. Race mixing was out of the question. Even the servants' quarters were segregated black from white, and there were no black grand resorters, none.

The Jekyl Islanders were perhaps the most exclusive of all resorters—they had sought out the island expressly to escape those pesky Newport millionaires. Their small number was also the most territorially expansionist, an urge encouraged by how far a Yankee dollar went in exchange for Southern land, especially land formerly deemed suitable for Negroes. Basically, they bought the coast. By 1947—before Jekyll (it had picked up an extra "l" in 1929) reverted to the state of Georgia, which opened it to tours by hoi polloi—only three of Georgia's 149 miles of beach were available to ordinary Georgians. Many of the crackers barred from their own coast came to swim at Fernandina, where they avenged their own exclusion by excluding blacks.

Up and down the Atlantic Seaboard, blacks already had beaches or island retreats they called their own: among them Oak Bluffs, on Martha's Vineyard; Atlantic Beach, in North Carolina; and Butler Beach and later Bethune Beach, in Florida. None were akin to American Beach. Few were residential and those that were had not been designed and built by a company, according to a company plan. Jacksonville blacks had long visited a spot on the coast called Manhattan Beach, which had a pavilion with changing rooms, a café, and a permanent "Fresh Air Camp" built by Eartha White for tubercular children. The pavilion burned down in 1938, the victim most likely of bad luck, though no one is sure it wasn't something more deliberate. What is sure is that after the fire, Manhattan Beach was no longer a black beach. Its closing lent urgency to A. L. Lewis's opportunity.

His larger opportunity was provided by the long history of exclusion. In contemplating a resort for "his people" as a reward for their ascendancy, Lewis was solidly in the mainstream of American economic experience. But once again the force of circumstance lofted his mundane ambition into the stratosphere of idealism. Even the elite among "his people" were at the very end of the line of exclusion. Cast out from everywhere, they had no one to cast out; defined by ostracism, they had no need to define themselves by rejecting wannabes. Walled in from without, they had no need to erect an exclusionary wall of their own. As a result, A. L. Lewis was free to create something no robber baron could: a socially coherent but democratically open resort utopia, a virtuous vacationland, a high-minded hideaway. It was a brief realization of an American ideal.

Not that American Beach was ever intended as a free-for-all. The restrictions and covenants governing the new township (in effect until the year 2000) stipulate that alcohol sales and gambling are permitted only on a certain few properties, that "noxious" behavior such as the playing of loud music is prohibited, and that no house can be constructed for under $2,500 dollars, a tidy sum in the 1940s. The first buyers were the executives of the Afro-American Life Insurance Company and other members of Jacksonville's professional class, but then, especially after the influx of those buyers had peaked, lot prices were lowered to within reach of many working-class families, and the Beach took on a permanent democratic cast. "Look, baby. That house belongs to a doctor and that one belongs to a maid," MaVynee likes to say to newcomers to the Beach. "Where else in America do maids own ocean lots and beach homes?" Across Gregg Street from the row of beachfront houses built by the company's elders, the Pension Bureau built cottages for Afro employees. The A. L. Lewis Motel was owned by the company but open to anyone with eight bucks a night, assuming that were a summer weeknight in the middle of the 1950s. The motel—designed, MaVynee told me, by John Betsch, who had been a builder before becoming an insurance executive and carried on a sideline in Jacksonville as a lay architect—had twenty-two suites, each with a living room, a dining room, and an electric kitchenette, all only steps from what the motel brochure called "the ripples of the tangy sea." There were several other hotels, owned by individuals. The social integration of black downtown Jacksonville was exactly what black Jacksonville preserved when it built an escape from the city.

The early chronology of the Beach is a mystery shrouded in the absence of Lewis's letters and the ambiguity of courthouse records. Ben Durham, a Beach old-timer, now dead, maintained with authority that the Afro bought the land in 1920; a deed for A. L. Lewis's lot—one of the first sold—is dated in the late 1940s (mysteriously, years after the letter whose letterhead shows the Lewis house under construction). Such confusion is not specific to American Beach, nor to the modern era. No less an authority than Alexander Hamilton would declare it only too typical. In 1823, Hamilton was sent to Amelia Island by President James Monroe to straighten out land claims after the island reverted from Spanish to American rule. He reported back that the surveyor of the island, George J. F. Clarke, was a man of "extravagant pretensions and inconsistent representations" and his deputy was a man "too contemptible for serious examination and too trifling to support or injure any other." After his experience on Amelia, Hamilton resigned his commission in spite of Monroe's insistent pleas, citing the damage that would certainly accrue to the reputation and character of anyone involved in Florida land transactions. Clarke is the surveyor responsible for many of the present-day property lines on the south end of Amelia Island, including those that define American Beach.

The records of those properties, their shifting lines and ownerships and worths, are kept in a walk-in vault in the basement of the Nassau County courthouse. The records there are stacked to the ceiling around every wall, and to enter the room is to feel that you have descended into an archaeological dig, where the sediment of history has been accruing page by page, the eons demarcated clearly by typeface: the recent computer printout gives way quickly to the electric and then the manual typewriter as the paper of the deeds gets older. If you chase the ownership of a property back far enough, you find yourself in broadsheet ledgers of handwritten entries, and the meaning of the transactions begins to speak more personally in a fine, italic calligraphy.

One day I was looking through the ledgers with Ernestine Smith of east Jacksonville and American Beach. Smith is ten years MaVynee's senior and as quietly refined as MaVynee is outspokenly outrageous, but she is akin to her neighbor in mischievous spirit and formidable history. Her paternal grandfather was E. W. Latson, one of the seven men who attended the conversation in the Bethel Baptist parsonage the night the Afro was conceived. Her maternal grandfather was L. D. Ervin, the Afro's first sales agent; a street in American Beach is named after him. Her father was an army captain during World War I—some people have told her that he was the first black man of that rank—and her mother was the first black dental hygienist in the state of Florida ("supposedly," Smith qualifies), with an office on the second floor of the Afro headquarters. Smith grew up in Jacksonville as a member of the invisible class—which meant also that the society's injustices were largely invisible to her, because her parents made sure to keep it that way. When the family went on motor trips, they took along a child's potty chair so that their daughter wouldn't have to use segregated rest rooms, and when they went to the movies, they only patronized the Strand and the Frolic and the Ritz, where their daughter could sit where she wanted. It wasn't until 1941, when Smith went back to Atlanta (she was born in Graves Hall, on the Morehouse campus) to attend Spelman College, that she learned about segregated seating; she had to climb the outside staircase at the Fox Theater on Peachtree Street to reach the colored balcony. "I don't remember prejudice as such until I was grown," she told me. "I was shielded. It wasn't till I had children of my own and I went into a store and they wouldn't let my daughter use a rest room."

She lives weekends at the Beach, in a house built by Mr. Ervin, several lots down the beach from A. L. Lewis's. "MaVynee's great-grandfather built the first house on the beach," she told me. "And my grandfather built the second." It is the only house on the beach row still preserved in its original condition, having survived killer hurricanes, nor'easters, and the era of general decrepitude as well as the remodeling vogue and all the sweet talk from potential buyers. When the Amelia Island Company was trying to buy up the Beach, they approached Ernestine Smith several times, but she held out, telling them that the house was the best thing her parents could have left her, and it would be what she left to her daughters, whichever of the five of them wanted it.

Smith is old enough to remember nearly drowning at Manhattan Beach, the beach where Eartha White had her Fresh Air Camp, and she missed by only four years overlapping with the life span of Eartha's mother, Clara. She remembers the beginnings of American Beach, when she was a teenager. There used to be a candy emporium called the Sweet Tooth where Lewis Street empties onto the sand beach, next to the bustling bathing pavilion. The Pavilion sold ice cream and hot dogs, and the children would play underneath it while the adults bought food and talked. Williams Restaurant served the best seafood in Florida at the end of Gregg Street, and the Duck Inn had dancing as well. Smith once explained to a young student inquiring about that time, "During my formative years, this was the best thing. The heyday of American Beach was a glorious, happy time." She has a talent for the trenchant phrase. Describing the strength of black business in Jacksonville, she told me, "We always had our own undertakers. That's the only business that's still flourishing." Noting that "every year someone drowned at American Beach," she said, "Looks like people always die at low tide."

But even Ernestine Smith was unsure of the Beach's early progress, and so it was that she came to be in the courthouse vault. MaVynee had come along with us, but the prospect of a full day in an open crypt proved intolerable to a nature that found even a night indoors claustrophobic. When she walked in the courthouse door, the protest buttons in her hair set off the metal detector, sending deputies scurrying and clotting the arrival of the jury pool. "Oh, it's MaVynee," a deputy called, darting his head around the corner. "Let her in." But she decided she would rather take a walk around town while we descended and dug.

Many hours later, we had put together a good chronology of the three transactions of the Afro-American that had compiled the Beach property. Thirty-three acres had come from the purchase of the Suhrer Tract in 1935, and in 1946 a land grant, signed by President Harry Truman, deeded eighty-three acres that included all of the southern beachfront and the site of the A. L. Lewis Motel. The land grant had been arranged through Eleanor Roosevelt, with the intervention of Mary McLeod Bethune, and through the good offices of Heimey Fishler, who went to Washington at the Afro-American's expense to consummate the deal.

The third property was the Harrison Tract. Samuel Harrison, the original owner, was a South Carolinian who fought with Cornwallis during the American Revolution and who decided, after his Tories lost to take refuge in English (later Spanish) Florida. He farmed the land, and died there in 1832. We followed the property trail into the old good heavy vellum with the slanted archaic hand as neat as any type-written page, in which one Robert Harrison Senior, Samuel's surviving brother, who had inherited the plantation, inventoried his possessions so that his wife, Mary M. E. Harrison, would have equal title to them and would retain them after his death. The date of the inventory was 1853, the twenty-fifth of August; and amid four long pages of lands delineated and goods enumerated and moneys accounted for was his profession of marital duty, phrased in the language of legalistic love and rank with the horror of his age:

> Now the said party of the first part the better to carry out the intention of said marriage . . . and [in] further consideration of the natural love and affection which the said party of the first part has for and bears to his said wife the said party of the second part: Hath bargained, sold, conveyed, remised, released, assigned, confirmed and by these presents doth bargain, sell, convey, remise, release, assigns and confirms unto the said party of the second part for her use, benefit and behoof during her natural life and for the use, benefit and behoof of her surviving children if any there are after her decease . . . all of the following property, to wit: Ninety-one negro slaves named as follows. . . .

And then began the interminable list, in some opaque order not consistently alphabetical, Christian names separated by commas, until eventually even the commas disappear and the names rush headlong into a single being:

> Prince's Grace, Judy, Hannah, Charles, Lane's Lizzy, little Prince, Phoebe, Jim, Paul Nancy Lucretia Grace Lucy Cato Gibson Martha Molly Scipio . . .

Lawyers and title searchers bustled through the vault in their customary lather, rifling through indices and slapping open leather-bound books of quitclaims and warranty deeds and mortgages taken and satisfied, the saga of their county's civic life spelled out in the hard code of ownership and sale. Amid them Ernestine Smith stood frozen over the Harrison estate as though struck by a bolt, with an expression that fell between incredulity and alarm, but frozen, as though she had spied the Devil in her morning cup of coffee and could not take her eyes off him for fear that if she blinked he would evaporate or grab her by the throat.

 . . . Billy Nancy Frank Tina Margaret Henry Catherine, Dinah, Thomas, Sue, Ned, Louis Richard, Betsy Henrietta . . .

After the names, the document would continue without cease or pause or barely even the ceremonial benefit of punctuation into tracts of land in Boggy Swamp and Thomas Swamp and then to horses and cattle and "other personal property," and all the "improvements, appurtenances and hereditaments to the same." But it was the names that transfixed.

 . . . Bogan, Patty, July Lydia, Paris Amy Cupio Peter Jane Clara . . .

"You know who that is?" I asked Smith of that particular name. She shook her head minutely, not looking away from the page. "That has to be Clara White," I said, "mother of Eartha White. She was a Harrison slave." The recognition seemed to jolt Smith a bit somewhere inside. At the time of the document's writing, Clara White, the woman who would be so devoted to the well-being of humanity that she would raise her daughter up into local sainthood, was an eight-year-old girl who had no inkling yet that she herself would ever be considered human. But it wasn't just that that shocked, wasn't the unthinkable state of a young woman whose own long life would miss crossing Smith's by less than the span of a hand—Smith had known that Clara White was born a slave. And it certainly wasn't the misfortune of some distant and indecipherable strange people, for there was nothing distant about it: this was the tangible immediate heritage of everyone Smith knew.

. . . Henrietta Rachel Maria Dwell Brooks Celia Dinah Chloe
Charles Bristol and Amy together with the future issue and
increase of the females, also all of the real Estate of said party
of the first part situated lying and being in the county & state
aforesaid . . .

There could be no doubt of what we were looking at, and we both
understood it in the terms we had come there to apply: the land the
Afro had bought to create American Beach had once been in its nature
legally indistinguishable from the mother of the Afro's founding clerk.
Both had been owned by the same individual. How could a thing so
simple as a courthouse contain such a mystery as this? The document
attested to a crime more base than ethical or cultural corruption; to
contemplate it was to encounter something lurid and miraculous, like
witnessing spontaneous generation: two vaunted *things*, slave and
land—two pieces of property owned and given in dowry by one man—
one of those becomes suddenly animate in the eyes of the law and pro-
ceeds in due course to own the other.

The white citizens in the old ledgers had familiar names, mostly—
Harrisons, Higginbothams, Sterrits—the roster more or less of modern Fernandina. In all the voluminous records those names had been
cross-indexed every possible way, and they switched back and forth
from one to another column as fortunes rose or fell: mortgagees
became mortgagers, debtors became lenders, rich men became pau-
pers, poor men became landed, and the landed became sadly landless.
But nowhere else did the metamorphosis rival this one, where those
things inventoried among the possessions could spring off a subsequent page as possessors, even if only possessors of debt and toil.

Such histories leave ghosts. Not only in the courthouse vault. The
old Harrison homesite, across the highway from American Beach, is
storied in Fernandina for its haints. I knew a woman who had lived on
the property in recent years who, though generally levelheaded, had
seen things she would only hint about, and would leave a party glumly
when the subject came up. Some of the ghosts preceded even the
tenure of the Harrison family, who were bedeviled by visitations: battle
noises, the night sounds of children's cries emanating from a cistern.
The plantation house itself burned down during the Civil War, with an

assist from Sherman's troops. Colonel Robert Harrison Jr., the last of the slave-owning Harrisons, returned from his service as a Confederate surgeon to a despoiled farm and a wild-eyed wife who had gone insane and who died within three years, and he lived out his remaining days in exemplary bitterness in a simpler house he erected on the spot.

That house, too, has been destroyed. The bulk of the old seven-hundred-acre Harrison plantation now belongs to new ones, Amelia Island Plantation and a development called Plantation Pointe. When the developers began putting in homes, their crews ran into skeletons. Archaeologists were summoned from the University of Florida who excavated back beyond the Harrison era to uncover a world the Harrisons themselves had been innocent of: the foundations of a seventeenth-century Spanish Franciscan mission. The mission had been established to proselytize the heathen indigenous tribes, and the mission enclosure had become a village of Indian converts. In 1702, the compound was raided by the English, who destroyed the mission and massacred the Indians. The university archaeologists exhumed the tally of that bloody day, the skeletons of 180 Indians, including children, many of whom had evidently died when they were tossed down the mission's cistern.

The local ghosts aren't always spectral. One April day in 1994, MaVynee called to tell me to hurry down to the Beach, that Samuel Harrison himself had dropped by for a visit. Indeed he had, driving all the way from Tallahassee in his Alfa Romeo roadster because he had read a newspaper article about American Beach and realized that the town was near the site of his family's old plantation. This Harrison was a tall, trim man in his forties, with blondish thinning hair and clad in tennis shorts and sandals. He was a nurse by profession—he had served as a medic in Vietnam—and was also a published novelist. He was considering writing a story based on family history. He had done a lot of research.

He wanted to find the old plantation cemetery, which MaVynee had once located back in the woods, across the main highway from the Beach. Amelia Island Plantation now owns the encompassing property but had exempted the cemetery acre and allowed an access easement, if we could find it. It turned out to be difficult to find. MaVynee dragged us down a long, abandoned fire road overgrown with tall grass and shrubs and blocked by the trunks of fallen trees. It was unseasonably hot and the June bugs were already complaining. "We're close," MaVynee said, fanning herself with a newspaper as she clambered over a tree trunk and kept an eye out for snakes. "It's here somewhere." But then the fire road ended.

Just as we thought there was nowhere farther to go, we discerned a weed-clogged, freshly-rutted trail, hardly as wide as a vehicle, cutting across the fire road in both directions, so we turned and headed up it until we had left the sound of the highway behind and were surrounded with the forest and the slow insistent buzzing of flies and the gentle slapping of MaVynee's flip-flops, and then that trail also ended, in a small clearing backed by a chain-link fence. In the clearing was a car, an old gray Ford, over which a man leaned, concentrating on a map he had spread out across the hood. He wore a white baseball cap and a large brass belt buckle that said "Private Pilot." A wood tick was crawling up his pants leg. My first reaction to the man was that he had been there for a thousand years, awaiting our arrival as the forest grew up around him.

"Hi, I'm Sam Harrison," our young charge said. "We're looking for the old Harrison cemetery."

"Oh, hi," the man with the map said. "I'm Robert Hamilton. Robert *Harrison* Hamilton. You've found it."

MaVynee whispered to me, "*I'm flippin' out!*"

Robert Harrison Hamilton and Samuel Harrison were cousins, in some dimension yet to be explored, and both were descended from the same local brood of Tory officers and Colonial planters. Bob, as he begged to be called, was from the Atlanta area; he had been to the homesite before to spruce up the graves, but not in a very long while. He had a key to a gate in the chain-link fence, and he led us through into the acre.

The first graves we passed were those of the reburied Indians laid out side by side, facing west, as per Indian custom, or so Bob said. Then we rounded a curve into a small field. In the corner, inside a low tabby wall and behind a Victorian wrought-iron fence with corncob finials, at the edge of a thicket of lush trees, were a few of the names that Ernestine Smith and I had seen in the courthouse vault. "Here's my namesake," Bob Harrison Hamilton said to Sam Harrison. "And let me show you yours. It's the simplest grave of all. 'Samuel Harrison. Died June 1832.' He'd lived here, let's see, thirty-eight years after starting the plantation. I don't know how he died."

Sam stood in front of the leaning headstone, overcome, with a tight grimace of a grin and his eyes all moist. He said, "In the letter I have, it says he was killed on horseback, fox hunting."

"I'd like to have a copy of that," Bob Hamilton said.

"Yoo-hoo! Here's his wife, over here," MaVynee called. As her voice echoed through the humidity under the vault of oaks, an enormous lizard slid off the lady's sarcophagus and hit the ground like a dropped brick. I realized we were in a sort of Cretaceous Eden. With modern predators fenced out, the reptiles reigned. At every step I made, something skittered away. Heavy blue skinks the size of squirrels, their heads a glans of glowing, menacing red, rattled sideways around tree trunks, wiggled fatly through the palmetto fronds. The entire enclosure seemed a hidden hothouse filled with the dense, still ozone of some other, more primitive epoch. Bob was telling Sam about his grandmother, born on the property in 1859, whom he had known when he was young—she died in 1946, after a life that encompassed both Abolition and the atomic bomb. When she was four, in 1863, she was taken to Jacksonville and placed on the lap of a visiting general, and that was her very earliest memory, peering up into the gray beard and kindly face of Robert E. Lee himself. When the war broke out, a Vermont relative had written to Robert Harrison Jr. that he should come north and fight for his country. He wrote back, "I am here fighting for my country, and if you'll be so kind as to pay me a visit, I'll gladly give you six feet of it."

"That's our Colonel Bob!" Robert Harrison Hamilton roared.

"Our Bob!" Sam Harrison agreed. With that, we drifted back toward the clearing beyond the chain-link fence. Colonel Bob's namesake locked the gate and got into his gray Ford and lurched down the rutted trail toward home.

Not all of the names that Ernestine and I had read in the courthouse were there on the property. Many of them could be found nearby, though. In addition to the family graveyard, the plantation Harrisons had maintained a slave cemetery. It was probably not thirty yards distant, but there was no longer a direct route between them.

The slave cemetery had ended up smack in the middle of a residential street in Plantation Pointe. Around it, houses had been built, in that sort of ahistorical, aregional, metastasized Cape Cod style, and in a gap in the subdivision the little cemetery sat, surrounded with a high, cheap fence. Although it was less overgrown than the Harrison plot, it was also visibly more humble. Many of the headstones there were concrete, their inscriptions scribbled with a finger in wet mortar instead of inscribed by a mason's chisel in imported granite. The other difference was this: the newest grave in the slave cemetery was a day or two old, its sandy soil still mounded raw from a recent funeral.

"Who's this, MaVynee?" I asked, when she and I and Sam Harrison found the plot.

"Oh," she said, "That's Ms. Drummond. You know, who lived on Lewis Street. She died last week."

American Beach residents may have assumed the role of property owners where once they would have been property, but they are still buried, if they are local stock, in the cemetery meant for slaves. That was one way to look at it. Another was that the success of a community can be counted in the continuity of its funerals. By that measure there was no doubt who had prevailed. The graveyard of the plantation owners had gone out of business a hundred years ago, while the graveyard of its slaves was still accepting bodies.

After the Civil War, some of the land of the old plantation had gone to its former slaves. It was sold off piecemeal by Harrisons or—like the fifty-four acres consigned by authority of President Rutherford B. Hayes in 1879 to one Stephen Drummond—acquired through government grant. In 1888, Gabriel and Edith Means, "in consideration of a desire to promote public morality and religion and of the sum of ten dollars to them in hand," gave the settlement land for a church, the Franklintown United Methodist Church, and a community was born.

Franklintown never grew beyond a dozen families, and never grew prosperous beyond the outhouse and pump-handle stage, but the water from the pump was sweet and not sulfurous, and the town was stable for generations, until a day described to me by a former Franklintown resident, Gabriel and Edith Means's great-grandson, George Green. "Somewhere around 1958 or 1959," he said, " I came home from school one afternoon, and I was surprised to see our house in a different place. I had to get the bus driver to stop. The whole thing came as kind of a shock. I said, 'Gosh, what're we doin'?' I had no idea what was going on at that time."

What was going on was that titanium had been discovered beneath the soil of south Amelia Island, and Union Carbide was quietly buying up property and moving the little Franklintown houses almost on the instant away from an intended strip mine. All the houses were hauled north, and the church followed. The families went from being independent landowners to being renters from a corporate landlord. But no mine ever got started. The price of titanium collapsed and the property went on the block. As it turns out, a new buyer was already on the way.

The whole Gualé coast was on the verge of being transformed. Strangely, the agent of change was an idea that A. L. Lewis had pioneered—the company-owned, company-designed, company-financed residential beach resort in a private, cul-de-sac enclave. The great innovator and practitioner who began the process on a large scale was Charles Fraser, who in 1956 began turning his family's South Carolina timberlands into Sea Pines Plantation on Hilton Head Island. His success ushered in a hundred imitations and began a runaway vogue for Sea-Island golf-course developments. Island after island was swallowed up, and a new stratum of economic history was laid like sod over all the old ones: just as it had been during the coming of the Northern industrialists, the black resident was suddenly not wanted on land where he had previously been relegated. As prosperity moved in, an old black culture was pushed into the sea. The most infamous instance of that cultural annihilation took place on Daufuskie Island, just south of Hilton Head and just north of Savannah. Daufuskie had been a pure, Gullah-speaking rural black enclave, reachable only by boat and inhabited by very few itinerant whites (including most famously Pat Conroy, the future novelist, who was then teaching school to Daufuskie's children). The white man who owned much of the island wanted to sell his property to the state of South Carolina and have it set aside as a park. He offered it virtually free of charge, but through the state's inaction it went instead to developers, who built another exclusive resort, à la Hilton Head. A golf course was put in and the local black families were pushed out—though the developers considered paying some of them to remain in their cabins as tourist attractions, sitting on their rustic porches making goat butter and grass baskets for the delectation of Bermuda-shorted shutterbugs parading by in jitneys. Fraser's company, Sea Pines, had gone on to build resorts as far afield as the Caribbean, and in the early 1970s he turned his sights on the greatest plum of all, Cumberland Island. Fraser intended to turn Cumberland into a mammoth new resort, and had gotten as far as buying up much of it and bulldozing an airstrip before a consortium of conservationists, Carnegies, and Jimmy Carter stopped him in his half-tracks with the institution of the Cumberland Island National Seashore. So Sea Pines licked its wounds and picked up its blueprints and island-hopped south to Amelia.

Through its new subsidiary, the Amelia Island Company, Sea Pines bought the Union Carbide holdings, and Franklintown was relocated once again, this time to American Beach. The old church was trucked intact to the upper end of Lewis Street. The old churchyard is now an Amelia Island Plantation tennis court. The Amelia Island Company built brand new homes for the Franklintown (now American Beach) residents—brick houses with modern plumbing. But the residents weren't universally grateful. As the true value of the land they had given up for a pittance became evident over the years, many of the Franklintown families began to feel gypped. They were especially angered when Plantation Pointe was built, across the highway from American Beach, and made access to the community's cemetery difficult—the cemetery that had served those families as far back as their enslavement on the Harrison plantation.

"They robbed us and took everything we had," Winifred Drummond, a veteran of the dislocations, told me. "And they put me in a wheelchair with a stroke and heart trouble." In 1994, Drummond was in his late eighties. He had lived most of those years in Franklintown, the rest in American Beach, and he had buried a lot of people in the old Harrison slave cemetery. Now, sitting in front of his newish brick ranch house, leaning on a cane, reminiscing slowly with visitors in a stroke-struck drawl or advising his grandson, Jeffrey Wilson, on such subjects as car mechanics and heritage, he talks frequently of his conviction that the green lawns of Plantation Pointe were sown over old black graves. On the morning of Sam Harrison's visit, after Harrison had found American Beach and approached the Titan and introduced himself to

MaVynee, she took him immediately back up Lewis Street to Drummond's house, her hairdo parting the air over the open roadster like a shark's fin cutting the water. The grandson of the slave shook hands with the great-grandson of the master; when I arrived, an hour later, they were deep into old times.

"You know," Drummond told Harrison, briefing him on political history, "I put up a good fight. But they were too powerful. They've tried to run us off of our land, but they can't do it. They're trying to kill us and run us off. Take everything we have. You see what too much money will do?" When we left to go across the highway to look for the old cemeteries, Drummond told us to hurry back. "You got a whole lot of my family to meet," he told Harrison. "Oh, we got a whole force of 'em. And they'll all be glad to see you. Oh, Jeff wouldn't take nothing to see you. Ol' Jeff will fall out. Jeff will fall out."

The two men laughed at the spectacle they would present together, and I marveled at the difference between Harrison's reception and that offered the white journalist whom MaVynee had scolded. "We are so grateful for your white ass coming here writing about us!" MaVynee had told the journalist, voguing the vehemence of Beach residents with a rolling shake of the head. "This is a two-way street," she had told her. "*Two-way*. You *bring* something." I could see that in MaVynee's eyes and those of Winifred Drummond, Harrison had brought something: a shared history. In an amnesiac world, where ghosts were figments and graves lay forgotten under lawns, where newspaper archives and historic papers became intentionally or accidentally bonfires but were not mourned, where churches fled from tennis courts and unique linguistic cultures from a pandemic of fairways and putting greens, where people strode past the monuments of their heritage not caring what they meant but only what they were worth, where worth was measured by the acre and the square foot and not by cubic volume of accumulated experience, Sam Harrison belonged to another way, the old way, the culture of memory.

Later in the afternoon, Harrison sat talking with MaVynee on A. L. Lewis's porch, as they sorted out their chance encounter with his cousin in the woods and his formal introductions to the gravestone of his namesake and the progeny of his namesake's slaves. Just before he left, he interrupted MaVynee midsentence with an inchoate thought that was clearly troubling him.

"Tell me if I'm wrong," he said, "but did I sense like an—um, uh—a feeling of family kinship? I mean, a relationship?" he asked, speaking of the welcome he had gotten from Drummond and his neighbors. "When I came up, they were ... I didn't really understand that *warmth*," he stumbled. "I really don't understand that. Because, you know, it seemed like they were genuinely happy to know that I was ... that I was a descendant of those people."

MaVynee looked at him a moment, taking him in: not the sandy-haired stranger, the tennis-togged scion of slave masters, but someone more deeply familiar, the great-grandchild of a patriarch whom the patriarch had drawn back home.

"They were, baby," she told him in her most consoling voice. "They were."

The spring of 1994, the spring of Sam Harrison's visit, was one of rejuvenation for American Beach. Not a lot of rejuvenation, but the signs were unmistakable. Several derelict buildings (that is, several buildings that were *monuments* of dereliction) had been demolished some months earlier, including the Blue Palace—the mansion with the driveway running through it onto the beach—which had been vacant since its clobbering by Hurricane Dora in 1964, and the house with the fallen balcony, across Lewis Street from the sand dune NaNa. Through the efforts of a Beach resident named Ruth Waters, an $18,000 matching grant had been secured from the state to buy palm trees to plant curbside all through town. They arrived in flatbed trucks. With their tops all trussed up, they looked like giant orange asparagi escaped from a Woody Allen comedy. A small sweating army of volunteers armed with shovels, under the generalship of Beach civic leader and Fernandina schoolteacher Annette Myers, and led by a motorized division consisting of a single front-end loader on loan from Amelia Island Plantation, began setting them in holes.

I'd rarely seen MaVynee in a more poisonous mood. "All in a lit-tul row," she droned as she cast an evil eye on the orderly phalanx of wooden sentries marching into position down her street. "It's that white man's disease," she declared. "White man has a Cadillac, so the black man wants a Cadillac. White man eats pork, black man's gotta eat pork. White man landscapes, *everybody's* gotta landscape. Just 'cause y'all white folks got straight hair, the whole world's gotta be straight." She soon forgave the palms, if not the Caucasian. "Look, it's just a widdle baby!" she crooned to the base of one rough column as, twenty feet above her, it sprouted its first new leaf. All through the hot summer to come, I would catch her in the evenings with purloined lengths of garden hose, watering the trees she had disparaged, lest they perish from inattention.

Things were getting better for MaVynee, too. An absentee home-owner who had decided to rent out his two-bedroom vacation house to tourists asked MaVynee to manage it, and so she had an occasional place to sleep and make phone calls, whenever the premises were empty. She let the yard grow up into a rampant tangle of herbs and wildflowers and spruced up the house's interior with a dozen bumper stickers.

The fate of the Beach seemed to be attracting some outside inter-est, which showed up in novel ways. One day a white stranger arrived in town and contracted to buy the largest building there, a three-story concrete structure known as the Candy Factory, across the intersection of Lewis and Gregg Streets from the old Sweeth Tooth. The Candy Factory had never opened for any purpose, confectionery or otherwise, since its completion in the 1970s, and had sat boarded up, as empty as a Jersey City warehouse. The stranger was from the North—at least, his accent was. He talked like a movie Mafioso, traveled with a bodyguard, and carried with him a little kidskin evening purse. He wanted to open a computer store in the Candy Factory, he said. He took a liking to MaVynee and let her see the contents of the purse: a pistol. He needed protection. He set out to explain to MaVynee why a computer super-store was just the thing for a commercially desolate stretch of empty coast, but his wife's chatter seemed to get in his way. "Shuddup when I'm tryin'a think!" he snapped at her. Eventually the deal fell through.

More promising seemed the black banker from the Midwest who wrote to MaVynee out of the blue because he'd heard of the Beach and wanted to come and invest in it. MaVynee envisioned him as the long-sought savior of the Harrison Tract—the terrible news had not yet been announced of its purchase by Amelia Island Plantation. But then he arrived and she disliked him on sight. She knocked herself out any-way, telling him of the heritage of American Beach, its significance, its natural beauty through the seasons, its cultural beauty in its heyday. But all the banker seemed interested in was finding another Hilton Head. "Black men're as bad as the white man—money's all they know and it's all they care about," MaVynee grumbled to me later. "I thought maybe if I kept on talking, I would reach back past all that yuck to some spot behind his brain and he'd see the light—I mean, damn it, see how they even got *me* brainwashed with all this '*light*' crap? Maybe he'd hear a bell go off."

The weekend following the banker's departure was stacking up to be a bad one. The radio reported that an anti-whaling protest boat whose operating budget MaVynee had helped supply had been sunk in Norwegian waters. Then the little two-bedroom vacation house erupted in a ruckus. The people from Jacksonville who had rented it had packed in thirteen friends, who had already busted out the screen door, and someone among them had been caught in flagrante delicto with the boyfriend of a woman who lived at the Beach year-round. The resulting conversation was a noisy one. MaVynee rushed over from the Titan, fearing that she would have a bloody mess on her hands in the house she was supposed to be managing. "I've always had too much imagination," she said to me. "I had to tell myself on the way down there: 'Nobody's murdered yet.'"

Nobody had been, yet. But she arrived to discover something almost worse, by MaVynee's standard of violence. The guests had mowed the lawn. The wildflower bed, only that morning in full glory, was hacked to boot-camp buzz-cut length. The result was no putting green: the yard resembled a mangy dog readied for a lice bath. In her furious grief, MaVynee became convinced that these particular guests might "forget" to pay their tab, so she walked along the street writing down license-plate numbers, just in case. A neighbor was amused by the Beach Lady's new hard-ass, bottom-line attitude. "Yeah," she told him, laughing, "all this capitalist shit. See why I'm not part of the system? I can't even handle this."

"I don't understand," she said to the same neighbor later, after the excitement had died down. "Why, if someone's going to play around on his girlfriend, does he do it right close to home?"

"MaVynee, you don't get it. That's the excitement," the neighbor explained. "Wondering if you're about to be discovered."

"You men!" MaVynee said.

"That's the hottest sex there is, when you might be found out!"

"In my next life," MaVynee told him, "I'm going to be a bird."

The morning of the following day was a beautiful one, and the agonies of guest cottage management and crisis resolution and cetology protection and capital solicitation seemed to MaVynee to be mercifully behind her. The sunrise was exceptional. The clouds were exceptional. It had so far been a spring of weird, extraordinary cloud formations, but these outdid anything. MaVynee watched them come over the big sand dune: some looked like lizards, some like birds, some like lizard-birds, like pterodactyls. As she stood outside her motor home, a bicycle rolled up and a roundish, middle-aged white man pulled off his safety helmet and said, "Howdy, MaVynee." The man was William R. Moore, director of planning and development for Amelia Island Plantation. "I wanted you to be the first to know," he said, and he told her that his company was buying the Harrison Tract, for their new Plantation Park project.

His announcement left MaVynee feeling like a restive volcano: "The steam's rising, but nothing's spilling out" is how she described her initial reaction. It wasn't until Moore had strapped on his helmet and ridden away, half an hour later, that what he told MaVynee began to register on her. "He pedaled off, and I said to myself, 'Bitch, did you hear what that man just said?'" And then she burst into tears. She had been crying most of the day when I arrived in late afternoon, her eyes all puffy behind her sunglasses—the made-in-China sunglasses that she had bought for herself at Kmart because she thought they made her look like a dragonfly. NaNa had been sold.

By the time that MaVynee became the "first to know" of the Harrison Tract purchase and with it the loss of her beloved NaNa, the Plantation Park project already had a history, and a lot of people knew it. It turns out that MaVynee's instinctive resistance to the landscaping of the streets had been prescient, for the palm trees were the vanguard of a white incursion more literal than she had imagined. When challenged later by suspicious Beach residents to provide any example of Amelia Island Plantation's goodwill toward the Beach, planning director Bill Moore would cite his company's recent loan of the front-end loader to help in planting the palm trees. But the day of that planting, as MaVynee interpreted it, was also a day of treachery and intrigue. Annette Myers, in addition to her supervision of the Beach beautification, had attended a walking tour that day for Amelia Island planners and developers around the Harrison Tract. The Plantation had invited her along on the tour and to dinners with Amelia Island Plantation executives because of her title: Myers was the president of American Beach, Inc., an organization that comes as close as anything in town to a governing body. It is actually more of a quasi chamber of commerce *cum* homeowners association, in which members enlist and pay dues. American Beach, Inc. meets every other month in the back room of the Franklintown Methodist Church; the meetings usually draw a quorum of eight or ten people. MaVynee was a sporadic attendee, in those years when Ernestine Smith paid her dues. The group was formed in 1982 by Beach resident and Stanton High School principal Ben Durham to present some organized and unified response to all the forces working toward American Beach's dissolution. But over time it had also become a field of intense internal division, where the coups were only barely bloodless and demonstrations could come dangerously close to legal action or blows. Annette Myers, the organization's fifth president, was a starched, aloof presence who administered with a high hand and did not encourage dissent. "Annette wants to keep control," Bill Moore told me of her method. "If she can get away with it, fine." She was the only person from American Beach invited early on into the Plantation's deliberations; she declined to relate her experience to other Beach residents, as she later told me, "so as not to start any rumors." When Myers called a meeting about the Plantation Park project, several weeks after MaVynee's revelation from Bill Moore, the entire town turned out. People filled the church's main chapel, a spare wooden room built by Franklintown residents. Facing the congregation in the front of the room stood three scrubbed-looking white men: Jack Healan, president of Amelia Island Plantation, Bill Moore, and Howard Landers, a land-use consultant from Jacksonville. This was to be their public announcement of Amelia Island Plantation's intentions, and they were eager to quell suspicions that had been at large since MaVynee had received the word and rapidly passed it on. "We don't want to do anything to cause concern in your community," Healan said. "Amelia Island Plantation and American Beach have been good neighbors. We want to work with your community to be sure that both our communities continue to exist in harmony."

The men had reason to think that their company's proposal for the Plantation Park development would meet with American Beach approval, and they spelled out why: the golf course they wanted to build would be a much quieter and friendlier usage than a half-million square feet of office and retail space, which was what the zoning permitted and what another developer might do. And the sixty or so housing units that the company wanted to put around its new golf course were just over half what the zoning allowed. "Great care has always gone into Amelia Island Plantation, where environmentally sensitive areas are looked at with great respect and are preserved forever," Healan said. "We go to great lengths to not cut trees down. What we like to think is, Man in harmony with Nature."

They had some portfolio in that regard. Part of Charles Fraser's success, beginning with Hilton Head, was his pioneering of a land-use model that set homes into the trees and spared the front beach dunes, which old-style hotel builders, eager to get their guests as close to the surf as possible, liked to level for foundation pads. In previous weeks, I had spent some time in the Plantation planning offices, and the planners, to hear them talk, were fellow travelers with MaVynee: they decried the disregard for trees and dunes displayed by other Amelia Island developers. The great sand dune, NaNa, which was tempting in that it offered the only ocean vista in the Plantation Park acreage, had itself been zoned to hold twenty-four houses, but Bill Moore took pains to let the congregants in the church know that the total number of residences that Amelia Island Plantation would erect on it was zero. "We plan on revegetating the dune and stabilizing it," he promised them. "We'll maintain it with a buffer of trees."

But with that said, the chapel was still tense with suspicion and resistance. No sooner had Jack Healan begun to speak, setting a tasseled loafer casually up on the front pew so he could lean conversationally on his raised knee, than someone interrupted his presentation and commanded, "Please take your foot off of our church pew!" Perhaps the church had something to do with it, since the building itself was a refugee from the territorial imperatives of Amelia Island

Plantation. When the questions began after the speeches ended, it was clear that some residents remained convinced that, environmentally sensitive or not, the project was an anaconda tightening around American Beach's future, the fulfillment of the forecast by the Amelia Island Plantation's previous owners that American Beach was headed for obsolescence. "American Beach has already been decimated by development. And this type of thing, without our input or involvement, will continue to erode the value of this historic site," one resident rose from his seat to say.

The locus of objection was centered in the fifth pew from the rear, where MaVynee sat. The Plantation's ecosensitivity seemed aimed directly at her; at times, as Beach residents argued both sides of the issue, everyone seemed to be addressing MaVynee. "When I first heard this plan—I guess I'm naive, but I was *happy*," Marsha Dean Phelts said. "When I came here, the plan was for a shopping center. So when I saw the golf course and the homes, MaVynee, I was *elated*. I put a sign out to sell my home for $75,000. And now if they put Plantation Park there, I'm going to sell it for $150,000."

When Healan called on MaVynee, her comments were aimed not at ecology but at cultural economy. "Mr. Healan, when you knew you were going to buy this, did you know that this was originally Afro-American land?"

"Yes, ma'am," Healan said.

"Did you perhaps think it would be positive to include us in your plan? In other words, why weren't we told this so perhaps we could have a joint venture, so we both would have benefited? You just assume that no black person would be interested."

"Now, just a second," Healan said. "The property has been for sale for ten years, and anyone who wanted to buy it could have, black or white."

MaVynee persisted. "Would you be willing to reopen negotiations with American Beach so that black people would be partly *owning* this? There's a difference. You could structure this like a corporation; we could have shares in it, so that we're actually benefiting by it."

Healan said, "I have no problem with that whatsoever." But their exchange left two things clear: First, that black or any other outside participation was impractical. (As Healan went on to warn, sparking a small commotion, "Taking on a partner is like getting married.") Second, that the center of the resistance, MaVynee's and others', did not really lie in what kind of neighbor the development would prove to be. It lay in the sorry fact that the land in question was once a monument of black ownership and was now just as emblematic of black loss. Even those in favor of the plan drove that point home. "There are some people in here who remember Mr. Ben Durham when he went to the Afro when he heard this property was going up for sale," Berenice Thomas scolded. "He brought it to the group"—American Beach, Inc.—"and tried to get some kind of commitment to buy this contract. And there are some people in this room who know what I'm saying. The property is sold now, and what we should do is stop all of the conversation and try to work with Amelia Island, because we had the *opportunity* to buy this property, we had the *opportunity* to get together, and we didn't." The audience responded with applause.

Listening to the ferment within the ranks of American Beach residents (who had applauded just as loudly some of the speeches opposing the project) and witnessing their continuing inability to "get together," I recalled MaVynee's description of American Beach, Inc. "It's like chess," she had told me. "I love it. Each homeowners' meeting, you wait and see which way the players are going to line up." I also wondered how it all must look to the visitors from Amelia Island Plantation. Bill Moore had earlier made it clear to me that their estimation of the prospects of their project included an assessment of American Beach political realities. "There are several groups there," Bill Moore had said. "The people I am in touch with are in the camp that in my rabble-rousing days we would call Uncle Toms. You know, middle class and traditional. Then there are the businessmen, like Quintin Jones"—Jones was a Florida juvenile parole officer who had run a now-defunct restaurant in American Beach called El Patio— "who will have a pragmatic outlook. And then there's MaVynee. She's somewhat of a fringe person in her beliefs and lifestyle. She doesn't represent the majority of folks. But she's articulate, and she'll show up at the meetings. It's good not to have her speak against you. She's smart."

What Moore didn't say, and couldn't know until the Plantation Park proposal had run its course, was how the proposal itself would further divide those local factions. Amidst the general falling-out, MaVynee Betsch and Annette Myers would come to seem the American Beach version of Hatfield and McCoy, Montague and Capulet. MaVynee raged against the dictatorial conservatism of "that bougie broad," and Myers found her counterpart's unsanctioned guerrilla activism so intolerable she had the bylaws of American Beach, Inc. amended to exclude the membership of anyone who didn't own property. "MaVynee's a snake," Myers declared to me.

Bill Moore concurred with both women. The antagonism Beach residents felt toward Plantation Park, he felt, was partly a reaction against Myers's imperiousness and partly inspired by MaVynee's contumely. "MaVynee is creating the issue," he told me after the Nassau County Commission meetings on Plantation Park, meetings far more rancorous than the one held in the church. "She's stirred it up. She's suggesting that we're taking something. We've been recast as the bad guys. That may be true or may not be true, but we don't feel that way. We feel that's an overemphasis." Now, after the hymnless recessional, Moore stood in the churchyard with the other Plantation emissaries, chatting with Beach residents and looking a little weary and a little unnerved. The resolution of the meeting had been no resolution. The closest to a verdict reached by any of the speakers had been pronounced by Eugene Emory, the psychology professor at Emory University who has a summer home at the Beach, who rose with a thought "on the heels of MaVynee's suggestion." His observation struck me as one that A. L. Lewis would have appreciated.

"I view the Plantation as a business entity," he said, "and you folks are about business. You're trying to make more money. You know, that's not illegal in this country, and so I think we all have to be aware of that. Now, you can do business with a human hand or you can do it in a vicious way. I think the perception—at least, from a historical perspective—is that it's been sort of inconsiderate and sort of vicious. And maybe both sides have some fault in that."

I didn't tell Annette Myers (and undoubtedly didn't have to) that MaVynee might enjoy being likened to a snake—though it wasn't as supreme a compliment as being compared to a butterfly or a spider. Spiders rank high among MaVynee's favorite things, in part because of the baroque formality of their nuptials. "Do you realize that if he even so much as plucks the wrong strand of that web, he's eaten alive?" MaVynee once asked me. I must have flinched at so splendid a protocol, because she said, "This might hurt your little male macho for a while, but you'll recover. Among the animals, courtship has to be of a certain kind, in a certain way, to a very precise degree. It's so beautiful, from an esthetic standpoint, and here we're supposed to be the higher animals and the best we can do is 'Hey, baby'? Oh, give me a break, y'all! I mean, this is the twentieth century? This is all we have evolved? Good God!" The season when the orb weavers drape their ornate doilies from the limbs of live oaks and sit in their centers like little gilded mice on billowing counterpanes of lace, awaiting both their date and their dinner, is an annual ecstasy for MaVynee.

Even before Annette Myers's comment on the reptilian nature of MaVynee's persona, I had heard MaVynee described in faunal terms—most profusely in the chilly lobby of a walk-up pensione in West Berlin, in the winter of 1993. The person I was visiting there was a professional acquaintance, a publisher's representative named Angelika Wellman. Our conversation echoed in the empty, high-ceilinged, sparsely furnished room; the acoustic was oddly old-fashioned, unmuted by carpeting, free of Muzak. The voice that Wellman channeled was over three decades old. It was the voice of a music critic. Wellman had volunteered to translate for me some old newspaper clips I had been carrying around, reviews of a series of performances that took place in the winter of 1959 in an opera house in Braunschweig, West Germany, a small city and important provincial music center south of Hamburg. Wellman's English was charmingly fractured; it transformed the reviews into something near poetry, or something nearly as incoherent as poetry. I inferred from her careful search for words that the thoughts expressed on the printed page had no precise equivalent. She did not translate the review so much as she described it. The opera was Richard Strauss's *Salome*.

"It says about the title role of the *Prinzessin* that she is at the same time as a princess an exotic cat," Wellman said. "It was sung by the *Halbnegerin*—the deminegro—Marvyne Betsch, from Florida. And the way she sang it was *hinreissend*, which means—if you see a woman and you say, 'Oh, she is so beautiful!'"

"Breathtaking?" I asked.

"Yes, breathtaking," Wellman said. "The way she sang was breathtaking. And the way she sang it and the way she acted and the way she danced, altogether it was breathtaking. 'The young American Marvyne Betsch, who is already well known as a concert singer, because of her the role of the princess from Judea doesn't only become this very touching glamour of exotic, but also with aspect of innocent creature'... You can say 'a human creature,' can't you? And you could make an adjective—'creaturous'? This is positive. You would say that maybe young animals don't know any bad. So it goes together with the innocence. You could say maybe some aspect of innocence and lack of responsibility. So, a person who is personally creaturous, very much at the beginning of everything: they don't have the feeling of responsibility, but in the positive sense." The description came so close to being the very best I'd ever heard of the MaVynee I knew that I had to remind myself that it referred to a woman I had never met—someone in her early twenties, just out of school, debuting simultaneously in adulthood and on the European stage.

Four years before those performances and that review, the *Prinzessin auf Florida* had arrived in Paris. She had crossed from New York on the SS *United States* in a storm so violent that it tossed the liner about, as MaVynee describes it, like a matchbox in a breeze, and the quantities of disinfectant required to swab the nausea-slick corridors of D deck, where the traveler's cabin was located, were sufficient to cause her to gag at the smell of Pine-Sol whenever she later encountered it. She landed in Le Havre and took the train to Paris. Within a month she had secured a room in the apartment of one Mme. Chantignon on Boulevard de Denain, a block from the Gare du Nord, and begun lessons with M. Boralevi, a voice tutor. She was truly at the beginning of everything.

The room on Bd. de Denain was tiny but tactically advantageous. Intended as the concierge's apartment, it had a private access to the street, and so an escape from Madame's custodial eye. On the street, MaVynee and her newly met companions—students from the Sorbonne, mostly—honed the time-honored art of surviving *la vie bohémienne* by dint of subversive savvy and youthful daring. They roamed the city, jimmying the gates of Métro stations and scrounging food from the kitchen doors of Chinese restaurants in the Latin Quarter. On days when it was cold, they took refuge in dance halls, where the thermostat and the atmosphere were marginally more tropical.

Mary Betsch sent her daughter a stipend on the first of every month; by the ides it had run out, despite MaVynee's much professed frugality: "I said, 'I tried, Mama.' God knows, I tried. But it just never worked." So the lower half of every calendar page provided early tutelage on surviving the privations of the Beach. "Do you know you can put red pepper in your socks to keep yourself warm?" MaVynee asked me one frigid night in the Titan, with a cabalistic whisper that was, thanks to the chill and the winter moonlight, more visible than audible. "You don't know that one? I'm teaching you all the tricks! And newspapers are the best insulation. My voice teacher had a studio that was cold, cold! Here I am freezing, and he's sitting up there warm as anything, and I said, 'How?' And he opened up his little vest and there were all these layers of newspapers!" She laughed delightedly at his inventiveness; he had taught her more than he realized.

Boralevi's room was not just cold, cold. It was also, in MaVynee's description, "Huge! Huge!" Her experience equated it with the central waiting room of Jacksonville's Union Station, but there was a serious distinction. The young black girl had been forbidden by Florida law to enter the station waiting room; Boralevi's Paris studio not only was hers to occupy but assured her transit to wherever she wished to go, artistically and professionally.

The fare sometimes seemed steep. "He insisted on making me sing Gilda, from *Rigoletto*," MaVynee said. "Oh, I hated that godawful thing! Oh, it's awful! *Arf-arf-arf-arf*," she sang, a poodle arpeggio. "I don't *like* coloratura—all that going up and down the scale. We called it 'going up the wall.'"

What she preferred—preferred to any opera, had preferred since her novice singing days at Oberlin—was lieder. This was artistic minimalism: just herself, in concert and contention with an audience; just a solitary voice in concert and contention with a solitary piano.

"It's like being naked," she told me. "There's nothing to help you. I mean, the piano is there, but it's not like you have an orchestra, or costumes and lighting, and all this other stuff. You're just standing on the stage. That's why the Germans give a singer who does lieder a title of

Kammersänger—chamber singer—which is even higher than *Opernsänger*. It's far more difficult than being in opera, because there's no way you can cheat, no way. You've either got it or you haven't. Just hitting the notes won't do."

Refining such a rigorous art required discipline, standing endless hours in the enormous room working through the most microscopic of musical details. When MaVynee described her regimen to me, she invoked her unmet inspiration, Zinka Milanov. "Somebody asked her in an interview, 'Oh, Miss Milanov, how many times have you practiced this one role?' She said, 'To sing one role, I would sing each aria sometimes a whole month.' And when I think about lieder with my teacher, we would sometimes do one phrase, I mean just *one phrase*, we would spend one month on it. Because it just wasn't right. It wasn't right."

With the success of her instruction—when some of it, anyway, seemed finally close to "right"—MaVynee left Paris for the concert circuit, and the circuit led her to West Germany. "I used to sing in all the little towns," she told me. "Marburg, that was one of my favorites, a college town. And I'd sing all the lieder. And that was good practice. Because it's bad enough I'm going to sing *Salome*, by Strauss, in Braunschweig—that's like singing the Mass in Latin in Rome. But first I had the practice of singing the lieder in all these small towns, and getting the criticism."

She sang Schubert, Schumann, Strauss, Wolf. "'Lebe Wohl,' that was one of my favorite lieder—oh, oh, oh! Hugo Wolf wrote it in that time in his life when he was very much influenced by Wagner. He had these real juicy chords. I was doing things like Schumann, his love cycle for Clara Schumann, on their wedding. It's a beautiful song cycle, I did all of that. And Schubert's 'You're Like a Flower.' It's one page. It's like haiku. But see, that's all good practice for opera, because you've got three minutes to set a scene, say something, say it *with* something—some passion or insight—and then it's over." At the end of some concerts, when she had run through her repertoire of lieder, she would dismiss the accompanist or quiet the orchestra and finish with a set of spirituals.

In that way, MaVynee worked her way up to engagements in the second tier of German cities—Stuttgart, Mainz, Hannover, Lübeck, Köln, and the like—those just a notch below Berlin in musical prestige. She was living in Hannover, studying with one Herr Hoffal (himself a former student of Richard Strauss) when the call to opera came. It came from a fellow student, a German tenor named Gotthard Kronstein, who telephoned to say that he was headed to Braunschweig to sing the role of Johannan, the prophet John the Baptist, in *Salome*. Why didn't MaVynee come audition for the lead—the willful temptress who falls so in love with the captive Johannan that she coerces King Herod, through the seductive Dance of the Seven Veils, into beheading him, and then sings her last exquisite aria on the existential power of love to the head, before kissing it on the lips.

A spider's courtship, indeed. "That's right," MaVynee said when she described how Kronstein had lured her into being his costar. "He fixed me up with the part, and then I chopped off his head. Damn sure did." And as a spider's courtship, clearly irresistible. It was MaVynee's first big break. "I had no reputation, coming to them. I was nobody, literally. Every time I think about it, it's unreal."

At the time of my conversation with Angelika Wellman, I had never heard MaVynee sing. I had seen her dance, once, a month earlier, at an NAACP banquet in Fernandina that was in its particulars a thoroughgoing catastrophe. It had been intended as a celebration of black history but became a parade of such folderol as a rap paean to an imagined African utopia filled with universal brotherly love and innocence until the arrival of "Mr. John." The stage of the Elm Street Recreation Center had been adorned for the occasion with several large ceramic statues of African deities, provided by a Fernandina resident who had brought them home from an African tour. They didn't survive the sound test; a microphone cord swept one after another crashing to the floor. MaVynee performed a sinuous free-form dervish dance—to a Dizzy Gillespie rendition of "Night in Tunisia" rasping tinnily from an underpowered boom box—on the rubble of someone else's shattered Afrophilia. She had looked forward to her performance, but its completion left her visibly glum. Afterward, she sat alone, across the room from her friends, stewing, I imagined from the expression on her face, in the gall of a treasured creativity toppled from its rightful stage. I was reminded that I knew nothing concrete about MaVynee's opera career—nothing other than her contention that she had had such a career, her late-night reminiscences of Kronsteins and Boralevis and Hoffals and Milanovs. In all her voluminous files in the Titan, she had not a single program or photograph or recording or review, no remnant at all of the time in her life she seemed to cherish most.

So while accompanying a friend on a book tour through Germany, I decided to visit Braunschweig. I wanted to look at the opera house there; it was a place I'd heard her mention. A taxi let me off at a Beaux Arts palace in an intimate urban square across from a hillside park that was, on this day, softened with falling snow. The Braunschweig Staatstheater is an estimable institution: Berlioz and Wagner conducted there, in a predecessor of the current hall. Goethe held a public reading there of Part I of *Faust*. "It's good I didn't know that," MaVynee told me later. "I'd have been too nervous to audition. Oh, my God! It was bad enough." Braunschweig was also renowned for its virtuoso interpreters of *Salome*.

It was the middle of a weekday morning, and the main doors of the Staatstheater were padlocked, the ticket *guichet* shuttered, the sidewalks empty. But the stage entrance, an unmarked door around the corner, opened to my push. Within was a shallow alcove guarded by a glass security booth, and beyond that a windowless corridor smelling of radiator heat and wet woolen coats. The uniformed woman inside the booth frowned at my unguttural consonants but brightened when I said "Archives," and summoned someone over the phone. Soon a woman in her mid-thirties with an archival look about her came bustling down the corridor.

"I'm trying to find information on a singer who performed here," I said to her.

The statement provoked a lot of nodding, but no response; the archivist had no more English than the guard. She pulled out a piece of paper and handed me a pen and I wrote MaVynee's name. She peered at it and showed it to the guard inside the glass booth. Both shook their heads. I took the paper back and wrote "1950s." They nodded again, as if pleased that we had numbers, at least, in common.

"She may have sung *Madame Butterfly*," I said. Nothing. "And maybe *Salome*." Nothing again.

"She's a soprano," I said.

"Ahh, *Sopranistin!*" the archivist said, and smiled hopefully, but the smile froze into an awkward stillness, and I could tell by the look she and the guard exchanged that I was on the verge of becoming a nuisance, and that the only question now on their mind was how to politely get me to go away.

"She's black," I said.

"*Blach?*" the archivist repeated, looking helplessly at her compatriot. The guard thought a moment, then pointed to the dark sleeve of her shirt. Watching it dawn on the archivist was like watching a flame crawl down a fuse and then suddenly the explosion came: her eyes flashed open and her face lit up. "*Die Schwarze!*" she cried, and made an exuberant overhand motion, something like a pitcher letting go a fastball or John Wayne urging his men down the Chisolm Trail. "*Komm mit mir!*" she exclaimed and marched off double-time down the corridor. Apparently MaVynee had not simply existed in these hallways; apparently she was storied: "The black one," famous even to those who were not around to witness her debut.

From a storeroom beside her office the archivist pulled down announcements of every postwar *Salome* until she hit the one in 1959, and there MaVynee's face shone up from a yellowed page, her hair in a chignon, her nails trim, posing with a theatrical mask of Johannan. There followed a flood of other photographs of her, and reviews and notes and programs—reams of musty papers tied in twine. I carried copies of some of them on to Berlin, where Angelika Wellman transposed them into the descriptions of the ingenue that fit so perfectly my image of an older, poorer woman on a Florida beach.

"'Marvyne Betsch is in the title role of somebody *Versunkenheit*'—which means, you could be lost in your daydreaming," Wellman went on. "So, she is in profound daydreaming but not really in fantasy—it's closer to contemplation. So she is in her profound contemplation. . . . Narraboth—I think he's a figure in the opera—somewhere describes Salome as a 'shadow of a white rose in a silver mirror.' And this description of the character of Salome being a shadow of this white rose in this silver mirror fits very well to Marvyne Betsch's figure, because she moves very nicely, delicately. It says here that this altogether was a conception which was very pleasant for your eyes, very nice to look at."

"They give it an exclamation point," I noted. "'Very nice to look at!'"

"Yes. Literally it says, 'It can go into your eyes!' And here it goes on to her voice. 'The most attractive aspect is her voice, which is astonishing, beautiful, and powerful and survived all demands of her part all the way through to the big final part at the end.'"

The review described MaVynee's voice as "sovereign." The next one Wellman picked up called it "noble, through all the different levels of the music" and noted that the audience, steeped in a tradition of fine Salomes, was a tough one. "'If Marvyne Betsch wouldn't be so capable, they would have just called her out of the room,'" Wellman read. "And it says it's Marvyne Betsch's first time on the dramatic stage, and because of this we have to raise even higher our estimation of what the artist has done. 'Marvyne Betsch is the real star of the night,' or 'of the presentation. The opening became a big success for all the people in the play, but especially for Marvyne Betsch, who got the highest applause and she had to go in front of the curtain.' Her art of singing, this adjective says, 'throws light into the future'— *Zukunftsreich*, that means that she has a big future. In January, she is billed to sing in Lübeck, north of Hamburg, again as Salome. But first, just after the premiere, she would take a plane back to Florida, and she would take a very fast plane. So I guess in the late fifties, the *Düsenjäger*, or this sort of machine, was the symbol of very fast planes, like futurist things. And it was nonstop. It says it was a six-hour, non-stop flight back to Florida."

Twice during her years on the European stage, MaVynee came home for Christmas. It was difficult, taking futurist planes to pay visits to the past. In her early days abroad, she had worn a diamond ring given her by a Jacksonville sweetheart, but then the engagement fizzled. She had lost touch with his old world, and she felt he understood little of her new one. She had suitors in Europe (among them Herr Kronstein, he who lost his head), but the most seductive suitors of all were success and celebrity and song and independence, in a world where MaVynee was—to say the least—a singular presence. The *hinreissend schwarze Kammersängerin* traveled throughout West Germany and Scandinavia and Italy and rode the Orient Express through the Balkan states, conversed with Erroll Garner and Yehudi Menuhin in England, saw Josephine Baker in the Moulin Rouge, dined in Hannover with the Modern Jazz Quartet, conspired in subversions and café revolutions with African expatriates in London, and sat front row center at Maria Callas's last London performances of *Tosca*. At a Louis Armstrong concert in Hannover, Satchmo himself strolled out into the audience to say hello. "I never shall forget it," MaVynee told me. "It was the intermission, and I look up and I see this black man say, 'Hey, baby!' It was so funny, because I'm so used to speaking German, and I hear that 'Hey, baby!' and I said, 'Oh, God, it's fabulous! It's just like being home!'"

Though of course it wasn't. It was just like being in Europe.

"Don't forget, this is the early sixties," MaVynee went on. "There weren't that many black people in Europe, period. You'd have a few black males, because of the military, but no black women. And I'm not exactly your run-of-the-mill black woman. I stand out, anyway. Give me a break! I would walk down the street and *everything* would stop. Hey! I had it way good!"

"I would love to go back to Germany," she said, on another occasion. "With all the bad publicity about how they treat foreigners, they could interview me and I'd tell them how they treated me: like . . . a . . . queen!"

She sang her Lübeck *Salome*, then returned to Braunschweig for the next step in her ascendancy: the role of Madame Butterfly in Puccini's thinly veiled anti-imperialist morality play (so very thinly veiled that it was originally banned in the United States). MaVynee provided me with her own interpretation of the plot: "They always make this death scene in the end almost sloopy-sloopy. I mean"—she adopted a goofus-y, *Gomer Pyle* voice—"'Oh, here, dum-de-dum, I got to die now.' *Nooo!* This is art! I mean, she's so proud! When I did it, this bitch was *ready!* It was much more of an honor thing, her whole killing. She's using her father's knife, get it? I'd read some Zen and asked a Japanese expert. I knew what to do. So I took the sash from the kimono, and I used that to bind my legs before I cut my guts out. *Ohhhhh!* It was fabulous! It really was."

The reviewers agreed. "Because of Marvyne Betsch, this presentation is liberated from all these sweet, romantic versions of Madame Butterfly," the *Abendpost* raved. "The public was touched by the detached expression of the role, and at the same time absorbed by the passion of her poetic and dramatic voice."

The reviews from around West Germany began going beyond descriptions of "exceptional talent" to talk about "rightful fame"—

about a person with a rare gift, destined to her art. " 'Marvyne Betsch always showed in the love poems of the first scene how her Butterfly would succeed at the end,' " Angelika Wellman read, " 'mainly with warmth and intense fire.' Actually, if you burn down the fire, the red thing that rests, what's it called?"

"Coals?" I suggested.

"I doubt that this is the right word."

"Embers?"

"It's the red thing which rests and then you can put the potatoes on. So, intense embers. 'With her gifted poetic ways of phrasing and the high register of voice without strain, and finally the way she acted, it was motivated from the inside. Touching and moving, this black Butterfly would go into death demonstrating the whole big abandon of her big disappointed life.' Oh! Nobody would critique like this anymore! 'The soloist had to go again and again in front of the curtain! And to the new Butterfly, what should follow for Marvyne Betsch is Aïda.' So it says they intend—"

"They're going to give her Aïda?" I interrupted, mildly stunned. This I had never heard a hint of.

"Yes," Wellman said.

MaVynee had sung Aïda in concert, but performing it in full production was a prospect she would have found especially gratifying—the chance to occupy the role that had drawn her to opera in the first place, to sing pianissimo that hair-raising high-wire A, to walk in the artistic footsteps of Zinka Milanov, and to do so in a way that even Milanov could not: as an Aïda *senza trucco*, Verdi without blackface. But it never happened.

Why MaVynee quit opera midstream and eventually professional singing altogether is a mystery even to those who love her. Johnnetta Cole, in her 1993 memoir *Conversations*, states that "something happened to my sister in Germany. When she returned to America she began to display very erratic behavior, but her behavior was not so erratic that she could not talk about what it meant to be an African American woman living in Germany." Germany, where even the compliments of the concertgoers displayed a buried bigotry: they could not admit the virtuosity of a black singer, even a *Halbnegerin* (as the press so pointedly described MaVynee), without attributing it to the Aryan blood implicit in her Germanic surname, Betsch.

For her part, MaVynee ascribes her rejection of a celebrated future to her own staunch independence. "See, after *Aïda* they had me doing *Carmen*, too"—another role she had sung in concert but not in production. "They wanted me to be part of the ensemble. Which is good, too, because then you get a regular contract. And then I would sing so many *Aïdas*, sing so many *Carmens*. But that's what I didn't want. I liked it the way I was doing it, where I would just come in, I'd have my concert, and get paid for just that one performance. I was free. Instead you got these contracts and *ohhh*, it's like a marriage: You got to go to bed with him, and go to bed when he says go to bed. I didn't want to deal with that. *No . . . way, . . . Jo . . . sé!* I didn't want to be married."

Between those polar explanations—of personal whim and pervasive racism—it would seem impossible to separate MaVynee's alienation from the subtler dictates of culture and history. She had gone to Europe and secured in remarkably short order a cherished aspiration of Radical Respectability. She had stormed the edifice of European art, had stood on the shoulders of A. L. Lewis's economic achievement and put her own education to the test and been acclaimed by a culture that would only too gladly have dismissed her. She had been accepted without reservation or caveat—and more than just accepted, because she did more than merely emulate. Within her purview, she had assumed the role of an innovator; she was creating the culture, and eliciting not approval but awe from her admirers, as the shadow of a black rose reflected in a silver mirror. And so she would seem to have demonstrated that the formula in place among the American black establishment since Reconstruction—that economic self-sufficiency and high achievement would earn release at last from the labyrinth of the Conundrum—was workable and not a delusional bourgeois conceit. But even as she lived out that triumph, something about it had not suited MaVynee. She refused to accept her acceptance.

Throughout her exalted exile, MaVynee had not escaped her roots. As she conquered foreign capitals, her homeland was never far away. One night in 1964, as she prepared for her entrance onto a West German stage, she solicited a news update from a stagehand on how a celebrated black woman athlete had performed that day in the Tokyo Olympics. "The black woman won," the stagehand whispered, "but they're killing black people in Mississippi." MaVynee replied, "Tell me after the performance."

Finally, in 1965, the performance ended. The curtain came down and MaVynee came home. She had been in Europe ten years. She had starred on stage in portrayals of a Gypsy cigarette girl, of Israelite and Ethiopian princesses, and of an abandoned Japanese mother who kills herself with her father's knife when her love brings dishonor on her family—in each case, a woman destroyed when she could not pursue her passion beyond barriers of politics, race, class, or jealousy. Not one of her heroines had survived the show. Not one among MaVynee's friends, watching her return, could imagine what she had given up her new life for. She seemed interrupted, caught up short, but by what: the world of her ambition or the world of her beginnings? By her reception in Europe, or the naggings of old Jacksonville?

In one clear way, her return restored a freedom to MaVynee—the freedom to pursue her future hand in hand with the future of her family's historic culture and community. On the surface, that community and culture were doing just fine. Jacksonville was as Jacksonville had always been, but better, with the successes of the civil rights movement and the building of the Afro's new headquarters on Union Street, and the attainment of a few precious political offices for blacks for the first time since Jim Crow. But in deeper ways, the culture was in crisis. Something had happened to America while MaVynee was away; her country was displaying very erratic behavior. MaVynee arrived home to a world she'd never known—a world that had crossed, at some imperceptible moment, a critical divide. MaVynee had departed for college and Europe from the land of What Might Be. Though she did not at first realize it, she had returned to the province of "What Went Wrong?" Regardless, she would never again be caught celebrating a false victory on a foreign stage when news reached her of casualties back home. Jacksonville was the place where MaVynee Betsch resolved to pursue her fate and to accept whatever that fate might bring: *Zukunftsreich*, or the whole big abandon of her big disappointed life.

While MaVynee was still in Europe, an article extolling her achievements appeared in *Ebony* magazine. The praise was more than journalistic laurels for a race emissary. It was a passing of the torch, a tribute from an icon of the old generation to a bright young prospect of the new. The author of the piece was Arnolta Williams, longtime friend of A. L. Lewis and a luminary of Jacksonville society ever since her arrival in that city as a twenty-two-year-old bride in 1918. Her husband was Dr. I. E. Williams, Meharry-trained physician and medical director of the Afro-American Life Insurance Company, a man so intent on the conservative application of etiquette that he refused to let his wife work. Restive, she wrote articles and sent them off each week to the *Pittsburgh Courier* or one or another black magazine, occasionally receiving the $5 or $10 honorarium those publications paid for submissions to their perpetual writing contests. "I bought a Ford car with the checks *Ebony* sent me," Williams told me, laughing. At our first meeting—at her Jacksonville house, in 1987—we talked for an hour or two about life in general, and the generalities gyrated compulsively around a vexing generational disappointment. Her outrage seemed sharper than the usual disaffection all generations feel for those who stumble along after them, but that made sense, for Jacksonville's oldsters and ingenues straddle a historic divide and would hardly comprehend each other's lives.

"Jacksonville, when I first knew it, was very rigid," Williams said. "Like any other typical Southern town. White, black, white, black, and ne'er the twain shall meet. But education and time marched on, and the Supreme Court made its decision in 1954, and you could see small cracks opening up. And today if you've got money, you can go anyplace in the world." To be sure, the elders had lived in the bad old days. But among them in their tribulation, giants strode. Of her friend A. L. Lewis, Williams said, "Yes, he was a fine man. He may not have had an education, but God! he had guts. They don't make them like that anymore." Of the era following his demise she said, "It's a sign of the times in which we live that we can't appreciate a man like that."

It was also a sign of the times that there was not much left to see, much less appreciate, of the tower of race pride that Lewis had built. Not much is remembered by the current generation; among the possessions lost to view is one particularly precious. It isn't the landmark buildings or influential black institutions or even the people, though those things were precious enough. As I traveled around Jacksonville trying to put together some account of the success of those people and their institutions, I became mired in the mystery of their destruction by theft and neglect. It began to seem to me that the most tragic neglect and grievous theft was the loss of the memory itself, the theft of history.

Arnolta Williams remembered. Many of MaVynee's generation did, too—caught as they were between both worlds, old and new. Of MaVynee, Williams said, "I put her picture in *Ebony*. She had a center-fold!" But the recollection of that triumph, that ritualistic passing of the baton at a moment of great optimism, clouded Williams's counte-nance. "What do you think of MaVynee?" she asked me suddenly. "Do you know that girl graduated from Oberlin? That girl went to Paris! She danced Salome of the Seven Veils. Why do you think she has led such a negative life? She's very intelligent to talk to. Why do you think she let her fingernails go? And you cannot blame it on mental illness; she's too intelligent. All I can say is she's a bit eccentric. Me, I'd rather be otherwise. Those fingernails are for the birds."

On that day, it was hardly a quarter century since Arnolta Williams had made her homage to MaVynee in *Ebony*. Parsed along the perplexing timeline of MaVynee's fingernails, the years since her return to America were a calendar of catastrophe; in those years the leaders of the Afro-American died, and the Afro itself, and a city imploded, and a society frayed, to be remembered only dimly and only by its survivors. A few decades was all the time it took for MaVynee's triumph and her community's prominence to come crashing back to earth.

In 1969, four years after MaVynee's return to Florida, the house that A. L. Lewis built in Sugar Hill and then gave to his granddaughter Mary—the house at the corner of Eighth and Jefferson with the flying balconies and Craftsman-style exposed-beam eaves and endless win-dows and limitless yard, in whose twenty-two rooms MaVynee had learned music on Mary's baby grand and a code of living at Fafa's Sunday table—was torn down. More than that, Sugar Hill itself was torn down—taken by eminent domain and bulldozed for the expansion of a county hospital. "They called it urban renewal," MaVynee said.

The plan was protested—Mary Betsch wrote personally to the governor—but it did no good. "They demolished the best neighborhood for blacks that they had," Jolita Simmons recalled. Simmons, the wife of the Afro's head actuary and at one time the secretary to A. L. Lewis, lost her house, as did many among Jacksonville's black establishment and among MaVynee's near relatives. MaVynee grieved as over a death, and still describes the protracted execution of her home—over which she kept a sidewalk vigil—through clenched teeth. "It took them three days to knock that house down, and they thought it would only take one," she told me. "It was too well built to die." Mary and MaVynee moved out to a brand-new ranch house in a predominantly white neighborhood on the Saint Johns River. When they tried to hang a painting on the thin unlathed wall, the hammer went straight through.

MaVynee's grandfather, James H. Lewis, moved to another lowslung ranch nearby, where, as he declined toward death, MaVynee nurtured the living; she tended the grounds and put in an extensive flower bed. "Oh, I loved that yard!" she told me. She described for me a Xanadu of ornamental trees and shrubs and shaded walks bordered by perennials, and a central fountain stocked with exotic fish, black moors that paled as their time under the implacable Florida sun wore on.

So it turned out that MaVynee, whom I'd heard rail so often against the insipid orderliness of domesticated gardens, had had one of her own. It had been years since she laid eyes on her creation, and one day in 1993 she insisted on taking me by for a visit. "There was nothing in white neighborhoods like it," she bragged as we sped down the highway into Jacksonville. "I'm not bragging, baby. The white garden clubs used to come and study that yard. Flowering quince, azalea. The traffic slowed to a crawl when it was in bloom." That sounded like pretty much constantly, I said. "By design," MaVynee said. "February was redbud. March was dogwood. May was persimmon. I'm serious! It was *the* showplace!"

The outlying precincts of modern Jacksonville, no matter their status, tend toward a sullen barrenness, and those we passed through to reach MaVynee's old haunts were no exception. Even the larger houses seemed forlornly out of place beside highway-wide, highwayfast avenues whose landmarks all bore trademarks: KFC, McDonald's, Burger King, McDonald's, KFC—the commissaries of a multiplechoice existence. These suburban neighborhoods had always struck me as the far-flung architectural rubble of some exploded city, places one might examine the way a scientist examines a meteorite for evidence of life in a faraway, long-ago world. Once I'd learned about the destruction of Sugar Hill, they seemed that all the more; these silent, sealed houses marked the places where lives had landed when they were blasted out of a close, old, proud community. In the light of their own history, the subdivisions we passed were funerary parks, the houses cenotaphs, their gardens *flores para los muertos*. Abruptly, MaVynee directed me into a narrow dirt trail beside a collapsing stone wall that surrounded what looked like a rusticated park. It wasn't James H. Lewis's lot, though. We had entered a graveyard.

The cemetery had the mark of erstwhile prominence—substantial mausoleums rose amid the headstones, which could hardly be discerned through the rampant thatch of grass and thistle and purple flowering phlox. MaVynee stepped through the weeds to a square whitewashed structure with an ornate iron gate guarded by broken urns. The gate was embellished with a large, cursive, wrought-iron *L*. Within, the marble floor was dank with puddled water and littered with peeled paint; marble walls reflected a dim, beatific light from a stained glass window bearing the banner "He arose." The names on the walls were names I knew. On the right was Abraham Lincoln Lewis, 1865–1947, and two other crypts: that of Mary Lewis, his first wife, who died in 1923 and to whose grave in this mausoleum, every Sunday, A. L. Lewis had paid a visit, sitting a while on the bench outside, where MaVynee now sat, alongside what had been but was not now a gravel path. And the crypt of Elzona Lewis, "Mama Zone," whom A. L. Lewis had married in 1925 and who outlived him, only to marry (or, as MaVynee would have it, "fall into the clutches of") a preacher who ran through her entire fortune (including A. L. Lewis's stocks and bonds and collected souvenirs from trips to Haiti and Africa) in order to fund his empire of "good works."

"He came to Mama Zone and told her, 'I had a dream that you built me a church.'" MaVynee told me, disgusted. "Doggone sure did. I'd have told him, 'Yeah, well, I had a dream, too, and you ain't in it.'" When Mama Zone died broke, after an extensive and expensive stay in a nursing home, her family had to pay for her burial by hocking A. L. Lewis's pocket watch.

Across from A. L. Lewis and his wives was James H. Lewis, who died in 1975 three weeks after his last surviving child, Mary Betsch, who was buried just outside. Outside, MaVynee kicked away the brambles to uncover her mother's headstone, next to that of her father, John T. Betsch, who died while MaVynee was at Oberlin. The cemetery had been established by A. L. Lewis and was run as one of the proudest of his businesses, for "it is a consolation to the Negro to know that he will be buried with proper ceremonies and his grave properly marked." It later became one of the properties—along with the Lincoln Golf and Country Club and the Harrison Tract—that James L. Lewis, in his frenzy to make ends meet, had sold off, and now it belonged to the city of Jacksonville. MaVynee had been lobbying various city and state politicians to rescue the cemetery from the disgrace of its current desuetude, with no apparent result. The enclosure even sounded like a fallow field, with a lonesome chorusing of crickets and, from overhead, a crow's dry rattle. Outside the gates, a line of black limousines passed in slow procession: a funeral cortege headed for somewhere else.

The disrepair of A. L. Lewis's grave was dispiriting, and we drove on, eager to reach the cheerier prospect of MaVynee's showplace garden. After a mile or so, she directed me again, this time up a horseshoe drive through a capacious acre of yard to the front of a sprawling house. The house was made of red brick, the fence by the road was of red boards. "My grandfather James had a thing about red," MaVynee explained. "Which was good because the butterflies loved it." But now even the bricks seemed faded, and whatever had once held paint was raw to the world. The fence was falling down. A television antenna sprawled on the roof; a lamppost leaned into the yard, its carriage lantern knocked catawumpus, swinging by a cord. In the circular drive, paved with white pebbles "bought for Mary's birthday," an encrusted Cadillac had expired onto its rims, its tires flat, its coachwork rotten with rust. "Lord have mercy," MaVynee said. She stepped out onto the drive as onto a foreign planet: "Unh, unh, unh." From one of a number of tall pecan trees, whose trunks MaVynee had painted each winter with lime ("Look how *huge* they are—and I remember when we put them in!"), a large limb had broken, squashing a feral hedge. MaVynee reached through the dry branches into the crushed greenery and came up with a red camellia. "Oh, my God!" she said, twirling the flower slowly as she surveyed the ruined yard. "Oh, my God!"

"This was my little world," MaVynee said. "Everything here, I planted. And look at it. I remember when my grandfather was dying and acting his mean self—that's what killed Mama, I'm serious, putting up with his agitation." Mary Betsch had spent more time in this house than in her own, attending to the old man. She would wake up at night and hear him in the next room slamming dresser drawers until the banging reduced her to tears, his senility focused on a long-lost five-dollar bill. "Who took my five dollars?" he raged and spent his days sitting in the window, with his back to the world, smoking a cigar and counting his money. "Counting his money over and over," MaVynee said. "And I'd just come out here and sit for hours in this gorgeous garden. I was literally being taken over by nature. Literally. So that, I don't know, it made the pain less painful, that's the only way I can describe it. Everything seemed less worse."

This house and yard, along with the cemetery and the Afro headquarters and American Beach, were the realm MaVynee inhabited in the decade after her return from Germany. Back then, when the ranch homes were new and bright and the garden still flourishing, it seemed a world intact, its residents still ascendant despite the loss of Sugar Hill. But the destruction of Sugar Hill was not a glancing or an isolated blow; the society that had lived there and the ideals it had professed were under inexorable attack, as often as not from the forces of "renewal" or progress, from within as well as without.

The true price of "progress" would not show up for decades—MaVynee was still assessing its violence on the day we went by her grandfather's old house and she saw what had befallen her garden. But the cost was accumulating beneath the surface of things long before the demise of the Afro, before even those dark days when James H. sat in his window oblivious to the glory of his garden, counting his money as his life ran out, before that day when Mary Betsch turned her face to the breeze on the hospital pillow and said to her eldest daughter, "The beach, MaVynee. The beach!"

Their nearly simultaneous deaths marked the next big change for MaVynee. She would spend the decade from 1975 to 1985 occupying the edifice of her family's grand creation even as that creation crumbled into dust. Her first move seemed to take her mother's last words as parental injunction—she went to American Beach. Along with the double inheritance came a share in a beach house, which she moved into: James H. Lewis's house, on Gregg Street, facing the sand and the water. For the first time, MaVynee was a full-time resident of the Beach, living in the oldest house in town, one that A. L. Lewis had built even before he built his own permanent residence, next door. MaVynee didn't just decorate the rooms, she integrated them. That is to say, she got out her hammer and knocked out interior walls. The ones that remained she painted blue and orange. ("Everything was orange! Like the moonrise!") Ringed with thirty-four windows and uncluttered with internal obstructions, the house made a passing fine wind funnel, which pleased its new resident. "That house was like I was returning to my own inner psyche, my own inner being," MaVynee said. "I just loved being inside it. I loved the view. I loved how every room had a breeze, after I knocked out the walls. *Ummm!* I was in Paradise." The house changed her as much as she changed it. "That house *healed* me," she said. "That house was absolutely a healing, holistic, spiritual place."

MaVynee had come home from Europe with a sickness in her that she had been fighting in one form or another ever since. Shortly after her return, a doctor diagnosed ovarian cancer, and she got a hysterectomy. Nevertheless, the pain continued, "but not real bad. You know, you'd have bad days and good days, but not real bad. It got horribly worse after Mama died. Really unreal."

Told she might now have colon cancer, but fed up with hospital rooms and doctors and tests and bills, MaVynee decided to combat it—whatever "it" was—on her own, with a regimen of fasting and organic food. "I was real sick then. I didn't let anybody know about it; I just told everyone in Jacksonville I was going back to the Beach. And so I went down there and stayed by myself. Just me and that ocean and wind. And I was really taking a chance, because I didn't know what I was doing. I was just playing it by ear." Her mortal grapple turned her tenure at the Beach into a mystical experience. "Seventy-five to eighty was the time, that was the horror," she said, "although I was enjoying the beach and my house. So the five years there were also some of the most beautiful of my life."

"It's a state of mind," she said. "I think everyone should have a life-threatening something-or-other. Because then you don't take it all for granted anymore. I mean, if you're enjoying a moonrise, and you think it's the last moonrise you're going to see, this obviously has much more meaning than just, 'Oh, well, another moonrise.' Humans are terrible—the way we take everything for granted. And America's worse—this whole culture! Look how you give kids presents for Christmas and nothing means anything: they play with them and throw them away. Everything's so instant. You get a house—yeah, so what? I hear people talk about their houses like *things*—'Yeah, I'm gonna go get me some wall-to-wall carpet. . . .' The way they talk! My house was like a temple for me. It was heaven, because I was living on the edge. Everything was as if tomorrow would not come, so every leaf became something to observe; a rain shower was something that was beautiful—you walked in it. Eating became such a sensual and even spiritual experience. Everything is as if *this may be it*, this is your last of everything. It's almost like the last act of the opera. You've saved up all this energy, now, for this."

Nature was her salve and her salvation. One day when she arrived home, the oleander bush in front of the beach house on Gregg Street had bloomed solid with butterflies, convening for their migration. "Talk about a religious high," MaVynee said. "I was speechless for half an hour." She read the miracle of the butterflies as a favorable prognosis, and it was. "It's been decades since I've been to a doctor," she boasts. Operating from her inherited house, she began spending her inheritance on the best cause she could think of—saving the thing she felt had saved her life.

"I had my little—it was almost like the MaVynee Betsch Nature Foundation, a one-woman show. I would select whatever environmental thing I wanted to support, and I would not only send them the money, I would also send them the game plan." She became a sustaining member of sixty organizations. "I supported biodiversity conferences in Brazil. I mean, I would support everything from Latin America to Africa to New Guinea. When they were killing the baby seals off Peru, Russell Train wrote me and said the World Wildlife Fund needed money to mount patrols. You know, no big deal, I just sat down and wrote a check for $2,000. That doggone Russell Train—if I had all the letters he sent me. . . ."

There were some, watching MaVynee mail away her fortune, who recalled an earlier heir to A. L. Lewis's wealth who lost it to the urgings of a more local doer of good works. MaVynee's generosity exasperated family friends—people like longtime Beach resident Selma Richardson. "Like a jackass, she took the money she got and sent it back to the wildwood forest, out in California," Richardson said. "I don't know whether that shows good sense or not, when she doesn't have a place to live now, does she?" One of MaVynee's contemporaries told me with sodden conviction, at the end of a long afternoon and the bottom of an empty glass, "*I* could'a been a butterfly, if I'd known that's what she wanted to spend a million dollars on!" I once asked MaVynee why she had to give away all her money. She said, "I don't know. I just . . . ," and paused for a long while. "The truth of the matter is, I'm not really good at adding up, and stuff like this. And I was just so enthusiastic and the whole nine yards. Everything was The Cause, and I just got caught up in it."

So in 1980, James H. Lewis's house at the Beach was sold, leaving the family for the first time since its construction. MaVynee's siblings, partners in the house, had wanted to get out anyway; their departure left the Beach with no resident Lewis. MaVynee moved back into Jacksonville. Without a place at the Beach or a house in town—without mother or grandfather to look after her, or funds to rely on—she relocated into the deepest redoubt of her great-grandfather's legacy. "I came home to the only place I knew to go," she told me, "and that was to the Afro."

I had been to the downtown headquarters of the Afro-American Life Insurance Company when the company was still operating, but only as far as the mahogany-walled offices of several Afro executives. In 1987, a couple of years after her residency there had ended but before the company closed, MaVynee gave me a top-to-bottom tour—or, rather, bottom-to-top, from the industrial-moderne, terrazzo-floored, granite-clad, chrome-trimmed reception lobby up to the glass-walled apartment atop the roof garden. The building was self-consciously a memorial—a million-dollar memorial in 1956, when it was completed. It boasted all the latest 1956 amenities, including a $24,000 Westinghouse Electronic-Eye elevator and a $7,500 door on the $12,700 Mosler vault, complementing what the building committee's final report, co-authored by Afro Vice President Mary Betsch, called "a structure modern in all respects . . . moderately ornamental and soundly monumental . . . at once as stately and as sound as the record of our company."

A plaque set into the lobby read:

TO THE NAVIGATOR WHO SAILED WITH THE EARLIEST EXPLOR-
ERS TO THIS CLIME AND BECAME THE FIRST AFRO-
AMERICAN...TO THE FOUNDING FATHERS WHO ESTABLISHED
THIS FINANCIAL INSTITUTION...AND TO THOSE GENERATIONS
DESTINED TO LEAD FURTHER ADVANCES IN SOLIDARITY
THROUGH THE AFRO-AMERICAN CONCEPT THIS EDIFICE IS DED-
ICATED AS A MONUMENT AND AS AN ENDURING SYMBOL OF
ACHIEVEMENT.

Another plaque reprised the "President's Message," A. L. Lewis's favorite verse from Micah. MaVynee led me past these presentations and through the warren of bright, paneled corridors to an older, darker annex, seemingly abandoned to storage except for a suite of rooms whose walls were papered with what looked at first glance to be floor-to-ceiling confetti. The confetti was punctuated with an occasional bumper sticker and a central portrait of Indian activist Russell Means. Decals on the windows declared, "Save the Wildlife." I recognized MaVynee's touch. Here had been her quarters during her half decade's residency in the Afro building. On closer approach, I saw that the wall covering was a collage of hundreds of canceled checks. MaVynee had turned her rooms into her own memorial, dedicated to her own Afro-American concept and testifying to the final use to which she had put A. L. Lewis's money. Each check was made out over MaVynee's signature to a conservation organization or researcher or activist.

At the Afro, the conservation efforts continued, but now more through MaVynee's presence than from her checkbook. She joined local protests against power plants and reckless coastal development. The Afro served her well as a command post. "That was the one nice thing about when I was at the Afro," she recalled, and threatened (with a laugh), "If you tell, I'll pin your ears back. I used to use the Afro stamp machine to send off all my radical environmental stuff—

druuum, druuum, druuum." She made the motions of turning the crank of an old-fangled 1956 stamp machine. "Fafa approved, because when I was down in the basement by myself I could feel his spirit saying, 'Go ahead, child. Go ahead.' "

As it happened, by then the Afro-American Life Insurance Company wasn't much more solvent than MaVynee. The company had long ranked among the top ten of black insurance companies nationwide. Over the years, it had bought out or absorbed the business of other major companies and opened branch offices throughout Florida and in Alabama, Mississippi, Georgia, and Texas. It had become the largest private employer of blacks in the state of Florida. But it was frail nonetheless. "After the war years," Charles Simmons, the Afro's head actuary, told me, "it was a toss-up each year whether or not we were still going to be solvent. Some years you made money; some years you didn't."

After James H. Lewis's retirement in 1967, the Afro presidency went to a man not in the family, I. H. Burney. The transition to a non-related, professional CEO was a crucial juncture that some of the Afro's sister companies—notably Atlanta Life and the biggest of them all, North Carolina Mutual, in Durham—had negotiated successfully. And Burney, a staid businessman in the mold of A. L. Lewis, handled it well. His tenure didn't survive the desire of the coming generation of Lewises to be back at the helm. In 1975, the year of James H. Lewis's death, the presidency passed to James L. Lewis, A. L. Lewis's great-grandson and MaVynee's cousin, and six years later to Lewis's associate and friend turned son-in-law, a New York attorney and former North Carolina Mutual consultant named Gilliard Glover.

Back when young Lewis was still a vice president and Glover still a consulting lawyer, they had arranged a life-prolonging loan from Afro competitor Atlanta Life, which was eventually paid back. During their successive presidencies, Lewis and Glover fired a number of the stodgy old hands—including some top managers whose knowledge was later sorely missed—and hired fresh blood. Tommie Pye was among the new recruits, and shared their optimism. "Well, we thought we were really great," Pye explained. "We thought we were the smartest things on Earth, and we could find the way in which to become very significant to black people. We were all young guys and we thought we knew everything in the world. And of course you never know everything in the world when you're that young." Pye would become head of administration for the home office, but his rise did not serve to preserve his youthful cheer. He said to me about the company's eventual demise, "It was probably inevitable." Prospering in the 1980s and 1990s required size—great size, at least 100 or 200 million dollars in assets, Pye figures, in an era when competitive white companies boasted assets of 50 or 60 billion. The Afro had twelve or thirteen million dollars in assets, but it had liabilities, as well. Pye reckons in retrospect that the company was probably insolvent in the early 1970s, and "certainly so by 1981."

The state agreed, and put the Afro under increasingly strict observation, first in 1980 by the Life Guarantee Fund, a coalition of consulting executives from other Florida insurers who worked to steer the company out of the rough, donating in the process $300,000, and then by the state insurance commission. Meanwhile, the Afro's top management was in disarray. Lewis's frantic attempts to raise money included means that many found questionable. MaVynee and others who knew him in the last years hint darkly at nefarious schemes and scenarios: of whimsical bookkeeping, customers bilked, funds raided and family businesses, like the cemetery and the country club, being pilfered before being jettisoned. MaVynee is given to the occasional exoneration of her cousin. "Remember, Little James needed the money to keep up the Afro's escrow, baby," she once admonished me, contradicting the invective she had recently been pouring on his head. She more commonly referred to him as "Greedy Guts," and she and others describe a man who needed cash to fund his own gambling and partying. His poker debts at Lincoln Golf and Country Club alone could run to the hundreds of dollars a day, and were often expensed to the Afro.

One time I asked MaVynee if she liked him. "Shoot yeah!" she answered. "James was *fun*! He had the most absorbing laugh. He was a charmer. He was more trouble to himself than to anyone else."

But the Life Guarantee Fund decided he was trouble to the company, and recommended his removal. In 1981, he abdicated (though he stayed with the company), and Gilliard Glover became the Afro-American's president. He would be the company's last.

"Little James just didn't know how to run things," MaVynee explained of the company's downward spiral. "He just didn't have that *cohesiveness*. Baby, you don't know how Fafa . . ." she stopped, and swerved away from looming nostalgia. "It just wasn't the same anymore. And then Gil comes in to rescue it from James, and then of course, once Gil gets in it just went on from there to worse."

James L. Lewis's personal decline was precipitous. In 1984, he was arrested for drug trafficking when a shrimp boat he owned was stopped en route from Colombia carrying 569 bales—fifteen tons—of marijuana. He turned state's evidence against his cohorts, and was sentenced to three years in prison.

Meanwhile, on Union Street, Glover was pushing some belated reforms; his lieutenants worked to convert the company from its reliance on premiums collected door-to-door, a system requiring a hefty payroll to service, into one whose customers paid by mail. But the company was still being swamped by market forces and bled by financial shenanigans and in 1987 the state, sure that the Afro's decline had proceeded so far as to put its customers at risk, placed it in rehabilitation and then in receivership, delivering its accounts and obligations to Atlanta Life Insurance Company. Some assets also went to Atlanta, including Tommie Pye, who moved to the Georgia capital and rose within a decade to become Atlanta Life's acting president. He remains haunted by an image from the Afro's final days, when the legal team from the state stormed in to take possession of the company. "Their elevator got to the second floor and the doors opened," Pye told me, "and there in the hall in front of them was MaVynee Betsch, and for a while it was a standoff—these people in suits and carrying briefcases, and this wild woman with her long hair and her nails, barring their path. They just stared. Nobody said anything. And then they marched around her and down the hall."

The team members took no joy in that day's work. "We're the doctors. We try to take care of the patient," one told me, years later. "That being our oldest company, we did our damnedest. We didn't want it to go down." The judge who signed the liquidation order, the man said, had been especially upset by his duty. The executive's account reminded me of what Arnolta Williams said, before the Afro's demise: "I don't think the good solid Caucasians of this state would like to see that company go." In the Jacksonville headquarters, the few last employees tidied up the final paperwork. The last day of the Afro-

American Life Insurance Company weirdly replicated its first, with
seven people sitting in a room. Then they all went home. The company closed its doors for good on July 17, 1987.

After the tour MaVynee gave me of the Union Street headquarters, she and I did not return together to the building until the day in
1993 when we visited A. L. Lewis's overgrown grave and James H.
Lewis's falling-down home. The finale of the ride was as depressing as
its start. The Afro's shining temple of granite and glass, the "enduring
symbol of achievement," was boarded up and empty, a three-story,
block-long coffin of weathered plywood. Months later, vandals broke
in and lit a fire and the back half of the premises—the annex where
MaVynee's suite had been—was gutted. The rest still stood, though—
sound, but hardly stately.

As remarkable as the company's sad demise was the decline of all
around it. Jacksonville's once significant black business center had dis-
appeared. Gone were the Linape, Tropicana, and KP ballrooms,
Manuel's Tap Room, the Strand, New Frolic, and Roosevelt theaters,
N. C. Paul's Interior Decorating studio, Harrison's and Anderson's
department stores, Sophia Nickerson Stark's cosmetics factory and
Nickerson's School of Beauty Culture, Reed's Tailor Shop, the Cuban
Tailor Shop, the Fifty-Fifty Bottling Company, the New Deal Cab
Company, Skinner's Florist, the Richmond Hotel, the Blue Chip
Hotel, Charlie Edd's Motel and Charlie Edd's Smoke Shop, Morris &
Son Bakery, Walker's Commercial and Vocational College, the
Harlem Pharmacy, the Speedway, the Swank and the Broad Street
cleaners, the High Hat Confectionery & Shoe Shine Parlor, the
Avenue Shoe Factory, Steven's Haberdashery, the J. C. Crummel Hat
Company, Maxey's Massage Center, the Courtney Duco Paint
Company, the Broadnax Service Station, L. G. Photo & Music Shop,
Bubba's Coffee Shop, the Waldorf Vandoria Cafeteria, the Blue
Dahlia Barber Shop, and hundreds of other firms large and small that
had made Broad and State and Ashley Streets and their surrounding
neighborhood—The Bricks—a thriving commercial center and the
locus of a self-contained economy. Nearby, Stanton High School was
boarded up as tight as the Afro. Out from town, three other monuments of black prestige had also died. Century Bank had collapsed in
scandal and been sold, and the Lincoln Golf and Country Club and

the Two Spot Night Club had both been demolished and replaced with housing projects.

Certainly, the same blight had ravaged other cities—in fact, every American city with a substantial black populace. Auburn Avenue in Atlanta and Central Avenue in Los Angeles are emblematic of the loss. But Sweet Auburn today at least displays the fossil remains of its former vitality. The businesses in The Bricks are not only closed; all signs of them have vaporized. Ashley Street, the once bustling urban boulevard, is now, along most of its length, a ragged pasture of uncut grass; the sidewalks of the Sunday promenade traverse a midtown tundra. A few area landmarks have survived, among them Mount Olive AME and Bethel Baptist churches and Broad Street's Masonic Hall, and the Clara White Mission, with its barbershop still operating on the ground floor. But the bulk of the black business district, Jacksonville's black downtown, has been obliterated as thoroughly as Sugar Hill, as thoroughly as Jacksonville itself was in 1901 by that year's "thundering, mighty, lurid, storm-wave of fire." This time the catastrophe was quiet. It might accurately be called friendly.

"Let me tell you a story," Charles Simmons said to me. We were sitting in the dining room of his house in Jacksonville, the house where his life had landed when he was bulldozed out of Sugar Hill, back when he was the Afro-American Life Insurance Company's chief actuary. Simmons in fact started the Afro's Actuarial Department; he and his wife, Jolita, who was once A. L. Lewis's secretary (not to mention the beauty-queen cover girl of *The Crisis*'s 1942 Jacksonville issue) live not far from the cemetery where A. L. Lewis lies buried. Simmons has a calm, kind voice and an actuarial deportment: discreet, precise, politic, averse to overstatement, incapable of bombast. The story he wanted to tell me was about a black man in the 1940s he described as "a good friend of my father's."

"This man had gone off to college and studied real estate," Simmons said. "And he came back home to Jacksonville and he had a little confectionery right across from the jail, on Liberty and Union. And all of the lawyers and judges and everybody would come over there and see him and buy canned goods and sandwiches and things like that. And so he decided to tear his confectionery down and build a two-story building with offices for lawyers and judges and so forth. And prior to building it, he talked to the people he was interested in and signed them to leases. He did all the groundwork necessary to build his building, and he built it. And when it was done not one person would move into it. They said, 'I'll pay you the first and last months' rent, and that's it.'

"See, they were friendly on a personal basis," he said. "But a public relationship was something else, and they couldn't move in." The hapless entrepreneur ultimately lost both his building and his business, the price of misjudging the intricate rules of racial association in a postwar world that was changing dramatically, if subtly. The story Charles Simmons told would have sufficed as a standard fable of the old regime, an expression of the long-reigning Southern ethic of "Get close, but don't get too high." But Simmons presented it differently— as a foretaste of what was to come, on a grand scale, when integration changed the world entirely and for the better.

Charles Simmons lived through those changes. He had an understanding nonpareil of the rules of association. When he represented the Afro-American in the Florida Life & Casualty Association, the insurance-industry lobbying group, or when he sat in Tallahassee in the 1940s and 1950s to help write the state insurance code, he had no trouble mingling with white executives on white golf courses, or eating with them and their wives at formal evening dinners. "I guess they made arrangements before I came," he said. But he knew the limits. "I was part of the group and yet not a part of the group."

"Even during segregation, there were relationships between black and white companies," he said, but the professional intimacy was no less imbalanced than the relationship between the ambitious confectioner and the whites who avoided his building. Call it one-way equality. No matter how often blacks sat with the white executives in meetings or mingled with them around the pool and buffet table, when it came to actual commerce the integration worked in one direction only, and ultimately to the black businessman's detriment. "The Afro-American was on the edge of the white community," Simmons said. "The community was real friendly with us. We had a lot of friends who were lawyers and insurance people and IBM people. Any information we wanted from a white insurance company, we could get it. I mean, we were integrated where our suppliers were concerned. But our market was limited to blacks."

The refusal of white companies to sell insurance to blacks—the embargo whose imposition had inspired the creation of the Afro—was finally breaking up. After the Afro and other black companies proved the market's profitability, white firms like Jacksonville's Independent Life began deploying white agents, and hiring black ones, to compete for the business. On the level of abstract virtue, the change was for the better—the decision of white companies to freeze out blacks had been an abomination, and its abolition felt like a true thaw—especially to those blacks hired by majority companies, but even to executives at the Afro. The only catch in the bargain of integrated markets was the unequal competition. It wasn't just the enormous sales force that Independent Life was able to put into the field, and it wasn't just the often lower rates of the majority companies (though they still charged blacks more than they did whites). "The main thing was that we didn't have as many people to sell to as they did," Simmons says, "because they could sell black and white, and we could only sell black."

Musing on that dynamic one day, MaVynee warned me, "Don't get me started on integration. All they were after was the black man's pocketbook."

It reminded me of something else she had said: "The only thing wrong with cynicism is it's wasted on the old." Even at her most cynical, though, MaVynee would not contest integration's importance in providing access to services and opportunities in housing and education and employment. It was a victory long sought and still relished, especially by those many blacks unshielded by immersion in the black economy or the insulating privileges of the black elite.

It was also relished by the elite. No one was more deeply immersed in or more insulated by privilege than Arnolta Williams. Until her death in 1995, she was at the pinnacle of prestige locally (and nationally, having received accolades for outstanding community service from both the Carter and Reagan White Houses), a woman who could afford to go to New York to see on Broadway the shows she was too proud to attend in Jacksonville. "My husband wouldn't let me go to the Jim Crow show, to sit in what we called the buzzard's roost," she told me. "He said he wasn't going to pay to be segregated." Her experience with segregation was the experience of much of the Sugar Hill crowd, and it was generally less violent than demeaning. Williams recalled coming home on the train from New York the day the Supreme Court removed from the dining car the curtain separating the races. "You used to have to go behind this curtain to eat. And they announced there was to be no more curtain," she said, and laughed ruefully. "Oh, it was a terrible day. They wanted us to be the first blacks to go back there, and we said, 'That's all right. We're not really hungry.'"

But having the wherewithal to avoid the worst indignities of Jim Crow could ease life only so far. "You know, the South was a terrible place to live," Williams said. "For me to tell you would sound like something out of a novel. Segregation's a vicious thing. To live in a seg-regated way is a vicious, vicious thing. That's the worst thing, other than a war, that one person can put on another—to *restrict* him. A human being is a human being, and you are no more responsible for being born white than I am for being born the way I am, because that's God's business. And a human being can stand so much. And no more."

Anyone needing to be reminded that integration was a progress from "darkness into light" (as Williams put it, though MaVynee would disapprove of her phrasing) can speak to those who paid the price of securing it—people like Rudolph Williams. Rudy Williams lives on the same street in American Beach where Arnolta Williams had her vaca-tion home. The two aren't related. Rudy Williams is a son of proletar-ian Fernandina—his mother was a domestic worker, and he was a worker in the Fernandina pulp mills for a tenure he once described to me as "forty-one years, four months, and three weeks!"

"I guess you loved it," I goaded him.

"Hell, yeah!" he said. "I loved to be away from it."

His fame among the millworkers, though, is for the successful effort he made to stay on the premises—to stay, that is, on his terms, back when the terms governing black jobs meant menial work only, and only of the thankless kind. His job was, as Williams describes it, "to do whatever those folks say do, or go home." He was denied a pro-motion to skilled "white" work, and when his job unloading railroad cars and log trucks began to ruin his back, he was relegated to the cus-todial detail. "Some of the most ignorant white people in the world, I had to listen to them," he said. "It was hard. But that's all right." Rather than truly integrate in the 1960s, the mill employed such devices as installing a window between rest rooms, so that blacks and whites could see each other washing up.

One day a co-worker yelled to Williams from the cab of his truck that there had been a meeting at the mill about "something you did you wasn't supposed to do." It turned out that the previous night while Williams was cleaning a water fountain in the white-collar area, he had taken a quick drink, and someone saw him. When his bosses notified him that he was being considered for reprimand, he said that he wanted to respond, and when they told him they would save a chair for him, he told them to save three. He showed up with an Urban League lawyer and a union lawyer and then told the two lawyers not to talk, that he would talk, that he just wanted them to witness. And then Rudy Williams read the riot act to the mill management about the slow pace of their desegregation and how he wasn't going to put up with it any-more. Afterward he filed a federal suit against the Container Corporation of America. His home was shot up, and KKK literature was scattered over his yard. Some workers, black and white, tried to curry favor with management by spying on his activities, but with the help of a few allies, black and white, he prevailed, and the mill was inte-grated. Still, Williams was unsatisfied. He helped mobilize the mill's black laborers and took them out of the black Hodcarrier's Union and forced the AFL-CIO to accept them into the more powerful Paper Makers Union. It was a serious coup, one still remembered in Fernandina.

While such fights secured essential rights for blacks nationwide, and while heroic showdowns such as Williams's form the emblematic image of integration in the nation's mythology, the broader effects of the era's changes were less pure, more perverse. For one thing, the immediate tangible commercial benefits of integration accrued exclu-sively to white business. Integration represented the greatest opening of a domestic American market in the nation's history, but the windfall only worked one way. Black customers flocked to the stores and hotels and restaurants—and beaches—where they had formerly been prohib-ited (drawn by the conviction, as the popular phrase went, that "the white man's ice is colder"), and forsook the black businesses to which they had been confined. Whites did not storm across the same open border to spend money in black establishments. For them the border had always been open—at least, officially. The only new opportunity for whites was the opportunity to sell to a new category of customer. Arnolta Williams noted of the effect, "I do know some of the Caucasians who might have been laughing at themselves or kicking themselves, to see what segregation had done to their business."

The results were predictable, if unforeseen. The whole economic skeleton of the black community, so painfully erected in the face of exclusion and injustice, collapsed as that exclusion was rescinded. "When society integrated, it all crumbled," Billy Moore told me. "That meant there were other venues you could go to, other things you were allowed to do. The rest of the city that had been forbidden opened up." Another American Beach resident phrased it in formula, "First we had segregation, and then integration. Then disintegration."

As in the past, the fruits of freedom had been offered on paper but not in coin. Without the coin, emancipation seemed suspiciously like the liberty to begin all over again at the bottom of every new economy. In the 1860s, that had meant tilling forty acres with a mule at the coronation of industrial capitalism; in the 1900s, it meant struggling six decades to establish an independent merchant economy even as the independent merchant was made obsolete by the chain store and the corporation. Now it meant being invited at last to climb the ladder of opportunity just as the lower rungs of that ladder—the rungs of industrial employment—were torn out by the triumph of the service and consumer economy, whose entry-level jobs led nowhere.

Regarding such a system, it is easy to understand Booker T. Washington's favorite diktat, that the success of black liberty required the fostering of black industries and the black ownership of black institutions. It was a shadow of this sentiment that MaVynee directed at the representatives of Amelia Island Plantation in the Franklintown Church: "Black people would be partly *owning* this. There's a difference!" That was the principle that had driven her great-grandfather and grandfather and mother and all the proprietors of all the establishments that had once lined Ashley and Broad Streets in Jacksonville—that blacks would someday own a big enough piece of the American economy to be able to instigate and profit from social change instead of being swept away and destroyed by it, even by change intended for their benefit.

Of the American Civil War, the historian and journalist Lerone Bennett has written: "The war which freed blacks created the economic structures that made black economic development—and hence black freedom—difficult and sometimes impossible." In the 1950s and 1960s, another war was fought, and another tidal wave hit the national fortunes. It brought the black man significant new freedoms on paper. And once again his ability to survive those changes economically was swept away, destroyed almost utterly.

The devastation of commercial black Jacksonville wasn't a refutation of the principle of black ownership. In a way, it reinforced it: black ownership suffered for the simple reason that blacks hadn't owned enough. At the height of black fortunes, there were many who thought that this parallel economy was on the verge of attaining a secure and sustainable state. Certainly the black media would have it so, as would white segregationists eager to demonstrate that separate-but-equal was workable. But there were warnings that all was not well. Sociologist E. Franklin Frazier wrote that the grand stature and glittering promise of the nation's black enterprise proved puny when not viewed through the magnifying glass of a wishful black press. "The total assets of all the Negro banks in the United States [in their heyday in the 1950s] were less than those of a single small white bank in a small town in the State of New York," he noted in 1962, and concluded that "the essential fact is that [blacks] still do not own any of the real wealth of America or play an important role in American business."

Frazier was not delivering a diagnosis of the ills of black business so much as an autopsy. A tad premature, but an autopsy nonetheless. Within a generation of his critique, the black businesses whose pretensions of strength he derided would be gone. His seminal essay, "Bourgeoisie Noire," appeared in 1955, the year that MaVynee moved to Paris, in *Recherches en Sciences Humaines*, an anthology of essays published in that city. When it was republished in the United States two years later, it drew a storm of protest from both white and black readers, before slowly entering the canon of respected sociology. Frazier professed suprise at the outrage, but he could hardly have been caught off guard. His book was a provocation, and as provocation it was not surgical; it was a bomb laid in the foundation of an edifice, aimed at destroying that edifice as thoroughly as the hospital bulldozers did Sugar Hill. In a way the edifice *was* Sugar Hill. Frazier's target was the black middle class and the myths and pretensions that sustained it. Since Frazier himself was black—he was the chairman of the sociology department at Howard University from 1934 to 1959—and firmly of the class that applauded academic prominence and would appreciate the panache of having one's book first published in France, *Black Bourgeoisie* could be seen as an inside job.

Frazier blasted the tenets of economic self-sufficiency—"the current faith," as he put it, "promulgated by Negro leaders, that business enterprise would open the way to equality and acceptance in white America. . . . One of the most striking indications of the unreality of the social world which the black bourgeoisie created is its faith in the importance of 'Negro business,' i.e., the business enterprises owned by Negroes and catering to Negro customers." A more generous critic might have honored the black entrepreneurs for what they tried to create, for the society they tried to foster, and even for the boosterism that was part of that attempt. Even if they eventually failed. After all, the banks whose fortitude Frazier ridiculed were struggling mightily against the handicap of one-way integration: they had to gather their capital in competition with white banks, which were glad to accept black savings accounts, but kept the risk of dispersing it to black borrowers all to themselves, since white banks wouldn't lend to blacks. Instead Frazier portrayed the apostles of black business as opiate vendors, purveying a cheerful myth to an oppressed people, thereby becoming an integral part of the oppression.

The dangers Frazier saw were intramural as well as imposed from without. He coupled the faltering material fortunes of his race with evidence of his race's growing materialism. As the financial structure that A. L. Lewis helped to build began to collapse, so did the philosophical structure that underlay it—the internal integration which had harnessed money and respectability to a moral purpose. In the system that was replacing the old one, things were considerably streamlined: money *was* respectability, and conspicuous consumption, not service, was the mark and obligation of success. The necessity of intellect and culture was omitted almost entirely. The enshrinement of money as a means in the early ideology had led to its apotheosis as an end. "In all the institutions, the canons of respectability were undergoing a radical change," Frazier wrote in *Black Bourgeoisie*. "Respectability became less a question of morals and manners and more a matter of the external marks of a high standard of living." Frazier characterized the black middle class emerging since the Depression as corrupt, pretentious, frivolous, deluded, and devoid of responsibility, especially the old responsibility toward less fortunate members of the race. Among the black institutions adopting the materialist persuasion, Frazier singled out the church for becoming a venue of worldly prosperity, offering a messianic materialism, a sort of divine guidance for the gambling life. It's a contention that does not shock MaVynee. "Didn't you ever go to church and see the hymn numbers posted on the wall, but no one is singing those hymns? The numbers are for the bolito, baby. They're to gamble on," she said, and continued, in her best "cynicism is wasted on the old" voice: "As far as I'm concerned, there's not a lot of difference between Christianity and capitalism anyway."

In *Black Bourgeoisie*, Frazier was describing a shift within a subset of a certain social strata and not every member of the race, but the shift was nonetheless notable because the subset was significant, the same set that both Booker T. Washington and W. E. B. Du Bois had trusted to lead the race out of its troubles. Johnnetta Cole and MaVynee Betsch, prominent members of that set, grew up in the old way: with money, but also with a conservative fiscal mythology. The mythology went beyond the Sunday afternoon lessons about pennies and nickels on the floor of the house in Sugar Hill, and beyond their great-grand-father's admonition that money, like manure, grew things when applied well but stank in excess. Both women recall the time when A. L. Lewis delivered, along with a new play ball, the admonition that "You are Lewises. I can give you gifts, but no one's obligated to give you anything. You have to produce." Even their toys came wrapped in lessons, indoctrinations into the belief that money should be accumu-lated through industry and discipline and thrift (activities worthy in themselves) and used to fund autonomy and dispel poverty and acquire culture, which would confer respectability, which would defend the race from attack and support its aspirations: in other words, the belief that money was a tangible agent serving a moral system.

Cole encountered the new ethic, the new materialism, as soon as she left home in the 1950s to become a freshman at Fisk University, in Nashville—a school that, despite its manifest virtues, was rife with "'bougie' young women [who] sat around boasting about their fathers' medical and legal practices, their mothers' fur coats, and speculating on which [medical student] they were going to marry," Cole wrote in *Conversations*. "I was distinctly turned off by what seemed like endless discussions about money."

The people ultimately elevated to prominence by this material standard were not the doctors and lawyers and exemplars of industry and thrift (and definitely were not the opera singers and the anthropologists) but those who made their money in the flashier rackets of sports and popular entertainment and gambling. The Jacksonville dentist's warning in *The Crisis* of January 1942, of "the danger to Negroes when members of the race, for purely selfish purposes, entered into certain types of business which are designed to drain the Negroes' purses but are destined never to lift the race one iota, either economically or morally," had proven prescient. The divide between those out to lift the race and those out to drain the purse had been the firmest barrier within the black business community; now it tumbled. Everyone sat at the gambler's table.

And why not? The prominence of the earnest businessman had, after all, been predicated on a straightforward wager—the wager that his earnestness, his uncynical subscription to the vaunted American ideal of honorable enterprise, would gain his race acceptance and respect. It had gained neither. As James Weldon Johnson noted, if industry and culture earned a black man anything in the eyes of whites, it was invisibility. Later, it earned him something even worse, when the captain of black business was betrayed by the "impartiality" of integration. The wager had been doubly lost. The winner was the cynic, the trickster who saw the ideal of honorable enterprise as a public relations front for an American economic system that was in truth a game without rules, a scam that deserved to be scammed and taken for whatever it was worth, and not something to be trusted or patiently courted with integrity and thrift.

Jacksonville's blacks might quibble with Frazier's condemnations, but their descriptions of the Afro-American Life Insurance Company's final years sound suspiciously Frazieresque. "You take the case of the

Afro-American Insurance Company and how they went under. That was a case of bad, bad management, all up the line," George Green, the Franklintown native and American Beach resident, told me one stormy day in his darkened house on Lewis Street (an antic bolt of lightning had knocked out the electricity). "Most of the older folks were passing away, and the younger ones were picking it up, and they couldn't handle it. They wanted to get rich fast, I guess you might say. They couldn't seem to handle it like their fathers and forefathers did."

Green's opinion echoes throughout Jacksonville almost without dissent. James L. Lewis and Gilliard Glover are chided for their style. What Tommie Pye described as youthful confidence, others in Jacksonville saw as a cocky ostentation. Lewis was a gambler and reckless social roué with an affection for the dog track and the Monterey Club; Glover was known for fine foreign cars, and expensive suits and jewelry. Whatever the merits of their corporate husbandry, they both gave the appearance of living high and fast even as their company languished.

"Little Jimmy did something he had no business doing," Arnolta Williams fumed to me one day, referring to the shrimp boat escapade. It seemed to her and others that James L. Lewis had been convicted of the lesser of his crimes. "Previous to that, he was not even conducting the affairs of the company! Had he done what he did, it would have been one of those things. But it was worse, because he represented a black business that was respected all the years. It was big business. Thriving. It was at the center of everything. Everything! Having that company, the first life insurance company in the state of Florida, was a nucleus of inspiration." Of the man who started that company and exemplified that inspiration she said, "He wasn't qualified academically to take a part in the stock market or whatever. Abe Lewis stopped school in sixth grade to run a turpentine still." But he built an institution "out of his own good brains," she said. "And from *that* to what that boy did to that company: giving it away. It's something, isn't it?"

Harriett Graham, a former Sugar Hill resident and frequent visitor to the house at American Beach owned by her daughter, Joyce, and son-in-law Billy Moore, told me, "A. L. Lewis came from a generation that had a lot of motherwit, if you want to call it that. And apparently they didn't have the fear, and they were smart enough to carry through on their vision." Graham worked as an accountant at the Afro, and her father was a district manager. "See, those people in those days, they did so many things that were *necessary* and *important*," she said in her careful voice. "And I guess that's why I'm a little taken aback when I come to think of that other generation I've experienced in my life—that they can't appreciate the necessity of maintaining this vision. Too many young people, I don't care what color they are, don't realize what has gone before in establishing something like the Afro-American Insurance Company. You know? They seem to take it for granted. But it's something that was *done*, and it takes constant *doing*. You don't have to have a lot of money. Just use your energy. But their attitude is, The quicker I get it, I destroy it. So they have taken to destroying . . . Well, I won't say 'destroy'—they have torn down."

The worst tearing down was of principle, not property. Long before its final collapse, the Afro had forsaken by increments its mission of elevating the black community, of fulfilling in a larger sense the motto on the company logo, "A Relief in Distress."

"I've heard stories," Tommie Pye told me. "Through the 1920s and 1930s, everyone who wanted their child seen by a doctor would come to the Afro-American, because there was a doctor there to be seen. There was an old scale there, and people would come by and get on the scale to weigh themselves. It was a beacon. What the Afro did also, it had a cadre of professional people and some money to offer a lot of support, in a lot of different ways, during the civil rights trouble. Most of the insurance companies did that. You may not be out there carrying a sign, marching, but you found a way. You provided the food. You bailed people out of jail who were in jail. You provided the attorney to go and represent someone. You found the homes for various people to stay in. The Afro-American did all these things. Again, a lot of people did not know that, but it was very well done."

Many people knew exactly how well done. Jacksonville resident Beverly Jackson grew up with the Afro. Every week of her Jacksonville childhood, the "'surance man" came to the door to collect the premium on her parents' policies. But her first encounter with the Afro's higher purpose came in her junior year in high school. It was 1972, and the civil rights and antiwar protests were roiling even Florida. When the Duval County school board decided to contain protests by erecting fences around its schools, Jackson led students in a coordinated response. "I got all the kids to walk out of the high school," she told me, and then added, almost as an afterthought, "Oh, the other thing I did was, we took over the principal's office, and I was at that time in eleventh grade, and it wasn't too cool to do that." Standing on the principal's desk with a megaphone, Jackson announced the walkout. Then she used the principal's telephone to call her family's lawyer. Sure enough, the police and the riot squads arrived in force and began wrestling students into police cars, "and of course everybody was fighting and it was getting crazy." Her lawyer, meanwhile, had called the place where such emergencies were brokered in Jacksonville, the home office of the Afro-American Life Insurance Company. The Afro building also housed the branch offices of the NAACP, and it was used to transforming itself into a rapid-response field headquarters. By the time the students began arriving in the city jail, the Afro's lawyers were there to monitor their treatment, post their bail, and file the legal briefs necessary to insure that they would not be held overnight. Beverly Jackson got off light, with a permanent expulsion from Duval County schools. She left Jacksonville to resume her education in Washington, D.C., with a high regard for the Afro-American.

The company's main expression of racial solidarity was in its daily dealings, a culture of small generosities that accompanied the culture of fiscal scrupulosity. Harriett Graham's father, LeRoy Bazzell, ran his own small insurance company before becoming an Afro-American district manager in Daytona Beach and Saint Augustine and, later, an independent contractor in Jacksonville with a house in Sugar Hill. He exemplified both sides of that culture. "He was a thorough person," Graham told me. "He was a real businessman. I was at one time his secretary." She laughed. "Boy, he was strict. If I was a penny off and couldn't find it, I had to work to find that penny. Sometimes I couldn't find it, it didn't matter how hard I worked with those books, and I'd go to bed and dream where that penny was." It stood to reason that her father would have an evil eye for light fingers among his agenting staff, and a stern response. But he also pushed hard within the company for policies lenient toward agents and customers alike. For years, white insurance companies were notorious for signing black customers to policies that would mature, and pay back dividends, in twenty years, only to drop them on a pretext in the nineteenth year. Graham's father pushed the Afro to accept the refugees of such cut-offs as new customers with immediate full benefits, so that they wouldn't forfeit the equity they had accrued, even though they had accrued it somewhere else.

The Afro's gradual betrayal of such racial responsibility weighed as heavily on the minds of its old employees as the fraying of sound business practice. For most of them, in fact, social solidarity and sound business practice were one and the same thing and their desertion all of a piece. When Graham's father encouraged a policy whereby the Afro would collect from some customers a year's premium in advance as a security cushion, so that customers would not get cut off when they missed a single payment, he also insisted that the agents be paid their commission on the extra income. The checks to the agents were already cut when the home office interceded, declaring that since the extra money had arrived in a lump sum and was not collected through weekly visits, the agents would not receive a commission on it. For the manager who had designed the plan, not to mention for the agents, it was a crushing affront.

As the idea fell out of favor that money's worth depended on its provenance, that gains ill gotten were thereby of ill repute, a new opportunism took over, and not just at the Afro. At its best, the opportunism was neglectful of social obligation, at its worst it was an everyman-for-himself ethic of willing predation. It might appear to hysterical whites that the gainful predation was mainly practiced by black criminals on white passersby, but the more significant predation was intramural. It could be lawful, through a commerce in which the dollar was the only thing of value, to be gained without regard to the circumstances of the race. But often it was larcenous, in instances where major black institutions, like banks and insurance companies and charitable institutions, used the language of racial solidarity and race pride to charm the money out of black pockets for services and benefits that were never rendered.

Beverly Jackson eventually witnessed the other side of the Afro's operation. She spent a dozen years in Washington after her protest got her evicted from the Duval County schools, earning degrees in communications and sociology and running an after-hours jazz club while holding "bread and butter jobs" in television and as a legal secretary.

Legal practice in the nation's capital provided a wide window on cynical business practices, and eventually Jackson got weary of the view and found her way back to Jacksonville, where she hoped to revive her idealism by working with blacks in black-run organizations. "I wanted to get away from what I thought was a European ethic" is how she puts it.

She secured a job with the bishop of the Jacksonville diocese of the African Methodist Episcopal Church, whose office was in the Afro-American building, and eventually she moved over to work for the Afro itself, as the staff assistant to the president for public relations. She reported to Gilliard Glover and coordinated at his behest public events of the charitable sort. The idea was to take underprivileged black children to the opera, to the planetarium, or arrange tutoring to help them get through school. Her office was the Afro's department of good works, and the programs she administered were textbook models of racial cooperation, since much of the money to run them was solicited from white corporations. They were also, Jackson related, models of race pride perverted to selfish ends. "It was a scam," she said. "A flimflam." The money collected for the programs, she claims, "just never materialized. These black kids never saw the money. It went to other places." The "scam" worked well for all its sponsors. "It was a give and take," Jackson said. The white banks and store chains got the public relations value of supporting a black cause, and black executives to present to their boards, and in return certain blacks got funding. But, as Jackson noted, they weren't always the blacks intended. In such ways, when the old ethic of racial uplift morphed from an honest battle cry into an advertising slogan, it simultaneously morphed into a weapon of racial destruction.

"Prior to integration (which for all its good definitely weakened some of our most valuable institutions), self-help was a way of life," Johnnetta Cole observed in *Conversations*. "Ironically, decades ago, during times of more overt and more brutal oppression than we now experience, we possessed a reservoir of values that enabled us to survive and in many instances thrive." That ethic of self-help was thrown on the same dust heap as the devalued respectability.

"It's weird how all this happened," MaVynee said. "When we were growing up, everybody was sticking together. We knew this was our survival. The Afro provided the money for the houses. It provided the money for the children to go to college. Everybody looked to the Afro. Daddy got up in the middle of the night to get people out of jail. Mama's whole reason was that if somebody didn't have money to bury people, she and Daddy would help them. Everything was like this *cause*. okay, now. Fafa's been a long time gone; integration is coming. It was like the Afro no longer had a reason anymore. And while the Afro was trying to adjust, it is as if the whole black society was also realigning itself. Because here before, we had to turn inward and help each other, because there was an enemy out there. Once the enemy is gone, whatever little minute internal conflicts you faced, they become exaggerated. So once the integration started, the thing that bound black people together was no longer there. So that capitalist dog-eat-dog psyche came out. Black people picked on each other to get to this world—this white world, whatever that garbage meant—that we were now programmed to be accepted into. We had to get this job, this house so we could be in a white neighborhood; we had to do this thing, even if this meant fighting another black. *Ohhhh*, I don't know. . . . It was just a time when things didn't end up just at all."

In the prominent absence of some of those people who could have explained the era to me—James L. was dead and Gilliard Glover, now a preacher in a suburb of Daytona Beach, refused to be interviewed—MaVynee pushed me to contact other survivors who would remember the way things were. Our trips to Jacksonville were punctuated with emergency yells and sudden swerving stops, whence she would bang on the door of some house and introduce me to whoever answered. "This is the young man I told you about who is writing a book on American Beach," she'd say, and sometimes she would go on to confide, "I even have a title for him." The title she had come up with, referring to the fact that American Beach has a dozen streets, was *Twelve Gates to the City*. "You know, like the spiritual," she would remind a startled, ambushed, prospective interviewee, and then break into a stanza in the back of her sovereign throat: "Twelve gates to the city, hallelu!"

Sometimes my journalistic reputation survived my introduction, and I would return for a formal interview. One of the people I talked to was Leota Davis. MaVynee came along. The woman who met us at the door was frail and straight-postured and wearing a gray dress with dark gray and red flowers on it, and a black brooch that read, "Praise the Lord." Her house had a porticoed dignity to it: on the dilapidated west Jacksonville street, it seemed forlornly haughty, like a Pullman in a freight lot. Her car, parked in her side yard, was protected within a paddock of chain-link fence, but her living room was inviting and relaxed. Bright colored lights blinked from a ceramic Christmas tree on a card table in the corner. Pink silk roses made a centerpiece for a marble coffee table in front of a couch, where she motioned for us to sit. MaVynee opted for the piano bench.

Davis began her career working in a laundry and as a cashier in a barbecue stand in a small south Georgia town, the town she was born in in 1900. "In Quitman, where I come from, it was almost slavery," she said, until the day she met one of the officers of the Afro-American Life Insurance Company. "Mr. Herbert said, 'Why don't you come and work at the Afro? You'll do good. You talk so much, you'll do fine.'"

Davis started out working the east and west quarters of Jacksonville, selling what Arnolta Williams called "under-the-arm accounts" in reference to the account ledger the agent had to lug around to every customer's door to collect the premium every week. Davis walked her rounds on foot and seized whatever opportunity arose along the way. "When I'd go to funerals," she said, "I'd sell insurance at a funeral." The policies cost ten cents a week for a family; Davis was paid thirty-five cents out of every dollar she sold, plus seven dollars a week. It was, relative to Quitman barbecue standards, prosperity— "Folks said, 'Chile, you've come a long way, for colored people'"—and soon she was in the office of the president's secretary, requesting an appointment to ask for a loan to buy herself a house. She had found one she wanted for $2,200, including a side lot. "And I heard his voice through the door, saying 'Anything she wants, you get it for her.'"

"A. L. Lewis meant business," Davis said. "But he was gentle and kind. He was a big deal. There were as many white folks as blacks in there, on the same-name basis with A. L. Lewis. None of this 'You're Mr. Barnett, I'm Abe.' He was *respected*. A. L. Lewis had built the Afro into a million dollars, and then the young people done run through it. It's a pity and a shame. It was the first colored company to be worth a million dollars. All Little James Lewis done was gamble that all away."

Davis recounted, seemingly for MaVynee's benefit, her last encounter with the company's last executive. "I looked at Gil and said,

'Lord, you have done closed the Afro,'" she said, shaking her head mournfully. "When I pass that building, I almost cry."

"You're tellin' me!" MaVynee said.

Many others felt a personal tie to the imposing headquarters building on Union Street, not the least among them Arnolta Williams, who was an Afro shareholder and whose husband, Dr. I. E. Williams, had served on the building construction committee with Mary Betsch, back in the fifties. On the day of our 1987 meeting, she had heard a rumor that the company was about to lose its headquarters, and she interrupted our interview to telephone President Glover at his office. "I'm going to find out what's going on," she told me, and the ensuing conversation, even just the half I could hear, revealed to me the kind of respect prevailing between the generations in Jacksonville and reminded me that steel magnolias also come in black. "Yes," Williams drawled to the secretary who answered. "How do you do today? This is Mrs. Williams. . . . That's right, that sweet old lady that has made Jacksonville sweeter for having me as a citizen of this great commu-nity. . . . Well, I'm not conceited a bit," she hummed, and then, with the suddenness of a bolt locking in a rifle breech, "Where's that boy? Where's Gil?"

There was another pause. "Now don't be fooling me," she instructed, a note of warning creeping into her voice. "Yeah, well, to leave a message for Gil to call me is for the birds. But you tell him, *Damn it, I want him to call me!* . . . Ex-*actly* what I said. Don't brush it off. Tell him I said, *'Damn it, he better call me!'* Okay?"

And in the moment it took her to slam down the receiver and turn her face to mine, she became once again the decorous nonagenarian aristocrat, her charm unruffled, patiently awaiting my next question. "I cuss 'em all out," she confided.

Harder than the threatened loss of the Afro building, the tangible embodiment of Williams's generation's achievement, was the deeper, more gradual loss of what it represented—the ethic that linked com-mercial practice, good works, and racial pride. The fall of commercial black Jacksonville left casualties. In the wake of the closure of the black-owned Century Bank, it was said, men had killed themselves. The fall of the Afro was hardly less traumatic. Ed Halfacre had come to the Afro in 1981 at the behest of Gil Glover, only to be disillusioned by the improprieties he uncovered that were undermining the company. "I'd read too much about A. L. Lewis. I didn't read enough about James L. Lewis. You understand what I'm saying?" When he termed what he discovered at the Afro "heartbreaking," Halfacre was being literal: he suffered a near-fatal heart attack in 1988. "I am sure it was due to the tension I had built up during that period," he told me. "Because I was mad as hell. I had a hair-trigger temper, and I was ready to fight about a lot of things. And I was mad at myself, because I saw a pattern for some things that I should have done something about. But I didn't want to have another heart attack. So I chose to forget all the junk that I'd seen." The larger community, likewise, chose to forget. Its wounds were of shame as well as anger, and the silence that healed them also sealed away the history of what was lost. As had happened with the incandescent life and igno-minious death of Bessie Coleman, pride in achievement became con-founded with its evil sibling, the humiliation of defeat.

On a spring morning years after the closing of the Afro, I sat in Harriett Graham's dining room, in a northern suburb of Atlanta, talk-ing about the importance to her of her father's teachings—her father, who would not excuse an agent's irregularity or his daughter for miss-ing a penny on the books, who had argued that forgoing an extra mea-sure of profit to aid a hapless customer might be a matter of decency. Graham is nothing if not circumspect, a poet and writer in her spare time, a resolutely introspective woman for whom uttering an ill word, even against her enemies, is difficult to the point of impossibility. Once, when I had asked her about the last regime at the Afro, she had said, "They lacked . . ." before pausing long seconds to pick just the right noun. "Precision," she said finally. That day, she had been talking about the decline of the Afro's climate of conscience, the hegemony of cold profit that, she implied, could turn nasty on those who resisted. It had turned nasty on her father, she said, and I inferred that as his con-servative "precision" and charity became anachronistic, he felt himself a target of ostracism and even abuse. Now, in Atlanta, Graham and I concluded our interview on the brink of the same hard territory but without venturing further, until I was preparing to thank her and say good-bye.

Then she said, "There's something I want to show you," and disap-peared off into the back of the house, leaving me to inspect a sideboard cluttered with sculptures she had glued together out of seashells she'd gathered at American Beach. She returned with a book, an anthology of poems containing several of her own. She opened it to a page, and I asked her if she would read her selection out loud. "Um-hmm," she said, in her birdsong voice. "Dear Dad," she read:

> 'Most thirty years you've been gone.
> It's still a fad
> To rub it in
> To destroy
> Knock down monuments
> Build impregnable walls
> To do dirt
> Cover with a lie
> Just as in time B.C.
>
> Unlike Job
> You lost patience
> Sanity
> Banged your head
> Took off for hell—
> (I won't believe)—
>
> If you're there
> Must be in company
> Of those who laughed in glee
> As their dirt drove you up the wall,
> Since most of them
> Went down the drain—
> "Company" and all.

"Get it?" she asked me as she closed the book. "Okay, my daddy committed suicide." Her whisper quieted to barely a breath. "And I can't talk about it." And she quickly left the room.

Two hundred and five years before MaVynee had departed her house in American Beach and made her way to the Afro, another traveler, equally besotted with nature, blazed her trail. William Bartram, a British naturalist, had come to Amelia Island to visit the Egmont estate, the elder sister to the Harrison plantation that would later be established to its south. He explored the same maritime oak forest that MaVynee would later exult in and that the developers from Texas would demolish, and then, as he continued his journey south, he endured a small, personal skirmish.

It was a trifling incident, really, but significant enough for Bartram to interrupt his celebration, in his *Travels*, of every leaf and cloud, the activities of every bird and spider, to record it. One of the other passengers in the boat that took Bartram down the coast had announced his intention of enlisting as Bartram's lieutenant and sharing his mission to explore the outback of this amazing new continent. But as the party approached Cow-ford on the Saint Johns River, the wilderness ferry crossing that would later become Jacksonville, this fellow decided that, after all, "not relishing the hardships and dangers, which might perhaps befal us," he could go no farther. Bartram noted their separation without remorse. "Our views were probably totally opposite," Bartram wrote:

> He a young mechanic on his adventures, seemed to be actu-ated by no other motives, than either to establish himself in some well-inhabited part of the country, where, by following his occupation, he might be enabled to procure, without much toil and danger, the necessaries and conveniences of life; or by industry and frugality, perhaps establish his fortune. Whilst I, continually impelled by a restless spirit of curiosity, in pursuit of new productions of nature, my chief happiness consisted in tracing and admiring the infinite power, majesty, and perfec-tion of the great Almighty Creator.

Thus, in the year before the American Declaration of Independence, Bartram described *in situ* a defining natural feature of the future nation's ecology—the estrangement of practical and reli-gious concerns, the divorce of money from mission, of commerce from "the cause." It would become also the essential internal struggle within the business ecology of post–Civil War Jacksonville and within the ecology of post-Depression black society. And also within the Lewis extended family. For a while, A. L. Lewis and others like him had managed to meld the two sides of the American character and create a vital synthesis of pragmatic moneymaking and enlightened motivation. But only for a while. Even as Bartram's footsteps described the course of MaVynee's coastal commute, the schism that cleaved him from his fellow traveler presaged her course among her countrymen, as A. L. Lewis's synthesis fell apart.

MaVynee's residency in the Afro headquarters wore on from three years to four to five, but even as she became a fixture, she was increasingly alienated. The building itself might be the ultimate material expression of her forebears' intent, but the scene within was more and more foreign to her eyes. To those at work there, she seemed lunatic. Even before her move to American Beach, she had begun a metamorphosis. Now, while the company drifted into what seemed to her like soulless opportunism unconnected with "the cause," she drifted the other way, into the sorcery of untrimmed nails and untrammeled behavior, a wild-haired Cordelia loose on the heath of generational betrayal. It was as if, while the connection between money and service cracked asunder, MaVynee fell to one side, giving up her fortune to heed the obligations of altruism, and giving up her security to better regard the power and perfection of nature. In pursuit of their fortunes, the necessaries and conveniences of life, her counterparts fell to the other side, forsaking altruism altogether.

One day in 1980 at the Afro, MaVynee sat talking with her cousin in the posh, mahogany preserve of the president's office, the office "Little James" had fought to secure as his birthright as a Lewis, from which he presided with a vainglory at odds with his kingdom's poverty, and he said to her, "MaVynee, I really envy you."

"I go, 'Whaaaat?'" MaVynee recalled. "My lifestyle had been getting weirder and weirder. And he said, 'I guess there's a little frustrated free spirit in us all.' I said, 'I guess so, James. I guess so.'"

Some while after Lewis vacated the president's desk and Gil Glover assumed it, the company wanted MaVynee's apartment back, and it was clear even to the freest of spirits that the time had come to go. In 1985, she moved out, leaving behind most of her belongings, such as they were, and the room papered with checks. "Anyway, I was sick of it at the Afro," she said. "I told myself come hell or high water, I was moving back to the Beach." It would seem like both, but she did. She had $70 to her name, and no place to stay.

The town MaVynee had left as a house-seller, she returned to as a vagabond. For all the purposeful intention she claims behind her current homelessness, it wasn't like that at first. She was not yet practiced as a gypsy. She wasn't pursuing any plan of protest. She was just a fifty-year-old woman at the end of her rope, on the street, without a home. "I was scared," she told me. Afraid of being mugged, she would walk all night, retiring to sleep on empty porches as soon as the sun came up. She hid her possessions under a vacant house and cooked on a Coleman stove. It was November when MaVynee arrived back at the Beach. When the weather turned cold, she took a lesson from M. Boralevi and lined her clothes with the *Fernandina Beach News-Leader*.

Slowly a life presented itself. "I know that I am destined," MaVynee once told me, "because whenever something bad happens to me, it always turns out to be good." She encouraged herself with the recollection of a catastrophe she had endured while traveling in Europe. She was coming north through the Balkans on the Orient Express, headed for the Wagner festival at Bayreuth, when someone stole her luggage. She never did make it to Bayreuth, but when she got off the train in Zagreb to report the theft, carrying no ticket, no money, no extra clothes, she was treated, as in Germany, "like a queen," only better. When the townspeople discovered she was an opera singer, they adopted her. She was invited to sing spirituals and arias in an impromptu concert (in a hotel restaurant, accompanied by a cabaret orchestra), and then led up the hill to visit the childhood home of Zagreb's favorite daughter and venerated diva, Zinka Milanov.

When MaVynee had been at the Beach some weeks, residents there began asking her to house-sit. One was the woman who owned MaVynee's former home, who now asked her to stay in it while she sojourned in Saudi Arabia. Another family, stumbling on MaVynee preparing a meal in a vacant lot, invited her to keep her few possessions in their basement. She "refrigerated" her food in a cast-off strongbox, using ice packs she chilled in the El Patio freezer. A New York philanthropist—a woman who shared MaVynee's interest in but-

terflies and remembered her aid to butterfly causes not so long ago
when MaVynee was flush—began sending her $25 or $40 a month,
now that the tables were turned. "It will come back to you," A. L.
Lewis had told her, of money spent in service, and a little bit of it did.

Even with MaVynee's newfound sponsors and friends, American
Beach offered no sanctuary from what she had been fleeing when she
fled the Afro. The schism that had sundered everything else had sundered the Beach as well. Integration pulled the rug out from American
Beach's historic raison d'être, as blacks flocked to formerly all-white
beaches. But that was the least of it. There was a more profound integration at work, one that insured MaVynee's continued isolation and
estrangement, her exile in her own country's heart.

The materialism that had transformed black respectability and the
opportunism that infected the black economy was not something
peculiar to blacks. MaVynee called it "the white man's disease," and
she wasn't far wrong. Even E. Franklin Frazier admitted, responding to
his critics' complaints, that conspicuous consumption and runaway
consumerism characterized equally the *nouveaux riches* of other minority and immigrant groups, whether Jewish or Italian or Irish. But it was
even more universal than that. The new ethic was quintessentially
American.

A. L. Lewis's ethic had also been quintessentially American, but of
an older America, the America of the patriot and the Puritan. His con-
flating of mission and profit was worthy of John Winthrop; his thrifti-
ness was a Ben Franklin hand-me-down. This was not only the
America Lewis emulated but the America he tried to integrate his family into. No wonder he failed. The rebuff of his generation of earnest
black entrepreneurs was a sign that his America survived in rhetoric
only.

Younger blacks read the majority culture more accurately. In a
generation they had leapt from Puritan to modern times, and the
America they saw was not that of the yeoman laborer and civic-minded
businessman but one of pervasive credit consumerism and retail
respectability. The way black culture translated that new ethic might
occasionally discomfit the majority, but it would be hard for the majority culture to disown. If black enterprise had moved into "certain types
of business which are designed to drain the Negroes' purses but are

destined never to lift the race one iota," was that so unworthy of a culture that made multimillionaires of pop stars and basketball players? If black children killed themselves over brand-name sneakers or over the color of their bandannas, was that unworthy of a culture in which even the clothing of the elite was transformed into uniforms by an ostentation of high-status logos? If those same children lost themselves in drugs, was that unworthy of a culture that had obviated the intermediate steps between money and fulfillment—a culture that promoted passive pleasure at the flip of a dial, and the grail of store-bought ecstasy? If gambling and entertainment have eroded the old injunction "You must produce," it's not just among blacks. In our age, the bolito is run by the states and the economy by speculators. International Telephone & Telegraph Corporation has downsized its bread-and-butter engineering to make easier money in Las Vegas as a corporate croupier and concierge. Arts and education languish in a society in which only insipid consumer images are judged wholesome enough to feed the American family, in which adulthood and success are devoted not to attaining complexities of introspection and knowledge but to securing a retirement playing games behind a gate.

The black bourgeoisie, Frazier observed, was in "its behavior as well as its mentality . . . a reflection of American modes of behavior and American values." Its members "wanted to forget the Negro's past, and they have attempted to conform to the behavior and values of the white community in the most minute detail." That their emulation would be "acute" only made sense. Such is aspiration. Frazier called the new black middle class "exaggerated Americans."

It wasn't as though the world of black business and black life had suffered an alien invasion at midcentury. All the elements that prevailed in the end had been there in the beginning. The shift was as subtle as it was substantial, as was the shift in America. But at the bottom of the shift was a role reversal: money now ruled the society it once had purported to serve. It wasn't business's fault, so much as the absence of other structures in church and community and college and media and art to challenge business's hegemony and assign a mission to life that transcended the material. When John Hope, the president of Morehouse College, delivered a speech in 1898 called "The Negro in Business" to the Fourth Atlanta University Conference, his formulation anticipated Frazier's by half a century. "We are living among the so-called Anglo-Saxons and dealing with them," he said. "They are a conquering people who turn their conquests into their pockets." His description of this culture was a mournful one, for all who resided in it and even for those who ruled over it. "Business seems to be not only simply the raw material of Anglo-Saxon civilization," Hope wrote, "but almost the civilization itself."

It was an open question whether or not such a civilization could escape the fate that Frazier predicted for the blacks enlisted into it: "suffering from nothingness," deprived of "both content and significance." The road of those compelled to give up a black culture they couldn't remember in order to court a white approval they couldn't attain led, in Frazier's words, to "the process of becoming NOBODY." In MaVynee's case, resisting that course had helped to make her an outcast. She was a wounded holdover of the old way, a woman whose cultural triumph was supposed to hasten an integration into an America that had already disappeared but whose wealth had tied her to an emergent America whose ethic she opposed. She plucked out her offending eye, and gave away the money that was no longer anything but money. But she was still an outcast, even on the beach resort of her family's creating.

"At the summer resorts where the black bourgeoisie gather to display their wealth," Frazier wrote, "the descendants of the old respectable families must defer to the underworld elements, who, through their money, have risen to the top of Negro 'society.'" American Beach's old guard would not recognize that statement on its face: they don't kowtow to criminals, and the Ritz-Carlton and Amelia Island Plantation, not pretensionless American Beach, are where the wealth parades. But everyone in the old guard would acknowledge the insight in Frazier's hyperbole, in an era when the town's most solid house (constructed of coquina block, and now belonging to Annette Myers) was built by Mrs. Hippard, the Fernandina gambling and saloon queen; an era when the amount of land at the Beach still controlled by the Afro's founding families is dwarfed by that controlled by the fortune of Jacksonville's one-time numbers king; an era when the town's only sustaining outside income is partying teenagers, in for a Sunday night. Surely the old order had been toppled, and the old sources of uplift dashed from their pedestals.

According to many among the early families, the seeds of the Beach's decline were being sown before its heyday, during A. L. Lewis's last years, when liquor made its incursion. "Mr. A. L. tried to keep it so that you would not have any whiskey on the beach," Harriett Graham told me. "And no businesses, of course, that would be on the beach-front, catering to the whiskey. Somewhere along the line, he was over-ruled."

MaVynee remembers the arguments that roiled her usually com-posed family when Evans's Rendezvous sought (successfully) the Beach's first liquor license. A. L. Lewis opposed the occurrence, but the trend was unavoidable. His son, James H., the Riverboat Gambler, would be one of the Rendezvous's most avid customers, and the Rendezvous would quickly become the institutional center of town, at the hub of a bustling covey of summertime juke joints and refreshment stands like El Patio, the Sweet Tooth, the Quick Snack, Net's Place, Little Zeng's Restaurant and Ice Cream Shop, and Reynolds's Sandwich Shop.

The new Beach establishments were mild enough by juke joint standards—though, as Marsha Dean Phelts expressed it in her 1997 book *An American Beach for African Americans*, "At Evans's Rendezvous, people checked every fiber of social refinement at the door." If they could get in the door, that is. By virtue of its popularity alone, the Rendezvous succeeded in defiling A. L. Lewis's dream of family-friendly quietude. It was the center of social life, the stage for band music and female-impersonator revues, the place to go for shrimp purlo or fried whiting on summer nights, where any self-respecting 1950s or 1960s teenager headed after the high school prom in Jacksonville, despite the parents' warnings. "They always said, 'You *cannot* go to American Beach after the prom,'" remembered Henry Adams, a current Beach resident and emeritus Matthew W. Gilbert High School promgoer. "Well, that was like handing out an invitation and a tank of gas. We all went."

"It used to be you had to wait for a space to get into Evans's Rendezvous," Adams said. "It would take hours to get in." Adams was a superior court judge, presiding over a courtroom in Fernandina until 1993, when he was appointed to a federal judgeship by President Clinton and moved to Tampa. He still keeps his house at the Beach.

On this day he was talking with his neighbor and friend Rudy Williams, who (even back when he was a custodian at the pulp mill, stirring up trouble for segregation) used to run one of the small restaurants near the Rendezvous. "And nobody got violent," Williams marveled to Adams. "If you bumped somebody, it was, 'Hey, brother.' 'Hey, cousin.' Now, there's this attitude. And where the kids got it, God knows. Everything's been ruined by money."

Today, when a far less festive Evans's Rendezvous is (aside from the parking lot and the motel) the only remaining business establishment at the Beach, its old role in subverting the town's sobriety remains a sore subject. There are those who keep it sore. "The other day I went down, especially for a meeting at American Beach, to see what all these young jackasses are doing," Selma Richardson said to me in Atlanta one day in 1993. "I sat down, and I told them I was the oldest one around there, and I didn't like some of the history I was seeing, but I said, 'If that's what you want, go on, because I'm getting too old to bother with it. But,' I said, 'I saw another Beach. I don't see what you see. And in the Beach I see, this liquor store shouldn't be there.' I'm very frank."

Richardson is a Jacksonville native—she was born in early 1903 in a house that had been charred in the great fire but survived, becoming a hostel for several homeless white families whom her parents took in. A merchant and mail-carrier's daughter, she taught child psychology at Tuskegee Institute, where her late husband, Dr. Harry Richardson, the first black man to graduate from Harvard Divinity School, was chaplain. She has seen black society from below and above and within. She lives in Atlanta, but in the 1990s, when she was closing in on a hundred, still maintained a house at the Beach. She is a woman of daunting refinement who has no use whatsoever for dainty propriety. Her approach to any subject is robust. Once, when I asked her about a painting in her living room of Egyptian pyramids, she responded with the most encyclopedic comparison of world equestria I've ever heard. "That's the worst animal to try to ride, a camel!" she exclaimed. "Tough, with that hump up there. The elephant is the most reliable one, and the nicest, softest. Because he watches where he puts his big foot. He's a comfortable ride."

"Not a camel?" I asked. It's remarkable where interviews will take you.

"No!" she replied. "He'll knock you off anytime! And I've been on a jackass. You get that in Port-au-Prince. That's worse than a camel."

Her view of history was equally intimate. She had known James Weldon Johnson ("Yeah, we knew him. He was just a down-to-earth person") and Mary McLeod Bethune, whose citrus ranch she used to visit, and A. Philip Randolph ("The people in Jacksonville all worshipped him") and the Martin Luther Kings, *père et fils* ("Martin was doing a good thing, except he was so nonviolent about it," she said of the latter. "Me, I'm a violent person") and A. L. Lewis. Of American Beach she told me, "It didn't go like Mr. Lewis wanted it to go. When we first went down there, when Mr. Lewis had it, it was quite different. The beginning was a good era. Then in between, something happened. He died, and he left it to his son, and then it went to his grandson, A. L. Lewis's great-grandson. And that's when the thing began to go down, that was a bad era, I think. And then you had those years in the sixties when they had the integration, and everyone went running to the white beaches. That was the era when it was quiet, but the businesses didn't like it, because they weren't making any money."

When the crowds came back, in the 1970s, Richardson reckoned them of a different sort. No longer refugees from white hostility, they were—at least, the worst among them—refugees from standards of comportment prevailing at other public beaches. Beach resident James Robinson calls them "the destroyers." "It used to be a nicer place. You didn't have too much fighting," Selma Richardson told me, though I didn't know what that meant exactly, coming from a woman who had successfully begged her mother, when she was a child, to return her to a public school, where she could engage in more frequent fisticuffs. "You had some," Richardson finished.

The new weekend partyers were rowdier, more given to drink and drugs and noise, with less respect for the privacy or property of the people who lived in the Beach homes the rest of the week. They parked in yards; they camped on porches. As early as the 1960s, Jacksonville neighborhood gangs arrived, sometimes by busload, to claim the Beach as their Sunday evening territory. In the early 1990s, one reputed gangster would parade around the parking lot with his entourage in tow, bedecked and bedazzling in clichéd drug-kingpin regalia—gold chains and gilded Mercedes—under the worried eye of a cluster of nervous Nassau County sheriff's deputies deployed at the base of the sand dune. In the summer seasons, the sheriff's deputies would cordon off the entry to Lewis Street and eyeball every incoming vehicle, in a move that some residents requested and others resented as an unconstitutional invasion. When the cordon was lifted, the intrusion on the ears and yards of property owners grew onerous; when it was in force, even longtime residents felt themselves treated with disrespectful suspicion and the Beach became as deserted on Sunday evenings (its traditional rush hour) as on rainy winter weekdays: nobody came at all, and the parking lot and Evans's Rendezvous stayed forlornly empty.

"You always had the weekend people in the summertime," Billy Moore told me. "But they weren't—how are you going to put it?—they weren't, uh, destructive like they are now. It was the way the society was. The society was much more mellow. You didn't have to go drinking and running around the beach and shooting at each other. It was just unheard of; you just didn't do that. Now it's like this. See, it's, uh, a different society. It's a different thing altogether."

Rudy Williams's restaurant, the Quick Snack, which he started with a loan from the Afro, is boarded up now, due to a lack of trade. Williams is retired from business, but hardly from devilment. His house is generally open to a random assortment of friends. It is a tidy gray saltbox at the end of Waldron Street, at the very edge of the township—a pretty cape house whose kitchen door opens into a shaded sunken glade of twining ocean oaks, and whose purchase was a family as well as a personal ambition. "My mother was always sassy and liked to tell you about your butt real quick," Williams once told me. "But she was real proud when I got this little place." He presides over it with a baritone hospitality and an easygoing nature that barely conceals the scar of the struggle of getting to such a house on such a street—a restive bitterness bubbling like hot tar beneath the bonhomie. "It's been rough—but, hey, thanks to the Lord, I'm all right," he'll say, taking an involuntary dive into that acid pool. "I didn't kill nobody. Felt like it. Many times, the son of a guns. People had no heart. When it came to black people, no heart, no feelings, we were just a bunch of nothings. There's been times it's been bad. But that's all right."

Williams is neither from the abstemious elite who founded the Beach—"I'm not a real bad-butt drinker but more or less I have me a shot every day of something"—nor is he a member of their behavioral antipode, the party kids who regularly overrun it. Williams is a true gentleman and an inveterate rascal. It has occurred to me, knowing him, that he is as close as anyone to being the man in A. L. Lewis's mind when Lewis wrote to Heimey Fishler, "I am very much interested in the temporal welfare of my people in the South"—someone for whom the option of a self-owned refuge was a matter of cosmic justice and emotional survival.

Once, when the several simultaneous jobs he was working as a young man gave Williams an ulcer, the white doctor in Fernandina called him over to the office window and pointed to a group of black men drinking and laughing in front of Mrs. Hippard's saloon, and what he said still bubbles away in Williams's pool of bitterness: "Now, Rudy, see those folks over there? Now you can't be a doctor like I am. You need to go over there and have a drink with those boys and sing and laugh a little and not try to push so high, and it will be better for you."

"And it was good advice," Williams told me. "But it was like kicking me in the face and throwing shit in my damn nose.

"Thank the Lord I've seen changes in my years," he said. "But not enough, and there's still no respect for the black man. Some white people you meet are all right, but most are not gonna expend any effort to find out what was our problem and honestly ask what they can help to do about it. They don't see any of us different from any of the rest. And there are blacks who, if you give them a quilt, they want to know why you don't tuck them in at night. But then there's me. I was the poorest man in Fernandina, but I always tried to maintain a decent home, and to always feed my children and keep clothes on them. I was too proud to go to the bank and get a damned loan. And if I was white, with my determination, pressing, pressing, always pressing, I guess I would have been a millionaire. But I found out in later years: the doctor was right." Then he slogged his way up out of the pool again, back into the sunlight of his home at American Beach, the cape home at the end of Waldron Street with the twisted, sunken forest just outside the kitchen door. "But it's all right," he said. "I thank God for it, really I do, and I didn't kill nobody."

In recent years, his home has been besieged. Just as the loud, young Jacksonville crowd has taken over the center of town, corporate development threatens its fringe. When Ocean Village was announced, the development whose enthusiastic land-clearing had Amelia Island Plantation planners shaking their heads in disapproval and caused MaVynee to weep, Williams was thankful for the county-mandated two-hundred-foot buffer, considering it was all that stood between his property and theirs. He was nevertheless open for new neighbors, whoever they might turn out to be: "Chinese, Blackinese, Pinkinese, or whatever damned-nese, if they're going to come up here and be good neighbors and holler, 'Hey, Rudy, how you doing?'" he said. "But them son of a bitches got money, and I don't have no damn money. And if they're going to come here and be all snob, I'm glad it's 200 feet between us." It turned out the 200 feet was little enough protection. The earth movers reworked the topography close enough to Williams's house to cause his walls to crack, or so he suspected when the walls cracked. He threatened a suit, and pronounced his intent to sell his house and evacuate. On the day of his conversation with Judge Adams, I wasn't sure whether his verdict on American Beach's decline was directed inward at the rowdy center of the Beach or outward at the encompassing development. Or perhaps he meant it universally: "Everything's been ruined by money."

After the midday ride of Bill Moore to warn MaVynee of Amelia Island Plantation's invasion of the Harrison Tract, her anger spun her into fits of raging vengeance. "Someone's about to get their white ass kicked—pardon my Ebonics—you just wait and see," she threatened. "This will make a Wagner third act look like nothin'!" For all that, her plans of counterattack were more fanciful than violent. She would sing on the sand dune, she swore, and when the national media showed up to film it, everyone would see how beautiful NaNa was, how worthy of being saved. She was only partially deluded. She never did sing, but USA Today and the NBC Evening News and National Public Radio did come, and did report on the conflict between the old black beach and the acquisitive white one. No reinforcements arrived.

MaVynee's better hopes and more realistic plans lay in her experiences while living at the Afro. She now saw the conservation battles she had helped to fight and the causes she had supported from her check-papered room as a warm-up. Hadn't she helped save an entire island, Fort George, from just such a fairway fate as now awaited the Harrison Tract? So from the summer of 1994 through early 1997, she pursued an established plan of action, contacting sympathetic politicians, getting biologists and lobbyists in to appraise the property for endangered species and cultural relics, attending every hearing in front of every controlling authority—whether they be county permitting boards or the Army Corps of Engineers or the Saint Johns River Water Management District—with power to thwart the project. Again she had a near brush with success. Over the Plantation's strenuous opposition, she convinced the state to put the tract on the CARL list, its inventory of Conservation and Recreational Lands whose value to the public made them candidates for government purchase. But eventually there was a problem. The state was averse to snatching property out of the arms of unwilling owners, much less from expectant developers. Amelia Island Plantation's unwillingness was emphasized by a phone call to the CARL board from a Fernandina attorney renowned for his Tallahassee connections. The property was dropped from the list.

The last best hope was local—convincing the Nassau County government that the development proposal should be given the heave-ho. Virtually all of American Beach attended the meeting of the zoning board on the night of December 5, 1995, where the Plantation made its pitch. "The development described here," Plantation consultant Howard Landers told the board, "is to satisfy the need the Plantation has for additional ability to play golf." Any thought that the audience was friendly to the concept evaporated with that remark, as a murmur of laughter rippled through the room. It was averred by the consultant that the golf course would not endanger American Beach by polluting its wells with fertilizer or herbicide runoff, nor through onerous tax hikes provoked by a rise in property values. Nor, according to another consultant, would it threaten the sand dune. "Very simplistically in my professional opinion," he declared, "I believe that the buffer that has been proposed to protect this dune is extremely adequate." Later in the hearing, Annette Myers and another American Beach resident—

Ben Sessions, the former Nassau County sheriff's deputy and Afro-American sales agent—rose to speak in the Plantation's favor.

Then the opposition queued up. "I saw in *USA Today* the 'mayor' of American Beach," the zoning board chairman announced with a smile, "and I want to call Her Honor first: MaVynee Betsch." And there she stood, in her flip-flops, at the podium just vacated by pinstripes and tassel loafers, her red felt wrap worn off the left shoulder, a large pendant whelk dangling by a black string from a neck also adorned with a choker of turquoise scarabs, handing out exhibits on sewage treatment capacities and forest canopies with a braceleted wrist clattering with small shells. Her presentation was hardly bureaucratic. "Everything that's green isn't good, Okay? Gangrene isn't. Golf greens either."

"I don't believe this," one Plantation executive muttered to another.

"Hold your applause down," the chairman warned the audience, pounding the table with his nameplate. "It messes up the tape!"

MaVynee moved on through her list of grievances and ended up with history. "All along the coast you will not see a black face from Charleston south. White developers have by devious means gotten all that land along the coast. Oh, they said very friendly things . . . but all that land was owned by blacks, and they have slowly like a cancer just bought it up bit by bit, until now they own us, at American Beach. It's not fair. It's just not fair."

When the chairman gaveled her out of time, Ernestine Smith—the same Ernestine Smith who had accompanied me to the courthouse to check the documents on American Beach's beginnings—rose in the second row in her blue dress to offer cheerfully, "She can have my five minutes."

"Oh, I love ya!" MaVynee said, and did a little quickstep behind the podium. A man rose behind Smith. "I'd like to give her mine, also."

"What's your name?" the chair asked.

"Rudolph Williams," he answered. Around the room, people began rising to volunteer more time. "No, no!" MaVynee said. "That's enough, that's enough." And when she finished and sat down to prolonged applause, they in fact used the time they'd kept, as the Plantation and its plan (which one opponent insisted on referring to as "the master's plan") came under a hail of criticism from a score of American Beach residents and also from white Fernandinans.

"Don't be fooled by the typical developers' language," Quintin Jones implored the board in stentorian tones. Jones is a Beach resident who grew up on Julia Street lugging baggage from the late night buses into his mother's hotel, and who, as the ex-operator of El Patio, had been included by Bill Moore among the contingent he described as "sensible businessmen." "The encroachment of the developers will accelerate the destruction and demise of American Beach," Jones said. "American Beach sits right in the middle of two multimillion-dollar resorts. As they expand, American Beach becomes more and more valuable to them. And to us. Don't be fooled. They've got their eyes on another piece."

The acrimony, and especially the insinuations of racism, upset the Plantation brass. "What they failed to do in that meeting last night was they focused on all the wrong things, on the racism and stuff," Bill Moore told me the next day. Behind the uproar, he spied the work of a not-so-invisible hand: MaVynee's. "I think the whole reason they haven't focused on the real issues is because of the driving force of MaVynee. She's leading a personal crusade, and using anything that's to her advantage to get supporters," Moore said. "She's capitalized on all the people's fears and suspicions. However much founded in reality they may be, she's managed to capitalize on them. She's pretty effectively built a constituency."

He understood where MaVynee might feel a bit riled. "First of all, back right before we purchased an option on the land, or right about the time when we purchased an option on that land, I saw MaVynee and she said, 'Gee, we really need to do something to save that land.' And I didn't say anything to her at that point. I really don't remember whether I knew what was happening—or I think I knew that we were looking at it, but I don't know if we'd done anything about it. But I wasn't at liberty to tell her that. Then when we got into it, I went and told her we had purchased an option on the land and told her that I'd like to get together and talk about it. From that point on, she just took a totally negative attitude.

"She feels that she has been taken advantage of," he said. "Maybe the closest analogy I could use to what I see her feelings being, is the feeling you get from some men when they feel they have been taken advantage of by a woman—you know, somebody who's divorced or had a bad relationship, or a woman that's had a bad relationship with a man, or one that's been raped. Or somebody that's been fired by a boss, you know, that whole thing, and that's what it's all about. It's the same thing, I think. In that regard. It's really a very personal thing with her. I think that deep down she thinks that it's her land. Everything she's done has been to say or imply that the land was being stolen from her by the white people. It's not that she's against the development, because she hasn't *thought* about the development."

"It's change MaVynee's fighting," Jack Healan concurred when I talked with him later. "And you can't fight change. She's like Davy Crockett at the Alamo, swinging her empty musket at the Mexicans."

"He died there, didn't he?" I prompted, drawing a knowing nod from Healan. "He couldn't get them all," he said.

Moore and Healan disparaged the link MaVynee drew between the Plantation's expansion and the long history of black coastal island settlements being displaced by white resorts. Communities were all the time being supplanted by other communities, Moore said. "These may be more like neighborhoods—a Jewish neighborhood in Brooklyn that evolved into a Puerto Rican neighborhood, or a white neighborhood evolved into a black neighborhood, and those things occur for certain reasons," he explained. "If you look at it from an urban point of view, from a planning point of view, the dynamics of community growth and change, it's all part of that process where a community coalesces around something. And what the people at American Beach coalesced around was the fact that they weren't allowed anyplace else. When that changed, the whole basis of that community dissolved. And now you have a group of people who are trying to rebuild that community, and they are trying to build it around what it was, which was a racially segregated, isolated community. And the only tool they have to build that is the only thing that built it in the first place, which is racism. To me, that's going in the wrong direction as progress is measured.

"Let me say this very clearly. I guess what I'm saying is, I'm very sensitive to talking about racial things. And that's what this whole thing is about. That's what this whole thing is about. That's the dynamic that's driving MaVynee." And because it also drove the internal dynamics of American Beach, Moore's experience promoting his development there had been like entering a fun house of fluid politics and magical thinking. "Because what's happening outside of American Beach is what's happening outside of American Beach. What's happening inside American Beach is what's happening inside. The two aren't connected. And that's what you observed last night," Moore said. "It wasn't the development. It was the history, the cultural thing that was the issue. The *issue* is not the issue."

Truly the two sides had seemed to be arguing on different levels— one side in the dry specificities of business and building code, to the letter of "the issue." The other, from the Beach, addressed the spirit of "the issue" in the general terms of justice and fairness and history. The zoning board, like all zoning boards, was empowered to consider specifics only. The chairman had sympathetically challenged MaVynee to provide them: "MaVynee, you've talked a lot, but tell me what you're asking for."

"I want more land behind that dune."

"What kind? How much? Be specific."

When MaVynee invoked a Bible verse to the effect that one might seek salvation by giving away what you could otherwise sell, the chairman said, in a voice sounding almost sorrowful, "They're not going to give you back the land, MaVynee."

The board recommended that the county commission accept the Plantation's proposal.

By the night of the county commission meeting, several weeks later, the political weight behind the reign of specifics had solidified. The commission was chaired by Jim B. Higginbotham, a patriarch of area politics whose family went back far enough in county history to appear in plantation records of the early 1800s. He announced at the outset his intolerance for any statement that "did not address the criteria," and showed soon enough what that meant to him. After the ensuing imbroglio, another white politician, former Fernandina city commissioner John Glenn, went on television to denounce the spectacle of "Chairman Higginbotham enforcing his totally arbitrary and capricious rules," and the "brutal" effect that enforcement had on an "inoffensive gentleman just trying to have his say."

The "inoffensive gentleman" was John Linnehan, a frail, bald-headed, sixty-year-old white man from Saint Marys, Georgia, just over the state line, who came to the podium in Hush Puppies and a Jimmy Stewart open gray cardigan and gold-rimmed glasses. He wanted to tell the commission of his experience on the advisory board of Kings Bay Naval Base, where chemical runoff had contaminated shallow residential wells—the sort of contamination the Plantation claimed could not happen with the wells at American Beach.

"I don't want to talk about this," Higginbotham interrupted him.

Linnehan then tried to describe the high cost and dubious effectiveness of well monitoring of the type that Amelia Island Plantation had promised to do.

"I don't want to hear it," Higginbotham said and, as the man tried to continue, met him with a loud barrage of "We've already heard this one time. . . . It's irrelevant to me right now. . . . I don't want to hear it!"

"It's not irrelevant to people who live at American Beach," Linnehan persisted in a pleading voice, beginning to shake with frustration. "You can say whatever you want up there in your high seat, but these people are the people who are going to be affected."

"Sit down."

Linnehan made a perceptible move to do just that, then changed his mind. "I will not sit down. This is a democratically held meeting. People's lives are at stake. If I can't have five minutes—"

"I'm going to tell you one more time, and then I'm going to put you outside."

"Why would I be put outside?"

Higginbotham pointed to the back of the room. "Because that officer right there is going to put you out."

Nassau County Sheriff Ray Geiger, in blue-blazer mufti, came up on one side of Linnehan ("Don't make us do this," he whispered to him) and a uniformed deputy on the other. They grabbed him around the waist. The man folded, collapsing onto the floor so close to Bill Moore, who was sitting in the front row, that Moore had to jerk his foot out of the way. Then, followed by stunned protests of "Outrageous" and "He's a citizen" and "Is this America? Is this the old Soviet Union?" they dragged the Georgian down the side aisle like a broken wheelbarrow. The sheriff then came back in to eject a Sierra Club official, David Queen, awaiting his turn to speak. Geiger had heard him object to Linnehan's removal. When

Queen shrugged off his grasp (not recognizing the un-uniformed man as the sheriff) Geiger told him, "You're under arrest."

After the two men spent a night in jail and endured a court hearing, the charges against them, of disrupting a public meeting and resisting arrest, were dropped. The county commission would draw media criticism from across the state. "In Nassau County, some public officials think they operate under a different Constitution," the *St. Petersburg Times* editorialized, and suggested that the county was becoming "a place where citizens fear to speak on important matters, where plainclothes toughs intimidate spirited citizens, where only the monied and the polished make their voices heard." But within the hearing room, the bullying had worked. The citizen testimony continued in a hushed, cowed way, before the commissioners voted to approve Plantation Park and pronounced the whole thing over. Before the hearing ended, Quintin Jones spoke. It was only a few weeks since his bravura call to arms at the zoning board meeting. His voice shook uncharacteristically at what he had just witnessed. "I'm very upset that those gentlemen were arrested for whatever reason," he said. "It's just a sad situation and it didn't have to happen."

His thoughts now were resigned and philosophical. "The developers of Amelia Island Plantation took advantage of a golden opportunity to purchase the land and expand their amenities for the members," he said. "The residents of American Beach missed a golden opportunity to purchase the land and will forever be in mourning about it. People are just upset that we didn't do it, and one half of American Beach is now gone. And that hurts us. So it's not just looking at Amelia Island Plantation as an enemy or adversary. It's like losing a member of the family and now it's gone, and we've got to get something out of it in whatever way we can."

Two years later, the last technicality had been signed away, and the earthmovers were unloaded onto the Harrison Tract. It took them less than a week to clear the bulk of the forest from NaNa to the highway, and prepare the place for "assisted living" retirement condominiums and the "needed" nine holes of golf. The denuding of the Plantation Park acreage (which had been renamed Osprey Village in deference to black sensitivities) stunned even some Plantation residents, and alienated even some at the Beach who had early on favored the project. In her 1997 book, Marsha Phelts observed that the Plantation employed landscaping and barbed wire to separate its "opulent sanctuary for the moneyed classes" from American Beach, but did nothing to camouflage the warehouses and service depots it built adjacent to American Beach property. "If the loss of nearly a hundred acres from the American Beach plat to the Amelia Island Company . . . is any indication of the community's future," she wrote, "it is bleak."

MaVynee kept up her advocacy, monitoring the development she had once hoped to stop. "Called SJRWMD last week and AIP still has not applied for the consumptive use permit," she wrote (referring to the Saint Johns River Water Management District) in a long list of complaints to the county's planning director. "Is this not required? Or will an exception be made for 'their convenience?' . . . Regarding the construction of a golf tee 150 feet seaward of the coastal construction line, they are already cutting the beautiful twisted trees. Yet as of today, THEY DO NOT HAVE THEIR PERMIT FROM DEP." Her militance belied her despair. On the copy she sent me of that particular letter, she scrawled in the margin, "Russ, NaNa cries out to me in my dreams! Her forest is dead, her wetlands, too. The Plantation broke her spirit."

I thought I knew the spirit she spoke of: wild, not contained, natural, not tamed. The Plantation consultants had promised the zoning board to redeem the sand dune from its current neglect: on a recent visit, they said, they had even seen tire tracks and footprints defiling the dune's eastern face. I could well believe that the dune might be better preserved under their care than it would be otherwise. It would have the benefit of a grounds staff and a landscaping budget, and if it did diminish due to the development behind it, the Plantation could, if they chose, haul in the dredges and the iron pipes and replenish it artificially the same way they did their beach, the way they employed fertilizer to keep the putting grass green and roving chaperones in golf carts to monitor the decorum of their neighborhoods. And they could do everything to insure that the dune did not suffer an iota, and MaVynee would still feel as bereft as if the Plantation had leveled NaNa outright. For while MaVynee argued that it was the dune's pristine magnificence she had sworn herself to defend, really it was something else. Really, it was the footprints.

MaVynee was preserving a history. But not a history of the corporate variety. The corporate history was something made and something kept. Hers just happened. If MaVynee felt, in Moore's word, raped, it was not her innocence that had been violated. It was her experience, the imprint on the face of things of all that had been lived. It was certainly that tracery of experience she treasured in her town, and expressed in her own unpredictable life, in her own appearance and dress. Interviewed on a local cable television show after the county commission meeting, she compared the Beach's value implicitly to her own. "It's like knowing a woman at twenty and knowing her at sixty," she said. "I know the Beach may not be what it was forty years ago. But it's something else, and that's okay."

About the same time, Moore told me that in the summer of 1994 Annette Myers had asked the Plantation to help American Beach, Inc., come up with a face-lift for the town. The Plantation funded a feasibility study and paid one of its land-use consultants to work with a small group of Beach residents handpicked by Myers. "So we met, and we developed a plan," Moore said. The plan had foundered at the time because, being concocted at the top instead of on the street, "it had all the connotations of something that whitey did, that somebody did. It didn't have a grass-roots basis," which would have provided what Moore called the "sense of ownership." Nevertheless, he told me, "the plan itself is very good; I think the focus of it was right. The whole thing focused on how do you create more identity for American Beach?" (I didn't interrupt him to protest that American Beach already had more identity than almost any place I'd ever been.) "The study recommended that maybe each of the seven beach walkovers have a little portal, a gazebo portal, each one with a little different design, named for one of the seven founders of the Afro-American Insurance Company. A plaque and maybe a little inscription or whatever. A scheme of maybe white with red and blue roofs. Good landscaping improvements and streetlights using white posts with decorative flags and stuff. All things to complement the concept of 'American Beach.'"

Were there really that many walkovers? I asked, so disoriented by the vision he was spinning that I could barely picture the beachfront. "Well, no, there are six. We had to stretch it a little bit," Moore said. "But you can see it starts to preserve the culture. It starts to say, 'Hey, this is American Beach!' You identify the image—red, white, and blue—with America, and then you start talking about the history of it through the founders of the Afro-American Insurance Company. So you start saying, 'This is an African American beach community created by someone who is memorialized in a bronze plaque.' And you have a monument. You could then go other places to start telling that story. And then what have you done? You have started to create something that people will come and look at. 'Wow! This was an African American community! These were people that accomplished something!'"

The plan could easily have accommodated citizen's suggestions, he thought. "Instead of doing individual little pavilions and walkovers, maybe you should do it in a single park. But obviously the Afro-American has a prominent part in it, right? And the American theme has a prominent part. Maybe you have a monument that looks like the Capitol. Or maybe it's the Washington Monument; I don't know what it could be. But the elements are there: American Beach. The Afro Insurance Company. Those are the two elements that won't change no matter what you do."

Of course, that was the problem. No matter what anyone could do, American Beach and the Afro-American Life Insurance Company had changed already. One was dying. The other was dead.

Moore's thoughts shifted back to MaVynee, and I asked him why he thought she felt so, as he had put it, "raped."

"I don't know," he answered. "I think you'd have to go back and look at a lot of things. You'd have to go a long way back. Why does MaVynee wear long fingernails? Have you ever asked her? I sort of see that being related to it. It's a physical manifestation of something going on inside. Because it's so different and so obvious and so dramatic and so unusual that it's got to represent some huge problem. And probably, in all reality, the problem relates to some big dealing with white people.

"She's a wonderful person," Moore exclaimed. "She's talented and she's thoughtful. And why she wants to focus on so much negativity, I don't know. There's a book by John-Roger and Peter McWilliams— *You Can't Afford the Luxury of a Negative Thought*. Great book for her. Maybe you ought to get her a copy."

*   *   *

When I had finished with my talk with Bill Moore, I drove into Jacksonville, guided by an address on a slip of paper. It turned out to be the address of a bungalow on a wide dirt driveway under a gloomy canopy of trees. A sign on a door announced the presence of a beauty parlor. The woman who met me inside led me through the parlor's ceramic, lavatory brightness and down a short corridor into a dim back room furnished with a cloth-draped table and a telephone and a lamp. A ceiling fan turned slowly overhead, making an irregular clicking noise. Some light filtered in from a high window. She put on a tape of dreamy, drifting piano music and lit some aromatic candles, whose sharp herbal scent competed with the smell of nail lacquer and hair spray wafting from the other room. She sat across the small table from me and rested her elbow on a book called *The Quest for Truth*.

This was Beverly Jackson's new office, where she read tarot cards and gave people advice of the metaphysical sort. "Isn't it odd?" MaVynee once said while describing the constant white parade that would visit a fortune-telling neighbor in Sugar Hill. "White people who consider blacks inferior in every other way will seek them out for instructions about how to lead their lives. I find that very odd." It wasn't the future, anyway, that I had come to ask about.

Jackson was in her early forties, a woman of personal ease and strength and professional assurance. She wore a shirt imprinted with a bust of Nefertiti and the words "The Beautiful Black Woman." Her right ear was pierced for a trio of earrings. Everything about her seemed a world away from her old identity as staff assistant to the president for public relations at the Afro-American Life Insurance Company. "I was so angry back then," she said. "When I left, I was very disillusioned. I was hurt. I could not believe that my people, so to speak . . . how shall I put it? I don't want to appear insensitive toward my people; I don't want to get caught up in that. I'm just talking about human beings. *Human* humans." Still, she could not believe what human humans could do to each other in the name of making money.

"It was a bad time," she told me. "The Afro was being investigated. It was going down the tubes. It was like plummeting, fast. Even the insurance end was a flimflam. I mean, if you go back to people and see if they really got paid, if their policies were really fulfilled and all—a lot of black people really lost out when that company went under. A lot of old people who had been paying in there, like my parents, for years and years and years, where that insurance man would come around and knock on the door, and he would collect that five dollars or ten dollars or whatever it was: they lost. They lost. The money didn't go to them, and it didn't go to the children, and it didn't get sunk back into the Afro.

"I tell you, when that company was closing down, it felt like the walls were bleeding," she said. "Those old people who had worked there for decades, you could see their spirits going down and down and down and down, and they knew that what they had been promised in terms of retirement, that wasn't going to be the real deal when it came down to the end, and it wasn't."

The experience left her, and not only her, with a complex sort of anger. "The kind of anger that can only breed shame. And then guilt, too. That's part of what I felt when I left there, I felt that guilt and that shame: 'Beverly, how can you walk away?'" Which in the end, after less than a year, is what she did. Oddly, Jackson said, her sanity was rescued not by a voice of complacency but by the angriest voice around, the voice of the madwoman in the attic, the woman everyone said was crazy, the woman they said had given away all her money, who walked the streets of Jacksonville and paced the halls of the Afro, fulminating against the sacrilege she saw being perpetrated right under the gaze of the founder's portrait hanging in the lobby.

"MaVynee feels real strongly about her family's name and what that stood for," Jackson said. "I started listening to some of her crazy stories, that people always said were crazy, and when I did, that's when I caught on to some of the things that were happening. About the Afro and how it was falling and how it was being bought out from under them, and the paperwork wasn't being kept, and people were losing out. MaVynee had a key to the Afro. She would sneak into the files. She knew what was going on. She was always afraid that the old people were going to suffer.

"So that's how I became involved with MaVynee. I started to listen to her, because she didn't always sound so crazy. And then, she could back things up. MaVynee could tell me certain things about people in the community and who they were dealing with, and when you looked beneath the surface, MaVynee knew all the dirt. She knew what was happening with these people's mamas, and their mama's mamas. She knew it from way back then. And like I say, I just got hip and started to pay attention. So in some ways, because I did start listening to MaVynee and I did start paying attention to the paper flow and the trail, I was able to help out some people, some kids, before I had to cut my losses and get out of there."

As Beverly Jackson talked, I had the sensation of two things happening around me. The room seemed to open up and fall away, into a landscape vast in space and time in which her words flowed through the agony of the Afro's dying days into the ocean of myriad lives. At the same time, it closed in. The walls grew darker and the tinkling of conversation and the sweet-heavy intoxication of spray and lacquer from the bright neighboring room grew distant and faint, and the words Jackson spoke fell into a still, dark private well, misting with the plumes of incense and dripping with the ceiling fan's *tick . . . tick . . . tick*. "She just sort of took me in," Jackson said of MaVynee. "And I just loved her spirit. And I saw part of me in her."

I'd heard a similar sentiment many times from other black women in Jacksonville: wealthy housewives with screened-in pools, women executives in soft-bow suits. A year or so earlier, MaVynee's friend Carol Alexander had expressed almost the identical thought, even as she told me, "And I still don't understand. Why does someone give up a profession and status and fortune? What makes a person lay it all down?"

So I asked. Jackson nodded. "People ask me, 'Did MaVynee have this split because she so disagreed with her mother and this whole Sugar Hill lifestyle?' That Sugar Hill," she said wonderingly. "That's a whole thing in itself. That's a whole culture that these black people devised for themselves, to set themselves apart." Jackson shrugged, and submitted a question of her own. "Or was it the fact that her parents wouldn't let her love whom she wanted to love? You have to remember that when MaVynee came back to this country it was really under duress, because her mother was sick. MaVynee was very in love with a man at the time. She very seldom talks about this. I want to say he's French, but something tells me he's German. She's very in love with him, and her family totally rejected that. They thought she was getting wild, you know, being out of the country and, as the old people say, smelling her top lip. But she's in love with this man, and talking about wanting to marry him, and they, the family, they just weren't having it. He was European and he wasn't from here. He wasn't from their segment. They hadn't chosen him.

"I think that it had something to do with that, too. The fact that she really found her freedom when she left here. She wasn't under the constraints of Sugar Hill. And as she got away from that, she lived, she breathed. She found real love. And what her parents, like all of our parents, had been teaching us about the *others*—you know, the white people, the foreigners, the others—she found out it wasn't true. She started to breathe for the first time. Guilt brought her back here. Her mother. Her mother dying brought her back here. Her family doing this whole big guilt thing about her being in love.

"For me, for Beverly, this is just how I feel. I never discussed it with MaVynee, and I could be totally wrong, I don't know, but I think at that point they broke her spirit. She gave in to not being herself. And you know what happens when you give in to not being yourself. You die. You die a slow death. And I think that when she made that choice, to come back here, somewhere in her mind she thought things were going to go quickly here and she would go back. But that karma didn't work out that way. Her mother got sick, she died, things happened, happened, happened. And her male friend went on to something or someone else."

"Did they ever meet, the man and Mary Betsch?" I asked.

"I don't know. But I know that once MaVynee came back here, she never saw him again. She never saw him again. And I never heard her talk about any other male person. After the mother died, and that kind of thing, that's when, from what I hear, MaVynee did this real personality split. They thought she was going insane and that she was a schizophrenic or whatever. She just split. And then when she did this thing with the money, giving it away to animal-rights organizations and that kind of thing—you know, black people hadn't heard of that. It was 'crazy.' When I met her—this was eighty-five? eighty-six?—she was breaking off from people even then. But as the Afro closed and all this was going on simultaneously—when that building started falling down—I swear it was like I could see slashes in her spirit field. She died. Each time I see her now, it's like she wants nothing to do with people. Humankind, they just let this woman down."

*   *   *

I couldn't know if Beverly Jackson's estimation of MaVynee's crisis was true. I hoped it wasn't, and consoled myself with technical quibbles. Was Mary Betsch really sick as early as 1965, when MaVynee flew home from Germany for the last time? Wouldn't I have heard of this Frenchman, this German, if indeed he had existed? But I sensed the rightness of Jackson's tale: the potent combination of Sugar Hill; of Radical Respectability, whose tenet requiring a "proper" marriage had turned from a defensive to an imprisoning wall; of MaVynee's loyalty and guilt over the deaths of Mary Betsch and James H. Lewis, people who left her, gave her up, after she had given up everything for them; and of her loyalty and guilt over the deaths of the Afro and the Beach and the sale of the Harrison Tract—the dispossession of things for whose possession she had been forced to give up everything. MaVynee had been raised into respectability, and had lived with its advantages until that day when respectability betrayed her. To escape its grasp, she gave up money and status and property and comfort, but those things weren't enough, and she had to give up the thing respectability most treasured in her life: her art. It was the only thing, among all those others, that Ma Vynee also treasured, but it had fallen hostage to the very restrictions of race she had thought she was escaping, and so it was renounced.

This seemed self-evident, that under the terms of the Conundrum, the trap that tightened no matter which way you pulled, one must inevitably define oneself in terms of race. No matter how far one had freely escaped, no matter how much one had seemed to establish an independent life—one's own life, uninflected by the considerations of color, of the history of color, the burden of color—one must eventually be called home. "That's the worst thing, other than a war, that one person can put on another—to *restrict* him," Arnolta Williams had told me. How subtly and horribly that control could work when the world made families do it to themselves, when societies condemned even their freest spirits to "pace the cage that wasn't there."

Beverly Jackson had called MaVynee's crisis "her split." But it seemed to me the problem was the opposite, the strain on a personality whose strands could not be conveniently separated, whose central knot could not be untangled, the personal from the public from the political from the historic from the racial. Sugar Hill and foreign loves and opera and sand dunes and sea turtles were in MaVynee's life indistinguishable, a single, coherent whole, an integrity. The "cohesiveness" MaVynee admired in her great-grandfather's character, what Johnnetta Cole called his "continuity" and his inability to "dichotomize"—that inner unity was MaVynee's, too. In the elder Lewis it spelled an enabling strength. In MaVynee, the strength was also a tragic liability. "I live in harmony," she told me. In harmony, she did not have the luxury of positive thoughts as things went bad, nor could she let her fortunes float in a world whose values had sunk.

On an afternoon some time after my conversation with Jackson, MaVynee and I sat in plastic beach chairs by the coast dune looking out over the beach. It was a warm, calm afternoon with a slight breeze and American Beach was deserted, as far as our eyes could tell, and resplendent under the sun. The railroad vine was blooming on NaNa's face, and clouds traipsed in convoy out of the forest, over the sea. The waves that pulled in softly to shore seemed old friends, friends of the family, familiar with all her people equally down through time, with A. L. Lewis and John and Mary Betsch, and James H. Lewis, and James L. Lewis, and with all the saga of triumph and cruelty that had played forth on that shore. The waves had greeted them all with the same bright sibilant applause. MaVynee was introspective, and invited talk about her past and, taking it as a proper opportunity, I asked about the man I'd heard she loved, whom the terms of her society had forbidden her to marry. MaVynee is dramatic. She once sang opera. Her sanity is protected within her artifice, her dignity within her sophistication, and I have never seen her, even in her most direct and unguarded moments, not perform. Except for this one time. She turned her head and stared out to sea a while, a long enough while that I knew the question had rocked her, and when she spoke, it was without theater. "Child, please," she said, so slowly each word seemed a sentence, and continued to look out to sea.

Later, when I pressed her, she stammered out a reluctant little: that he was German, that she had written home about him, but that Mary rejected him out of her own social conceits, her own driven sense of the role MaVynee was expected to play in Sugar Hill respectability. Essentially, she told me that Beverly Jackson was right, and that the social ethic MaVynee had been brought up to pursue as a method for breaking down walls had become a restrictive code, a wall itself.

Eventually, she told me just that much. For now, on the beach, MaVynee turned her talk toward something else. "Do you know, you can get into or out of more situations with music!" she said brightly, and launched into the day in Yugoslavia when she was headed for Bayreuth on the train and her suitcase was stolen and she was escorted to the home of Zinka Milanov, and the day in Braunschweig when Herr Kronstein was losing his voice to a dry throat and played his Johannan stage right instead of stage center and broke for the curtain at each gap in the dialogue so the stage hand could spray mist down his gullet. "He shouldn't have gone on at all!" MaVynee said, and laughed at his audacity. Then there were the days when the concert ended and she stood on the empty stage panting with exhaustion and she could hear them through the curtain, shouting "*Brava!*"

"Do you know what they do?" MaVynee asked. "When they want an encore, they beat on the curtain. Oh, I loved it! From behind, it looks like waves. It was so sensual!" Sometimes, she said, on gentle days like this one, she looked out at the sea and saw in its swells that fervent, animated curtain, ready at any moment to divide and invite her back in front of the crowd.

In 1967, the librettist and opera critic Richard Plant wrote an essay dealing with "American Negro artists"—specifically, singers—"who don't feel at home in Anglo-Saxon business civilization" but find a sanctuary in the world of German song. His observations grew out of decades of experience as a reviewer, but were rooted in a concert he attended during his youth in his native Germany. The singer was a yet unknown black American. Her name was Marian Anderson. Few if any in the audience, which Plant described as "rather stiff, and reticent," had ever heard a black woman sing anything, much less German lieder, but as Anderson dispatched songs by Schumann and Brahms and began Schubert's "Death and the Maiden," Plant remembered, the mood in the hall "changed radically, as though clouds had been swept away by a gentle wind." The audience "went wild," and gave a "roar of approval." This black American was not merely sufficient to the task but "interpreted

Schubert in such a manner that the concept of many German singers appeared superficial in comparison. What Miss Anderson had caught and projected was a deeply ingrained sadness, a knowledge that life is a short procession of vanities, in which our most passionate longings can never be fulfilled." She had transformed lieder into "a sort of blues." The experience left Plant to ponder a mystery, which deepened over the years as he heard other black classical singers in Europe and America: what was this kinship (Plant, borrowing from Goethe, called it an "elective affinity") between black American experience and German song? Spirituals and lieder, he said, "display so many similarities that they can't be accidental. [In] their basic mood of sadness, alienation, helplessness before hostile ministries of power . . . both share a feeling of loss, of a despair so beyond words that only music can express it."

Plant wrote, "German Lied demands more than the dazzling technique. . . . It has to be felt from the heart; its deepest layer must be understood, caught and projected from a basement of the unconscious—and here the American Negro singers and the German romantic composers reveal that rare and stunning elective affinity which makes one the fated partner of the other."

The affinity was forged in history. "German lyricists and composers of certain periods felt as unfulfilled in their society as did the Negroes in America. And so, both groups turned inward, so to speak," and some toward a hermetic reverence for poetry and nature. "People shut out from the mainstream of their nation often find consolation in nature," Plant said, "[in] the fields, the winds, the rivers; these bestowed their blessings on everyone regardless of station or color, and they never betrayed you, because they were more constant than humans."

In all her time in Europe, MaVynee said, her mother never heard her sing.

On a blazing mid-August afternoon, I pulled up to a time-worn house on Evergreen Street in Jacksonville, to interview Maude Aveilhe, a woman who had worked long years for the Afro. She had actually worked long decades, over five of them, and at the end of her career she was in charge of data processing. She oversaw, collated, catalogued, and archived every bit of official information about the company, and that was why MaVynee had recommended her, and why I wanted to talk with her. If anyone represented a corporate memory, Maude Aveilhe did.

She met me at the screen door, a tiny, fine-boned woman with still-refined features beneath the wrinkles, and especially when she smiled. Her smile displayed a lot of mischief and spark. Her small, enclosed front porch was wretched with the smell of kitten shit, and there were, indeed, three cats tied by lengths of string to chair legs—a momma cat and two of her brood. "Want a kitten?" Aveilhe said, and invited me inside. "It should be cooler there."

It wasn't. It was, if anything, another five degrees hotter and certainly over a hundred degrees, and immediately I could feel the sweat running under my shirt like tent caterpillars in a tent-caterpillar tent. The windows were all closed, and the ceiling fan in the next room was off. I looked at its still blades longingly, wishing for any movement, for even an illusion of breath. The rug was sculpted shag, the lamp shades were red velvet, and the curtains a heavy gold velour. I felt I had entered a sort of upholstered incinerator, a crematorium just getting fired up. The TV was blaring, and when I asked Aveilhe if she could turn it down she laughed and said, "I don't need it," and walked into the dining room to cut it off. Then she came and sat across from me, displaying no hint of perspiration.

"I was in charge of the IBM machines," she started when I asked her about the Afro. "I worked there till I retired. Look here, I'm ninety-one, and I can't remember everything I did. But anyway, I was in charge of it. But don't look at me," she said and giggled. "I'm ninety-one, and I retired from there."

As we talked, I realized with dismay that the grand saga that was lost to Jacksonville's memory would soon disappear entirely even from Maude Aveilhe's. The history I had come to hear, and that she had lived, had escaped from her mind's embrace and now flitted only occasionally into sight, like some furtive iridescent bird loosed from its cage into the forest.

"It was quite an institution," she said when I persisted in discussing the Afro. "But the thing about it, they changed managements, you know how those things run." She shifted her hands as if they were resting on a billowing sheet, to indicate a sort of nebulous uncertainty.

"You know," she said wonderingly, "people will steal, won't they? So the company went down. They had a way of bringing their people in, and when you look around there's nothing left. But when I went there, old man A. L. Lewis was president, chairman. Mr. Ervin was secretary. It's been so long ago, I can't remember."

"What kind of man was A. L. Lewis?" I asked her.

"Oh yeah, he was impressive. He was productive, like. He founded the company. Oh, he was chairman of the board. And his son was president after he was. So it went, on down the line." She stopped and drifted through her thoughts for a moment. "It looks like it was quite a progressive company," she said. "An outstanding company, with a lot of business. But you know, sometimes, when they put people in, you don't know what they're doing. The old people died out. Looks like—you know how they do in the business world." She gave a delightful, easy laugh. "They're swinging from here and swinging from there and a little from here and a little from there," and she made a plucking motion with one hand and then the other. "And they bring in their people and begin to dillying and dallying and messin' with the figures. And after a while, nobody knows where the figures are. Those things happen."

"It was a shame it had to happen," I offered.

"I don't guess anyone's interested to that extent," she said. "And I guess it's gone so far, do you think? It's gone too far. I had charge of the IBM machines when I was there. Unh! Times bring on changes. Are they trying to sell the building now?"

For a minute, she shifted, remembering her years as a social worker on Ashley Street, her office above the Clara White Mission. "It's changed," she said of the street. "I guess the whole world has. In Roosevelt's day, it was the town: Ashley Street, State Street, Broad Street, there was a lot of activity. You know, segregation was the big to-do, and Ashley Street was really the street, in those days. For the blacks. And Broad Street. And Negro businesses were isolated mostly in those areas right in there. It was just times, I guess. My cousin had a beauty parlor. I guess the whole world has changed. People have special ideas."

She stood and walked out of the room and came back with a framed photograph. It was black and white, but it instantly became the most vivid thing in the room, the only thing not faded with heat and age, though it was old: a photo of her and her late husband. He had been a musician, she said, leader of his own five-piece orchestra, and when the Depression hit he became a sleeping-car porter. The photograph was of the good days, the early days, when they were young and she was very beautiful. Aveilhe looked at it a while. Then she said, quietly, "It was quite a company. Mr. A. L. Lewis, it was going good when he lived, you know. But sometimes, people just don't value what they have. Ervin, A. L. Lewis, they were sincere people. They would never understand the way the world is now. I didn't even get a pension."

"Shouldn't you have?" I asked.

"Yeah, I thought I should have, but you know with all this wrangling and tangling and I never did get it. I wasn't there. I had retired. I didn't get a pension. I didn't even get my pension from the company. It's terrible, and I've retired. When I left, I didn't get a dime. Didn't get any pension money."

"Didn't that make you mad?" I asked.

"Yeah, sure did. But when it's all over, it's too late."

On a subsequent morning, as I was heading back to the Beach from Aveilhe's east Jacksonville neighborhood, I decided to detour through downtown, and because it had been a long while since I passed the boarded-up Afro, I turned down Union Street. A pickup truck was parked on the sidewalk in front of the building, and the plywood had been ripped off of part of the lower façade, and so I stopped and went in. A construction crew was milling about, getting the size of the place, and a job foreman explained to me that the AME Church had bought the building, and was starting its transformation into the bishop's new offices. I introduced myself, and he offered me a hardhat and a tour. The building was magnificent, he said. Possibly the first use of pre-stressed concrete beams in the area, and the mahogany on the officers' walls was not veneer but thick solid planking. We walked through piles of gypsum dust and skirted heaped debris. The elevator was jammed open, and filled with bent metal molding. A lot of vandalism and looting had gone on, the foreman said. In the basement, someone had set up a sawmill and run quite an efficient salvage operation, cutting up the old brass fittings, the aluminum stair railings. We climbed the terrazzo, cantilevered stairs—missing, sure enough, their banisters—to the second-floor lobby, where polished granite panels had collapsed

from water-damaged walls and lay like giant cobbles across our path.
The foreman hopped between them down the hall. He stopped to
sweep the dust from one with the sole of his shoe. In the swath of clean
stone, I could see the words "A. L. Lewis" and some other names, and I
bent down and wiped the dust from an inscription. The tablet was
green marble, and the size of a tabletop. "It's two inches thick!" the
foreman marveled. The inscription read, "He hath shewed thee, O
man, what is good, and what doth the Lord require of thee, but to do
justly, and to love mercy, and to walk humbly with thy God?"

"Can you imagine what that would cost today?" the foreman
asked.

Back downstairs, we passed the gaping Mosler vault and entered
the old conference room. The room was half filled with a table saw and
stacks of lumber and, along two walls under broken windows, with
dust-covered heaps of papers. The papers were mounded like snow by
a plow, or like sand by a great wind, into an unruly drift or dune some
five feet tall and equally wide and more than three times as long.
Where they had been piled too high, the papers cascaded in avalanches
across the floor: letters, ledgers, account books, stock certificates, pay-
rolls, legal briefs, receipts, reports, calendars—the accumulated
records, so long presumed missing, of the Afro-American Life
Insurance Company. "They told us to throw it all in here," the foreman said. "There's a lot more in the basement." With his blessing and
some boxes he brought in, I remained in the room and started scoop-
ing the papers up out of harm's way, sorting them crudely as I went,
and stacking the boxes against a wall. The foreman said the bishop
would arrive soon, and would want to say hello.

From under the sawdust, under the mangle of footprints, I pulled
what I began to see was not only the detritus of a company but the substantial history of a people. The boxes began filling with what I knew
from my vain searches over the years to be the greatest financial profile of black Jacksonville in existence, extending back day by itemized
day past wars and depressions, past Red Summer and Jim Crow and
the Great Jacksonville Fire almost to Reconstruction, for the oldest of
the records were older than the company itself. Here were the hand-
penned letters of a young A. L. Lewis, and responses from such lumi-
naries of the age as Morehouse president John Hope; here were the

minutes of meetings of the Afro-American Pension Bureau, in the years when lynching was at its peak and the need of a financial bulwark most dire, the years when A. L. Lewis was newly anointed as president and discussing with his directors the possibility of a black beach. Here were the time cards for each individual employee, and bundled weekly receipts from every field office around the Southeast, and the paper-clipped contents of James H. Lewis's last wallet, his gasoline bill included, and planning memos for charitable events, and solicitations for band instruments for schoolchildren, and occultly ornamented initiation diplomas for nineteenth-century mutual-aid societies, and thousands of signatures on deeds and mortgages and envelopes and paper scraps detailing private transactions in money and land that spelled the birth and growth of The Bricks and Sugar Hill.

When I had been at it for a couple of hours, I heard footsteps and the foreman returned, smiling, accompanied by a stark, thin, important young man in a black suit and heavy black-framed sunglasses with gold monograms, who turned out to be a reverend with the AME Church. The reverend looked expensive, but not happy. "No, no, no, no, no, no, no, no, no," he said, waving a diamond ring in what I could tell right away was not going to be a benediction. I rose to introduce myself and held out a hand, which he didn't take. "No, no, no, no, no," he elaborated to the foreman. I explained that I was trying to get some documents out from underfoot, that they seemed important histori-cally, to which he responded perceptively that it was none of my con-cern. To my mention of black Jacksonvillians who could vouch for my sincerity and for the need to preserve the papers, he said, "They don't tell me what to do" and "I don't recall them helping the AME Church get this property." Accompanied by the now silent and seemingly mis-erable foreman, he "showed me out" to where his car a large new-model custom black-and-gilt Mercedes, was parked on the sidewalk behind my car. "Has he taken anything?" the reverend asked. "No, nothing's left this building," the foreman assured him hurriedly.

But a few items escaped. The object I was holding when I stood to greet the churchman was still in my hand as I walked outside, and once I had survived the bum's rush and was securely in my car, I perused it for the first time. It was a small black book the shape of a deck of cards, with two pieces of paper stuck into it. The tarnished gold letters on the book's face said, "The Afro-American Insurance Co.—Jacksonville, Fla." and its pages held a fine-print catalogue of rates and benefits for all the types of policies the company sold. This was an agent's rate book, carried by some debit agent on his or her neighborhood rounds in the year of the book's currency, 1922. I pulled out the pieces of paper. The first was a dollar bill, an old-style large-format World War I era, Federal Reserve Bank Note redeemable for gold. The other was a piece of lined parchment, seemingly a page from a chapbook, yellowed now, folded in quarters for so many years that the folds had become permanent pleats. On its back two words had been carefully scrawled in pencil: "Anachronism" and "Oligarchy." Was this an old penmanship exercise? I wondered. A spelling drill? The other side of the paper held a brief moral essay, and I surmised from the few misspellings that it had been dictated rather than copied, perhaps in one of the literacy *cum* citizenship classes the Afro sponsored in its early years. The essay read:

> Sometime the smallest men have the most money. The dollar mark is no standard in heaven. Money is the lowest kind of wealth. Fools and knaves may have wealth of coin, but only a true man can be rich in character. A good name is great riches. Poverty may be either an honor or a stigma, and so may wealth. Gold has never yet been able to Purchase either Peace or Purity. Peace in the mind is better then Plenty in the Purse. A true life is true riches.

For a moment, as I held these papers, it occurred to me to walk back into the building and return them to their source, like fishes tossed back into an obscuring pond. But then I thought of another and rightful owner who would appreciate them more, who might even display them in her Titan for anyone to see. So with these things beside me—a rate book, a credo, and a dollar bill—I headed back to the highway, and back toward American Beach.

The Three-Walled Room

Zora Neale Hurston in Washington, D.C., in early 1920s.

Battles of national destiny bear the names of ordinary towns. The wheeling armies stumble on each other in the darkness and whatever small place lies between them in their encounter is lifted by mischance out of its insignificance and donates its name as a synonym for honor or disaster or triumph or retreat. The forces that converged on American Beach in the 1990s were less visible and bloody than those that contested Gettysburg or Lexington or Chancellorsville. They bore no bright insignia and followed no clear banner. In a time of peaceful civil war, they vied for the nation's future in one of its tiniest and most hidden hamlets; in a war whose landscape was the geography of history, the history of American Beach gave the town a tactical importance. The Beach was not alone. Skirmishes were breaking out everywhere. It wasn't until I watched the same forces contest another small Florida town that I saw them emerge from the mist and display themselves for what they were, and declare what it was they wanted. In the roster of American battlefields, Eatonville warrants mention.

It's hard to know whether Eatonville and American Beach are identical or opposite places. They share a set of circumstances, both being historic black towns endangered by development. But while American Beach is on the state's watery fringe, Eatonville is a suburb of Orlando, a metropolis in the center of the state. In the realm of urban Florida, it would be hard to get farther from salt water. Since Orlando is also the home of Disney World, and since Eatonville is surrounded by the suburban sprawl that Disney World has generated, it could be said that Eatonville is also at an epicenter of common American experience, in ways that isolated American Beach is not.

Eatonville is the oldest incorporated black town in the United States. Like every town—like America—it has striven since its founding to accrue the necessities of civic life: a working government, a sustaining economy, a culture, and a history. Of these four, culture and history are the more problematic, in that they can't be established by constitution or run by a board of directors. Yet they are vital. No other poverty—not even economic poverty—is as destructive to civic life as the poverty of culture and history: they form the abiding link between generations; they give coherence and meaning to the lives of families and towns and countries. America, being (as it seemed to its colonizers) brand-new, had a special task in establishing a culture and a history. It is laboring mightily still. Black Americans had the most extraordinary task of all. No other people, in their passage here, were more violently stripped of their culture, history, religion, and language. To a greater degree than the European or Asian or any other New World settler, the African started over when he got off the boat and set his foot on the continent; for that, he deserves to be recognized as the quintessential American, the self-invented, home-grown, native immigrant.

As black Americans set about their task of building a new identity and establishing a place in their new land, they did so under an onerous burden, which transcends the burden of slavery and thus remains heavy still. They had to create themselves from scratch in the glare of the white man's scrutiny. The scrutiny was not benign, because it was not disinterested. White Americans were engaged in their own desperate struggle to create an identity for themselves, and in that struggle they found black people useful in many subtle ways as a counterpart and foil. To that end, white Americans plundered whatever they approved of in black life and demeaned the rest. The experience of A. L. Lewis and his family down through the generations to MaVynee Betsch is testament to the distorting power of that acquisitive gaze: nothing that blacks could do, whether it was building a company or singing opera, was free of the intrusion of race appraisal. Their every act was submitted to white inspection, and the inspection of blacks worried about white inspection, and thus taken away from them just as the historic culture of Africa had been taken. It would be as difficult to build a new culture in such an environment as to amass gold without a vault; in this century, and increasingly as this century draws to an end, black cultural capital has been whisked away or shattered nearly as fast as it could be accumulated. The often-stated desire of blacks to *own* something is at its root the need to own that: the privacy within which to properly construct a culture and build a history. Without that privacy, nothing authentic can flourish. Seemingly every act and thought is warped by its need to reflect or deflect the majority opinion. In this way, expression is perverted into performance.

Even or especially in this particular, black experience is profoundly American. America at the turn of the twenty-first century finds itself in a bind that A. L. Lewis would recognize. As Americans continue with the vital task of building their young culture, their efforts are subverted. Their families and polities suffer from the weakness of the cultural glue, and are unable to concoct a stronger one before the acquisitive eye of an overweening power. The power belongs to consumer capitalism, which once made products for our culture to use but which increasingly, in the so-called entertainment and information and service economies, considers culture a product and history something to be merchandised. Media saturation and advertising distort the very values of informed democracy and historical literacy that the commerce pretends to promote. Whatever cannot be marketed is dismissed; the authentic is supplanted by the ersatz. In the face of that plunder, submission and protest are possible, but true culture-building is difficult to the point of impossibility, and requires a fight.

That was the fight whose armies careened into each other in a corner of central Florida and made it a battleground. On one side were the forces of make-believe and money and corporate-sponsored society, on the other the forces of self-determination and cultural integrity. Each side had its Mecca in one of two Orlando suburbs built as explicit expressions of their respective ideals. Both towns predicated their existence on a reading of history, but their readings of history differed. One of the towns was called Celebration, and it was created by one of the greatest of America's corporate empires and inspired and championed by that empire's patron saint, Walt Disney. The other town was Eatonville, created by Negroes and championed by a non-profit organization operating off folding tables on a shoestring and led by a local schoolteacher named N. Y. Nathiri.

Knowing N. Y. Nathiri as I do, which is to say professionally, I picture her in two places. One is in a box, the other on a stage. The box is her office, a square, cramped, windowless storage closet at the rear of an art gallery on Eatonville's main street. From here Nathiri administers a civic organization known as PEC (for Preserve Eatonville Community). The stage is often just that, when she is giving a speech or introducing a symposium. Or she may be outside the public hall but still in the public eye, racing around Eatonville simultaneously hoisting a cell phone and several walkie-talkies as she coordinates the far-flung mayhem of PEC's annual street festival. I say I imagine her in two places, but really she is the same in each, for even onstage facing an audience she seems as private and enclosed as she does when she is ensconced in her boxy office with her door shut, plotting Eatonville's ascendance.

I met N. Y. Nathiri in Jacksonville. We were introduced by MaVynee Betsch. In the cause of protecting black history, the two women are geopolitical allies, philosophical counterparts, and comrades-in-arms. Because Nathiri grew up in the shadow of Afro-American Life Insurance Company, for which her mother worked as an Orlando-area agent, she and MaVynee are also linked by family happenstance. Nevertheless, I'm not too sure they like each other. They are dispositional opposites: one is an ecstatic, the other an ascetic. To the degree that MaVynee exudes a tragic, artistic bohemianism, to the degree that MaVynee is onstage even when she is alone, Nathiri displays the controlled, precise sobriety of an academic librarian—which she was, at Cornell in the 1970s. Like MaVynee at American Beach, she is the most visible member of her community, but without the flamboyance of shell bracelets or witchy coifs. She dresses in shapeless monastic robes and covers her head with a black hijab or sometimes a white one. She is a practicing Muslim, an orthodox Sunni, which explains some of her formality, and explains why her friends tend to hold their breath (as I have learned to do) at the inevitable moment—one that recurs more frequently as her reputation spreads and her profile heightens—when a friendly dignitary will welcome her to the podium with an outstretched hand or, God forbid, a kiss, which Nathiri resolutely declines. In Islam, even in Islamic Florida, it is impolite for men to touch women in public. In Nathiri's life, as in Eatonville's history, walls are worth defending. Freedom lies within.

To a drive-through visitor, Eatonville is an eight-block-long, gap-toothed business district of cinder-block stores and churches grand and modest, barbershops, and juke joints. There is a motel and a nightclub and a firehouse and a school. Twenty-eight hundred residents live in a surrounding neighborhood of neat, modest, postwar ranch-style homes. The town is enveloped by greater Orlando and overshadowed by an interstate, which does not acknowledge it even with the courtesy of an exit. It is tiny and poor, relative to the neighboring towns of Maitland and Winter Park, and thoroughly black.

Eatonville holds the distinction of being, as Nathiri puts it, "the oldest incorporated city in the United States founded by Americans of
African descent." It holds the further distinction, for such a town, of
having survived with its black sovereignty intact to the brink of the
twenty-first century.

In 1987—coincidentally, the year of Eatonville's centennial—its
walls were finally breached, by a construction project devised by
Orange County. The county intended to widen an existing road linking Interstate 4, west of Eatonville, and U.S. Highway 17, east of
Eatonville. The problem was, the linking road was Kennedy
Boulevard, the main business artery of Eatonville. The widening, from
two lanes to five, would take out or crowd out most of those businesses, replace the municipal park with water-runoff retention ponds,
and divide the tiny town with a barrier all but impassable to pedestri-
ans, in order to allow the high-speed passage of eleven thousand extra
cars a day. In effect, it would spell the end of Eatonville.

Eatonville has no appreciable political weight and little political
coherence. Some of the town's politicians—including the mayor—supported the road project. Many citizens feared it. They protested to the
Orange County Commission but got nowhere. The project was
approved. "The wolf came in sheep's clothing and said, 'Wouldn't you
like to participate in progress?'" Nathiri explained to me one afternoon in her office. "And the people said, 'No.' So they said 'Okay,
we're gonna take this and make it a road, so you're gonna *be* a part of
progress one way or another.'"

In 1986, Nathiri was teaching part-time at a community college
and raising her three children on the same parcel of Eatonville land
where she herself grew up. The threat galvanized her to action. "Our
outside friends were calling us to say, 'You really understand what's
going on here, don't you? I hope you are not being naive and thinking
that this road is for the benefit of your community. Please understand
that this is an effort to destroy the community so that development
can come in.' Here, in order to bring in the Kmarts and the strip malls,
you know—you can't do it on this little road. You have to expand it. So
that was it. This was a community-busting road."

It was beyond the eleventh hour. The project seemed inevitable.
"There were stakes," Nathiri remembers. "Oh, you could only say they

were trying to put the fear of God in our hearts. There were surveyors' stakes every which way. We had stakes everywhere. Everywhere."

Nevertheless, the townspeople decided to fight, and not only through their elected city government. They formed PEC and took the county to court. "We didn't just have one of these hearts-and-flowers initiatives," Nathiri said. "We went to their gut and confronted them on their own information." They called in lawyers and engineers to challenge every assumption behind the road project. In a short time, they ran up $30,000 in legal fees.

But as it turns out, the legal fight was only a part of their defense, and maybe the least part. PEC, with Nathiri at the helm, turned to Eatonville's history and summoned from it an ancestral champion—a woman who, like Nathiri herself, like MaVynee Betsch at American Beach, had left her home for success in the wide world, only to give up the bright lights and return. It's unlikely that Orange County trembled in its boots at this development: the woman's prominence in the wide world may have been great at one time, but she was only an author of books and not even a well-known one, like Stephen King or John Grisham. Besides, she was dead. The champion's name was Zora Neale Hurston.

Zora (her first name is such an exclamation of onomatopoetic eponymy that few can resist hailing her in the familiar) was one of the stars of the Harlem Renaissance, that creative outburst which began with the publication of Claude McKay's poem *If We Must Die* during the Red Summer of 1919 and lasted until the Harlem Riot of 1935, and comprised the most concentrated literary movement in American history. She was also Eatonville's child. Most likely, Hurston was born either in Eatonville in 1903 or in the tiny eastern Alabama town of Notasulga in 1891. Stetson Kennedy, her boss when she worked for the WPA Writers' Project in the late 1930s (her office was in the Clara White Mission, on Ashley Street in Jacksonville), commented in a short biographical essay that "the time and place of the birth of Zora Neale Hurston are among the Great Mysteries." Hurston was famously secretive on this score, and her reply to such observations was, "Anyway, I can guarantee that I was born." Whatever the case, she grew up in Eatonville, and except for brief sojourns, lived there until adulthood, when she left to seek her fortune in the North. No matter how high her fortunes soared, Eatonville remained her center. It was certainly her professional center; she documented Eatonville's folk life in short stories, nonfiction pieces, and novels, including her 1937 masterwork, *Their Eyes Were Watching God*.

Hurston's career traced the same sad trajectory as those of some other eminent American authors; after all her success, she died forgotten and broke, in Florida in 1960. This explains why she can be introduced as famous but still needs introduction. Hurston spent her last years working as a maid near Miami and was living in an indigents' nursing home in Fort Pierce when she died. She was buried in an unmarked grave in a segregated graveyard.

So it was that in calling on Zora Neale Hurston to resurrect Eatonville, N. Y. Nathiri and PEC were joining in the resurrection of Zora Neale Hurston. Their idea was simply to create enough awareness of Eatonville's first citizen to make the town seem less conveniently expendable to the county despoilers. Nathiri was convinced that the most substantial object the town could place in the path of the bulldozers was its history. To highlight that history, in 1988 the group began organizing a street festival they named the Zora Neale Hurston Festival of the Arts—or, less formally, *Zora!*—and they set about trying to solicit some interest and some funds. Both came, in a different form and to a greater degree than they had expected. N. Y. Nathiri told me about the moment when those expectations surged—the night PEC's bookkeeper called her at home to tell her they had received a check for $1,000. It was signed by an A. Walker. "And I said, 'A. Walker!' And she said, 'It's from San Francisco.' And I said, 'Mrs. Brown, that's *Alice Walker!* Alice Walker has sent us a thousand-dollar check!'"

Walker's interest was not out of the blue. She had long championed the revival of interest in the ostracized author and her denigrated works. Of *Their Eyes Were Watching God*, Walker wrote: "No book is more important to me than this one." In 1973, she had traveled to Fort Pierce and found the weed-choked cemetery where Hurston lay buried, and placed in it a granite headstone reading, "Zora Neale Hurston—A Genius of the South."

As PEC's plans progressed, it became evident that Eatonville was a spiritual homeplace to many more Americans than anyone had suspected—to people who felt an intimate connection with the place through Hurston's descriptions and the travails of Janie Mae Crawford, the heroine of *Their Eyes Were Watching God,* but had never seen it. Now they came to see it: ten thousand of them the first year; hundreds of thousands in years following. "Eatonville as created or reflected in the work of Zora Neale Hurston represents a state of mind," Nathiri told me, "and people are just anxious to be here. It's like a cultural homecoming."

Interest flowed into PEC from the likes of Stetson Kennedy, actress Ruby Dee, and Hurston biographer Robert Hemenway—who, like Walker and others, volunteered to come to *Zora!* and speak at their own expense. "So when we got Alice Walker, we knew we were on the way," Nathiri told me. "After the first festival, the genie was out of the bottle."

Zora! was followed by *Zora! 2* and *Zora! 3,* and now, in the last week of every January (deliberately timed to avoid Black History Month), crowds descend on Eatonville to listen to jazz, watch plays, dance to rock and roll, buy Nubian perfumes and oils, batik robes and kente umbrellas, T-shirts, fried fish, barbecue, and beer from outdoor vendors shaded under arrays of funeral tents—in short, to do all the things that people do at street celebrations of African-American life. They also convene in auditoriums and conference rooms around town and on regional campuses to hear invited ivory-towerites chew on the meaning of Hurston's life and work, and often on each other.

This is *Zora!*'s distinction. While street festivals and academic symposia are legion, they usually stay as far apart on the continuum of convocations as Reverend Ike and Cotton Mather on the continuum of divines. It would be hard to imagine Taylor, Texas, for instance, inviting the National Herpetological Society to conjoin its convention to the annual festivities of the town's Rattlesnake Roundup, but Eatonville has accomplished just such an amalgam of high and popular culture. For a week each year, an important provincial capital of black intellectual endeavor is a large party in a very tiny town.

By 1994, the year of *Zora! 5,* the poor black town slated for demolition and the dead writer whose reputation was only beginning its climb out of obscurity had come so successfully to each other's rescue that the road project seemed a dead letter. Orange County, which had so recently plotted the town's demise, was now promoting its existence in tourist brochures as a must-see local attraction. Meanwhile, Eatonville was being extolled by such eminent academics as Elinor Traylor, who chairs the Department of Literature at Howard

University, as "now one of the most important regions on the literary map of the world." It would seem that the battle was over. In reality it had just begun. The forces that had mustered to defeat the new highway remained bivouacked in the town for a grander fight, which had nothing to do with roads and less to do with the future of Eatonville than with the future of American society.

"Eatonville is a colored town, and concerned with colored affairs," Hurston wrote in 1932. The festival held in her honor has managed a sort of unforeseen cultural prestidigitation. "When I speak from an ethnic or heritage point of view, yes, I'm saying what we're doing in Eatonville can be a rejuvenating force for *this* community of people in the country," N. Y. Nathiri told me, and by "this community" she meant the community of "colored affairs." "But of course I am also confident that what we are doing has a rejuvenating aspect for the society at large. It has a universal application; it has a global application. I really do believe that the work we are doing in Eatonville is a paradigm for a resurrection in the country."

Nathiri and Eatonville weren't the only ones adopting a messianic urban mission. In 1994 a massive construction project was announced: an entire town—a place intended as the eventual home for 20,000 people—was to be built in Osceola County, just across the Orange County border. Its charter was idealistic: to restore the American community through a return to old-fashioned American small-town values. The town was to be called Celebration and, like Eatonville, it based its existence on heritage. Like Eatonville, Celebration saw itself as a template for cultural salvation. "I hope in fifty years they say, 'Thank God for Celebration. It's set up a system of how to develop communities,'" the CEO of the development company told me. The developer was the Walt Disney Company, and the CEO was Michael Eisner. His enthusiasm had percolated through the ranks even to the part-time Disney receptionist, who gushed, "It's a gift. I think Celebration is, if anything, a gift to the nation and the world."

Disney, of course, was already something of a local presence. The Disney World theme park is the largest private employer in the Orange County area. More than that, it is the largest single-site private employer in Florida. Since 1972, when Disneyworld opened, Orlando has been in its economic thrall, down to the tenor of Orlando's road-side marketplace. "They opened Disneyworld," an Orange County commissioner once told me. "And we got Muffler World, Carpet World, Pants World, Pie World." They also got Busch Gardens, Universal Studios, and a host of other such gargantuan playgrounds. Orlando is now the greatest tourist destination in the world, ahead of second-place Paris. People come there from everywhere, but they don't come to see anything indigenous to Orlando or Orange County, unless it's alligator wrestling at World Famous Gatorland. They come to see precisely what they could see at home—to a place where, as the promotional slogan for Universal Studios says, "what happens in the movies happens to you." They visit mass-media cartoon characters, ride through reenacted movie scenes, and buy mass-marketed mass-media product tie-ins.

The interstate and other arteries that course through Orlando are stacked with billboards proclaiming the local product. They do not hawk oranges, as they once might have, nor the missiles of Martin-Lockheed, which opened a factory there in the 1950s. Like the rest of America, Orlando's economy has gone through generations: agricultural, industrial, and now the economy that is the whole country's future, dedicated to service, entertainment, tourism, and make-believe. The allures beckoning from Orlando's billboards range from the outlandish—Survive a Towering Inferno! Flee from Rampaging Dinosaurs!—to quaint Americana. In fact, there is little distinction between quaint and outlandish, between fundamentals and fantasy. "Main Street" is the antechamber to Disney's Magic Kingdom and so lies at the heart of the heart of the extended tourist Mecca; it is a five-eighths-scale replica of a traditional downtown, graced with the gingerbread storefronts of folksy small-scale merchants, along streets undefiled by automobiles. Millions of people pay millions of dollars to come and enjoy that townscape. It is a vision right out of Orlando's agricultural past, but its visitors arrive by car through Orlando's present, down jammed highways lined with corporate hotels and chain restaurants. It's the rare visitor who gets a glimpse of the genuine, erstwhile Orlando main street, which Disney helped to destroy.

In 1963, when Walt Disney himself flew over Orange County in Arthur Godfrey's private jet and pointed to the place where he wanted to build his empire, Orlando was a tidy, claustrophobic, lake-cratered, moss-draped, brick-paved Southern citrus burg, its municipal history an accretion of local genealogies. It was a place where few looked out and fewer in, its identity yet undimmed by suburban sprawl or the scrim of corporate fantasy. The bricks, most of them, have by now been asphalted over to accommodate faster traffic. Especially on its outer fringes, Orlando is an endless migraine agglomeration of throbbing highways lined with endless ticky-tack. The Orlando cityscape has become a preeminent victim of the Florida chain-store massacre.

Orlando's experience is more the rule than the exception among American towns. One of the problems unleashed on the nation at large by prosperity and growth in the decades after World War II was the problem of pervasive uniformity. Everywhere, the mall filled with chain stores has replaced the old independent-business downtowns; the highway has supplanted the sidewalk and the public rails; television has supplanted the town square and the active forms of recreation and culture; and the old close-knit neighborhood has been replaced with the subdivision's anonymous cul-de-sacs, its sweeping avenues empty of life, friendly only to unimpeded traffic and leading to nothing in the way of services or jobs, to nothing resembling a real and vital center.

So Orlando is not unique. But in few other places in America is the Siamese connection between mall and sprawl, dystopian main street and utopian Main Street, so visibly demonstrated. N. Y. Nathiri's contention that Eatonville was targeted for "community busting" to clear the way for the Kmarts and Targets makes more convincing and sinister sense when you see what lies around Eatonville. It is the only municipality rich or poor in the region which can boast that it has not a single franchise. Nowhere in Eatonville can you find a McDonald's or a Best Western or Häagen-Dazs or Circuit City, but nowhere outside of Eatonville can you find the Mop City Barbershop, R & R Groceries, Gil's Auto Parts, Smith's Eatonville Motel, Boswell & Sons Tavern, Scoops Ice Cream Parlor, or the Zora Neale Hurston National Museum of Fine Arts.

In 1984, the corporate conquest of Orlando nearly consumed Disney itself. The excess of undeveloped land in Walt Disney's Florida holdings had been made exceedingly valuable by encroaching commercial sprawl and was attracting corporate raiders. To forestall losing the entire company to unwanted suitors, the empty land had to be sold off or developed. Disney's managers didn't want to sell it off, precisely because they didn't want to live with whatever suburban outrage some developer decided to erect next door to their park. So they decided to develop it themselves. Disney could have gone with the default model of development: the gated, golf-centered, monocultural enclave—a model known within Disney as the "Arvida pattern," after one of Florida's most successful developers of such plans, the Arvida Company. Disney owned Arvida. When the time came to develop Celebration, though, Michael Eisner (who grew up the son of an urban planner on Manhattan's Upper East Side) didn't want to do things the Arvida way. "I went on a tour of all the Arvida properties," he told me. "By the time I had seen—I don't know—fifty of the exact same kitchens all over Florida, the exact same houses, the exact same walls and exact same feeling that is shared with Palm Springs, I became convinced that there was a better way, a more interesting way to do it. Celebration is not what I used to call 'Palm Springs kibbutz.' We're not doing that."

Instead, Eisner turned the project over to planners and architects who were in revolt against modern subdivisions, who see in the recent progress of urban design a conspiracy to promote civic emptiness. The architects were loosely identified with a movement called neo-traditionalism, a term that makes some of them nervous (Disney has rechristened the movement Family-Friendly Planning) but which accurately indicates their leaning. The plan they devised for Celebration turned the civic clock back to a more gentle, coherent, and self-confident hour in American history—ironically, to precisely that hour before corporations began developing communities. Celebration would, at least in its outward manifestations, recall a town out of the 1930s or 1940s. Its street plan would encourage the pedestrian and restrain the car, with narrow roads laid out on a grid instead of in swooping curves and cul-de-sacs. Garages would be behind the houses and would open onto alleys. The houses would be set close enough together to make neighborliness unavoidable and walking distances manageable. There would even be places worth walking to—a downtown with markets and cafés and a City Hall and post office, and a school placed centrally enough to play a ceremonial as well as a utilitarian role, instead of being shunted off to cheaper land on some industrial fringe. There would be no guard or gate to challenge visitors at the town's border. Mixed in with million-dollar custom-built mansions would be more affordable homes and apartments sufficient to ensure a modest socioeconomic mix. If the community's eventual residential makeup reflected that of the brochures, the town would be racially diverse. The residential buildings would all reflect pre-1940 housing styles, with columns and front porches and sash windows and high ceilings, and they would be *erect*—none of this spreading, sterile, jet-age, A-frame, split-level, minimalist modernism! In all, Celebration's outward attributes would be those that characterized the more livable American cities before World War II.

Nothing in the way of neo-traditionalism had yet been essayed on the scale of Celebration—but no previous project had enjoyed the imprimatur or pocketbook of the Walt Disney Company, or the Disney aptitude for mixing sentimentality with idealism to imbue a commercial project with a mission. Disney would reportedly spend $2.5 billion developing and building Celebration. The town's mission was no less grandiose: defying and perhaps reversing the decline of community in postwar America. Michael Eisner stressed to me that Celebration was not meant as a cure for all the deep social problems Americans faced, "the vast problems of gun control and drug addiction and the rest of it . . . HIV problems." But just as suburban blight and its attendant social decay were not confined to Orlando, Disney's remedy was not meant to be an isolated whim. "This is needed so much, in so many places, that this is just the beginning," Eisner told me, though he felt that any future Celebrations would have to be built by some company other than his own. "We are a silly company," he said. "I'm happy that we're a silly company. At the same time we are a very serious company *trying* to be silly,"—his voice grew more intent—"and here we had this piece of land, and this is not a silly adventure we're on here!"

In 1994, Celebration's site was still just pasture and swamp, and its mission was evident only in a prototype sales brochure, in which the proposed town certainly sounded neo-traditional. "There once was a place where neighbors greeted neighbors in the quiet of summer twilight," the brochure proclaimed.

Where children chased fireflies. And porch swings provided easy refuge from the cares of the day.

The movie house showed cartoons on Saturday. The grocery store delivered. And there was one teacher who always knew you had that special something.

Remember that place? Perhaps from your childhood. Or maybe just from stories. It held a magic all its own. The special magic of an American hometown.

One clear-skied Sunday in early 1996, two years after reading that brochure, I paid a visit to the (now former) pasture. I left my car near the corner of Market Street and Celebration Avenue and took a walk through America's newest town. It was in a miraculous state of midcreation. The shell of a downtown was clustered at the shore of a brand-new lake. A short, straight canal (fed by a water pump and clarified of Florida silt by regular infusions of alum) divided the north- and south-bound lanes of a boulevard called Water Street, which sales agents touted as "the Champs-Élysées of Celebration." Vast acres of trucked-in sand were laced with a mesh of newly asphalted streets, dotted with the concrete foundation pads for hundreds of future homes. A school building was up, though it was windowless; a crane towered over the steel skeleton of the medical center. I had the sensation of being in a town undergoing a cataclysm in reverse, arising in a flash of dust, playing out backwards the advent of the atomic age.

No one was about; the workers had taken the day off. The business district was littered with the residue of a week's construction labors— piles of sand, stacks of shingles and bricks, assembled roof trusses, a reposing front-end loader, the cast-off bandoliers of nail guns. In the shell of a future restaurant, a sawhorse table held a banquet of fast-food wrappers, scurrying slightly in the warm eddies of a breeze that moved through the open honeycomb of offices and stores and apartments. Farther up the empty street, I encountered the only other human figure in the entire town, a little girl riding a bicycle past a picket fence under a spreading oak, chased by her dog. It was the town insignia, embossed on the manhole covers like some coded clue in a time capsule—an icon of innocence and freedom bearing a Disney copyright.

There were still no completed houses. But all four hundred and fifty residences planned as part of Celebration's initial stage already had eager buyers. On November 18, 1995, a lottery had been held to determine who could buy one of these residences. The event took place out of sight of the town construction, in a field by the highway, overshadowed by the Disney corporate offices and next to the Celebration Preview Center, a prefab sales office whose exterior had been glamorized with the trompe-l'oeil façade of a quaint Colonial house. Carnival tents were set up in the field. Cartoon characters entertained the kids. The event was called Founder's Day. When I asked a sales agent who the founder was, she told me that there wasn't any, technically speaking, though coincidentally November 18 was Mickey Mouse's birthday. The agents had had no idea how many people would show up, especially since there was nothing much to look at yet other than the Preview Center—not even a model home. But when the day came, five thousand people attended. Twelve hundred put down the $1,000 deposit to qualify for a chance to buy a house, demand thus outstripping supply by nearly three to one. Some people, I was told, had quit their jobs and sold their homes in distant states and moved into hotel rooms or (in one case) the family car, awaiting the Founder's Day auction. It seemed that Celebration was a spiritual homeplace to many more Americans than anyone had suspected, and for the same reason that Eatonville was: America was looking for its roots.

"We just happen to believe that we lost something when we turned our backs on the neighborhood concept," a fundamentalist minister from south Florida told me in the Preview Center, after winning the lottery and registering to buy a Celebration home. "And that's what this community's about. It's going back to when this country functioned best as a country, with neighborhood-type arrangements where people were really neighbors. They weren't just living side by side without knowing each other. And we like that idea. We think it's time we turned around this nation and got back to where we were."

Thus, simultaneously, across the span of a county, Eatonville and Celebration enlisted in the vanguard of the struggle for the survival of the American town. Each year when I came back to spend a week in Eatonville, I would also drive to the other end of Orange County to see how Disney was coming along with its project. The two towns did not seem so very different from each other in their attempts to hold disastrous development at bay: they were both eminently well-intentioned. Each was working against the standard urban script. Eatonville was trying hard to stave off the kind of decline that had befallen American Beach. Celebration was determined not to become another Amelia Island Plantation. Both were eager to represent a solution to the American dilemma and lead the nation, if only by example, into a better future.

In truth, though, the towns were different in ways more important and intrinsic than the one's newness and opulence and the other's age and poverty. The distinction between them, and the reason one would fail in its mission and the other succeed, could be found in the life story of Zora Neale Hurston.

To read Hurston is to be invited home. *Dust Tracks on a Road*, her 1942 autobiography, is in great part a biography of Eatonville, and *Their Eyes Were Watching God* presents the town's early years as a sort of Genesis myth, stylized but not disguised. The novel's protagonist is Janie Mae Crawford, who ambles into Eatonville with her second husband, Jody Starks, who will become the town's central citizen, first mayor, and sole storekeeper. (Eatonville's renowned storekeeper since the 1880s and during Hurston's childhood was named Joe Clarke.) The town Janie Mae and Jody help to build was, when they first saw it, a "scant dozen of shame-faced houses scattered in the sand and palmetto roots," prompting him to comment, "God, they call this a town? Why, 'tain't nothing but a raw place in de woods." Starks mobilizes the settlers to civic improvement, starting with the blazing of Kennedy Boulevard. "A day was named for roads and they all agreed to bring axes and things like that and chop out two roads running each way."

In real life, all this occurred a hundred years before the county brought earthmovers and things like that and threatened the widening of that old road into a highway. Between Reconstruction and the turn of the century, that era when Eatonville was founded, similar black settlements were springing up all over the South and the Midwest. Some thirty of them were incorporated, for the towns aspired to legal recognition and to full participation in the American democratic experiment.

In light of that, Jody Starks's speech to his fellow residents is not as pre-posterous as it might sound. "Ah kin see dat dis town is full uh union and love," he says. "Ah means tuh put mah hands tuh de plow heah, and strain every nerve tuh make dis our town de metropolis uh de state. So maybe Ah better tell yuh in case you don't know dat if we expect tuh move on, us got tuh incorporate lak every other town. Us got tuh incor-porate, and us got tuh have uh mayor, if things is tuh be done and done right." Of those black incorporated towns, few remain, but among them is Eatonville, the pioneer: "the first attempt at organized self-govern-ment on the part of Negroes in America," Hurston wrote in *Dust Tracks*.

Only by seceding from the surrounding society could the founders of Eatonville enlist themselves in it. In their insistence on democratic norms, they made it clear that they were not creating a refuge from America but a redoubt from which to participate in America. The extraordinary audacity of that is evident from the experience of Hurston's contemporary, July Perry. Perry was black, and lived in Ocoee, a town about as far west of downtown Orlando as Eatonville is north. In 1920, on election day, some black citizens showed up at the Ocoee polls and asked to vote. Their boldness sparked a white riot, in which the entire black population of Ocoee was driven from town and more than thirty were killed, in a massacre Hurston later claimed to have witnessed. Defending his home and family, July Perry killed two white marauders. He was lynched from a telephone pole on the Eatonville road. Ocoee to this day is a place blacks hesitate to visit. By contrast, throughout the long nightmare of black disfranchisement Eatonville had a black elected government, black-run public services, and a volunteer black militia strong enough to check violent raids from the Ku Klux Klan at the city limits.

The town also had the active goodwill of many whites, who helped secure its land and build its first church, Saint Lawrence AME, which was established in 1882, before the town's incorporation, and whose congregation still prays in a modest white-frame successor to the orig-inal building, also on Kennedy Boulevard. The walls of this church are, tellingly, lined with paintings depicting the stations of the cross as experiences of black Eatonville citizens, all painted in the 1930s by André Smith, a white artist who lived in neighboring Maitland.

"It means something to me, it really does," Clara Williams

explained to me one day in 1994, when I asked her about Eatonville's importance as a self-contained and self-determining town. Williams was seventy-one at that time and is counted among Eatonville's eminent, though she was then living in Orlando. She had been christened in Saint Lawrence AME and has seen her grandchildren christened there, too. Her grandparents moved to Eatonville from southern Georgia in 1892, when the town was five years old and her father an infant of one. Her father met her mother when they were students at the local Hungerford School, where her mother later taught. Her parents, grandparents, and great-grandmother are buried in the town cemetery, and their memory underscores the necessity of Eatonville's existence; her father was murdered by a Klansman when he was forty-two, walking home down a county road. "Him and his friend, they were coming from fishing," Williams told me in her precise and gentle voice. "The man just ran over them and killed them for nothin'. Just 'cause he could. And nobody told my mother, and my mother was worried about my daddy hadn't come home. And the next morning a friend of the family was at the post office and heard this policeman talk about this man was killed last night and he was comin' from fishing. And he asked the police if he knew who the man was, and the policeman said, 'No, just two more niggers dead.'"

Like many in Orlando, Williams knew exactly who the killer was. There was no secret about it. Her only small recourse to justice was to refuse to buy sheet music in the store where he was employed.

Zora Neale Hurston's father was pastor of Eatonville's other large church, Macedonia Baptist, and was one of the men mustered to the town's defense. Hurston recalled him going out one night armed with his repeating Winchester rifle when cries from the swamp raised fears that a black man had fallen into the hands of the Klan. He also served three terms as Eatonville's mayor during the World War I era, allowing Hurston to boast in *Dust Tracks*, "The village of Eatonville is still governed by the laws formulated by my father." Hurston herself grew up on Taylor Street, in a house with a five-acre garden and two giant chinaberry trees by the front gate, and a front walk lined with Cape jasmine bushes. She attended the Hungerford Normal & Industrial School, Eatonville's largest and most prestigious institution, a residential academy with an agricultural campus modeled on Tuskegee

Institute. She received her more informal education in black story-telling (which she didn't yet know to call folkways) lingering in front of Joe Clarke's general store and listening to the adults compete in the vivid extemporaneous exaggeration that Hurston later designated "patented porch lies."

Hurston left her little town to head north, spending two years at Howard University under the guidance of literary impresario Alain Locke, the man she called a "presiding genius" and whom the poet Claude McKay classified as "a Philadelphia blue-black blood, a Rhodes scholar and graduate of Oxford University, and [one] I have heard . . . described as the most refined Negro in America." Howard was followed by a scholarship to (and eventual degree from) Barnard College, where Hurston was the first black student. She went on to study anthropology at Columbia with the esteemed Franz Boas. Boas sent her back south to apply her training to collecting folktales in various rural enclaves. Packing a pistol and a two-dollar dress, she took her anthropology as far afield as Haiti and New Orleans to study voodoo (for her 1938 book *Tell My Horse*) and to Florida locales like American Beach, which she visited in 1939 while doing oral histories of Franklintown residents. She also brought her work home to Eatonville, to study systematically the mannerisms of her "kin-folks and skin folks" in the town where she grew up.

On her visits, Hurston gave back to Eatonville the gift she had received on Joe Clarke's porch. "I saw her all the time when I was growing up," Clara Williams said to me. Williams is one of only two surviving Eatonvillians who can say that. "Whenever Zora came to Eatonville, she came up on what we called the Hill, behind Saint Lawrence church, and all of us children would follow her wherever she was going, and she'd read to us or tell us stories and have us playing games. And we just sat down on the ground under a tree, and she kept us spellbound with stories."

Hurston also told stories *about* the town, in articles and factual books and in thinly varnished fictions, and it caused no little animosity. "She wrote about the people," Williams said. "Some things she wrote, she didn't have to write. Tellin' people's business. Some of the things she said, she didn't have to tell. Some of the things the men would do, the wives didn't know anything about, but she said it in her books. That caused confusion.

"She had friends," Williams said. "A lot of people. Some of the older ones she got on their nerves tellin' tales on them. And some of them, I've come to find out, weren't tales. Some of them were true. But at the time, you know, people didn't want it to be known. You don't want all your business in the street, and putting it in a book, that's indiscreet."

Hurston was also resented because she was able to thrive among big-city whites while her friends remained caught in constricted lives. Worse, she thrived by turning the material of those constricted lives into salable commodity. When Hurston first arrived in New York, she was astonished to see vendors selling the same flowers that had lined her front walk in Eatonville in wild profusion. Except in the North they weren't called Cape jasmine; they were called gardenias and cost a dollar a bloom. Some of the people back home felt that the stories she told to black and white listeners in Harlem and to readers around the country enjoyed the same astronomical markup. They were ordinary porch lies sold for a dollar a bloom. In the course of that commerce, Hurston seemed to have accomplished what the Ku Klux Klan could not, and opened her little closed town to white inspection.

It was as though the creativity that made Hurston Eatonville's pre-eminent patriot had also made her Eatonville's greatest traitor. "Because she, it seemed, was catering to whites," Clara Williams told me. Williams had direct experience with the anger this engendered, on a day when Hurston was in Eatonville and drew the Williams children over to her home to hear some stories. "On this particular day," Clara Williams said, "she had this photographer there, and she had these big long watermelons she had raised, and she gave each of us a quarter section, and we were just eatin' watermelon, and he was takin' our picture." At home that evening, the children related their adventure to their father, "and he said, 'Wait here till I get back.' He left. And we never knew what happened until after I grew up. I had finished college. And one day we were all talking about it, and I said, 'You know, we never saw those pictures.' And Mother said, 'You never will.'" Williams's father had threatened Hurston with jail if photographs of his exceptional black children eating stereotypical watermelon ever reached publication.

"There were whites that looked at blacks, you know, with a difference," Williams said. "And this is what they wanted. And, uh, some people resented it."

The runaway ambition and wayward direction of Eatonville's experiment occurred to me one evening at *Zora! 5*, during a presentation in an auditorium—really, a converted basketball arena at the University of Central Florida, in Orlando—at about the moment when a woman in the front row of the VIP section went into diabetic shock, stopped breathing, and fell apparently unconscious from her folding chair. No other woman, doing such, would have been suspected of refined artistic effect. But this particular woman was Jacquelyn Torrence, who is nationally known as the Story Lady, a collector and performer of Southern black folktales and an adept at dramatic timing perhaps unsurpassed in the country. This night, her timing, though morbid, was impeccable.

Like the others in the arena, she had come to watch Maya Angelou trade patented porch lies and general wisdom with her longtime friend and colleague Elinor Traylor. The audience was thick with headline intellects. Every time Angelou invoked some authority's name, such as that of bell hooks, or Spelman College's Beverly Guy-Sheftall, Berkeley's Barbara Christian, or Emory's Richard Long ("the only polymath I know," Angelou called him), a yell from the audience told her they were present in the room. Finally she said, "Good grief, you all should be up here!"

The onstage conversation had been introduced as one that would be full of "love and laughter," and there was plenty of that, if you counted love for Hurston. She was called a pathfinder and a lifesaver, was credited with a cosmic utility unusual in a mere writer, and before the hour was over had been likened to Sojourner Truth, Harriet Tubman, Frederick Douglass, Martin Luther King Jr., Malcolm X, Mary McCleod Bethune, and the Queen of Sheba. There was a lot of laughter, too—most prominently from Traylor, whose brass-gong bray of delight greeted the anecdotes and verses flowing out of Angelou's memory. "The woman I love is fat, and chocolate to the bone," Angelou sang, her voice slowing through the nineteenth-century folk song until its savoring of each syllable verged on the salacious. ". . . And every time she shakes, some skinny woman loses her home."

The audience was roaring before she was half done. But behind the fun crept something less good-natured—something urgent, in a tone by turns cautionary and pleading and so at odds with the expectation of general good cheer that it might have seemed impolite, except that it so perfectly reflected the larger transformation of a simple, small-town street festival into a venue of national mission and racial destiny.

"The truth is, we have not just come to extol and export Zora Neale Hurston, or any writer, or any teacher or preacher or rabbi or any priest," Angelou said. "It's not just for that. If it is of any use at all, it is to encourage the race to continue. To continue with some passion. That's it! Otherwise, what's it all about, Alfie? It's an intellectual exercise otherwise. In truth, Ms. Hurston's books can make a difference in our lives. We are desperate now. You all know it. The truth is, our communities are dying. Our children are running crazy in the streets. We, of all people, are afraid to walk down the streets inhabited by our children. That's real life. It's no plaything. We may laugh and joke, but it's no plaything. The children need us, and somehow we've taken our hands off, and yet we come out to celebrate, and festival, and gala, and sometimes we do it superficially, and we have the form and not the thing."

That calling up of peril and promise, that connecting of culture to civic survival, inspired something in Traylor. She said, "Sister, I want to tell an anecdote."

"Please, I bet you will," Angelou responded, and it was then that Traylor put a name to the subtext that had underlain the festival all week long, and it was also then, at that particular moment, that Jacquelyn Torrence, the Story Lady, collapsed in the front row and chairs began scuffing and people in the audience began rushing to her and running to call paramedics.

Traylor's anecdote was of a visit she paid to the home of a museum curator in Haiti. "When I walked in his house I was stunned," she said. "What he had was a collection of the carnival art of Haiti. Papier-mâché pieces. I admired them so that he said, 'You may have one. Just select.' And I did, I selected. Then I changed my mind, and I selected another. He said, 'Have what you will.' I brought it home. And that year wasn't too good a year. Things happened. . . . One particularly anguished night, I was reading Hurston's *Tell My Horse* . . . and as I read through, I discovered what I had brought home. I had brought home Damballah, the god of creativity. But there are two, Ms. Hurston said. One is *destructive*, and the other is the essence of *constructive*."

Traylor's voice rose through the last of the story until she half stood to shout her final line, "I had selected first the constructive and then the destructive Damballah: I had brought destruction in my house!" she yelled. "And Ms. Hurston said to me, '*Get it out!*'"

The audience all the way up to the top of the bleachers were thus treated to the arresting spectacle of one of the nation's leading black folklore enthusiasts screaming about the lethality of ill-chosen creativity while another lay before her on the floor receiving mouth-to-mouth resuscitation, as though struck down by it. When Maya Angelou spoke next, it was unclear for a moment whether she was calling for help for Torrence, for her race, or for a nation afflicted with the duality of a creativity it seemed unable to harness or evade.

"Is there a doctor in the house?" she said.

I couldn't vouch for the strict accuracy of Traylor's description—Damballah Ouedo, the "great source," and "suprême Mystère," is the patriarch of the voodoo gods of Haiti, but he does not have a dual nature. Other voodoo gods do, though. They can show up either as good ("Rada") gods or bad ("Petro") gods. The distinction in their appearance may be subtle, but one is wise to observe it. By placing evil alongside good within the character of individual gods instead of segregating it in a separate Satanic antagonist, voodoo emphasized a subtle truth—that the greatest enemy of good may be not its polar opposite but its approximation, its simulacrum. If Traylor's specifics were loose, her general observation was dead on the money: were creativity a god, it would surely exhibit a destructive as well as a constructive incarnation. The struggle between the two was at the root of Hurston's work, her life, her town's experience, and the festival that commemorates them all.

The Rada and Petro gods of creativity conspired to earn Hurston's prominence among black writers in the Harlem Renaissance, and conspired to shame her from their ranks. Her first renown among New Yorkers was as an unexcelled raconteur. "Of this 'niggerati,'" Langston Hughes wrote (cribbing the appellation from Wallace Thurman),

"Zora Neale Hurston was surely the most amusing. Only to reach a wider audience need she ever write books—because she is a perfect book of entertainment in herself." Among all that flowering of black creativity called the Harlem Renaissance, Hurston was not only the most prominent woman, she was also, remarkably, the only prominent emissary from the deep main well of American black culture, the rural South. In New York, she held a monopoly both on the folktales that her comrades found so irresistible and hilarious and on the folk manners that terrified them. For all that the black intellectuals of the time championed the black common man—the man Hurston called "the Negro farthest down"—they also found him embarrassingly backward, especially in his rural and Southern incarnation. They mistook his mannerisms and his elliptical tale-telling, saturated with magical religion and hyperbolic humor but absent of political realism, for Uncle Tom subservience.

So it was inevitable that Hurston would be misperceived. Just as she was an oddity among the Renaissancers, she was also, eventually, isolated. Her strength was her undoing, for her strength was Eatonville. The town gave her more than material. Its uniqueness permitted hers. There is no avoiding the connection between creative and democratic forms: the only deep and small-town Southerner of rank among the Harlem Renaissance writers, the first black graduate of Barnard, the most prominent black woman writer and only black academic folklore anthropologist of her time—that person hailed from the oldest township in the country governed by African Americans. "I was born in a Negro town," Hurston wrote in the beginning of her autobiography. "I do not mean by that the black back-side of an average town." By and large, the other celebrated black writers had all grown up in just such urban "back-sides"—black neighborhoods appended to white cities, where black perspectives were, in convoluted ways, appended to the injustice of white society and the indifference of white culture. They could hardly appreciate the profound distinction of Hurston's charter with the world, how untrammeled she was by the implications of otherness or any indoctrination in inferiority. Hurston's Eatonville was like a four-walled room, but the worlds her companions came from were rooms with one wall missing, exposing their lives to the white man's intentions and inspection.

Hurston was living testament to a black nationalist credo—that free of the predations of the white man a black child could grow into genius not only unbent by the weight of white attitudes but unresponsive to them. At her best, she applied her gift the way white American writers had the luxury of applying theirs—to larger questions of her relation to God, love, work, and nature—undistracted by the question that preoccupied her brethren, of their relation to the white man. Thus in its inimical way, Eatonville made its poet black. And Eatonville bid her sing. Things would not remain so clear or easy once she got to Harlem.

The Harlem Renaissance was distinct among American artistic movements not just for its geographic and racial concentration but for its pervading self-consciousness. It wasn't just a forum for art, it was also a forum *about* art. It was about itself, and its expression was attended by furious self-analysis. The analysis was in no way gentle or generous or kind; it was critical to the verge of fratricide. At issue was the enigma of authenticity, an enigma that exists outside of racial experience and that all artists of all ages have had to confront, but one that black experience in America was especially equipped to illuminate. The enigma's inner mechanism was essentially that of the Conundrum, the trap in black American life that tightened no matter which way one pulled.

In black street life, the trap worked along such lines as this: If you worked for success within the general American system, you would be dismissed by whites and denounced by blacks as an obedient Uncle Tom, but if you rejected such success and opposed the larger society, you still predicated your life's struggle on someone else's domination, and so were no freer than your "Tom" counterpart. Either way, the issue of race enmeshed you as it did not a white man, and absorbed all of your efforts in a miasma of self-reference. Likewise, if you assented to the white man's oppression you were deemed servile, but if you reacted you were called a savage, and either case warranted the oppression. As Alain Locke phrased it in an essay titled "The New Negro," "The ordinary man has had until recently only a hard choice between the alternatives of supine and humiliating submission and stimulating but hurtful counter-prejudice."

Locke wrote "The New Negro" as an introduction for an anthology bearing the same name, which he edited and which was published in 1925. The anthology contained pieces by Zora Neale Hurston, Langston Hughes, Melville Herskovits, Claude McKay, Countee Cullen, James Weldon Johnson, E. Franklin Frazier, and W. E. B. Du Bois, among others. It would become recognized as a sort of bible of the Harlem Renaissance, a movement Locke saw as a "spiritual Coming of Age," opening "constructive channels" through which "the balked social feelings of the American Negro can flow freely." But if Locke foresaw a time when "the ordinary man" would be free of that "hard choice" and be liberated from the Conundrum, then *The New Negro* itself provided evidence to the contrary—it contained the germ of a dispute that would transpose the hard choice full-blown into the literary world. Even his own contributors disagreed vehemently with him and with each other over the proper role of the black artist.

"In all sorts of ways we are hemmed in and our new young artists have got to fight their way to freedom," W. E. B. Du Bois wrote, in "The Criteria of Negro Art." Like the black businessman or black mechanic, the black artist was not free simply to create—he was bound to create in a way that reflected on his race, one way or another. Du Bois himself argued that each piece of black writing must contain an argument against injustice and what he called "racial pre-judgment." "All art is propaganda, and must ever be, despite the wailings of the purists," he wrote. "I stand in utter shamelessness and say that whatever art I have for writing has been used always for propaganda for gaining the right of black folk to love and enjoy. I do not care a damn for any art that is not used for propaganda. But I do care when propaganda is confined to one side while the other is stripped and silent."

Some protested this: "My chief objection to propaganda," Alain Locke wrote, "is that it perpetuates the position of group inferiority" to a "dominant majority whom it harangues, cajoles, threatens or supplicates."

But other black writers amplified Du Bois's formula: in his essay "The Negro Artist and the Racial Mountain," Langston Hughes condemned Countee Cullen (without naming him) for once having told Hughes, "I want to be a poet—not a Negro poet." Hughes considered this to mean that Cullen wanted to be white, but he missed the likely alternative—that Cullen was merely objecting to being placed in the jaws of the Conundrum. In order to escape the white definition of blackness, Cullen (like A. L. Lewis in a business sense) was obligated to defend blackness with his art and with his life, but that left him no chance at the real duty of the artist: to become transparent, to have no alliance, to speak from a self so basic and private that it was divested of identity, and thereby to be honest. In short, being black, he was proscribed from culture building as long as the white man watched.

In America, the luxury of writing from the assumption of no-self was conferred easily only on white men. (Virginia Woolf's *A Room of One's Own* presents the same dynamic in terms of gender.) That was the white man's greatest tyranny: not that he forced blacks to defend their blackness and not that he wrote from a position of whiteness, but that he could pursue his life and art in the illusion that he was generic, faceless—an Everyman, alone in the room with God. The white writer certainly would not have had debilitating confrontations such as that endured by Claude McKay when a black American journalist accosted him violently in Paris for exploiting "Negroes to please the white reading public." McKay, with his dangerous and unrepentant characters and angry poetics, was one of the most militant of the era's writers; the late Harvard historian Nathan Huggins called him "the voice of black defiance and bitterness." But even McKay would need to protest, with a pained mystification over his role, "Frankly, I have never regarded myself as a Negro poet."

Hurston sympathized with the accused in these instances, and lauded their courage in flouting prevailing doctrine. "I have always shared your approach to art," she wrote to Countee Cullen in 1943. "That is, you have written from within rather than to catch the eye of those who were making the loudest noise for the moment. I know that hitch-hiking on band-wagons has become the rage among Negro artists, . . . but I have never thumbed a ride and can feel no admiration for those who travel that way."

Well she might identify with Cullen and McKay. More than other writers, Hurston endured the accusation that she was "pleasing the white public." Undoubtedly she invited the charge, partly through her use of black dialect and her eagerness to employ her colored antics to entertain impressionable whites—"some of whom simply paid her just to sit around and represent the Negro race for them," as Langston

Hughes sniffed in *The Big Sea*—but more through her apparent uncon-
cern (in her books) with white injustice toward blacks. "Zora has a
simple solution to the problems of the race," the Harlem Renaissance
poet and Hughes collaborator Arna Bontemps once said. "She ignores
them."

In her writing, she ignored them purposefully. "Negroes were supposed to write about the Race Problem," Hurston opined in *Dust
Tracks on a Road*. "I was and am thoroughly sick of the subject. My
interest lies in what makes a man or a woman do such-and-so, regardless of his color." Still, she felt the sting of the injunction to write racial
propaganda: "I was afraid to tell a story the way I wanted, or rather the
way the story told itself to me."

Neither Hurston's anthropology nor her fiction concerned itself
much with relationships between the races. She presented black life as
self-contained. She was born of Eatonville and bore its mark:
Eatonville and the culture she depicted were worlds unto themselves.
Hurston did open and expose that world to view through what she
called "the spyglass of anthropology": cultural anthropologists deign
to pry open only those rooms they see as closed. In her autobiography,
she transformed Joe Clarke's porch into a stage, even footnoting black
idioms, as though for her natural audience her native tongue would
need translation.

But if her fiction seemed similar, it was actually written from the
radically different vantage point, as Robert Hemenway puts it, of cultural dramatist rather than cultural interpreter. *Their Eyes Were
Watching God* is now recognized for presenting a world that is more
authentically and faithfully black for being entirely black, for avoiding
the preoccupation of most black writers with the black relationship to
white America. Thanks to that virtue, it comes closer than almost any
Harlem Renaissance novel to being art, to observing its own internal
logic undistracted by imposed social responsibilities, to being its own
world.

That is the event that *Zora!* is founded on: the crowds come to
Eatonville each year to commemorate the discovery of a cultural grail,
the grail of an artistic creation founded in race but not bound by race,
a creation that is more universal for being more ethnic. *Their Eyes Were
Watching God* was a thoroughly black book, in the untranslated vernac-

ular of rural black life, in which not only the dialogue but the framing exposition was couched in black English. Here, though, the jargon and folk mannerisms were not codes for moral or mental simplicity or primitivism. Hurston gave them full (even classical) values of complexity and dignity and stylistic grace, and fashioned a tale more purely transcendent and less conscribed than any yet told by her compatriots. As did Eatonville, she ignored the larger world as a way of participating in it. As N. Y. Nathiri's freedom would be a generation later, Hurston's freedom lay within walls.

She had brought to the stage something worked out in the privacy of her heart, not something tailored to the expectations of the audience, and she would make the audience love it, though not immediately. *Their Eyes Were Watching God* was not recognized in 1937 as a profound and modern text—at least, not by everybody. Alain Locke lamented, in a review in the magazine *Opportunity*, that Hurston hadn't yet "come to grips with . . . social document fiction." The master of social document fiction, Richard Wright, blasted her with a review in *New Masses*: "Her characters eat and laugh and cry and work and kill; they swing like a pendulum eternally in that safe and narrow orbit in which America likes to see the Negro live: between laughter and tears," he wrote. "Miss Hurston *voluntarily* continues in her novel the tradition which was *forced* upon the Negro in the theater, that is, the minstrel technique that makes the 'white folks' laugh."

There—it was said. That was the dread name and awful face of the Petro god of creativity: minstrelsy. All the works of the Harlem Renaissance, all the efforts of singers like MaVynee Betsch to dignify spirituals on the European operatic stage, were propelled in part by the demon shadow that black artists could never quite outrun—the legacy of the blackface minstrel, who had paraded before white America in step-'n-fetchit farce from before the Civil War through the early 1900s. The minstrel was the caricature that made the authentic impossible, the stereotype so strong that it could supplant the meaning and content of actual lives. And because it partook perversely of those lives, and even engaged the talents of talented blacks, it was impossible to disown. Disowning it required the constant self-censure of black artists. It required, for instance, the dedication of black Harlem Renaissance writers to "social document fiction" and "propaganda" that would rescue black art from the emasculating cartoon and allow black Americans to, for the first time, own their image and their output, and thereby own themselves.

It also blinded black critics to the virtues of Hurston's work. She spoke in the black dialect and humor popularized by the minstrel and exposed the ways of common black folk, the same folk that black Renaissancers wanted to champion but whom the minstrel had made embarrassing, the same folk whose folksiness could be respectably displayed in public only when coupled to face-saving demonstrations of black resistance and anger. Hurston's sin had been to neglect the imperative of artistic and racial defensiveness and write as though she had nothing to defend. Even in her daily life, she seemed unusually impervious to affront and derision. When wheeling down the main street of Chapel Hill in her red convertible in 1939, on her way to the seminars of Professor Paul Green, the Pulitzer Prize–winning dramatist at the University of North Carolina, Hurston would be taunted by students' cries of "Hi, nigger!" "Hi, freshmen!" she yelled back cheerfully.

Nevertheless her life was a cautionary tale of the corrosive effect of a powerful, needy audience, even if that audience was sympathetic, even a sponsor. Hurston's sponsor during her early career was an elderly white woman with a Park Avenue address, whom Hurston called Godmother. Her real name was Mrs. Rufus Osgood Mason. Like many whites in that era, Mason was interested in black artists; more than others, she devoted her pocketbook and guidance to their labors. Mason sponsored Langston Hughes, paying some of his college tuition and supporting him through the writing of his novel, *Not Without Laughter*. She bankrolled Zora Neale Hurston's anthropological forays through the South and the Caribbean in the late 1920s, giving her $200 a month for two years and providing her with a car. Hurston flourished under the arrangement, and played Godmother blithely along with the same down-home diction and ribald stories she later turned into master fiction. But here, at the heart of her early creative striving, her ostentatious blackness seemed not proud but convenient, a way of satisfying the terms of the loan with the primitivism required to sate white expectation. Some of Hurston's compatriots thought she was playing the trickster, pulling a scam on a credulous

Godmother. (Hurston professed not to mind "'Tomming' if it's done right . . . [I]t has its uses like feinting in the prize ring.") Others thought her pandering distasteful and denigrating. Was Hurston hiding behind a minstrel screen or promoting herself through a minstrel image? Either way it came to the same thing.

Hughes loved Mrs. Mason, and knew that her interest in black arts coincided with an interest in all arts and was not simply condescending. But when he said good-bye to the contract and asked Mason to become his friend instead of his sponsor, she dismissed him with such a detailed disquisition on his every fault that he saw the relationship in its essence. "That beautiful room, that had been so full of light and help and understanding for me, suddenly became like a trap closing in, faster and faster, the room darker and darker, until the light went out with a sudden crash," he wrote in *The Big Sea*. Hurston would eventually suffer a similar crash, but not before her labors had acquired the taint that had sullied the efforts of earlier black writers in the eyes of Richard Wright, writers he described as "prim and decorous ambassadors who went a-beggin to white America . . . dressed in the knee pants of servility."

In the end, Hurston wasn't sullied by her art or her critics. She was sullied by her audience. The problem of the minstrel is and always has been the problem of the audience. All artists have one, and all cultural innovations have one, too. But the distinction is profound between the innovations born in four-sided and three-sided rooms—between those forged in private and presented with integrity to an audience, and those whose author is merely an agent for the audience's expectations. The minstrel show was inauthentic because it was commercial in a way that reflected its white spectators as much as it did black life. Hurston once noted of the black fondness for anthropomorphic animal stories that "We throw the cloak of our shortcomings over the monkey." In the same fashion, whites threw the cloak of their shortcomings over the blackface minstrel. The minstrel offered a proxy relief for a Victorian America unhappy with its own anti-libidinous puritanism, and eased the anxiety of an insecure white culture that saw itself as unsophisticated compared with Europe. Blacks weren't bushwhacked by their own cultural infirmities; it was the infirmities of white American life that black minstrelsy was carefully tailored to fit. That's what made the audience so relentlessly acquisitive, and why it had the effect of usurping black creative effort and black identity. But if blackface was really whiteface, it still fell to blacks to escape the stereotype.

The tyranny of the audience is evident in every breath out of the Harlem Renaissance. "Negro writing has been addressed in the main to a small white audience rather than to a Negro one," Richard Wright complained in "Blueprint for Negro Writing," a claim he dusted off for his diatribe against *Their Eyes Were Watching God.* "In the main, [Hurston's] novel is not addressed to the Negro, but to a white audience whose chauvinistic tastes she knows how to satisfy. She exploits the phase of Negro life which is 'quaint,' the phase which evokes a piteous smile on the lips of the 'superior' race."

It was ironic that for presenting a book whose characters were oblivious to white concerns, Hurston would be vilified as a minstrel by an author who was ever conscious of the reaction of white observers. Between the two authors, it was the more militant Wright who was unable to shake the white gaze. This was the Conundrum exquisitely at work: by insisting that black writing protest white hegemony, Wright insured that no writing happen that did not keep whites in mind. Thus was the insurrectionist made overseer. Black rage could be no less a minstrelsy than black laughter and tears. Instructively, the only black-authored books that white publishers would pay good advances for and that white readers happily purchased were books concerning the injustice of whites toward blacks. Wright was remunerated. The woman he accused of minstrelsy never received more than $1,000 in royalties for any of her books. Hemenway noted of Hurston, "She never really compromised with the American economic system."

The problem of white usurpation of black culture would have been of slightly less consequence if it had been confined to literature. Even in its heyday, the whole Harlem vogue suffered the debilitating effects of a "patronage" that echoed the unequal relationship between Hurston and Godmother. The world center of black pride had become a staged spectacle for white voyeurs. "There is laughter, color, and spontaneity at Harlem's core," W. E. B. Du Bois wrote in a 1926 denunciation of Carl Van Vechten's *Nigger Heaven*, "but in the current cabaret, financed and supported largely by white New York, this core is so overlaid and enwrapped with cheaper stuff that no one but a fool could mistake it for the genuine exhibition of the spirit of the people."

"It was a period when Charleston preachers opened up shouting churches as sideshows for white tourists," Langston Hughes lamented in *The Big Sea*, a period when "the Cotton Club was a Jim Crow club for gangsters and monied whites." In an era when even the booze was unlabeled and homemade, Harlem began to seem trademarked. "It became utterly commercial, planned for the downtown tourist trade, and therefore dull," Hughes wrote. "Harlem nights became show nights for the Nordics."

Two years after the infamous Harlem Riot solidified the return of cultural home rule and white neglect, Hurston published her master-piece and saw it condemned by black critics as rank minstrelsy. That denunciation contributed to her final homecoming to Florida and her exile from literature. In terms of authentic history, her coming season of oblivion would turn out to be a blessing.

On my visits to Celebration, it became apparent that the principles that the architects there were invoking were the same as those that had undergirded the literary movement in Harlem over half a century ear-lier. Both places were laboratories for the idea that the quality of civic life was connected to the quality of esthetic expression. True, the idea was arrayed in different clothing. The Renaissancers thought that being "rated as human," in Du Bois's phrase, required a demonstration of excellence in literature and art. Disney's designers maintained that human existence was enhanced by excellence in municipal design.

But sometimes there was a convergence, as when Celebration architect Joe Barnes described his craft in literary terms. "I'm a big believer that architecture is a language that we use to communicate about our culture, our society, our goals and aspirations," he explained to me, "and it's a language that's been developed over time." Barnes was one of the visionaries that Disney had drawn into the Celebration pro-ject. Like everyone around him, he saw his practical duties as serving an ideal. "If you're building a house at Celebration, you're building more than just an individual house on an individual lot," he said. "You're creating community." Substitute the words "writing a book" for "building a house" and you could attribute the thought to Alain Locke or Langston Hughes.

As with the Harlem Renaissance, Celebration's sense of mission also imbued it with an orthodoxy. "We just don't want people sort of willfully inventing architectural languages," Barnes said. Barnes is a keeper of that orthodoxy; he is in charge of developing and enforcing the Celebration Pattern Book, a document that stipulates which design elements (that is, architectural languages) are permissible and which are not, right down to the fine points of the joinery of columns and the proportions of windows and the density and placement of shrubbery and flower beds. "Things like proportion and scale add value to the community," Barnes contended.

Such control would ensure the beauty of Celebration's classical architecture, a beauty that Barnes described in terms of necessity or purpose and whose highest virtue was a quality he called "rigor." He described in glowing terms how traditional Florida homes were rarely built of brick because Florida didn't have the mud; how chimneys were placed outside the houses in the South but inside for warmth in the North, where roof pitches were canted steep to shed snow. The lovely uniformity of window dimensions in an antebellum Southern town derived from the fact that there had probably been only one window maker, who had made them all. The overall dimensions of classical homes, Barnes said, were predicated on the length of a wooden truss that could be lifted into place by several men. The beauty of these things arose from the necessity that inspired them.

So, Celebration not only echoed the Harlem Renaissance belief in the connection of beauty to civic life and in the insistence on an orthodoxy. It also echoed the principle supporting that orthodoxy: the importance of authenticity, the renunciation of artificiality.

Yet Barnes's authenticity, his rigor, seemed rooted in an artificial preservation of such things as roof-truss dimensions limited by how much a few men could carry. "Now we have steel trusses, and cranes that can set the trusses in place and we can span anything we want," Barnes admitted. I asked him if that didn't mean the classical home designs had lost rigor and become fashion. "There's a potential for that," he said. "We're not doing things because we have to. We're doing things because we want to. It's an esthetic. But I think it goes beyond that."

I wasn't sure what his esthetic implied about architecture; likely it was harmless. But Celebration carried the concepts he proposed beyond the limits of the Pattern Book and the framework of buildings and streets that the planners referred to as Celebration's "hardware." "We decided early on that the software was going to be more important than the hardware," Tom Lewis told me, a statement elaborated by the man whom everyone at Celebration considered the spirit behind the idea, Peter Rummell. "I've been around enough places to know that unless it has some kind of heart to it, there's just not much to it," Rummell told me. "Some point of view, some—I don't want to say 'soul' or 'heart'—but something more than tee times every Saturday morning to hold people together."

I spoke with Rummell in 1996 in his office in the Disney headquarters in Burbank, California, a Michael Graves–designed building on whose façade the seven dwarfs serve as caryatids. Rummell was the president of Disney Design and Development, which oversaw the empire's real estate ventures, and also its theme park "imagineering." He can claim, and did, to come by his belief in the virtue of small town life honestly, having grown up in "an Ozzie and Harriet family" in a town of 350 residents in New York's rural Mohawk Valley, "where everybody knew everybody and everything was safe and you could walk anywhere and my bicycle was my complete mode of transportation and it was, you know, the 1950s and it was pretty idealized."

Rummell has an architect's fastidiousness—on his immaculate desk the day we talked were little mounds of paper clips arrayed in neat rows, segregated by color—but his real background is in the hurly-burly of business, amplified by a Wharton MBA and a "Ph.D. in real estate," as he calls it, courtesy of his initiation into the commercial world, working for Charles Fraser on Amelia Island—founding and building Amelia Island Plantation. "That's why I know about American Beach," he said. "I have two vivid memories of the early days of things, two environmental issues that we all felt strongly about." One was the Jacksonville Shark Club, which would spend drunken afternoons reeling in fourteen- and fifteen-foot-long sharks out of the surf onto the Plantation's beach, terrorizing the customers to whom Rummell was trying to sell vacation homes. The other issue was American Beach, "and God forbid that somebody might have to see a black person." It was clear from Rummell's tone that he disapproved of the concern the issue caused among the Plantation's creators. "I can tell you stories about these, for the most part, white, waspy, Northern and Southern business school guys sitting at Amelia in the early years watching American Beach fill up on summer weekends, trying to figure out how we were going to explain that to our clients. It was interesting!"

By the time he began working on Celebration's concept, Rummell was tired of retirement- and recreation-centered villages and wanted to do something more interesting, wanted to create some place "big enough to have a there there": a town. "I really have been very insistent on that word, with all the images that word conjures up," he told me. "Celebration's not a city, it's not a resort, it's not a place, it's not a development. It's a town. And I want it to be a town." When Disney's executives searched out older towns that had the "soul" or "heart" that Rummell desired—towns like Savannah, Annapolis, and East Hampton —the qualities they shared that made them work all centered on something Celebration didn't have: roots.

To the Disney people, the self-styled imagineers who confected the five-eighths-scale Norman Rockwell past of the Magic Kingdom's Main Street, that seemed doable. "One of the things we do particularly in imagineering when we're creating something is we often create a story, a back story, and you write a whole mythology about something, because then it helps you stay true to your design of a show or a ride or whatever you're doing," Rummell told me, "and it's actually a very helpful tool that the imagineers have honed to a fine art over the last forty years, and we do it all the time."

Meetings were held about how to provide Celebration with an appropriate back story. Names were suggested that implied a hallowed history—implied, for instance, that the town might have risen from the flames after being sacked by Sherman. Those ideas were discarded. "It just didn't feel right," Rummell said. "People gravitate to things that are real. You can't fool the public. Now, we didn't have a hundred years of tradition to rely on, so we did it with the tools that we have, these place-making kind of tools that hopefully will make Celebration feel random yet planned, and done over time, though it was done over a relatively short time frame. So the whole effort here is to try to convey—without being dishonest—to give some sense of those things we feel good about, even though by definition you don't have them.

Because the one thing you can't buy, you can't buy time, which is the only sort of true way to day by day build that sense of tradition.

"We haven't created a mythical history about the place," he said. "But I think we have tried to create a sense of place that is comfortable, and perhaps you could hopefully someday walk down a street and sit some place and kind of close your eyes and get some comfort that you've been here, or that there's people who have been there before you, and that it feels like a place with tradition, even though it doesn't."

Celebration's historical plight is one many black Americans can commiserate with; they appreciate the vital necessity of culture and history precisely because they have been forced to try to subsist without them. "They, unlike the immigrants, had no immediate past and history and culture to celebrate," Nathan Huggins observed in his 1971 history, *Harlem Renaissance*. Slavery had severed black historical continuity, disrupted whatever linguistic and artistic and religious community black people had enjoyed before their abduction, so that they did not have, as Huggins phrased it, "ready at hand the surface manifestations of a former culture which, no matter how diluted and distorted, could serve as a link with the past." Or, as Janie Mae Crawford heard it from her grandmother, "You know, honey, us colored folks is branches without roots and that makes things come round in queer ways."

It certainly did. Nothing so magnified the distorting force of the black minstrel as did the absence of black roots. Other immigrant groups (European Jews, notably) had their buffoons and court clowns and ethnic comics whom they put onstage and laughed at, but they also had the cultural ballast of an uninterrupted history strong enough to keep their minstrels from overtaking their identities. Having to make a culture more or less from scratch has given blacks an ironic position in the American cultural landscape: no one contributes more copiously or ambitiously to it, devising art forms almost hourly. And no one stays more in need of a cultural base. This is because nothing the black community devises is not immediately "contributed." Nothing it builds is not sold off. There is no privacy in which to nurture a cultural innovation to its maturity before presenting it to the world; the audience for black culture is too voracious to allow that.

At the turn of the century, the audience of concern was the white consumers of blackface minstrel shows. During the Harlem Renaissance, it was the white Manhattanites who commercialized Harlem and the white Godmothers who sponsored its arts. Today's audience is exponentially more powerful. The sponsors are entertainment conglomerates that promote one and then another "ghetto" teenager until their untimely and violent deaths, and make millions in the process, marketing even the mystique of the violence that killed them. The leading audience for the entertainers is the largely white, largely teenage consumer.

The "antisocial" attitude of young blacks—the pathology of gang signs and drive-bys and in-your-face antagonism—is in some small part an attempt to retreat from the acquisitive audience, to offend the approving gaze and buy some privacy, to close the three-walled room. At the same time, ultimately, it is profound compliance with the audience and the sponsor. In a commercial world where even the bloodiest and baddest behavior is transformed overnight into lucrative product, the search for privacy through antagonism is vain. The "safe and narrow orbit in which America likes to see the Negro live: between laughter and tears" has been expanded; America likes its Negroes confrontational and dysfunctional, and the angry rappers and gangsters are the media's new useful primitives, the new minstrels, cut to today's fashion of white expectation.

The avarice of that white audience for black images betrays the fact that blacks aren't the only ones being robbed by America's new sponsors. Whites have been robbed too. White consumers covet black ghetto experience because it is one of the few places left in American life which seems to them to be still authentic, still (despite the concentration of trademarks and sports logos) posturing defiance against simpering commercialism. The majority culture has already been plundered by pop. White popular culture maintained its own reserves of protest against commercial uniformity—the 1960s were full of such expression. But as advertisers and marketers figured out how to turn even protest into commodity, as Bob Dylan became elevator music and even the ironic detachment and slope-shouldered cynicism of "Generation X" was remade instantly into the hip new sales pitch, the corporation seemed to be chasing down and consuming American experience faster than American experience could escape. Just as tourism is always on the lookout for the getaway that hasn't been discovered by tourism, modern commerce seeks desperately for the authentic that it hasn't already adulterated. Commercialism has chased black culture into increasingly angry demonstrations, and as each form of angry authenticity draws the fascination of the white consumer, it too is made into commodity. In this way, all of America is becoming a three-walled room, where the only values are pop values and nothing is nurtured in the privacy of the heart before being dragged onto the minstrel stage of the marketplace.

In such a climate, the only popular expressions that maintain their integrity are the old ones: those that were nurtured longer in the privacy of the community because they were born before the audience grew quite so avaricious. For blacks, that means gospel, for instance—born out of the ultimate four-walled room of black experience, the church—or jazz: those things that are weighted by the ballast of hoarded history.

The urgency of the black quest to establish a history attests to the desperate need for weight to ballast the popular culture. The responsibility presented to the modern artist is to somehow gather that ballast. "It means," Richard Wright said, "that the Negro writers must have in their consciousness the fore-shortened picture of the *whole*, nourishing culture from which they were torn in Africa, and of the long, complex (and for the most part, unconscious) struggle to regain in some form and under alien conditions of life a *whole* culture again." Everyone, even non-artists, shares the burden. As the Renaissance-era historian Arthur A. Schomburg phrased it, "History must restore what slavery took away." Because of the need for a history, a usable past, he said, "we find the Negro . . . apt out of the very pressure of the present to become the most enthusiastic antiquarian of them all."

He might have been predicting N. Y. Nathiri. One day, I asked Nathiri to sum up her work in Eatonville, and she said, "It was a positive asserting of the role of heritage." We were speaking in her office, after an eventful afternoon during which she had unceremoniously deposed the deejay of a local radio station from the *Zora!* festival bandstand because she found the lyrics of the rap songs he was playing demeaning to the race. "For our people, for people of African descent, there is a recognition that there is a certain dignity to knowing your heritage," Nathiri told me. "We are desperate to make sure that the children know of their heritage, because what we have found is, the result of not knowing is self-destruction."

Just as she calls Zora Neale Hurston a cultural preservationist, Nathiri calls herself a historical preservationist. But as she describes her role, the distinction between history and culture seems negligible. In conferences around the nation where the meaning of historical preservation is debated, Nathiri argues for a new definition that will better honor black contribution. Before a meeting of the National Trust for Historic Preservation, she insisted that historical value should not be attributed only to places with beautiful buildings (which naturally favored the class of people in the American past prosperous enough to erect and own beautiful buildings) but should also be recognized in places beautiful for their social importance—in which case, flea-bitten locales like Eatonville and American Beach would take a deserved position alongside columned mansions and districts of Victorian gingerbread. History's importance to a culture, after all, lies in its intangibles.

Black Americans have struggled on many fronts to reconnect themselves with a usable past, often through an insistence that their new land recognize the heritage of the land they left. Pre-Diaspora Africa has the attraction of being distant enough in time and space to insulate it from usurpation by modern commerce, but it is also distant from the lives and concerns of modern black Americans. As an ancestor from a more recent and distinctly American past, Zora Neale Hurston offered Nathiri another route, one closer than any ancient society across the sea and therefore, in Huggins's phrase, "ready at hand."

Zora offered more than that. She was insulated by virtue of her long neglect, and like Africa could be rediscovered in her unsullied state. She had not been commodified or turned into advertising for any popular point of view, the way Malcolm X had been turned into fodder for movies, to be consumed with popcorn, an icon on baseball caps to be worn by teenagers eager for an attitude but not for any comprehension of his life. Hurston was, in a word, authentic, a quality that eluded much of the black attempts to reconnect with a past. For it turns out that Africa, though distant from the white man's intentions, was vulnerable to those of the black man. Afromantic texts minstrelized African history by insisting that it display such inventions as alphabets and Bronze Age flying machines sufficient to compete with European history on European terms. Alex Haley's family saga, *Roots*, was distorted by its need to propagandize. "My people need a myth," Haley responded unapologetically when the falsities of his document were revealed.

His instinct was no different than that of the Celebration planners, whose "people" needed a myth as badly as anyone else. Providing one was the mission of the Celebration Foundation, an organization funded by Disney and corporate partners like General Electric and Sun Trust Bank, and by donations from Celebration homeowners. The Foundation is overseen by Charles Adams, a Celebration Company vice president in charge of Celebration's cultural aspects. "We're putting together a program called Celebration Traditions," Adams told me. "One of the things that most communities have today is a heritage. You know, it's been there for a while, there's a history to it. Celebration is starting from scratch, so it doesn't have the advantage of having families grown up in the town that really can facilitate and bring in and embrace people as they move in. But we do have some history, really going back to the original vision from Walt."

Celebration Traditions is a two-day course designed to brief arrivals on the thinking behind Celebration. "This is very similar to what we do when we bring in a new cast member to work for the Walt Disney Company," Adams said. "We take them through something called Disney Traditions, and it's one of the ways that we've been able to perpetuate the culture that you see when you go in those parks out there over all these years. As we bring them in, we immerse them in the heritage of Disney and, you know, what sets us apart from other employees at other companies. We might be offering similar types of things in Celebration Traditions."

Adams hastened to add that participation in the course is "elective," saying that he was trying to avoid giving the impression of engaging in social engineering. However, the struggle to manufacture a tradition for the town hints at something more troublesome—a hollowness at the core, the lack of something even Celebration's inventors deemed essential, a history of struggle motivated by a bona fide purpose, such as inspired the creation of Eatonville, and to a different degree most towns. Such manufactured history, like Afromanticism,

held the peril that Arthur Schomburg observed in the early hypings of
black American heroes. "This sort of thing was pathetically over-
corrective, ridiculously over-laudatory; it was apologetics turned into
biography," he wrote in an essay in *The New Negro*. "A true historical
sense develops slowly and with difficulty under such circumstances."

It seemed that the good Rada and evil Petro gods of history were
no different than those of creativity: Petro history was also a minstrel
out to serve the deforming needs of propaganda. When E. Franklin
Frazier, in *Black Bourgeoisie*, decried the black middle class, with its pretensions of wealth and refinement and its illusions that black commerce would carry it to a golden future, the sin he condemned most
strongly was that of engaging in "make-believe." He didn't just mean
fantasy. He meant delusion, essential truth distorted to suit the sponsor. Make-believe was a fundamental scourge of black commerce and
black bourgeois society. The voices of the Harlem Renaissance
unveiled it as the scourge, likewise, of black art and expression, and
black history: the contaminant that would thwart any young culture
from creating itself, thereby unleashing violence and entropy on the
community addicted to it.

It was also, certainly, the scourge of an entertainment-addicted
nation and of its spiritual capital Orlando, where the technicolor fan-
tasies float over an increasingly barren urbanscape, where make-believe
has not enriched the host culture but undermined and supplanted it.
The day in 1994 when I approached Orlando headed for my first *Zora!*
festival, the interstate billboards trumpeted the Yoruba word for creativity, *Kuumba*. The word had become almost household in recent
years, popularized by creators of the annual Kwaanza celebrations as
one of the seven tenets of the African spirit. It had even been made into
a title in its own right, of Kuumba festivals around the South. Those
festivals sprang up spontaneously at first but have since drawn the pernicious sponsorship of cigarette and malt-liquor manufacturers, who
see no conflict between good works and a little product insinuation and
so have volunteered as Godmothers. It seems that even black history—
which was supposed to rescue black community and creativity from
corporate co-option—was itself being usurped by commerce. The billboards greeting me on the interstate announced the enshrinement of
African creativity on a new and empyrean level: as the theme of a new

thrill ride at Universal Studios, alongside "Kongfrontation" and "Back to the Future." Between the gaping painted jaws of a jungle lion, the Universal billboards read, "KUUMBA: Feel the Roar!"

It was hard to find Eatonville for all the signs.

Two years later, on the Sunday when I made my solitary walk through Celebration's empty and unfinished downtown, my mind was occupied with Eatonville, and with N. Y. Nathiri's views on the vital importance of history. I knew that the creators of Celebration agreed about that importance, except for Nathiri's insistence that historical value not be confounded with the prettiness of old buildings. History, of the intangible sort that Nathiri craved, was to a society what experience was to a person; the prerequisite of responsibility. To have it and to understand what one had was to be elevated into cultural adulthood. Democracy was an expression of that responsibility, and the city halls of towns such as Eatonville were the places where the adulthoods of persons and that of societies joined forces.

The admiration that Celebration's planners expressed for a bygone America seemed on its surface to be a regard for civic maturity—for a time when American citizens reigned from every front porch over the structure of their communities and the messy responsibility of democracy held sway and society worked. But the nostalgia prevailing in the sales presentations in the Celebration Preview Center was of a different sort. On my way into town, I had stopped there to watch the video presentation that greeted all prospective home buyers. The video purveyed an escape from adulthood, an invitation to reclaim a childhood paradise, where (in the words of one of the announcers) "playtime doesn't end until Mama calls you in." The soundtrack continued, "There is a place that takes you back to that time of innocence. A place where the biggest decision is whether to play kick-the-can or king of the hill. A place of caramel apples and cotton candy, secret forts and hopscotch on the streets. That place is here again, in a new town called Celebration."

In the real, new town called Celebration, the City Hall, not yet clad with marble, stared empty-eyed, like some classical ruin over a forgotten Acropolis, through a bewildering forest of columns. The Celebration City Hall has forty-six exterior columns. It was designed

by Philip Johnson and sits next to Michael Graves's post office in the
Town Center cluster of what Disney calls "icon buildings." Inside the
City Hall are offices for the Osceola County Sheriff's Department,
the town's community association, and its Community Development
District, and public meeting rooms. "Not these nasty little rooms you
get in the back of a country club or a condo rental office for community to gather together," Robert A. M. Stern, Celebration's master
planner, told me. "I mean these are rooms that have a certain public
dignity to them. Setting is important."

What the setting won't have is a real city government. Celebration
has neglected Jody Starks's advice that "us got tuh incorporate, and us
got tuh have uh mayor, if things is tuh be done and done right." No
future daughter of Celebration will be able to say, as Zora Neale
Hurston did of Eatonville, "The village of Celebration is still governed
by the laws formulated by my father." Celebration is unincorporated,
and its services are provided by (and its authority delegated to)
Osceola County. Considering that subdivisions generally are not self-
ruled and that Osceola County might not have welcomed the creation
within its borders of something as nettlesome as a new municipal government, the arrangement would not seem notable, except that other
subdivisions don't claim descent from the American charter and don't
sport City Halls.

When Joe Barnes talked to me, a few months after that visit, about
"architectural rigor," I mentioned that the columns so popular with
Celebration architects were used by Thomas Jefferson as a direct
American homage to the Greek ideal of— He didn't even let me finish
the sentence. "Democracy," Barnes said. "Yeah. But I don't think ours
is a political reference, though we use the classical column."

Why erect the temple I wondered (though not aloud). Why commission one of the nation's most celebrated architects to design it,
when its central democratic function was, in Barnes's word, an
esthetic? Why invoke the sibling esthetics of history and tradition,
when those very things truly expressed were so often antagonistic to
the goals of commerce? I knew well that commerce did not like to
trade in that which is not fungible. The job of authentic history is to
provoke; of authentic tradition to hold fast; of authentic democracy to
popularly establish the popular will. From an advertising standpoint,

they were all thorny properties, which made them inconvenient guests at any corporate picnic. So why were their ghosts—the "sense of" those things—invited?

In short, why was Disney building Celebration? Was it, as described, a corrective, an attempt to resurrect the American civic values of the time before corporate hegemony over American culture? Or was it an experiment in extending that hegemony? The corporate hegemony of postwar America was surely at a moment of trial. It was like a parasite that discovers it has nearly consumed its host. It had chased down more and more of America's cultural output, and replaced more and more of America's spontaneity and industry and creativity with its own mass-produced product. It had transformed even American protest into movie cliché and advertising minstrelsy. It was seeking, through myriad small-scale portrayals, to become the arbiter of America's sense of its own history. Often the portrayals weren't that small. In the early 1990s, Disney fought to build a 3,000-acre history theme park, called Disney's America, in Virginia, outfitted with "playlands" where visitors could relive, among other experiences, the travails of Ellis Island, the Vietnam War, and slavery. ("We want to make you feel what it was like to be a slave, or what it was like to escape through the Underground Railroad," Disney vice-president Robert Weis explained.)

Ultimately, for all its efforts, commercial America had seen the devastation of emptied cities and lives, and seen Hallmark sentiment and the cult of competitive self-interest substitute for cultural values, and seen cynicism and eager obeisance substitute for self-determination; and now the corporate culture had to find a way to correct those imbalances, to replace the qualities it had robbed from the society. Those lost qualities were the ones that Celebration grouped under the word "community," but the word was deceptive. In the old American town that Celebration pretended to re-create, businesses served a community built by citizens who were enveloped in a society. Celebration's real mission was to see if the chain could be reversed—if a true society could be fostered among people living in a community built by a business.

Once you understood Celebration as an expansion of corporate power and not a renunciation of it, then you saw why those troublesome qualities of history and tradition were replaced by approximations, simulacrums: they were needed as esthetic to permit their absence in fact. Walt Disney's abiding genius, after all, was his use of an esthetic of history to defeat the more troublesome reality of history, just as he created Main Street as an idyllic replica of the Missouri town where he had endured a dreadful childhood. As one imagineer explained in a Disney publication, "What we create is a Disney Realism, sort of Utopian in nature, where we carefully program out all the negative, unwanted elements and program in the positive elements." Walt Disney was the Louis Pasteur of history, who perfected ways to protect people from the viral effects of memory by injecting it back into them in a denatured form. It was a voodoo formulation, wherein similarity of appearance disguised opposition of intent. But would it work with democracy, too? Disney did, after all, have a real experience with democracy, for Disney World is, before all else, a governmental entity. Walt's greatest feat of imagineering was his vaulting of a theme park into a polity. Back in the late 1960s, the Florida legislature granted his holdings an unusual status: while they would remain part of Orange and Osceola counties, they would be given the powers and privileges of an autonomous county. This allowed the Disney World district to do things like levy taxes and enforce building codes—powers that were normally granted only to popularly elected governments. Walt Disney had a long-standing enmity for popularly elected governments. So he laid out a governmental organization in the new district comprising Disney World, in which a few Disney executives were made the resident citizenry and given the power to vote for what the company wanted done.

When I asked Michael Eisner whether Walt was a fan of democracy, he replied, "No, because he was afraid the process would not keep up the quality, I guess. I never knew him. He didn't live long enough to shape his own vision. I mean, he had some ideas that were brilliant and some ideas that didn't work. In what he was doing, he would have evolved."

But the Disney World property is still run by the same rigged polity. Celebration has been de-annexed from that property, and an admitted reason is to keep its residents from having any say in Disney World decisions. Meanwhile, the only official voice that Celebration

residents have in Celebration is through their community association—and even there, Disney is retaining veto power over any decisions the citizens make. Behind the columns of Celebration's City
Hall, the disruptive god of democracy is honored in elaborate cere-
mony precisely to keep him at bay.

The lack of power does not offend Celebration residents I talked
with. On the contrary, many seemed to have been attracted to the
town by the prospect of living under the protective wing of a corporation. The fundamentalist minister from south Florida who had
expressed an eagerness to "turn around this nation" explained to me,
on the morning he closed on his house, "Well, you have to sign a contract, and one of the things you have to state is your willingness to go
along with whatever is determined best for the community. In a sense,
to a great degree, you're trusting in Disney and their ability to do
things right." He had asked questions about his new home that the
Disney sales staff couldn't answer. "So, do I say I want the answers
before I sign?" he asked me. "Or do I say, you know, I think these people are really honest, and I think they've got some of the best people in
the business working to make this the best place, and I'm going to
trust them? That's the reason I did it."

Others spoke similarly. When I mentioned such conversations to
Robert A. M. Stern, he nodded. "In order to get your point across, you
sometimes need to have a strong management," he said. "People will
succumb to a single management in a resort setting. In fact they
almost glory in the fact that someone runs the show. People love to
come to Disney, because the very word 'Disney' means a certain
authoritative standard, which they will succumb to. The problem is, in
a democracy, if everybody has a God-given right to be a rampant individual, everyone will be throwing his gum wrappers all over the place,
abusing it. So how in a democratic society do you achieve some mea-
sure of decorum when you don't have class? A beneficent dictator—
like a Disney—can set down certain rules. We're not saying anybody
has to live in Celebration. This isn't some sort of gulag. It's a place you
want to live in. And to live in a community you have to give up some of
your freedoms. This is what being in a community is. You have to give
up some individuality to be in a community. Democracy does not
mean rampant individuality. It's not the Wild West anymore."

If there is anything about Celebration that represents an authentic history, it is that autocratic notion. In 1990, Richard Foglesong, a Rollins College professor of politics researching Disney history in the Disney archives in Burbank, California, found a memo scrawled with Walt Disney's handwriting. A librarian identified it as being one of the papers in Disney's desk drawer when he died. It was an attorney's dissection of the political complications of a possible Disney town, where residents would vote. The attorney suggested that Disney control the town for two years, as other developers sometimes do, then cede the vote to residents.

"And when he said that, Walt put a 'No' in the margin an inch high," Foglesong told me. "He switched from pencil to red grease pencil." Disney sketched an alternative organization of governance in which the citizen would be omitted from any except a cursory advisory role. In the same archives, Foglesong came across a Disney grant application from the era when Disney was still intending his Experimental Prototype Community of Tomorrow as a working town. It stated flatly, as Foglesong related to me, that "we need to reconsider whether democracy is the best way to organize a city."

Listening to Foglesong, my mind was seized with conflicting images. The first was of the town I had just visited, its boutique City Hall presiding over a boutique business district owned and administered by a corporation renowned for excellent planning, with a founding landlord who would not let things deteriorate into the messiness of the urban world of Orlando, right next door. The other images were out of the messy world: out of a town just up the road whose founders had risked death to insist on their democratic birthright and pursue their cultural adulthood, and out of another town in a distant corner of Florida: Fernandina Beach, a place rapidly being changed as Orlando had been changed, surrounded with gated resort communities and anonymous developments housing an influx of rootless residents, while the hardware and grocery and office-supply stores of its commercial center were replaced with knickknack shops and bed-and-breakfasts to feed an influx of tourists. Unlike some other places I'd lived in—whose average residents had an attachment to their town no thicker than the adhesive holding a tourist sticker to a paper suitcase— Fernandina was still a town whose citizens were pinned in place by their histories. Their houses had been built, their churches founded, their businesses created, their battles fought by parents and grandparents whose struggles they knew as their own and whose portraits, like as not, hung over the mantel. Their future grew out of their past, and was still shaped by their rude hand. The specific image that washed over me out of Fernandina was of a humid near-midnight, and a hushed throng of townspeople had gathered in the dim yellow porch lamp under the live oaks in the dirt yard behind the county annex. It was an election night, and sporadically, as the returns rolled in from precinct ballot boxes around the county, a clerk climbed a stepladder to scribble the new numbers on an enormous white board. Opposing candidates and their constituents watched the accumulating tallies and calculated, digit by digit, in breath-quiet solemnity, the future of their town and their lives.

If there was such a thing as a secret soul to an American town, that was it—in the machinery by which it handled its problems. It wasn't a machinery meant for prettiness and calm, because a town had reasons for being and people had reasons for being in the town, and with those serious purposes came conflict, and conflict was the predicate of democracy. That was the strange secret of American innocence—that those people had convened in the lamplight not in consensus, but in contention over their differences, and in the ongoing progress of that contention, when all the returns were in, they had adjourned.

I couldn't envision that scene being played out amid the glamorized comity of Celebration. I wasn't sure how such a messy system could contest with the modern pressures of a business-driven America. But in Fernandina, as in the unglamorous and uncomitous Eatonville so close by, I couldn't imagine things working any other way.

In the years when Celebration was unveiling for the nation its futurist traditionalism, Eatonville was undergoing more than usual paroxysms of democratic angst. A new young mayor was elected in 1994, who promised to reinvigorate the town but who by 1996 had alienated nearly everyone with a backroom deal allowing a permit for a strip club out by the interstate. Permission was revoked by citizen revolt, but not before the incident had illustrated exactly the weakness of popular government against the spread of commercial decay—certainly no strip club was being considered for Celebration's downtown—and not before the politics of Eatonville were angrily rent. In the cramped office of PEC, N. Y. Nathiri considered the fate of her town— "Eatonville is still struggling for its survival," she told me—and decided that the vitality of Eatonville's conflicts was a sign that the town had prevailed. "We see people from Indonesia, we see them from the Caribbean, and I know from the questions they ask they are interested in understanding how we, who are obviously a minority—how is it that we have been able to maintain this little village in the belly of the beast. You can see it in their eyes, they're just amazed: 'How is it you still exist?'"

The festival was thriving. *Zora!* 7 was dedicated to exploring the Harlem Renaissance, and the festival continued to attract enthusiastic crowds to discussions that were not euphemistic or mythologizing, that partook of creativity without indulging in make-believe. At the center of the pervading tone of exultant realism was, as always, Zora Neale Hurston, who was treated as indelicately as she was respectfully, as a complicated exemplar of both Rada and Petro creativity. The critiques offered at the festival had begun to include critiques *of* the festival and the danger it faced—the danger of its success.

The warning had echoed through a *Zora!* 5 panel discussion in which the notion of Hurston as a feminist was batted around by Beverly Guy-Sheftall, bell hooks, and Barbara Christian. Christian said, at one point, "I'm interested for black women to chart a journey of self-determination and self-sufficiency that may in fact be oppositional to the motif of capitalist success." Her sentiment was made more urgent by a question from the audience revealing that *Their Eyes Were Watching God* was being transformed by a screenwriter into a possible Hollywood movie. Hurston was losing her privacy, becoming enough of a draw that she was already being donated to the entertainment economy. "We still have to remember," bell hooks cautioned from the dais, "that even as Hurston is canonized, the way in which she is being canonized might very much be a way of destroying what she means to us African American women and African American folk, as a writer."

In Nathiri's mind, that is the ghost stalking all their efforts. The festival as it grows has attracted sponsors. This is fortunate. Speakers like Henry Louis Gates Jr. and Maya Angelou have come without charging their customary speaking fees, but the cost of getting them and their intellectual and artistic compatriots there in the numbers demanded by each year's program is prohibitive. Corporations have helped defray the costs that the gate could not. Black entrepreneurs have donated. The Walt Disney Company has, too—generously. After the Maya Angelou speech, a private reception for the author was so packed with sponsors who could not be ignored that most Eatonville residents were excluded, as were some Hurston family members, to their disgust.

It was only a skirmish in a larger and more problematic war. "I would say the challenge for authentic culture, once it gets itself established, is to be particularly mindful of its charge," Nathiri told me. "And so I have no doubt that the real challenge for us is to keep from becoming crassly commercial. There's no doubt that what we're doing has a nice preciousness to it: we have to keep from falling off the edge. I don't want to hear anybody say we've become overly commercial. That to me is a death knell. It's a warning. What we have here, what we've been able to create, and what we know is successful is that authentic culture can be successful. It can attract people. It can mold things."

Of the festival, Clara Williams says, "It's good for some people. Not for me. It's a little rich for my blood." She had been priced out of the big events. Nevertheless, she revels in Eatonville's comeback. She is living in Orlando, having given her Eatonville property to her son with the instruction: "Don't ever sell it. If you ever don't want it, give it back to me. And I'll give it to one of my nephews or someone in the family. I don't ever want it out of the family." About the importance of Eatonville, she says, "It depends on whether or not you have roots in it. Now if you're just moving there, you don't understand. But if you've been there all the time, you understand it."

Things have changed everywhere. Williams's mother's old home in Orlando has been torn down for a new county office building. The county has named it the Hurston Building. Up in Eatonville, Joe Clarke's store has also been torn down, in a stretch of Kennedy Boulevard dominated by the massive new Heroes nightclub; another landmark, Mrs. Dash's store, has been demolished to make way for a beauty parlor. "It's not the same Eatonville at all," Williams says. "There's too many houses out there."

But the oil portraits of old Eatonville life still line the walls of Saint Lawrence AME church, and in the cemetery, now overshadowed by the rumbling interstate, the headstones mark the passing of Williams's father and mother, who grew up in Eatonville, her grandparents, who moved there in the third year after Eatonville's incorporation, and even her great-grandmother, whose story is the one at the center of all Eatonville stories, the hard stone of necessity clenched tightly in the root of Eatonville's deep history. When I went into Orlando to talk with Clara Williams, she pulled out a heavy Bible and laid it on her dining room table. It had belonged to her great-grandmother, and its inside cover was dated 1863. Her great-grandmother had died in Eatonville, free, after being born a slave.

"When she came to Orlando, she was working for the Bass family," Williams said. "Fred Bass was head of the Ku Klux Klan. And that's who she lived with and worked for until she died." Williams recalled her childhood visits to the Bass house, where she was allowed to use the back door and forbidden to enter deeper into the house than the kitchen. She remembered one visit in particular.

"We went to see my great-grandma," Williams told me. "And I had ridden my bike, because I had my little brother on my bicycle. And we went naturally to the back door. That's where we had to go. So we went in, and my great-grandmother was setting the table, because the Klan was getting ready to have a meeting. She had just finished ironing all of these starched sheets, and had them all on the table, all the hoods. And I missed my brother. I didn't know where he was. And there was a swinging door going out of the kitchen into the dining room, and I noticed that the door was kind of cracked. And I looked, and just as I walked around and peeked, there my brother was, and he had taken one of those hoods and had it on his head. And my heart sank. And just as I was taking it off of his head to put it back on the table, Mr. Fred came down the steps from upstairs, and he saw us.

"I handed my great-grandmother the hat. I said, 'George had it on.' And I grabbed my brother and I flew. And when I got home I was so nervous I couldn't stand up, and Mother wanted to know what was wrong, and I couldn't tell her the truth, I just ran out. And my mother was trying to calm me down. She said, 'They aren't goin' to kill him.'

"So, a couple of days passed. And we looked up and here was Mr. Fred in the door. He was about the biggest man you have ever seen. He couldn't get in that door without bending over, he was just that tall. And he came in that door and he said, 'Where is that George?' And we had told George just go on to the back of the house and just stay. And instead of George staying back there, he came runnin' in. He said, 'Here he be! Here he be!' Mr. Fred he started to pick him up, and he was holding George, and I was just cryin' down. He said, 'What you cryin' for, Clara?'

"'Cause I want my brother. I don't want you to have him.'

" 'Well, here he is. I'm not going to take him anywhere.'

"And Fred Bass said to George, he said, 'Boy, you a boy after my own heart.'"

Williams told the story without moral inflection, in the steady, bemused tone of a woman who has lived with a story most of her life and has turned it around innumerable times in the light of fresh experience and each time marveled anew, knowing that it holds the truth but that the truth is beyond her knowing. It is the story of a boy who didn't comprehend the price of life's distinctions and the older sister who did all too well, because she could remember their father, who had walked with a friend down a county road and had been killed for nothing more than that, in a world that allowed such things. It was the story of a woman born a slave, who had owned a Bible even while she was owned, who after her emancipation worked the remainder of her life even unto its penultimate week starching and ironing the uniforms of the men who hated her kind; and of the man who was the leader of those men, who had traveled all the way to their family home to meet the black child who was the natural enemy of every law he laid down, who had transgressed one of those laws, and to whom the man said, "Boy, you a boy after my own heart."

The story was a history, and not a history of the sort that could be invented. Its mystery was that it was humorous, in a certain sort of light, but was the more unfathomably horrible for being so. It was a truer story than all the political or public formulations of black and white and the Race Question in America, because it was private, and being private went deeper, and at its deepest and most explanatory answered nothing. It was a story out of an America built by two races

of people who imagined they were opposed either over their differences or over the question of whether or not they were different. They
were opposed, though neither lived in a culture the other had not
helped to build, though they both were fervent about the same dignity
and liberty, and though they were united in the danger their children
would face in the world they'd created together. Their children would
live with the consequences of their story, even as their story was forgotten or misplaced, even as their history declined into dust or was
elevated into spectacle but either way was lost. Lost except in the quiet
closed room where the old woman studied the Bible of her forebear
and wondered what it all had meant.

Some days after that conversation with Clara Williams, I attended
a service in her church, Saint Lawrence AME, on Kennedy Boulevard
in Eatonville. The *Zora!* festival was over for the year, and the people I
had seen in action as its coordinators were convening in their real and
everyday faces, in the Sunday regalia of citizens and congregants. The
open room of their town had closed about them once again. There was
a visiting minister, a woman minister from some nearby Florida
municipality. Sister Ella Dinkins, who is N. Y. Nathiri's mother, read
the announcements, and the choir sang "Amazing Grace" and "Time
Is Filled with Swift Transition," and the plate was passed. As I looked
around at the people and the room, another of Clara Williams's stories
came back to me. It was also a story about Fred Bass and Williams's
great-grandmother, and she told it in the same bemused, uninflected
tones. "About a week before my great-grandmother died, she had
taken sick over there," Williams said. "And she wanted to go stay with
my grandmother. So we took her to Eatonville. And when she died, I
had to go tell Mr. Fred. And he came to the funeral. When people
looked up and saw Fred Bass comin' through that door ..." Clara
Williams laughed a little at the marvel of it. "And he was so big and
heavy, the floor just creaked when he walked. The church was old. And
it just creaked. And he went up to view the body, and I wouldn't tell
you no tale, that man leaned over that casket and he broke down crying, he boo-hoo cried. He just cried and cried. And finally he got himself together and he went on back out and went outside the church,
and we didn't see him no more."

A few nights before I came to the service in Saint Lawrence AME church, the *Zora!* festival had wound up with a gospel concert in an auditorium in town. The room was filled past comfortable capacity and overheated even with the doors ajar, and the main singer was a professional tenor who had grown up in Eatonville and whom Clara Williams had once had as a pupil. The audience tried to join in, as though this were not simply a concert performance. They clapped some, but through most of it they just listened, too respectful to rejoice—in marked contrast to their renditions of the same songs in church on Sunday mornings. But on the Sunday following, when the visiting minister took the pulpit, it was clear that some of the manners of the festival's "gospel" concert had laid the distance of decorum over everyone's heart. She looked out over the room and saw a room of spectators, and, not abiding that, she stopped dead in the middle of her thought and summoned her congregation to her point—that in this old room there was to be no actor and no audience, that here they were all engaged in the same fine effort, the same desperate ecstasy. "Now, you seem to think that you have come to hear me preach," she said in the tone and cadence of a measured reasonableness. "Now . . . you know . . . I am not from Eatonville . . . And you may not understand . . . what Eatonville means . . . to those of us not from here." And her voice shed its patience and rose to a full bellow. "*Because I don't come to Eatonville to preach!*" she thundered. "*I come to Eatonville to shout!*"

Epilogue:
Twelve Gates to the City

MaVynee Betsch, 1994.

On a recent spring morning in Ft. Worth, Texas—at a little after nine, according to a watch which I had just adjusted to reflect a change in time zones—I rode down a hotel escalator with N. Y. Nathiri into a capacious lower lobby crowded with conventioneers. The whole town was crowded, besieged by attendees of the annual conclave of the National Trust for Historic Preservation. This was the event that had drawn Nathiri to Texas; she was to be one of the convention's featured speakers. I'd come to Texas partly to talk with her. Over a year earlier, I'd moved from Florida, deserting quiet little Fernandina Beach for bustling Los Angeles, and I was experiencing withdrawal, being stuck so far from the action. In the hotel, Nathiri had spent the breakfast hour catching me up on the goings on in Eatonville.

Now as we rode our mile-long escalator down into the maw of convention central, the teeming masses scouring the lobby for floor passes and name badges turned one by one and then en masse to stare. The room, from above, seemed almost to congeal. I wasn't particularly surprised. The crowd was visibly divided between those convinced the party required a suit and tie, and those others who found it an opportunity for a Hawaiian print shirt and a funny hat. Nathiri was the only one present who interpreted proper convention attire as a white habit and white head scarf. Descending from on high, she must have looked positively ecclesiastic. As it happened, though, the upturned gazes weren't even aimed at us, but at something above and behind us. Without glancing around, Nathiri asked, "Is MaVynee here?"

"Why do you say that?" I kidded her, and she laughed.

"When I'm invisible in a room like this, there's usually only one explanation," she said.

Sure enough: twenty steps behind us was the Beach Lady. MaVynee was the other reason I had come to Ft. Worth. I had picked her up at the airport the day before, at the conclusion of her first plane ride since the one that brought her home from Germany, thirty years earlier. Fittingly, the flight presaged her reemergence onto the formal stage: she, too, had been invited to address the convention.

Time, as the hymn would have it, is filled with swift transition. Nathiri's increasing prominence and MaVynee's decreasing isolation are only two of the recent changes to the people and places I have described in the stories in this book. Since I left Amelia Island, several of the old Afro hands I had come to know, notably Arnolta Williams, Maude Aveilhe and Ed Halfacre, have died. But the history they lived seems to be drawing some attention, at last. Ernestine Smith's house at American Beach, the only one of the old beachfront homes still in its original condition, has been put on the National Register of Historic Places. In Jacksonville, A. L. Lewis's grave site has also been declared an historic monument, and the cemetery it resides in is being better maintained. Down in The Bricks, renovation has begun on the old Ritz Theatre. The Ritz was never the grandest of the grand black theaters in town—that honor may have gone to the double-domed Strand, where Duke Ellington and Count Basie came to play. Nevertheless, the cultural contribution of the Ritz remains a cherished memory in black Jacksonville, if for no other reason than the gala children's talent review it hosted every April, a production courtesy of Jacksonville impresario Charlie "Hoss" Singleton, the author of such venerable standards as "Blue Velvet" and "Strangers in the Night." In recent years, the Ritz had a sadder distinction: it was the only one among those eminent theaters whose building still stood. It was crumbling and derelict, but it stood. Now, behind its old facade and original marquee, it is being entirely rebuilt—with a new, modern auditorium and with offices and an exhibit hall for permanent and travelling installations. In 1999, it will be dedicated to its new purpose as the Ritz Theatre and LaVilla Cultural and Heritage Museum (LaVilla being the historic name for the old neighborhood roughly coinciding with The Bricks.) The museum is touted as "the gateway for a cultural rebirth in Jacksonville." Its director (announced by Mayor John Delaney after a year-long search), was a woman who had first engaged local black history when she discovered its total absence from her sons' elementary-school curricula and volunteered to read and perform historical anecdotes for the students. She'd gone on to found her own cultural and historical resource company, CJA Associates, in 1993, and was poised to direct a large civic institution. She was Carol Alexander, MaVynee's close friend and confidant. Presiding over the center, Alexander will build on the work of earlier champions of black Jacksonville history—Camilla Thompson, Charlotte Stewart, and Hortense Gray. The credentials of these three lay historians are enhanced by their personal heritage—they are daughters of some of Jacksonville's oldest and most eminent black families—but their efforts have never received their limelight. The LaVilla center begins to provide a proper venue for the story they and others worked through adversity to preserve, and a sanctuary for the tattered culture of memory. To commemorate that sinew of generational connection, Carol Alexander wears a bracelet given her by Hortense Gray that had once belonged to Gray's mother, Arnolta Williams.

Something the LaVilla center won't be able to spotlight are the documents that I stumbled on in the headquarters of the Afro-American Life Insurance Company. Immediately after my expulsion from the building on the day of my last visit, I called several black historians in Jacksonville and around the country and also called Johnnetta Cole, to advertise the material's existence, and its peril. The renovation undertaken by the African Methodist Episcopal Church was interrupted soon after my visit, the victim of financial distress within the church, and for a couple years the building again sat empty and boarded up. Eventually, though, the church persevered, and in April 1998, the beacon building on Union Street was open to the public for the first time in over a decade. Inside, the old mahogany panelling is gone, irreparable after its years of neglect and vandalism. But the marble walls and brass and granite plaques still adorn the lobby, whose industrial-moderne reception desk is restored to original lustre. "When I first saw the building, I thought, 'If I blew on it, I could blow this thing down.'" Frank Cummings, bishop and presiding prelate of the Eleventh Florida District of the AME Church, told me. The bishop seemed a warm and enthusiastic man, who extolled the significance of the Afro-American Life Insurance Company, though he'd come to his Jacksonville post after the company's close. He understood that the home office had an emotional significance that compensated for its outward frailty: "Then I realized that this building was more than brick and mortar, and was solid at its core."

The only papers remaining in the refurbished building were some books on a shelf, he said. He wished the enormous trove of documents could have gone to a university like Edward Waters College, but instead they had been removed by some individuals, and he offered to have his secretary put me in touch with the man who knew exactly where they'd gone. After the bishop and I finished speaking, the secretary came on the line. "Call this number," she instructed me, "and ask to speak to Reverend Gil Glover."

Gilliard Glover had undergone a curious odyssey in the years since he was president of the Afro-American Life Insurance Company—his old colleagues often noted the apparent humbling of his material fortunes—but he persists. Instead of returning to New York or to the practice of law, he became an AME preacher, with a church outside of Daytona Beach. That was where I'd reached him on my several fruitless attempts to procure an interview, and that's where he was in the spring of 1998 when I dialed the number the bishop had supplied. Glover again brusquely rebuffed my invitation to discuss his tenure at the Afro. "Don't even want to think about it," he declared, at his most effusive. "Time wise, in terms of time allocation, it's not something that's going to be profitable for me, so it's just not something I'm interested in opening up." He pled ignorance about the papers, except to tell me to check with Johnnetta Cole, that they were "probably" with her and another Lewis descendent he named who also lives in Atlanta. "I don't have any of them," he averred, and then ended the conversation. Johnnetta Cole, when I reached her the next day, vehemently rejected Glover's assertions: neither she nor her Atlanta cousin had seen a single one of the papers; she was disturbed about it and was considering petitioning the AME church for possession. Apparently the treasure of the abandoned Afro has disappeared back into those same mysterious shadows that have obliterated so much else of Jacksonville's black heritage.

Other things were changing, only to remain the same. Peter Rummell, whom I interviewed in California, has returned to Jacksonville—the man who got his start building Amelia Island Plantation and rose to become vice president of the Disney Company is now chief executive of the St. Joe Corporation, which is the largest private landowner in Florida. He has responsibility for developing a million acres of Florida real estate, much of it along the coast, into new communities. Rummell expects those developments to be designed according to the tenets of neo-traditionalism; he cites Celebration as a model of how he plans to proceed.

Meanwhile, in 1998, the entire town of Eatonville was placed on the National Register of Historic Places. Cultural survival secured through a "community" model of historic preservation—the model employed by Eatonville—continued its quiet vogue, inspiring some new national organizations. Among them, two in particular promise to affect the fate of American Beach. The Gullah/Geechee Sea Island Coalition, though headquartered in Brooklyn (where its founder, Marquetta Goodwine, a native of St. Helena Island, South Carolina, resides and works), is striving to preserve and disseminate the folk culture of Gualé, the coastal islands of South Carolina and Georgia, and is simultaneously trying to stem the eradication of that culture by golf resorts and second-home subdivisions. Similarly, in Indianapolis, the National Association for African American Heritage Preservation is targeting at-risk relics of black history, and lobbying to salvage them from oblivion. In that spirit, Claudia Polley, the organization's founder and president, brought American Beach to the attention of the National Trust for Historic Preservation, which considered in 1998 placing the township on its ten most endangered American sites list.

Despite Polley's professional polish and MaVynee's overt bohemianism, the two were as familiar to each other as sisters on first sight. Like MaVynee, Polley is the daughter of an old middle-class family. She was raised in the strict disciplines of service and music and race consciousness and spent her childhood summers at a black beach, Fox Lake, which was attached to no ocean, but served Indianapolis as American Beach served Jacksonville. She, too, was educated as a singer, at Julliard, and performed in Europe before coming home to advance the fortunes of her community. Asked to chair a discussion on black heritage at an annual convention of the National Trust for Historic Preservation, Polley wrote and invited MaVynee to join her.

It had been quite a number of years since MaVynee had left the Jacksonville vicinity. As it turned out, leaving wasn't easy. She showed up at the airport holding her travel kit under one arm (containing her speech and a jar of organic honey), and holding her hair under the other, and even succeeded in getting her buttons through the metal detector, but was stopped cold at the gate by a ticket agent demanding identification. In lieu of a driver's license, MaVynee hauled press clippings out of her bag: photograph after newspaper photograph with her name in the captions, but they did no good, and MaVynee was refused a boarding pass and was delayed by a day. "How can we be sure that's you?" the agent asked.

" 'Cause in the whole world, she's the only one like her," Carol Alexander told him. An old Sugar Hill lawyer at the next gate, and Congresswoman Corrine Brown, who was rushing through to catch a flight to Washington, saw their long-time acquaintance and stopped to offer assurances that she was no terrorist, at least of the violent sort. "But you're the Beach Lady; everybody knows you," a child in line exclaimed.

So MaVynee arrived in Texas just in time for the show. The National Trust panel on which she spoke convened right after lunch in an anonymous, windowless, hotel ballroom, a forest of folding chairs lit with Lucite chandeliers. The other panelists were academics, or executives of standing organizations, and they looked it: silk ties and magenta Chanel suits, collars of linked gold, ropes of cultured pearl. Their talks were heavy with grant advice and bureaucracy objectives. At the end of the row, and the last to speak, was MaVynee, dressed in a royal blue drape, her cowrie anklets clattering whenever she crossed her feet. For a moment as she awaited her turn at the microphone, she thought she'd lost her notes, and I could hear her whispered self-castigation, "Oh, Mahv! Oh, Mahv!" as she rifled through her tote bag. Polley introduced her as "the soul, physical and spiritual," of her community's revival, and MaVynee took the floor. Within a minute she was all confidence and spunk, and the audience (of several hundred) that had been soberly attentive through the previous presentations began applauding and laughing appreciatively, and there was even a cheer or two. MaVynee had added some new lines to her standard bus-tour recitative. As she listed Florida's first black millionaire and first black supreme court justice and all the other pioneers that had called the Beach their home, she exclaimed, "We have so many firsts, it's like being a perpetual virgin."

"I brought down the house," I heard her brag to a friend, months later, in Florida.

But the words that most impressed me were the first she spoke, before her voice had lost its nervous quaver. They were not words about preservation, but about restoration—restoration not of a town or even of a society, but of herself. MaVynee was back before the world, and she was changed importantly from the woman who had given up her first grand stage, half her life ago. She had given up that stage partly in the inchoate comprehension that she must do so to defend her community; now, the defense of her community was the cause that brought her back before the crowd. Her introduction held a certainty of identity she could not have mustered at thirty, despite the telltale trill affecting her voice as she began to speak. In the simplicity of her claim, it was evident to anyone who loved her that her person and her performance were one, now. No wonder she had stage fright. This was a debut. "Hello," she said to the audience. "My name is MaVynee Betsch. I'm the great-granddaughter of A. L. Lewis, and I live at American Beach."